W9-BAA-740

W. Larry Dandridge

PRAISE, REVIEWS, AND RECOMMENDATIONS ◄

"We follow Larry and his fellow birdmen into the treacherous Vietnam landscape, hoping for their safety and amazed by their skill and bravery. These are brutally honest stories about the young men who flew 24/7 into dangerous situations and helped save many lives. You won't soon forget them. The narratives and descriptions are wonderful—very real and powerful. Blades of Thunder is literally edge-of-your-seat reading. I also have enjoyed learning about the other "characters" in the book; that is, the guys Larry went to flight school with and all who play a part in his experiences. I find myself frequently thinking about the book. It is very moving and very real, and simply heartbreaking at times. The character arc from new soldier to seasoned warrior is right on target. It should be made into a movie or mini-series!"

Kim Catanzarite
Freelance Editor, Writer, and Writers Digest Instructor

"An action packed, fact filled, and provocative story about some of the bravest of the bravest in Vietnam—our helicopter pilots, crew chiefs, and door gunners! This book is filled with many valuable lessons and helpful advice that today's US military services, troops, the Veterans Administration, and civilian leaders should read and remember."

Major General (Retired) James Livingston
USMC, Medal of Honor Recipient

"*Blades of Thunder, Book I* is the sort of gripping narrative of conflict that can only be created by someone who was really, truly there. Author Larry Dandridge captures life as an Army aviator in Vietnam through stories, letters, and images, all with a pervasive commitment to detail that puts the reader on the ground—and in the air—with a wide cast of G.I.s. Beyond technical coverage—well-supplemented with multiple, thorough, appendices—we are shown the spiritual and psychological toll of a war whose long shadow is still cast across our nation. An act of service just as powerful as his military missions, Larry Dandridge's *Blades of Thunder, Book I* is not to be missed."

Robert Salvo
Managing Editor, Charleston Mercury

"An interesting and accurate account of Vietnam Helicopter Crews courage, motivation, and love of the troops they supported. This work is full of factual aeronautical knowledge, gunnery information, military innovations, and lessons learned. Every military aviator, logistician, aeronautical engineer, crew chief, and door gunner serving today needs to read this."

MG (Retired) Rudy Ostovich
Past Army Aviation Center Commander

"Wow! Well written and well documented first-hand stories about the real lives of pilots and crews involved in the Vietnam conflict. Dandridge does a fantastic job of educating the reader who may not be familiar with the intricacies of the mechanics of helicopters and armament, and the limitations of the technologies now nearly 50 years old. Letters exchanged among fellow pilots and crewmen, expressing their innermost thoughts and feelings while experiencing the rigors of war, introduce each exciting episode. This format draws the reader into their personal stories. This book is hard, if not impossible, to put down. A must-read for anyone interested in the history of the Vietnam conflict and the men who served their country so proudly."

John Schmied
(121st Avn Co. 1966-1967 – SP-5, Maintenance)
Current Secretary of the 121 Avn Association 28 Feb 2015

BLADES OF THUNDER

OF

BOOK ONE OF TWO

The True Stories of Army Helicopter Pilots, Crew Chiefs, and Door Gunners in Vietnam

Author: LTC (Retired) W. Larry Dandridge

1969 Air Force, Navy, and Marine Corps Fighter Pilots Prayer:

"God, please give me the eyes of a hawk, the wings of an eagle, the agility of the cheetah, and the balls of an Army helicopter pilot!"

-Unknown Source

The letter and mission titled "Milk Run" described in Chapter 13 of this book was written by BG (Retired) Dan H. Hickman and is copyrighted ©2014 to Dan H. Hickman. BG (Ret) Dan H. Hickman has authorized the letter and mission titled "Milk Run" in Chapter 13 of this book to be printed in Blades Of Thunder Book I of II. Dan H. Hickman has authorized all royalties and profits resulting from the publication of "Blades of Thunder" to Tigers, Vikings, & Vipers Publishing, Limited Liability Company (LLC) and the Fisher House Charleston. Anyone wanting permission to reprint Chapter 13, "Milk Run" must get permission from BG (Ret) Dan H. Hickman.

Contributors: US Army BG (Ret) Dan H. Hickman, COL (Ret) Sam DeLoach, USCG Captain (Ret) Rick Thomas, LTC (Ret) Tom Jameson, Major (Ret) Bill Schmidt, ex-Captain Laurie (Bubba) Segrest, ex-Captain Gene Booth, Chief Warrant Officer 4 (Retired) Jim Zeitler, CW2 (Ret) Brian King, CW2 (Ret) Roger Howell, Chief Warrant Officer (Retired) and ex-Specialist 5 Wayne Zander, Ex-Specialist 5 Michael (Mike) Dewey, ex-Sergeant George Quackenbush, and too many others to mention here. Each of the contributors has generously supported the Fisher House Charleston by asking for no fees or royalties for their contributions. 2015 profits from the sale of this book will be donated to the Fisher House Charleston.

The advice, contributions, editing, and assistance of all who contributed are greatly appreciated!

Edited By: Kim Catanzarite, Freelance Editor and Writer
www.editandproof.com, (843) 367-2252, email: kim@editandproof.com.

Designed By: Spot-On Branding LLC
Spot-OnBranding.com, email: nora@spot-onbranding.com

For more information or to order additional books, please contact:

Tigers, Vikings, & Vipers Publishing LLC
A Service Disabled Veteran Owned Small Business - SDVOSB
236 North Ainsdale Drive, Charleston, South Carolina 29414 U.S.A.
1-843-276-7164, FAX: 843-573-9241, *LDandridge@earthlink.net*
TVVPublishingLLC.com

ISBN 978-0-578-15637-8

eISBN 978-1-4951-3906-2

Printed in the United States of America.

First Printing June 10, 2015.

This book is dedicated to

Warrant Officer 1 Gerald "Jerry" David Markland

...and 41 other members of Warrant Officer Rotary Wing Primary Class 68-13 and Advanced Class 68-21, and the other service men and service women who laid their lives on the altar of freedom in Vietnam. Jerry Markland was the honor graduate of our advanced flight class, a great patriot, a gifted leader, a loving son, one of our Army Aviation *band of brothers*[1], and a fine young man and fellow officer. He was a slick (troop and supply transport), gunship (attack helicopter), and smoke ship pilot.

Jerry was killed in action flying a UH-1C Huey helicopter smoke and gunship named **"Smokey"** with the 187th Assault Helicopter Company, Crusaders.

"Smokey" was shot down on a low- level run, while putting down a smoke screen so the command and control (C&C) aircraft could safely land in and take off from a hot landing zone (LZ), under heavy enemy fire. Two of the smoke ship's crew, Specialist 4 Stephen C. Ponty Jr. and Warrant Officer Gerald David Markland were killed and the Aircraft Commander, Warrant Officer Roger Howell, call sign Crusader 25 and Specialist 5 Marshall were seriously wounded. Jerry Markland was born on January 6, 1948, and died on December 28, 1968. Jerry's contagious smile, bravery, quick wit, excellent flying skills, athletic abilities, and love of his brother aviators, fellow crewmen, his parents, and this great nation will not be forgotten.

CONTENTS ➤

▲

PRELUDE ◄

This work is about six young US Army pilots and green officers, all between 20 and 21 years old, arriving in Vietnam where they each become men, highly skilled pilots, and proficient officers within a few months. None of them will be the same after their first combat tour in Vietnam. All of them will bear the scars of war for life, either physically or mentally or both. All will be strengthened spiritually and none will ever be the same. Some will soon be dead and most will be injured or wounded within the next 12 months. One will become an amputee and all will suffer from varying degrees of Post Traumatic Stress Disorder (PTSD) for the rest of their lives. All will become beloved brothers and all will honor their families, friends, and this great nation with their dedication, sacrifice, courage, and love of family, country, and God!

This book is about Army aviators (commissioned officer pilots and warrant officer pilots) and their enlisted (private through specialist 5 and noncommissioned officer (NCO—sergeant) door gunners and crew chiefs in Vietnam. It is also about the unbreakable bond they formed with their aviation warrior and maintenance team mates and the combat, combat support, and combat service support troops they supported. A bond that could not and has not been broken, not even by many horrendous wounds and injuries, long decades of separation, some post traumatic stress wounds and other service connected disabilities, and the deaths of over two-thirds of all Vietnam veterans. This book is not a history book, but there is much historical and accurate information in this work and the letters that introduce each chapter.

1

Except for Chapter 2 which contains no aerial combat mission, the "true war story and aerial mission" in each chapter of this book is nonfiction. Each mission is what actually took place based on the memories, and I must say, now 47-year-old memories, of the crew members who tell the stories. The letters that introduce each chapter are fiction, but those letters are the kinds of letters many aviation soldiers wrote to each other during their combat tour in Vietnam. The letters that begin each chapter were primarily written by Larry Dandridge. Each letter includes much factual information about Vietnam and its history, climate, culture, geography, religions, and character. The letters also include much factual information about America's war in Vietnam, our troops, the stress and emotions our troops felt, the weapons used, and the units and places these soldiers were assigned to.

Unlike today's age of email, satellites, text messages, social media, facsimile, and cell phones, the letters that American troops wrote while in Vietnam were the primary and almost only way soldiers and their families kept in touch during the Vietnam War. As in all previous wars, the letters and war stories in this book tell about the almost universal naivety and lack of knowledge about Vietnam of the young soldiers when they first arrive in the combat zone. The letters and war stories tell about the rapid maturing, accelerated aging, war-fighting skill building, team-building, and frequently demoralizing effect that war has on troops, their families, and the nations involved.

The book describes some of the traumatic and detrimental effects that the following have on young and old soldiers:

- combat, loneliness, danger, fear, and stress;

- violence, death, disfigurement, suffering, and pain;

- disease, clouds of mosquitoes and many other biting insects, and leaches;

- black ants, stinging caterpillars, black scorpions, and poisonous snakes;

- wild and dangerous animals, continuous discomfort, lack of sleep and rest;

- good and bad leadership, bureaucracy, nightmares, and loud noise;

- separation, total darkness, and the stifling heat, and cold monsoon rains;

- soaking wet 100 per cent humidity, sucking mud, low and high altitudes; and

- razor sharp grass, stinging trees, and strangling vines.

This book also describes some of the *fog of war*[2] and the down ward progression that some troops followed towards mental, physical, and spiritual exhaustion:

- From arrival, wanting to prove their manhood, invincibility, enthusiasm, "can-do" attitude, and optimism that the United States could and would win this war quickly, and then on to slow frustration and doubt about the abilities of US top civilian and military leadership, the credibility of the news media, the patriotism and wisdom of the anti-war demonstrators back home, and the United States ability to win;

- From compassion and empathy for the Vietnamese to cynicism and disgust towards the motivation less, lethargic, and corrupt South Vietnamese military and government;

- From a high esprit de corps and gung ho attitude to grief, depression, numbness, disappointment, and sometimes ruthlessness;

- From wanting to fly troop transport (slicks) or medical evacuation helicopters to avoid combat to volunteering for gunships (attack and aerial artillery Hueys, Cobras and armed scout helicopters) to get even, seek retribution and revenge, and ultimately survive.

Throughout this book the reader will see references to **"slicks,"** which was the slang name given to the troop transport and utility UH-1B, D, and H model Huey helicopters flown in Vietnam. The reader will also see reference to **"gunships,"** which were the Huey B and C model attack and aerial artillery helicopters used in Vietnam; **"scouts,"** which were the armed reconnaissance OH-6,

OH-23, OH-58, and other observation helicopters used in SE Asia; and **"snakes,"** which were the fast, sleek, and highly lethal Cobra attack helicopters. Numerous acronyms, military terms, and slang will also be used in this book and they are briefly defined when used. More detailed definitions and explanations of technical terms and acronyms are in the Glossary and Acronyms at the end of this book. Your reading will be easier and your understanding of many military terms will be fresh in your minds if you scan the Glossary and Acronyms before you begin reading the following chapters.

CHAPTER 1: MARCH 28, 1969 ◄

"Viking 21 is Going Down!"

US Air Force, Navy, and Marine Corps fighter pilot prayer: "God, please give me the eyes of a hawk, the wings of an eagle, the agility of the cheetah, and the balls of an Army helicopter pilot!"
– Unknown Source

"Tiger 3, Tiger 3... Viking 21 is going down! Viking 21's tail rotor has been blown off and he is crashing!" screamed the wing ship aircraft commander, Viking 23[3]. Viking 23, flown by Aircraft Commander Warrant Officer Robert Johnson and Pilot 1st Lieutenant George Taylor[i] was covering our fire team lead gunship helicopter call sign Viking 21. Tiger 3 was the flight mission commander and he was a young 22-year-old first lieutenant named Claude Stanley. 1st Lt. Stanley was about to lose a valuable crew, some friends, and an expensive UH-1B helicopter gunship. Viking 21 was Warrant Officer, Gunship Aircraft Commander (the AC), and Fire Team Leader Brian King's call sign.

It was a clear day with a bluebird's eggshell-colored sky and a few wisps of cotton-white clouds and it was March 28, 1969. Our Viking light fire team of two UH-1B Huey Gunships had just returned to the battlefield and completed the cover of a text book perfect, 121st Assault Helicopter Company (AHC), five UH-1D Huey slick, combat assault. The South Vietnamese Army (ARVN) soldiers had jumped off the slicks and were on line advancing towards an enemy infested tree line. The slicks we were covering were the famed Soc Trang Tigers in *V* formation and they were exiting the landing zone (LZ). Only one of them had called out "taking fire."

As always, Viking 21 began this mission fully combat loaded and over maximum safe gross weight. Viking 21's aircraft had about

1,000 pounds of fuel on board and a full load of armament including 7,600 rounds of 7.62 millimeter (mm) minigun ammunition, 2,000 rounds of 7.62mm door gun ammunition, and fourteen 2.75- inch (70mm) folding fin aerial rockets (FFARs) with ten pound high-explosive war heads. The maximum effective range of the 2.75-inch rocket is about 8,000 meters. The UH-1B model gunship was a very unstable weapons platform and our old pull-down rocket sight and a grease pencil mark on the windshield was at best Kentucky windage. We had to be flying "in-trim" with our turn and slip indicator ball centered to hit anything.

We also had to be within 300 to 600 meters slant range, and sometimes closer, to expect any kind of accuracy with our rockets. The rocket-firing button (switch) was on the aircraft commander's (AC's) cyclic stick, located between the AC's knees. Brian King was famous or perhaps *infamous* for shooting rockets at close range to the enemy to ensure accuracy. This was something that at times made me, as the left-seat pilot and minigun operator, quite nervous. Looking the Viet Cong and North Vietnamese Army soldiers in the eye was not my favorite pastime, and we were subject to flying through the debris from the exploded rocket.

The 2.75-inch rockets came in two high-explosive varieties, a 10-pound war head and a 17-pound war head. Also available was a white phosphorous rocket for burning things and marking targets and an antipersonnel flechette rocket, which we called nails. The flechette rocket would burst just short of the target and shower the area with 1,180 hardened steel and extremely *lethal* darts. We were restricted from firing nails over the heads of friendly troops and from using them near our troops. In the past few days, Brian had been showing me that the flechette round emitted a puff of red smoke at the point of rocket detonation, but the pilots could not really see the impact of the darts. My aircraft commander and fire team leader told me that the length of the impact area of nails was dependent upon the steepness of the angle of attack and that the slant range to the target determined the spread of the nails.

We UH-1B and C model gunship pilots almost always fired rockets in a cruise forward flight mode at approximately 80 to 90 knots forward airspeed and motion. Eighty to 90 knot running fire had to be used because we did not have the engine or rotor power to

PICTURE 1: UH-1B VIKING GUNSHIP TAKING OFF AT SOC TRANC

Picture courtesy of George Taylor, ex Tiger and Viking Pilot

1. 7.62mm minigun mounted on each outboard pylon.

2. The lighted perimeter fence at Soc Trang. Note that it is not kept clear of brush and vines. I am sure that the VC made this note also.

3. One seven shot 2.75-inch folding fin aerial rocket pod on each outboard pod.

4. Note the luxurious asphalt runway at Soc Trang. Unlike most other Army airfields we had much less problems with dust and mud.

hover out of ground effect or, for that matter, "in ground effect" when loaded and fueled. I was told that gunships had resorted to hovering rocket fire in emergency conditions, as when the Vin Long US Army Airfield was about to be overrun by VC in Tet of 1968 or when the aircraft was trapped on the ground and could not take off due to the extra weight of perhaps rescuing other downed crew members or troops. I would learn much more about rocket ballistics when I started my right seat training in gunships. For now, I was content being the best minigun operator and, when flying the one hog (sometimes called frog) 40mm configured gunship we had, the best 40mm M-75 chin turret operator and gunship pilot that I could be.

Brian told me that the 2.75-inch Folding-Fin Aerial Rocket (FFAR)[4], powered by the Mark 4 and Mark 40 rocket motor was originally developed by the US Navy for use as a free-flight aerial rocket in the late 1940s. I knew the 2.75-inch rocket was used extensively in the Korean War and now it was serving as the helicopter's Vietnam aerial artillery and most powerful helicopter ordnance in 1969. The UH-1B and C model Huey gunships and AH-1G Cobra that we Army aviators were flying in Vietnam used a variety of launchers including the M158 seven-tube rocket pod and M200 19-tube rocket launchers. Therefore, our standard B Model Huey gunship, like the one we were flying on this mission, was armed with two seven shot rocket pods, one on each side, giving us a 14-rocket pay load. The one UH-1B gunship "Hog" in our gun platoon had two M200 19-shot 2.75-inch rocket pods installed, giving it a 38- rocket capability. The Hog was also armed with a 40mm gun mounted on the nose turret—and of course our two door gunners M60 machine guns.

The minigun XM-21 gun system installed on our gunship included two electric operated, six barrel, M134 7.62mm miniguns, one on each weapons pylon on the right and left side of the aircraft. Both miniguns could be fired simultaneously or one at a time and each gun had a rate of fire of 2,000 or 4,000 rounds per minute. The miniguns flexed in unison up and down and side to side. The guns also had stops to prevent the gun from being flexed so far that it would shoot the aircraft. We always operated one gun at a time to extend our ammunition and to ensure that both guns would not jam before we could use all of our ammunition. If the guns were being operated simultaneously (in the both mode), both would fire 2,000 rounds per minute until one gun hit the inboard stop, which would stop the inboard facing gun from firing and switch the outboard facing gun to the 4,000 rounds per minute rate of firing.

The 7.62mm minigun ammunition was loaded and carried in two rows of metal boxes fixed to the floor of the cabin area between the crew chief and door gunner seats. One row of boxes fed the ammo to the right side minigun, and the other row fed the left side minigun. Ammo moved through a flexible metal chute from the row of ammo boxes, through the floor, and under the crew chief and door gunner's seats. The miniguns were designed to fire

PICTURE 2: THE FLECHETTES (NAILS) IN THE 2.75-INCH AERIEL ROCKET

Picture courtesy of Larry Dandridge.

We had 10-pound warhead and 17-pound war head High Explosive, White Phosphorous, and Flechette (nails) war heads (munitions) on our 2.75-inch Folding Fin Aerial Rockets with a mark 40 motor that we used in Vietnam. Smoke and flare rockets existed, but the author never used them or had them available for use. The flechette is a pointed steel projectile, with a vaned tail for stable flight. The name comes from French **fléchette**, "little arrow" or "dart" round. Our standard UH-1B Model gunship had two XM-158 seven shot rocket pods, one pod on each side.

in three-second bursts and would then stop firing until the pilot pulled the trigger again. These guns jammed frequently because of feed problems. Every fifth round was a tracer round, so at 2,000 rounds per minute there was a red continuous streak racing toward the target. The rockets would interrupt the minigun when fired for safety reasons—mother nature and the aircraft commander did not like it if the minigun shot down a rocket!

Even with its upgraded 1,100 shaft horsepower engine, the old B model gunship, serial number 64-14063, was already an outdated

PICTURE 3: LITTLE HELPER

Picture courtesy of George Quackenbush.

The children of Vietnam were the true picture of why we were fighting there. This little man wanted to help George Quackenbush load rockets, so George gave him a rocket with 10-pound war head to hold and pose with in front of his gunship. One of the most wonderful things the 121st Assault helicopter Company did in Vietnam was adopt the local orphanage at Soc Trang. The good work the entire Soc Trang US military community did for the Soc Trang Orphanage will never be forgotten by the local Vietnamese people and those of us who served there.

aircraft, unable to keep up with the UH-1D and H model slicks it was designed to escort and cover, and it was unable to hover out of ground effect when combat loaded. The B model's fuel capacity and range was limited and its short 44-foot main rotor, with only 21-inch chord (rotor width) was not capable of allowing the fully loaded or overloaded B Model gunship to make a safe auto-rotation in the high heat and humidity of Vietnam. If they lost an engine or had to auto rotate due to another emergency such as the loss of a tail rotor, the best a UH-1B model crew could hope for was to "crash and walk away!"

Viking 21 also had one galvanized Igloo water cooler on board, with much cherished ice and water and sodas in it. I, Pilot and Minigun Operator Larry Dandridge, had my dad send the Igloo cooler to me in Vietnam, just a month before. Our aircraft was also carrying a case of C-rations, pilots hand guns and M16A1 rifles, the two enlisted men's M14 rifles and personal pistols, each crew member's approximate 15-pound, ceramic, bullet-resistant (30 caliber at 100 yards) breast and back plate—fondly called a "chicken plate,"[5] boxes of smoke grenades, two spare flight helmets, one PRC-90 survival radio, a small bag of the crew chief's tools, two M-60 machine guns, spare M60 machine gun barrels, asbestos mittens (gloves) for each gunner to use to change hot barrels, and about 200 rounds of personal small arms ammunition.

Brian King was leading our light fire team of two gunships near the small village of Mi Da near the Cambodian Border, west and north of Dong Tam and Vinh Long. Brian was 20 years old and had been in country for eight months. I, his pilot and minigun operator, was a 20 year old warrant officer who had been in country six and one half months. Both Brian and I had been slick (utility helicopter) pilots and aircraft commanders before being selected for gunships. Brian had just a month before performed an emergency auto-rotation and thereby successfully landed a UH-1B Viking gunship that was suffering engine failure, so he was recently experienced with a real in-flight emergency.

Successfully auto rotating and performing a no power emergency landing in a small rough area, in an overloaded B model with its short 44-foot main rotor blades is a major feat in itself. Brian had proven he could do this difficult maneuver and emergency procedure. When I first joined the guns, our gun platoon leader, Captain Gene Booth said, "Brian King is the best pilot in our unit!"

This day, the 28th of March 1969, like every day we flew, Brian King, our enlisted crew, and I knew we had a hard-earned and glorious reputation to uphold. We were US Army helicopter pilots and crewmen. The ground troops knew that no matter how bad

Picture 4: UH-1B Viking Gunship Left-Side Rocket Pod and Minigun

Picture courtesy of Tiger and Viking George Quackenbush and Tiger Bill Schmidt.

1. First generation helicopter seats gave almost no protection in vertical crashes. Thousands of crew and passengers suffered compression fractures in crashes.

2. The Crew Chief's seat. Note there was "no armor" seat protection (bottom, rear or sides) for our brave enlisted crew members! All they had was the front and back body armor plates in their vest.

3. Minigun shown without safety bullet catcher installed.

4. Fifty-five gallon drums filled with sand and dirt revetments gave some protection from small arms, rockets, and mortar fire.

things got, we slick (troop transport) pilots were there to take them in and get them out. The ground troops also knew that if we were gun pilots, we were there, no matter how bad things got, to cover them and, if needed, to land and get them out of harm's way! We knew that the noise of our main rotor blades, the thunder of our blades, was a sound of great comfort to every US soldier in Vietnam! We knew that our thin-skinned flying crates were the infantryman's ticket out of hell and we would, if necessary, give our lives trying to successfully accomplish any mission that we were given, whether it be troop transport, troop insertion, troop extraction, medical evacuation, reconnaissance, attack/gunship, resupply, defoliation, night fire fly, or aerial artillery.

I was thinking and laughing inside about the chin bubble (the Plexiglas lower window in front of our feet and pedal controls) that First Lieutenant Bubba Segrest and I had to replace on the B Model Huey gunship we had flown yesterday. Bubba was flying low-level and had hit a dead tree limb that he did not see until it was too late to avoid it. Our gunship pilots too frequently hit trees and cracked or broke chin bubbles due to the helicopter flying so low, but flying low was the best and really only way for us to avoid most of the enemy ground fire. I chuckled to myself at how the crew chief scolded us and told us we would have to replace the chin bubble as punishment for our screw up. As I recall there are about 100 screws in a chin bubble and it would take two pilots about three hours to perform such a simple maintenance task that would take a crew chief 20 minutes, because the crew chief was that good at it.

The crew chief, who was also our left side door gunner, Specialist Five Malcolm Rose had been promoted to the 121st flight operations sergeant position and had stopped flying for the past few months until today. Malcolm Rose was respected and loved by all of the flight crews and he seemed to enjoy my sense of humor. He had earned a safe job at Soc Trang, where the 121st Assault Helicopter Company was stationed in IV Corps of South Vietnam and he was *short*, meaning he had less than one month before he was going home and getting out of the Army. It was Malcolm's bad luck that he wanted to fly one more time in a gunship before he rotated back stateside to safety and civilian life. The other door gunner, Specialist 4 Gomez, whom I knew little about, was the right-side door gunner, and he was at least half way through his combat tour of duty on the 28th of March 1969.

Malcolm was an aircraft mechanic and crew chief by Military Occupational Specialty (MOS), and like all crew chiefs he elected to fly on the left side of the gunship so he could see and monitor the engine and transmission instruments located on the center and

13

PICTURE 5: THAT SON AIRPORT BEING USED BY 13TH COMBAT AVIATION BATTALION JOINT OPERATIONS ON SEVEN MOUNTAINS

Picture courtesy of Mike Shakocius.

This is a picture of a 13th Combat Aviation Battalion Operation with aircraft from all the delta units. We used the airport at That Son, which was an ARVN Camp between the mountains and the border to Cambodia. The Special Forces Camp at Ba Xoai is close by. The 121st flew many missions with the Green Berets and Rangers from there. The Cambodian border was about five miles to the north. If you look at the photo of the airport you can count 16 aircraft, including Tiger Mike Shakocius' Huey. There were at least 17 aircraft on the field including OH-6's, AH-IG's, UH-1C's, UH-1D's, O-1 Birddogs, and a C-123.

right side of the cockpit instrument panel. Although the aircraft commander ran the show in flight, the aircraft was "owned by the crew chief" when it came to maintenance, preventive maintenance, daily maintenance inspections, flight line needs, and calls on whether the aircraft was flyable or not. Malcolm and the door gunner had smoke grenades attached to the litter (stretcher) poles near their seating area on each side of the aircraft, ready for them to grab and throw out to mark the spot they were taking fire from and to mark the positions of bunkers and other targets they spotted. They also used the bottom of the litter pole as a brace for their inboard foot, when standing "outside of the aircraft" with their outboard foot on top of the rocket pod. There is a floor microphone button near each litter pole for the crew chief and door gunner to use to talk to each other and the two pilots, thus leaving their hands free to operate their machine guns.

The crew chief and door gunner had the most hazardous and difficult jobs as they were frequently hit with and sometimes burned or injured by rocket blast, blistering hot spent shell casings, tree limbs, bugs, and debris from exploding rockets and targets. The injuries were normally not very serious, but they were painful and irritating to say the least. The crew chief and door gunner had to wear their sunglasses and keep their helmet visors down, or they were sure to lose an eye or worse. These brave men were in a much higher-risk situation than the pilots as they did not have armored seats like the pilots to protect them.

The crew chief and door gunner were not buckled in like the pilots with standard seat belts and full shoulder harness. Instead they stood much of the time with one foot outside the aircraft on the rocket pod looking for targets, calling out enemy fire, clearing the aircraft in turns-climbs-descents to prevent mid air collisions, and firing their M60s! These courageous sky soldiers would watch the enemies' small arms and 51 caliber and (God forbid) sometimes enemy 37mm anti aircraft and rifle-propelled grenades (RPGs) arch up towards their aircraft like hungry monsters trying to destroy our aircraft. Of course tracers looked much larger and more threatening at night.

The 51 caliber had a range of over two miles and would go through everything in a Huey including both sides of an armored seat and the pilot's body armor and the pilot sitting in the seat at 2,500 feet above ground level. Most helicopters flew at or above 1,500 feet to avoid the maximum effective range of enemy smalls arms fire (7.62mm, 5.56mm, 30 caliber, 45 caliber, and a variety of other size weapons), but the aircraft would need to be at 5,000 feet or higher to avoid the destructive fire power of the Viet Cong and North Vietnamese Army 51 caliber weapons. No one had the time to climb to, fly, and descend from such high altitudes in a helicopter in Vietnam. To get caught in an enemy ambush with three or more of their dreaded 51 caliber weapons firing on a helicopter or formation of multiple helicopters was one of a helicopter crews' worst nightmares. Unfortunately, it happened all too often. The VC and NVA were experts at camouflaging and setting up three 51 caliber heavy guns in a triangular formation around a potential landing zone or pickup zone or even a base camp. Many times they waited long periods, avoiding detection from patrols and flight surveillance, allowing aircraft to come and go, before opening up on unsuspecting US Army helicopters when they least expected it.

One of our door gunners described the 51 caliber tracers flying past him as softball-size fireballs. Hell, they looked like orange and sometimes green basketballs to me! It was impossible to forget that for each tracer we saw, there were four more rounds somewhere nearby that were not tracers that we could not see. Dan Eismann, one of our excellent and brave crew chiefs used to say that he just chose "not to be afraid" and concentrated on shooting the enemy before they shot him. I could not force myself to not be afraid, but I tried my best to do my job, stay focused, and pray we would live to fight another day.

Because of the high operations tempo of Vietnam helicopter operations and because of the high humidity, high salinity, extreme heat, dirt, sand, insects, monsoon rains, battle damage, and constant over-gross weight operations, we were flying our aircraft every third day into a major 25-hour maintenance inspection, and every 12 days into a 100-hour periodic inspection, and every month into an engine overhaul. We were also wearing out our main rotor blades in the sand, dust, debris, grass, leaves, and small branches we were encountering, every 200 hours versus the 1,000-hour designed life span for the blades. These adverse and hostile environmental conditions required our beloved crew chiefs to frequently live in their aircraft 24 hours per day. They had to fly as crew chief and left-side door gunner all day and then perform the daily maintenance inspection, cleaning, and working on the aircraft most of the night fixing things that broke or were damaged. They were fortunate many nights to be able to sleep in the aircraft a couple hours before the early morning flight launch the next day. They frequently had to catch cat naps in the aircraft between missions just to keep going.

Both door gunners Rose and Gomez had free guns, which were stripped-down versions of the infantryman's M60 Machine Gun. Each door gunner, was attached to the aircraft only by their "monkey harness"—the only thing keeping them from falling completely out of the aircraft during violent maneuvers. In flight, the crew chief and door gunner were forever vigilant and scanning the ground, jungle, forests, rice paddies, and other areas we flew over. They were constantly listening for the tell tale pops of ground fire and they were experts at spotting muzzle flashes from enemy gunners on the ground. Attached to each gunship door gunner's M60 was a metal box holding 200 rounds of 7.62mm ammunition. Malcolm Rose was right-handed and, like all right handed door gunners, he held the heavy 23-pound M60[6] machine gun by the pistol grip with his right hand and by the plastic forearm grip with his left hand.

When we were attacking the enemy, conducting reconnaissance by fire, or just providing covering fires for the slicks or ground troops, the door gunner on the side in the direction of our turn would be firing in front of the aircraft and on his side of the aircraft. The door gunner on the opposite side would be firing in the area that we had just flown over. These famous helicopter soldiers and gunners would frequently lean out so far that they were nearly upside down as they were firing and covering our asses. The names of some of our gunships, Birth Control, Here Comes the Judge, Cherry Buster, Till Death Do Us Part, and Viking Queen reflected the bravado of our Viking team-mates. And, like the pilots, they were flying a grueling 100 to 120 hours per month. During emergency periods like the VC and NVA Tet offensive of 1968 they flew over 200 hours per month!

Another important responsibility of the door gunner and crew chief was to pull the red emergency seat release handles in the event that one of the pilots was shot. These handles were located near the floor on the back of the pilot's seat. Then the door gunner and crew chief would lower the seat down, extract the pilot from his seat, and administer first aid. They would then raise the seat and sometimes the crew chief would get in that seat and help the remaining one pilot get the aircraft back to the nearest hospital. We always taught our crew chiefs the fundamentals of helicopter flying in case both pilot's were seriously wounded and unable to fly, or killed.

The gun platoon had a very selective and competitive process for inducting new pilots and enlisted members. Much to the two Tiger slick platoon leaders displeasure, the Viking gunships were frequently taking some of the best slick pilots from the slick platoons. I had loved flying slicks as an aircraft commander, but the call to fly attack helicopters (gunships) was irresistible, especially since my dear friend, Jerry Markland, had been killed. I wanted to shoot back at these VC and NVA who had been shooting at my slicks for the past six months.

On that day, Brian King was having trouble with his helmet mike and could not transmit, so he changed helmets putting on the spare helmet we Vikings carried on each aircraft. The spare helmet's mike and ear phones worked, but the helmet was two sizes too big for my fire team leader. There was no time to complain about that now. The assault aircraft were landing, and the enemy was engaging the slicks, us, and the ground force. Brian was in charge of covering those Tiger Hueys that were landing directly in front of an enemy bunker line in the trees about 50 meters in front of the slicks. My hands were full rotating the minigun from target to target using the flexible miniguns control hanging down from the ceiling of the helicopter and firing short bursts to cover the landing aircraft.

There were two light fire teams with two gunships in each fire team on this day's mission. One fire team would be rearming and refueling while the other was on station covering landings and pickups and attacking targets. One of my best friends, First Lieutenant Laurie "Bubba" Segrest, was leading the other Viking fire team. Thus far the enemy fire had been sporadic and none of us were particularly worried about the mission. We each believed that we would go home safely that night, like we had been doing over the past many months in Vietnam.

As we flew that day, I thought, *We are the sons of the greatest generation and our president has made a national pledge to help the South Vietnamese government defend itself against communist aggression. Although none of us wants to be at war,*

PICTURE 6: 1ST LT. GEORGE TAYLOR STANDING BY 121ST A VIKING GUNSHIP.

1. Viking parking and ready line, in revetment, with Soc Trang buildings and water tower in background.

2. George Taylor[i] went from slick pilot to gunship pilot to become a Viking aircraft commander, wing ship commander, fire team leader, and eventually Viking 26.

3. Note green log book in windshield and hanging helmet.

4. Note the nose low attitude of the old B-Models and its low ground clearance gave the pilots better forward visibility and the feel of a sports car. Taking off and flying these over loaded and underpowered aircraft took great skill.

we know that if our leaders say we are needed, then we knew we have to be here and represent the greatest country on earth. Our fathers fought in the great war (World War II) against people who put innocent people in ovens and now it's our turn to stop communism and its form of evil, which killed so many people in Russia, Poland, Hungary, Korea, and other places worldwide.

It also ran through my mind that morning that the VC had a $25,000 reward on helicopter pilots' heads. Army attack and scout helicopters were finding the enemy and killing them with great frequency. The enemy had a special fear and hatred of us. I reminded myself that these VC and NVA soldiers were extremely talented and highly motivated adversaries. But then, like Scarlet O'Hara in *Gone With the Wind*, I said to myself, "I am not going to think about that today. I am too busy and the Vikings are too good to get shot down or captured."

It was the dry season, and the rice fields were bone dry, hard as reinforced concrete, brown as an old pine cone, and extremely dusty as evidenced whenever the helicopters got close to them. We gunships were flying southwest, at about 100 feet altitude above ground level, at 90 knots, with skids just above the tree tops, in a moderate right turn, when the tail rotor exploded! Parts of the tail rotor flew by the left side, "my side" of the aircraft, and the aircraft immediately went into an extremely nose-low and tail-high attitude and began a violent spin to the right. I said, "Oh shhhiiiiiiiit!"

With the loss of weight of our 90-degree gear box and tail rotor components from the extreme tail end of our aircraft and the loss of the anti-torque rotor (tail rotor), our aircraft's center of gravity shifted dangerously toward the nose of the gunship. In flight school we pilots were taught that in some situations the aircraft might *stream line*, nose right when a tail rotor is lost, if there was enough forward airspeed, but this time the aircraft went into a rapid spin and nose-low attitude immediately even though Brian entered auto-rotation as soon as he heard, felt, and diagnosed the violent explosion and spin. We were in big trouble! We were going to crash damn hard!

A few months earlier, Brian King had experienced and successfully handled an engine failure and at first moment he thought this emergency might be the same thing. So he chopped the throttle expecting a normal auto-rotation, but instead the aircraft went extremely nose low and started to spin. Both of us pilots' and both door gunners' eyes were wide open with surprise and fear. We thought the aircraft was going to invert to an upside down and spinning position, a guaranteed fatal situation. Our adrenaline levels spiked and our *fight, freeze, or run* instinct kicked into maximum gear. We could not choose the freeze or run option in

PICTURE 7: TIGERS HOT REFUELING

Picture courtesy of Tom Jameson.

Picture of 121st Assault Helicopter Company Tiger slicks hot refueling. US Army aircraft seldom shut down to refuel, especially during multi aircraft operations. The crew chief usually did the refueling while the door gunner or pilot served as fire guard. Only one pilot stayed in the aircraft during hot refueling. With everything properly grounded this was a safe and combat expedient process. Air Force guys thought we were crazy.

a spinning and out-of-control helicopter, at 100 feet above ground level, going 90 knots—we would have to fight!

With no other choice, Viking 21 pulled in aft cycle to pull the nose up and avoid a fatal upside down or diving crash attitude thus slowing the forward airspeed but at the same time aggravating and accelerating the spin. I dropped my minigun sight and control and got on the flight controls with the fire team leader and called out "Mayday, Mayday, Mayday, Viking 21 is going down! Mayday! 21 is going down hard!"

Brian had entered auto-rotation by rolling off the throttle, which disconnected the engine from the main rotor system, slowing the spin slightly, but the spin was still so fast that Brian King's loose fitting helmet flew off from the centrifugal force of the spin before we hit the ground. The extreme heavyweight (really over allowable gross weight) of the gunship and the small main rotor blades of the UH-1B caused the aircraft to go into a rapid and deadly sink rate. Like me, all of the crew members lost orientation to the ground as the aircraft turned clockwise in a death spiral. Brian and I tried to control this wild, spinning, bucking bull of an aircraft, but being experienced pilots, we both knew the odds were against landing this runaway helicopter safely. Our best hope was to crash as softly as possible.

By the grace of God, the aircraft in its death plunge flew past the tree line, still spinning and falling with lightning speed. The crew had only about five or six seconds before the aircraft would violently strike the ground, at almost zero forward airspeed, and at an almost unsurvivable rate of descent! The crew chief and door gunner dropped their M60s and hung on, they had no time to fasten seat belts and only their seat belt extensions were holding them in the aircraft. Each of the enlisted men in the back were about to become unguided missiles upon impact.

I could hear Warrant Officer Bob Johnson, our wing ship AC, yelling on the radio, "Stay with it, Brian, stay with it!" His high-pitched voice gave away the fear and concern that he felt for each of us flying in the fatally injured and out-of-control gunship. We wished that we could make an emergency run-on-landing to an airfield like Soc Trang with crash rescue, but that was impossible in a spinning and overweight helicopter. We were falling almost straight down.

To make matters worse for us, the UH-1B model Huey had much smaller main rotor blades than the larger and safer blades used on all later C, D, and H model Hueys. Those UH-1B lighter, shorter,narrower blades did not produce enough inertia. The short narrow blades were not adequate to perform a safe auto-rotation in our wildly spinning and over gross weight situation. The spinning aircraft made it very difficult for us to know exactly what altitude the helicopter was at or when to apply collective pitch (pull up on the control lever in the pilots left hand) to cushion the imminent crash landing.

Aircraft Commander and Blue Tiger Platoon Leader 1st Lieutenant Sid Seitz[ii], who was the flight leader of the Tiger slicks we had been covering five minutes earlier heard our Mayday call. He immediately turned over his flight of slicks to the lead aircraft and started heading back to the landing zone to render assistance and evacuate any of us who might become injured in the imminent crash. He flew his slick as hard and fast as it would go, coming back to our aid.

After four or five 360-degree spins in a nose low attitude, our fatally wounded gunship impacted the sun parched and cement hard rice paddy surface like 20 tons of lead. First the landing skids and cross bars smashed hard into the belly of the aircraft disappearing completely into the aircraft's fuselage. They were almost pushed through the floor of the aircraft. The doors buckled and all windshields shattered. The fuel cells broke out of the sides of the aircraft. Then the main rotor blades smashed down into the ground and snapped the entire main rotor system off from the six inch diameter, steel, main rotor mast that connected the main transmission to the main rotor system. In spite of being strapped on snugly, my helmet and the two enlisted crew members' helmets flew off upon impact. It was a miracle that the aircraft and crew did not catch on fire and burn, as there was no crashworthy fuel system in use on Army aircraft at that time and the crew was totally incapacitated and seriously injured.

The crash actually crushed the helicopter to about one half of its original height and broke the aircraft almost into two large pieces at the midpoint. Both door gunners were thrown from the aircraft, breaking their seat belt extensions off, as they flew out of the aircraft, at high speed. Both pilots' backs were broken immediately by the extreme sudden stop after the rapid vertical descent. Both pilots were knocked unconscious and had traumatic brain injuries (TBIs) caused by the extreme force of the crash and their helmetless heads impacting the rocket and minigun sights and the heavy chicken plates.

Aircraft Commander Brian King's face, smashed into the fixed, steel XM-60 reflex rocket sight, breaking his nose and pushing it flat up and under his right eye, giving him a concussion, and cutting his face in several places. Brian also broke his right hand, broke his right ankle, damaged his right hip, sprained his knees, and severally whip lashed his neck and back. The crash knocked him unconscious and he was bleeding so much out of his nose that he was in danger of drowning in his own blood.

The left door gunner, Malcolm Rose, who also served as the crew chief, was thrown from the aircraft. The force of the spin and crash was so great that his seat belt broke and he severely broke his upper right leg in several places[7]. The right door gunner remained near the aircraft and was dazed, disoriented, and bruised, with a broken ankle.

Unfortunately, I did not have a vest (carrier) for my chicken plate so I had worn the roughly 15 pound ceramic bullet resistant plate under my shoulder harness and above my seat belt. When the aircraft impacted the ground, my back was broken, both of my ankles were shattered, and that heavy chicken plate became a dangerous and high speed battering ram. The chicken plate smashed down on top of both of my thighs bruising them and nearly breaking both of my upper leg femur bones. The chicken plate then flew back up and struck my left mandible (jaw), at an estimated 100 miles per hour, breaking my jaw, lacerating my neck deeply (2 inches deep and five inches long) , whip lashing my neck, giving me a Traumatic Brain Injury (TBI), and almost taking my head off. My deep neck and jaw line laceration was showing my tongue through my neck and squirting blood everywhere. Mercifully I was knocked unconscious by the tremendous G forces and trauma.

I awakened in my pilot's seat in severe pain, in a weird and hypnotic state. As my head semi-cleared, everything was blurry, and seemed to be in slow motion. I wondered what that red fluid was splashing up on my face and on the windshield and instrument panel—hydraulic fluid I guessed. I unbuckled my seat belt and reached for my M16 rifle that had been strapped over the side of my armored seat only to find it gone. I passed out again. I awoke a few seconds later, concerned about advancing troops and the fact that we'd crashed not far from the tree line of a heavy forest and jungle area. I wondered how I would help set up a temporary defense with only a 38 caliber pistol and 18 rounds of pistol ammo—

not to mention the disadvantage of not being able to remain awake for more than few seconds at a time or move?

I also wondered how I could be in Vietnam in 1969, seven years after the first Army Aviation combat units deployed, and so many aviators (especially me) still did not have chicken plate vests. The chicken plate vest (holder) was truly an essential piece of safety gear! Napoleon and Hitler had invaded Russia without proper winter clothing and equipment; Custer left his heavy guns in garrison; and now the US Army is without chicken plate vests, without proper rifles for air crews, without enough magazines for our 45 caliber pistols, and without enough clips for our M14 rifles for us air crews. We're the richest country in the world and still not properly equipping our soldiers. That really sucks! Then I passed out again from the lightning bolts of pain shooting from my lower back.

Again, I awoke and my head cleared a little more. I looked down and saw that red fluid pooling in and around my white-colored chicken plate was blood—and, my God, it was my blood! I then realized that my throat was lacerated deeply and bleeding profusely. I put my Nomex gloved four fingers inside my neck wound, felt my tongue through the six inch hole, and passed out again. I soon awoke and tried to pull myself up but passed out again from the extreme pain caused primarily by the compression fractures in my lower back.

In a few seconds I awakened again and I looked at the aircraft commander, only to find Brian with his head low, leaning forward, blood pouring from his face, and passed out. "Brian, are you OK?" I shouted, but Brian did not respond. *What is that loud noise?* I thought, unaware and not conscious enough to recognize that miraculously and now dangerously our aircraft turbine engine was still running and should be shut down before it ignited the fuel leaks throughout the aircraft.

A cloud of dull brown dust was slowly settling around our broken and smashed gunship. I thought, *Is this dirt and dust to be my death shroud?* Fear crept into the minds of each of us crew members, but survival, training, and shock overrode much of the fear. All four of us semiconscious crew members knew help was on the way.

Looking out the left side window, I saw the left-side door gunner; Specialist 5 Malcolm Rose was sitting in the dry, hard rice paddy with no helmet and no weapon and he was looking back at me.

"Help me get out," I called out to Rose, and he shouted back, "I can't" and pointed to his mangled right leg. I hadn't noticed that his right leg was facing directly to his rear and twisted grotesquely. His left leg was facing forward as he sat and his right leg was twisted 180 degrees and facing directly behind him and appeared almost amputated. Rose was seriously injured and in agonizing pain, with a broken and splintered leg. His dazed and ashen face was a sad sight. A shiver and coldness ran through my veins. Rose probably needed more help than I did.

Aircraft Commander Brian King awoke sitting in his armored seat thinking that a fire would surely soon engulf the aircraft. He wanted out of his seat and the aircraft. The AC reached with his right hand to release his harness, but for some reason he couldn't get it to release. He then realized that his right hand was broken and would not work properly. Brian used his left hand to release his shoulder and lap belts. He then rolled out of his seat to the ground, which was only a foot from the bottom of his seat. Once on the ground he found he could not get up or walk. So there Brian sat, on the ground, drifting in and out of consciousness. All he could do was look at me on the other side of the aircraft. He saw that I, too, was alternately waking up, moaning, and passing out again.

Brian could not breathe through his smashed and broken nose and he could hardly breathe through his mouth due to his massive nose bleed. The blood from Brian's nose was running into his mouth causing him to believe he was drowning.

As soon as our wing man had called out to Tiger 3 that we were crashing, one of the slicks in the formation that we Vikings had been covering turned around to help rescue us. Tiger 3 had also landed to help extract the badly wounded and injured crew and ground troops moved to protect the crash area and our Viking 21 team. Two soldiers from the Tiger rescue helicopter pulled me from my seat as I yelled obscenities at them for causing me so much pain. Then I passed out again.

When I woke up again, I was lying on the floor of the Tiger rescue slick with one of my rescuers applying a bandage and direct pressure to my neck wound. The rescue helicopter was taking off, at low level, and headed for trees. Both pilots were looking back in horror at the wounded Viking 21 crew and expressing concern for the injured on board their aircraft. I thought, *Damn, who is flying this aircraft? Both pilots are looking at us, and no one is flying this Huey, and they were heading straight for a tall tree line! Here I am almost killed by the enemy, rescued by these Tigers, and now the two idiots flying this slick are going to fly into a tree and kill all of us.* I tried to scream at the pilots to stop gawking at us wounded and please fly us to safety, but I could not quite break through the fog of pain and mouthful of blood and get myself to say it.

It only took about 15 to 20 minutes to fly to the US Army's 29th Evacuation Hospital at Can Tho. The helicopter landed directly in front of the Quonset Hut type hospital emergency room. The two door gunners and I were quickly put on litters and taken into the ER. Brian was foolishly and dangerously allowed to walk into the ER where he collapsed. The ER looked just like the ones in the popular TV show *MASH*. Medics, nurses, specialists, and doctors were frantically working on other wounded and injured troops and triage was in progress. A doctor told us, "Not to worry, we will take care of you. You guys are going to be all right."

Within a few minutes of arriving at the 29th Evacuation Hospital at Can Tho, our 121st Commanding Officer, Major Harold Ramey, and my good friend and fellow Gunship AC, 1st Lt. Bubba Segrest arrived. Bubba walked up to the foot end of my litter, looked at me, and asked a nurse, "Where is Warrant Officer Larry Dandridge? The nurse pointed to me. Segrest was white with shock and disbelief. He tried to look optimistic, to hide his horror. He said, "How are you ole man?"

I replied, "What do you mean 'Where is Dandridge?' You were looking right at me. To answer you, I am doing great, because I am leaving this hell-hole. You are the one that has to stay here another six months." Segrest grew whiter and he was sweating when he said, "I have to go out for some fresh air and a smoke, but I will come back and check on you Larry. Hang in there pal." Bubba walked to the door of the ER, staggered outside, and unbeknownst to me, my poor and dear friend passed out, fell forward like a limp rag, and smashed his head hard on the bumper of a jeep parked in front of the ER. Bubba had cut his forehead, banged the heck out of his head, and now he lay unconscious on the ground in front of the jeep.

One minute later, two medics carried Bubba inside on a stretcher and laid him down next to me. I was alarmed. "What has happened to Bubba? I asked. Was he shot by a sniper?" The medic replied, "No, he has just passed out from shock and dehydration, and he hit his head." I would never let my dear airborne ranger buddy and *Charleston SC News and Courier News Paper* Star Football Player" forget this fainting incident. We since have had many laughs over a beer together about this scary day in Vietnam.

Within a couple of hours, all of us Viking crew members had received our initial medical evaluations and first phase of our medical care. My gaping and bleeding neck laceration was sewn up and x-rays had been taken of my back, but unfortunately no x-rays were taken of my head, ankles, neck, or jaw. A few days later both of my ankles were found to be shattered and my left mandible (jaw) broken. Door Gunner Malcolm Rose's leg had been set and repaired as much as possible. Aircraft Commander Brian King's broken back had been x-rayed, but not his head or neck. Brian's severely broken and bruised nose had also been set, but it oozed blood continuously. The door gunner's ankle also had been set. We were each taken to a ward to prepare for ten days to two weeks in Can Tho. After that we would take the long journey back to the land of round eyes, the good ole USA, by way of Can Tho, Saigon, and Japan.

My broken jaw was not discovered until they gave me some hard food on my second day in the Can Tho hospital. King and I were placed in beds by each other, near the far end of a Quonset hut type ward, and far from the entrance to the ward, where doctors, nurses, and medics would come to us from time to time. Neither of us banged up warrant officers had the strength to roll over for about four days. Both of us suffered major back pain and what seemed like head to toe bruises that made moving even a little on our own almost impossible.

On about the fifth night in the Can Tho hospital, at about 2:00 AM in the morning, I awoke to a strange gurgling sound and the sound of liquid splashing on a metal surface. Brian was lying on his left side, facing me, and bleeding like a stuck pig from his nose. He could not talk and was holding a bedpan under his head catching the red tide pouring out of his face. I began to yell for help through my wired jaw. I could not sit-up, stand, or walk. My weak calls for help were muffled and the medic sitting at his desk reading his book under a dim light about 20 beds away could not hear my calls for help. It took 10 minutes to get the medic's attention and some help for poor Brian.

The second week in April 1969, I was medical evacuated by an Air Force C130 Hercules aircraft to Saigon, where I spent three days awaiting transport to Japan and the 249th General Hospital there. All I remember about the C-130 flight was it was loud, dusty, hot, and bouncy. I spent three days and nights in Saigon and was medical evacuated on to Japan in a C-141 Star Lifter, where I spent two months recovering. Thinking I could finally get a chance to sit up a while and tired of lying on my back for the past two weeks, I made the foolish mistake of changing my medical tag from litter to ambulatory just before getting on the C-141. After sitting for about 30 minutes, I was totally exhausted and nauseated, and my back was aching. It was actually torturing me with severe pain, but there was no place to lie down. So I was completely spent, and my back was killing me when the C-141 landed in Tokyo, Japan.

The hospital in Japan was a horrifying experience for me. Much worse than my own physical, mental, and spiritual wounds and injuries was my having to see so many and much more seriously wounded troops in great pain and agony. Most of the soldiers and marines in this orthopedic ward at Camp Zama, Japan, were amputees. The daily cleaning of their amputee stumps was an excruciatingly painful treatment—and resulted in much screaming, cursing, and crying from those poor legless, armless, burned, and broken soldiers and marines. Some troops were so badly injured they looked like mummies on a rotisserie and were being slowly turned 24 hours a day to prevent bed sores and blood clots, assist with their breathing, and promote healing. These mummies would occasionally moan but could not talk, and the sight of them depressed my innermost soul.

PICTURE 8: VIKING UH-1B MODEL HUEY GUNSHIP PILOT'S COCKPIT

1. Flexible minigun sight and control that helped terribly injure Larry Dandridge.

2. Brian King's helmet flew off before impact from centrifugal force of spinning and tail rotor-less helicopter.

3. Fold down and rigid rocket sight that Brian King smashed his face on and broke his nose on.

4. AC's M14 rifle barrel. These rifles were too long, heavy, and cumbersome for air crew members.

Then it was on to Scott Air Force Base, IL, for me where I spent four days waiting for a plane to Fort Gordon, GA, where I spent 30 days in the hospital and 60 days on convalescent leave, mostly at home in Charleston, SC. Luckily for me, my dad owned a small chain of hardware stores there called "Superior Hardware Stores," and he gave me a job loading and unloading trucks at his lumber company and hardware business. Working at my dad's store allowed me to slowly rebuild my back muscles, work at my own pace, and take breaks as I needed.

After the crash, Brian King was evacuated to Japan and hospitalized where he, too, witnessed much tragedy and suffering of his brother soldiers and marines and a few sailors and airman too. Brian King was then sent to Walter Reed Army Hospital in Washington, DC, where he expected to have back surgery. He stayed at Walter Reed for two months and, because he was not ready for surgery, he was sent to Fort Wolters, Texas as a classroom instructor. Much to his disappointment, Brian did not return to flight status. After four months he was sent to Brooke General Hospital in San Antonia, Texas, and had back surgery in November of 1969. Brian King was medically retired September 29, 1970, as a chief warrant officer.

For two years after leaving the Army Brian could not breathe through his nose. So he had nose surgery in 1973 to enable him to breathe through his nose again. Later he would have knee surgery to reconstruct his badly injured left knee. The Veterans Administration also wanted to repair his right knee, but he said, "No, when I can't walk on it then I will have it repaired."

I did not see Brian King[iii] again until 1971 when Brian visited me in Savannah, GA where I was a flight instructor and instrument flight examiner at Hunter Army Airfield. Brian's back never healed properly. It turns out that Brian had a scoliosis (curvature to the spine) that was not discovered during his induction physical. That scoliosis significantly magnified the injuries to his back. Brian had numerous operations to his back, but could not return to flying. He lost much weight, and was medically retired. He lives with excruciating back pain to this day. Brian is 100 percent military service connected disabled and legally blind. In spite of his serious injuries, Brian went on to have a successful career in insurance and a family. He is retired in the Orlando, FL, area with his wife. His son is a young Army aviator and warrant officer flying Apache attack helicopters at Fort Hood, Texas, in the 1st Air Cavalry Division and is a combat Veteran of the current War on Terror.

I would go on and serve 24 years and one month in the US Army and retire as a Lieutenant Colonel in 1991. As I grew older, my many physical and mental combat injuries would cause me more and more pain and disability. Today I am a proud but 100 percent military service connected disabled veteran. However, my injuries and

PICTURE 9: MARCH 28, 1969, CRASHED VIKING GUNSHIP WITH TAIL ROTOR AND 90 DEGREE GEAR BOX BLOWN OFF COVERING COMBAT ASSAULT

Picture courtesy of George Quackenbush.

1. AC Brian King, in right seat, had almost identical injuries as Dandridge.

2. Crew Chief Malcolm Rose was sitting here and was ejected upon impact and suffered a femur (upper leg) fracture and other injuries. The door gunner was on opposite side and suffered a broken ankle.

3. Pilot Larry Dandridge was sitting in left front pilot's seat and suffered traumatic brain injuries (TBIs), broken back, broken left jaw, shattered ankles, broken right hand, a severe laceration of left neck, sprained knees, and a horrific neck whip lash.

wounds did not prevent me from working as a regional manager, program manager, proposals manager, business development manager, engineer, and analyst in the aerospace and defense industry and a CEO and board chairman in the medical industry.

With a number of other partners, I founded a highly successful hospice in St. Louis, MO in 2002 and sold it in 2012. I continue to write part-time. I live and work in my beautiful home town of Charleston, SC, with my lovely wife, Judi, who is a retired school teacher, and our two beloved Italian (miniature) Greyhounds. As a state of SC and American Legion trained and certified Veterans Service Assistant and as a VA Trained and Certified Patient and Family Centered Care (PFCC) Instructor, and as an Army Combat Related Service Compensation Ambassador, I also do a lot of volunteer work for the local and first class Ralph H. Johnson VA Medical Center. My five children include two nurse practitioners, a lawyer, a dietitian, and a programmer, and my nine grandchildren are the true blessings of my old age.

Neither Brian nor I have been able to find out what exactly happened to Malcolm Rose or Specialist Gomez after that bad day in March 1969 in Vietnam. In 2012, Viking Door Gunner Wayne Zander told me that Malcolm Rose did recover from his wounds and had been living somewhere in Washington State. Both Larry and Brian would like to contact their door gunners and crew chief some day and thank them for their selfless, unwavering, and brave service to this great nation—and for keeping them alive in Vietnam! Both Brian and Larry have tried to follow the "Lead, Follow, or get Out of the Way" principle of Army Aviation leadership since becoming Army Aviators, and they are still close friends.

Back to March 1969

Back to March 28, 1969. As I lay there in the hospital in Can Tau, Vietnam, unable to move and high on a heavy dose of the narcotic pain killer Demerol, I though back about my graduation date of September 10, 1968 from US Army Rotary Wing Flight School and my classmates' and my anticipation of Vietnam.

Picture 10: UH-1D Tiger Slick Loaded with 15 ARVNs

About the US Army Enlisted Sky Soldiers and their M60s: The crew chief served as a door gunner and flying mechanic and the other door gunner assisted the crew chief and manned his M60 machine gun[8]. The M60 used on the Huey slicks is pedestal mounted. The M60 used on the UH-B and C Model gunships was a hand held, free gun that was sometimes attached to the aircraft with a bungee cord. The M60 is air cooled and has fixed head space allowing quick barrel changes for cooling. The gun weights approximately 23 pounds with a rate of fire 100 rounds per minute sustained fire, 200 rounds per minute rapid fire, and uninterrupted continuous fire. The gunners are issued an asbestos mitten for changing barrels, a ruptured cartridge extractor, screwdriver and reamer combination wrench, and cleaning rod. Maximum range of the M60's 7.62mm round is 3,725 meters and tracer burnout takes place at approximately 900 meters. The 7.62 ammunition in Vietnam included ball, tracer, and armor piercing. Bandoleer capacity was 100 rounds. Gunners frequently linked bandoleers together.

PICTURE 11: WO1 BRIAN KING AND CPT BILL FERGUSON

1. WO1 Brian King[9] was a 20-year-old fire team leader and gunship AC who trained many of the Viking real life officers (RLOs) and warrant officers. He bravely and skillfully led hundreds of dangerous missions. He is credited with saving his crew by flying a wildly spinning helicopter that was far out of center-of-gravity, without a tail rotor and 90 degree gearbox to the ground in an uncontrolled but survivable crash. Brian went on in civilian life to be a very successful business man and family man. He and his wife are retired and live in Florida today.

2. Captain Bill Ferguson[iv] was shot through the shoulder flying fire team lead and was awarded the "Silver Star" for staying on station to cover the troops on the ground that day. Bill and Brian are wearing the Vikings distinctive black berets and tee shirts. Both officers remain friends today.

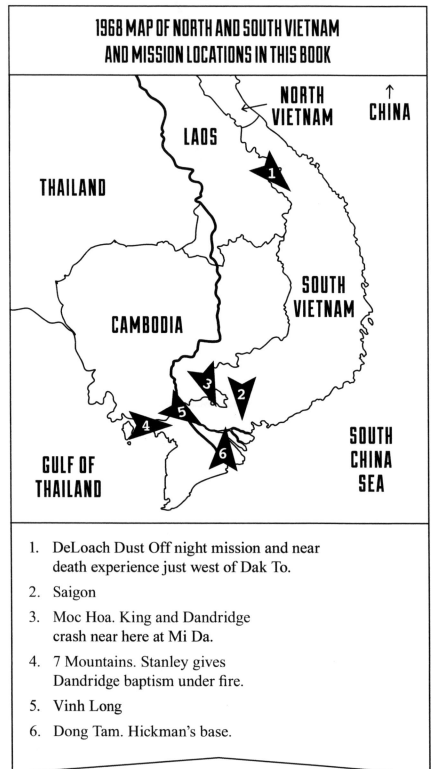

1968 MAP OF NORTH AND SOUTH VIETNAM AND MISSION LOCATIONS IN THIS BOOK

1. DeLoach Dust Off night mission and near death experience just west of Dak To.

2. Saigon

3. Moc Hoa. King and Dandridge crash near here at Mi Da.

4. 7 Mountains. Stanley gives Dandridge baptism under fire.

5. Vinh Long

6. Dong Tam. Hickman's base.

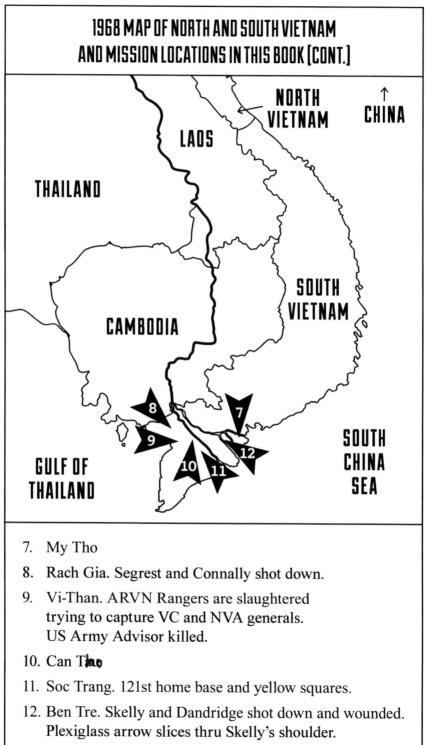

1968 MAP OF NORTH AND SOUTH VIETNAM AND MISSION LOCATIONS IN THIS BOOK [CONT.]

7. My Tho

8. Rach Gia. Segrest and Connally shot down.

9. Vi-Than. ARVN Rangers are slaughtered trying to capture VC and NVA generals. US Army Advisor killed.

10. Can Tho

11. Soc Trang. 121st home base and yellow squares.

12. Ben Tre. Skelly and Dandridge shot down and wounded. Plexiglass arrow slices thru Skelly's shoulder.

CHAPTER 2: SEPTEMBER 10, 1968 ◄

"US Army Leadership—Lead, Follow, or Get the Hell Out of the Way!"

Army Helicopter Flight School Graduates Decide to Keep in Touch and Share Interesting War Stories with Each Other

I, Warrant Officer 1 (WO1) Larry Dandridge and Warrant Officers Danny Hickman, Sam DeLoach[10], and Jerry Markland had just graduated from the US Army Warrant Officer Rotary Wing Flight School. Jerry Markland was my warrant officer class honor graduate. My good friend from high school and college, First Lieutenant "Bubba Segrest," had gone through flight school at the same time and was in the real live officer (RLO) graduating flight class that had paralleled my warrant officers' flight class and graduated on the same day.

Like our 219 fellow flight classmates, each of us were young men, in excellent physical and mental condition, and some of us were also in strong spiritual condition. Only two of our classmates were African American and they both served with great distinction and valor. Each of us had orders to Vietnam and would be there within a few weeks. By the end of October 1969 over two dozen of my warrant officer classmates were killed in action (KIA), one would be missing in action (MIA), and approximately half of the rest would have been wounded, injured, or become ill with a tropical or other service related disease. The majority of the survivors would suffer from mild to serious Post Traumatic Stress Disorder (PTSD) for the rest of their lives and many would become seriously or fatally ill from exposure to Agent Orange. All would give a great deal of their physical, mental, and spiritual strength and health fighting the Viet Cong and North Vietnamese Army in 1968 and 1969 and some would give everything!

PICTURE 13: WO1 JERRY MARKLAND (Center), WO1 ROY BUSH (Right), AND WO1 WILLIAMS (Left) AT GRADUATION ON SEPTEMBER 10, 1968

Picture courtesy of Larry Dandridge.

1. WO1 Gerald (Jerry) David Markland, Flight Class Honor Graduate.

2. WO1 Roy Bush on Jerry's right as you look at picture.

3. WO1 G. Williams on Jerry's left as you look at picture.

4. Warrant Officer Rotary Wing Flight School graduation day September 10, 1968[11] at Hunter Army Airfield, GA. Little did these young men know what they would face in the bloodiest two years (1968 and 1969) in Vietnam. Roy Bush would accompany Jerry's remains back to the USA. The two warrants (Williams on left and Bush on right) standing on each side of Jerry were his best friends throughout flight school. Jerry Markland and Larry Dandridge tried to eat and drink San Francisco dry en route to RVN and had been good friends throughout 1967 and 1968. If anyone can please send Larry Dandridge at *Ldandridge@earthlink.net* the address of any relative of Jerry Markland's, please do. The author wants to tell Jerry Markland's family what a great person, officer, brother-in-arms, pilot, and soldier Jerry was and to send them an autographed copy of this book.

Standing outside the auditorium at Hunter Army Airfield, GA, we congratulated each other and promised to keep in touch by letter while we served our combat tour of duty in Vietnam. Only one of our classmates had orders to someplace other than Vietnam. We warrant officers had each completed almost one year of flight training and we had simultaneously completed a year of warrant officer candidate (WOC) training. Each of us was proud to be a soldier, Army warrant officer or real life officer (RLO), and aviator. We were self-confident and ready to help the US Army, US Marine Corps, US Navy, US Coast Guard, US Air Force, and South Vietnamese military to kick the Viet Cong and North Vietnamese out of South Vietnam.

No longer would we be wearing the green winter walking out dress of the US Army with the warrant officer candidate (WOC) brass on our lapels and the orange shoulder strap loops with the Army Primary Helicopter School Crest pinned on it, indicating senior warrant officer candidate students. Instead we had proudly replaced those things of students with the rank insignia of a Warrant Officer 1(a gold bar with one brown rectangle in the middle) and silver US Army aviator wings. By order of the president of the United States, we were now officers, gentleman, and aviators—well, truthfully, we were at least officers and aviators with some of us still having a way to go to becoming gentleman.

We had our shiny, new silver aviator wings, a tactical instrument ticket, a Geneva Convention Card (which the NVA and VC did not recognize), our infantry basic training from Fort Polk Louisiana, our Escape and Evasion (E&E) two-day ground course certification, and our Handbook for US Forces In Vietnam. We were ready to save the world from communist aggression. Most important, the daily routine of inspections, running, doing push-ups, living in a state side barracks, studying, flying, taking tests, and being yelled at were over.

The tactical instrument ticket was supposed to provide enough skill and knowledge flying on instruments only and under Instrument Flight Rules (IFR) and Instrument Meteorological Conditions (IMC) to safely fly out of an inadvertent encounter with bad weather, smoke, or loss of horizon orientation at night. This lack of instrument (bad weather) flight training and lack of navigation aids in Vietnam would cost the lives of some Army aviators and their passengers and crew.

IMC or IFR flying essentially means flying with no visibility of the ground or horizon and in obscuration from clouds, smoke, haze, rain, snow, ice, dust, sand, or night conditions. IMC and IFR are essentially bad weather flying where the pilots cannot see the ground or anything else outside of the cockpit. Flying in bad weather was a "dangerous and emergency situation" for pilots with a tactical instrument rating. Without continual and frequent practice and good navigation aids, the tactical instrument ticket did not provide pilots with enough training to guarantee the successful execution of Very High Frequency Omni Directional Range (VOR), Automatic Direction Finding (ADF), and Instrument Landing System (ILS) approaches. Adding to the hazard of bad weather flying in Vietnam, was the fact that time for IFR practice did not exist in Vietnam.

Fortunately the limited instrument flight training that we received in flight school did, in most cases, teach us enough, to stay upright and to be talked down using a Ground Controlled Approach (GCA) or just to climb up to a safe altitude to clear terrain and ground obstacles and fly heading and maintaining a safe altitude until clearer weather could be found. The tactical instrument ticket did teach us how to navigate from point to point using ADF and VOR, but there were very few navigation aids and GCA sites in Vietnam. Since there was very little time for instrument flight training in Vietnam, the longer pilots were out of flight school, the rustier their instrument flying skills became and the more dangerous going inadvertently or on purpose into clouds became. Most pilots elected to fly low level, in easy range of small arms fire rather than to try flying on instruments in clouds. Flying formation in IMC conditions was impossible.

There were no cellular phones, laptop computers, desktop computers, e-mail, texting, Global Positioning Systems (GPS), Distance Measuring Equipment (DME), Night-Vision Goggles (NVG), and almost no radar altimeters, in Army Aviation in Vietnam at that time. There were also no active or passive infrared suppressors, passive heat reduction exhausts, chaff dispensers, flare dispensers, or radar jammers on helicopters back then to help evade and fool heat-seeking and radar-guided weapons. Because there were no crash-worthy fuel systems installed back then, many helicopter passengers and crew members, who would have otherwise survived crashes in an aircraft with a crash-worthy fuel system, lost their lives or were seriously burned due to frequent post-crash aircraft fires in Vietnam.

The main transmission and tail rotor gear boxes in the UH-1s, AH-1s, OH-6s, and other helicopters used in Vietnam were filled with oil. The oil drained quickly out of gearboxes when they were penetrated by small arms fire, the 51 caliber NVA machine guns[12], and heavier enemy anti aircraft weapons, thus forcing the aircraft to rapidly make an emergency landing or risk the transmissions seizing from heat and resulting in a fatal crash. Today's modern Army helicopters have grease in those gear boxes thus allowing them plenty of time to safely fly back home to be repaired. Finally, the aircraft and crews, especially the crew chiefs and door gunners, had little armored protection. Helicopter vital controls, components, and the enlisted crew members and passengers in the back, were highly susceptible to small arms fire. This vulnerability would lead to the demise of Jerry Markland and one of his enlisted crew members.

Army pilots in Vietnam used maps, very limited ADF radio stations, FM homing, some radar vectoring, and dead reckoning to find difficult locations all over Vietnam, Cambodia, and Laos. They also flew at night in the worst weather imaginable and sometimes used flares at night to help conduct their missions, which destroyed the crew members' night vision and made flying out of the flare illumination zone very dangerous. One good thing going for all Army aviators was the terrific "on-the-job-training" (called OJT) that all Army helicopter crew members went through in country, during their first 60 to 90 days there. The first female Army helicopter aviators were trained after Vietnam, so this book does not address their many later and current significant contributions to Army aviation.

As I walked away from my comrades and flight school graduation, I could hear the "thunder" and the loud "wop-wop-wop" sound of hundreds of UH-1 Huey, TH-13 Sioux, and AH-1 Cobra helicopter rotor blades in the background, as a thousand or more instructor pilots (IPs) and student pilots took off, performed maneuvers, and landed at Hunter Army Airfield and dozens of surrounding training areas. I thought about what I had been taught about leadership since joining the US Army, and I started formulating a personal style and philosophy of leadership. And I began writing a speech on leadership that I would eventually give at the Armed Forces Staff College in Norfolk, Virginia, in December of 1983 as a senior major.

That award winning speech would later be published in over 20 magazines, professional journals, and news papers, as well as two books in the US, Germany, and Great Britain. It would be published as a provocative training aid at many US Army and other schools and organizations, including: The US Military Academy at West Point, the German War College, the Department of Home Land Security, the Military Order of World Wars (MOWW), the Association of the US Army (AUSA), the US Army Berlin Brigade, the US Army Europe, the Warrant Officer Association Online Magazine, the US Army Field Artillery School, the US Army Air Defense School, the US Army Engineer School, the US Army Military Police (MP) School, the US Army Adjutant General (AG) School, the US Army Chemical School, the US Army National Guard, and the US Army Aviation School to stimulate discussions and thinking about leadership.

That speech embodies the high degree of training, technical skill, leadership, compassion, kindness, optimism, enthusiasm, understanding, wisdom, and courage exhibited by the warrant officers and commissioned officers, non-commissioned officers, and enlisted men and women of all of our armed services yesterday, today, and tomorrow. The speech is also the frame work of the high standards and moral character of the US Army Officer and Noncommissioned Officer Corps. The speech is shown in this book and is the essence of how these officers have tried to live their lives since graduating from officer and flight training. As in all professions, some did much better than others as leaders, but all could fly helicopters well and all loved their fellow birdmen and the troops they supported.

With the grid lock we see in our federal government today, with the lack of moral and ethical behavior in many of our nation's present and past top leaders, and with the tremendous challenges the United States of America faces around the world, our nation's members of the congress, presidents, cabinet members, and other federal, state, and local government officials and our nation's top leaders in industry need to read this speech. They need to try to emulate the high standards that our military officers, warrant officers, and noncommissioned officers follow! Of course some of our military leaders also would do well to reread this speech and rededicate themselves to high moral, ethical, and military standards.

Military Leadership Speech

Lead, Follow, or Get the Hell Out of the Way!
(A Personal View)

Leadership is taking the point position when your flight or unit is expecting contact with the enemy[13]. Leadership is flying a crippled bomber to the ground when one of your wounded crew members cannot bail out. Leadership is keeping your young soldiers, marines, airmen, sailors, and coast guardsmen alive and never leaving your wounded behind. Leadership is duty, honor, and country. Leadership is writing a dead trooper's family a personal letter immediately after the battle.

Leadership is not glorifying war. Leadership is not doing "anything" just to get promoted. Leadership is not winning the battle at all costs, nor is it losing a war to avoid causalities. Leadership is not found in the security of a well-fortified command bunker, nor is it found in a plush officers' field mess. Leadership pulls motor stables with the mechanics and operators of all ground equipment. Leadership stands up to bullies, cowards, fools, and the indecisive—no matter what their rank or position.

No compromise of the integrity of one's word, deed, or signature is leadership. Setting high standards and seeing that they are met is leadership. Intelligence, dedication, creativity, and selflessness are leadership. Stamina, vigor, and commitment are leadership. Spontaneous, contagious enthusiasm is leadership. Initiative,

PICTURE 14: WARRANT OFFICER CANDIDATE LARRY DANDRIDGE IN AUGUST OF 1968

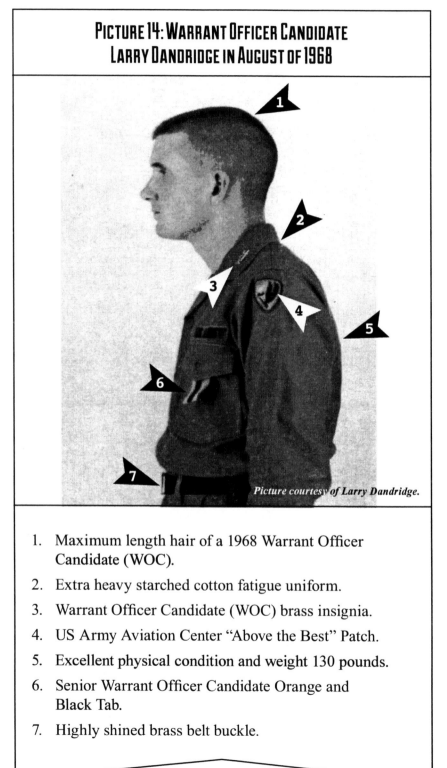

Picture courtesy of Larry Dandridge.

1. Maximum length hair of a 1968 Warrant Officer Candidate (WOC).

2. Extra heavy starched cotton fatigue uniform.

3. Warrant Officer Candidate (WOC) brass insignia.

4. US Army Aviation Center "Above the Best" Patch.

5. Excellent physical condition and weight 130 pounds.

6. Senior Warrant Officer Candidate Orange and Black Tab.

7. Highly shined brass belt buckle.

self-improvement, and professionalism are leadership. Pilots helping their crew chief and door gunner, immediately after each flight, complete the post flight inspection, weapons cleaning, and maintenance is leadership.

Leadership is rewarding a soldier, sailor, airman, marine, coast guardsman, or civilian with the appropriate recognition immediately after exceptional service. Leadership is commanding and managing. Leadership is establishing and meeting, by priority, specific objectives. Leadership is managing by exception, using job enlargement, and seeking job enrichment. Leadership knows that leading is more than just "follow me," but also "follow my orders."

Believing in God, family, and country, in that order is leadership. Being humanistic is leadership. Trusting the ideas and decisions of well-trained troops is leadership. Knowing where the mission is at, when the troops and material are to be there, and how many troops and systems are needed to win is leadership. Blocking out periods of "private time" to accomplish creative work and recharge is leadership. Compromising for the good of the whole with sister services and partner leaders on budgeting, planning, and executing is leadership.

Leadership is treating men and women equally without regard to race, color, creed, religion, age, or custom. Leadership is visiting your wounded and sick frequently. Leadership is knowing and living by the Constitution, the Code of Conduct, the Geneva Convention, and the basic human rights of all mankind. Leadership understands the tactical and strategic nature of war. Leadership shares the misery, exhaustion, and dangers that his or her troops face.

A leader is assertive but not aggressive. Leadership is neither ruthless nor mindless discipline, but it is the ability to do the right thing at the right time, by putting the whole before the parts. Leadership is not a good efficiency report, nor is it paper readiness. Leadership is not a court martial for every mistake nor is it leniency for serious violations. A leader is fair, predictable, persistent, consistent, and tough.

Giving a superior sound professional advice, even when you know he or she does not want to hear it is leadership. After you have given your best advice, following all legal, moral, and ethical orders, even when you do not agree with them is leadership. Leading when you can; following when you should; and getting the hell out of the way when you have nothing to offer, is leadership. Learning the language, culture, and customs of a host country is leadership. Staying in top physical condition is leadership.

Leadership is a general who knows the friendly and enemy situation, knows the immediate action sequence for the M16 rifle, knows his driver's first name and family, and can recite the Lord's Prayer. Leadership is a private who knows that he or she is in the chain of command and will have to take over when senior in rank. Leadership knows that a water truck in the desert is worth more combat power that an extra armored cavalry regiment.

Not forgetting that the past is our heritage, the present is our challenge, and the future is our responsibility is leadership. Not being overweight, not smoking, saying no to drugs, and not drinking alcohol in excess is leadership. Delegating authority, commanding confidence and respect, and accepting full responsibility for your actions is leadership. Ingenuity, sociability, tact, and tenacity are leadership. Cross training is leadership. Rapid sharing of intelligence is leadership.

Leadership is not being right all the time, and it is certainly not being wrong most of the time. Leadership fixes problems—not blame. Leadership is adaptability, appearance, cooperation, and decisiveness. Leadership displays knowledge, manages resources efficiently, and plans beyond the immediate requirements of assigned duties. Leadership creates an organization of mutual respect. Leadership is building an organization and environment where it is not necessary to tell troops what to do. Leadership knows that combat without conscience is evil.

A leader knows why there are air, land, and sea forces; why there are cavalry, infantry, armor, artillery, aviation, amphibious, special operations, prepositioned, recon, and logistical forces; and why combined arms and concentration of combat power are important. A leader knows about air, land, sea, and cyberspace battle and defense in-depth, civil affairs, urban operations, counter insurgency techniques, the advantages our forces have at night, and how to use them. A wise leader knows that young soldiers spend most of their time worrying about and planning tactics, while older more experienced soldiers spend the majority of their time worrying about and planning logistics.

Leadership can be good or bad, centralized or decentralized, warm or cold, offensive or defensive, macro or micro, or expensive or free. Leadership can be Catholic or Protestant, Jewish or Moslem, Hindu or Mormon, Atheist or Agnostic. Leadership prevents over mobility of junior leaders and troops, by keeping them in their jobs long enough to really learn their jobs and common and collective tasks and to work as team members. Establishing and promoting worker and troop certification and team certification programs are leadership. Leadership provides their troops with plenty of clean water and hot food. Leadership keeps their troops as comfortable as possible, keeps them feed, keeps them clean, keeps them supplied, keeps them informed, and keeps them from becoming depressed and suicidal.

Leaders hope and pray for the best and plan for the worst. Leaders know about the need to wage "total war" to win and about the special advantage the defender has in cities, mountains, and jungles. Leaders know how to "own the night" and take maximum advantage of all of the combat arms team, and they are skilled in the use of snipers, attack helicopters, counter artillery, naval gun and missile fire, and close air support. Leaders know not to keep weapons of their troops locked up and away from them, but rather to train troops to live with a clean, safe, secure, and serviceable weapon that they can expertly handle and fire.

Leadership is embodied in Jesus, Joshua Lawrence Chamberlain, George Patton, Abraham Lincoln, Lewis Burwell "Chesty" Puller, Doctor Martin Luther King Jr., Pope John Paul II, Moe Berg, Robert E. Lee, Winston Churchill, Joan of Arc, John Paul Jones, Winston Churchill, Sister Teresa, Margaret Thatcher, Nelson Mandela, Moses, Audie Leon Murphy, and many other well known figures.

Also leaders are less-known people like: Robert Lee Lightle, Dan Hickman, Bill Whatley, Dick Orrell, Sam DeLoach, Mendal Ackerman, Wes Komulainen, Frank Gordon, Rick Maull, John Schmoncees, John. C. Dandridge, Bill Waters, Brent Edwards, Kristy Krumwiede, Ron Williams, and thousands of others.[14]

Commitment to the team and a participatory form of leadership that draws on every troop's knowledge and skills, at every level, is leadership. Encouraging and rewarding suggestions and complaints is leadership. Having an open door and "open mind" policy is leadership. Empowering troops, civil service employees, and support contractors with the tools, responsibility, authority, and "accountability" to get the tough jobs done is leadership. Making troops multi-process, multi-weapon, and multi-functional experts is good leadership. Good leaders practice servant leadership and they know that potential suicidal thoughts can quickly seep into a depressed, stressed, and fatigued soldier—especially if family problems back home are present.

Leaders know that "the bitterness of low quality remains long after the sweetness of low price." Leaders allow talented soldiers "long leashes" for experimenting. Leaders find ways to satisfy the essential need of troops and civil servants to be both part of a team and be recognized as individuals. Leaders know how to use "internal and external bench marking," observations, and inspections to rate their organization's readiness, products, services, and processes against those front runners in their specialty.

Leadership is guiding. Leadership is legendary. Leadership is foresight. Leadership is absorbent, abstinent, and, unfortunately, at times it is abominable. Leadership is baccalaureate, balanced, basic, and too frequently backward and barbaric. Leadership has saved lives, killed, stopped wars, and started wars. Leadership has walked softly and carried a big stick, but it has also been loud and nonviolent. Leadership knows that a positive attitude will take you further than ability.

Saying what you do in clear, concise Standard Operating Procedures (SOPs), Plans, Processes, Value Streams, and Operations Orders and doing what you say (following those processes) is leadership. Breaking down communication barriers between staffs, line units, support organizations, and sister units is leadership. Getting at least a green belt and preferably a black belt in Lean Six Sigma techniques is leadership. Asking deep probing questions (five whys), finding root causes, and developing sound counter measures to "mistake proof" processes is leadership.

Changing problems into opportunities is leadership. Knowing that you can seldom wait until you have all of the answers is leadership. Repeatedly doing simple things that demonstrate sincerity is leadership.

Leadership is honesty, enthusiasm, loyalty, courage, and wisdom. Taking care of your soldiers', civilians, sailors, airmen, coast guardsmen, and marines and their dependents is leadership. Leadership includes being a good boss, good comrade and friend, father or mother, son or daughter, sister or brother, and husband or wife. Leadership is creative, aggressive, and drives for perfection. Leadership is not about coddling troops, but it is about challenging them.

Knowing that the profession of arms is much more than just a job is leadership. Being an unquestionable friend to the environment is leadership. Basing decisions on facts is leadership. Promoting and rewarding continuous improvement and value are leadership. Being a champion of safety, security, and quality is leadership. Staying focused on internal customers, external customers, and the enemy is leadership. Finding and eliminating the eight types of waste (waiting, overproduction, rework, motion, transportation, processing, inventory, and intellect) is leadership.

Performing preventive maintenance, knowing what cellular techniques involve, being skilled in set-up reduction, understanding mixed model methods, and understanding rocks-in-the-river problem-solving and inventory management is leadership. Knowing how to level and balance workload, understanding that distance (to supplies, replacements, ammunition, fuel, etc.) is usually evil, and ensuring things are at least "in-time," if not "just in time," is leadership.

Leadership is enthusiasm, optimism, helping, training, encouraging, understanding, motivating, disciplining, crying, laughing, standing firm, giving way, counseling, correcting, giving a second chance, and trying again and again. Leadership moves to the sound of the guns. Leaders are tall, short, thin, heavy, male, female, black, brown, white, yellow, old, young, and naturalized and un-naturalized. Leaders are from the city and from the farm. Leadership works hard to close the gap between a soldier's potential and his or her performance.

51

Knowing how to use teams, flow-charts (value streams and process maps), simple yet powerful statistical methods, simplification, continuous improvement, responsive complaint and suggestion programs, five-why, and standardization to get the tough jobs done is leadership. Leadership makes quality easy to see, feel, smell, taste, and hear, by finding root causes and permanently fixing the problem. Leadership is clarifying processes, identifying the detailed steps of each process, eliminating all non value added activities, and making every troop an expert at soldier common tasks—everyone should be an Infantryman first!

Leadership is sharing a common center, spirit, and cause. Leadership is caring, compassion, empathy, fierceness, and leading by example. Leadership is having the moral courage to convince troops to act contrary to their natural instincts. Leadership knows that treating all prisoners and detainees in accordance with the Geneva Convention and other appropriate protections is absolutely essential to having any kind of chance of getting the same humane and dignified treatment for our Prisoners of War (POWs) from our enemies.

Leaders look you in the eye, kick you in the ass, cover your flank, and take your place on the most dangerous mission. Knowing there is "a place for everything and everything in its place" is leadership. Leadership shares the dangers, admits mistakes, and learns from them. Eating last is leadership and leaving the pickup zone (PZ) last is leadership. Going up the hill first and "pulling your troops up behind you" is leadership. Sharing the pains of heat, dirt, cold, wet, insects, leaches, fleas, lice, and other harsh environmental conditions is leadership. "Packing your own roll and digging your own hole" is leadership.

Leadership comes from experience, but experience comes from making mistakes. A leader changes the odds and knows the risks. Leaders develop teamwork. The tides, the channels, the seasons, the winds, the hazards, the weather, the enemy, the terrain, and the best forecast are all known by leaders. Leadership knows that the one most important word is we and the least most important word is I. Leadership knows there is no end to change, except failure. Leadership knows that if you treat every customer (and trooper) like your last or first, you would never have to worry about repeat business.

Leaders often make good grades in school and have numerous years of formal education and many important degrees. But they also have been known to fail math, English, and other equally important subjects. Leaders make sure the enemy gives his life for his cause. Leadership ensures his or her troops always have the tactical advantage, best training, best equipment, and the highest morale, plenty of clean water, rest, and hot food. Leaders work hard at ensuring the workload is distributed equally among all troops.

Leadership comes from family, friends, teachers, coaches, and pastors. Simple, easy-to-understand orders come from leaders. Complex tasks are changed into short and accurate plans through leadership. Leadership can be learned and taught, but it cannot be forgotten nor brought. Leadership can be seen, tasted, smelled, felt, and heard, and it can come from a blind person with no hands who cannot hear, speak, nor walk.

Leadership knows that US citizenship is a duty and not a privilege. Leadership knows that, "For those who have fought for it, life has a special meaning the protected will never know![15]" As Thomas Paine said, "Lead, follow, or get out of the way." Finally, a leader is so in love with life that he or she is willing (but not wanting) to die to ensure that others live, and our great nation will go on![16]

Bubba, Danny, Jerry, Sam, our other flight classmates, and I said our final congratulations, goodbyes, and promises to stay in touch by mail, and each of us went immediately on leave for 10 to 30 days before catching a flight to San Francisco or Oakland and then on to Vietnam. We each knew that 1968 had already been the bloodiest year yet in Vietnam and that over 13,000 US troops had been killed during the first nine months of fighting in Southeast Asia. It was also glaringly evident that helicopter crew members were paying a heavy toll in Vietnam.

All of us knew we had to face an unusually complex challenge in Southeast Asia. We knew we would be told that we were fighting in support of a US national policy of helping an emerging nation, South Vietnam, to choose its own destiny, free of communist coercion. We knew we would be facing the frustration of conducting anti-guerrilla and conventional war operations. We knew that we would be conducting military campaigns against well-trained and determined (even fanatical) enemy regular army units. I wondered how we each would handle fighting an enemy who attacked only when he wanted to, vanished quickly underground and into safe havens in Cambodia and Laos, and was almost always indistinguishable from the populace of Vietnam.

Each of us prayed in our own way that all would have safe and successful combat tours, but each shuddered and wondered who might be coming home maimed or in a body bag. The following letters and true stories would document the next year of fighting, flying, serving, sweating, shivering, itching, crying, cursing, maturing, bleeding, grieving, numbing, denying, feeling guilty, becoming hyper-vigilant, becoming compulsive, being confused, becoming angry, becoming sensitive and frightened by loud noises, and in some cases dying or becoming crippled and disabled in Vietnam.

CHAPTER 3: OCTOBER 10, 1968 ◄

"Beware of the Yellow Squares."

*Letter from Warrant Officer Larry Dandridge to
WO1 Jerry Markland 15 October 1968*

Date: 15 October 1968

From: Warrant Officer W. Larry Dandridge,
121st Assault Helicopter Company (Airmobile Light),
13th CAB, 1st Aviation Brigade, APO 96296

TO: Warrant Officer Gerald David Markland
187th AHC, 11th AVN BN, 12th AVN GRP, 1 AVN BDE
APO SF 01213

Dear Jerry,

Hope this letter finds you safe and enjoying your tour. I
have been assigned to the 121st Assault Helicopter Company
(Airmobile Light) here at Soc Trang, Vietnam. The town of
Soc Trang is about 95 miles southwest of Saigon and has a
population of about 30,000. The Officers, NCOs, and enlisted
men here have been great to me, and I am getting used to the
routine here of getting up at O dark thirty, gulping down a
can of C-Ration fruit, drinking some water and orange juice
or a coke, pre-flight inspecting my aircraft, getting briefed
by an aircraft commander, taking off by 0530 hours for a
day of 12 to 14 hours of flying, helping the crew chief and
door gunner with post-flight clean up, eating supper, having a
beer, writing a letter home, asking God to forgive my sins and
to please protect us, and then going to bed.

It was sad to leave behind, in SC, my lovely wife, Nancy,
whom my friends and I affectionately call by her nickname,
"Muggs," and my 17-month-old beautiful and precious

55

daughter, Lori Shay Dandridge. I just listened to John Denver's song "Leaving On a Jet Plane," and it sure says it all about how each of us soldiers feel about leaving the good ole USA and heading out for Vietnam![17]

My wife and mom were crying as I walked out to the plane at the Charleston, SC, airport when I left for Vietnam. Being a soldier is certainly harder on families than it is on us warriors. I left Muggs and daughter in a nice apartment, in a safe area in Charleston called Park Dale, and our used car was running well, so hopefully they will be fine until I return next September. I am going to try to live off of $20.00 a month here in Vietnam and send the rest of my $600.00 per month (total pay before taxes) back to my wife.

Hope you can visit Soc Trang sometime. Soc Trang is a strategic combat support base and Army airfield in the Mekong Delta, a little over a mile southwest of Khanh Hung. It is located at about 8 degrees north latitude, very near the equator, and is the hottest place I have lived. Soc Trang was originally a World War II Japanese fighter base, then a French Military base, a US Marine Corps Air field, and now a US Army Airfield.

This place has everything I need to survive this combat tour including, old but sound barracks left by the Japs and French, a Ground Controlled Approach (GCA) capability facility and a low frequency-medium frequency Automatic Direction Finder (ADF) Beacon, an Air Force operated Tactical Aid to Navigation) (TACAN) station, a USAF Weather Station, a small Post Exchange (PX), maintenance hangars, a control tower, and one large paved asphalt runway.

We also have showers and latrines with running water most of the time, free (but censored) out bound mail, a mess hall with an ice machine, a barber shop, a high wire fence with too many vines growing on it, wooden and sandbagged guard towers, eight or nine cement bunkers along the fence, revetments[18] for our aircraft made out of 55 gallon dirt filled drums, and an Officers-Club. There is also an enlisted club, an ammunition dump, an Army of the Republic of South Vietnam (ARVN)

105mm artillery battery on the north end of the airfield, a US MP Detachment, a sister Assault Helicopter Company—the 336th AHC (T-Bird Gunships and Warrior Slicks), a fixed-wing Bird Dog (L-19 airplane) detachment, the 82nd Air Ambulance (Dust Off) Medical Detachment, an Engineer Unit, and even a swimming pool that is always closed due to no clean water and contamination. This place is really quite comfortable compared to the way the grunts and the cavalry live. I really have nothing to complain about.

Unlike most other Army Aviation locations in Vietnam, which have Perforated Steel Planking (PSP) or dirt runways, parking areas, and maintenance areas, which cause huge dust, blowing sand, and mud problems and discomfort—Soc Trang actually has a wide paved runway and paved parking and work areas. A person would just have to be here and feel the filth and discomfort of the blowing sand and dust and the gosh-awful and gooey mud at other Army Aviation bases, to appreciate Soc Trang. The terrible dirty and irritating feeling of getting sand and dust blown into your ears, eyes, neck, hair, and everything else from the sand storms created by hovering helicopters is something we all hate over here.

As much as helicopters are loved by our fighting men—no one likes the sand storms and clouds of dust they (especially Chinooks) create. I thank the good Lord everyday that my orders were changed from the 25th Infantry Division to the 1st Aviation Brigade's 121st Assault Helicopter Company (Airmobile Light)! I really did not want to fly those old OH-23 Raven scout helicopters for the 25th.

The guys here tell me that the 121st is the "Senior Army Aviation Unit" in IV Corps and one of the very first US Aviation units in Vietnam. The unit history book says that the 121st deployed to Da Nang, Vietnam, on 15 December 1961, as the 93d Transportation Company (Helicopter). In Da Nang this unit, flying the CH-21 Shawnee, called the "Flying Banana" helped develop helicopter assault techniques, aerial supply and medical evacuation methods, and they provided aerial transportation for the ARVN troops. The unit then relocated to Soc Trang in September of 1962 and became the first Army helicopter company in the Mekong Delta. In January 1963, the unit was presented with a fifteen-week-old Bengal Tiger.

Although the tiger, named Tuffy, only stayed with the unit until June of 1963, his gift to the unit was the name, "The Soc Trang Tigers." On 25 June 1963, the 93d Transportation Company was redesignated the 121st Aviation Company (Air Mobile Light). Only a few days later, on 4 July 1963, came the activation of the "Delta" Battalion, the higher headquarters of the 121, which later was renamed the 13th Combat Aviation Battalion (CAB)[19] located at Can Tho, South Vietnam. In 1964 the H-21 flying bananas were replaced by the UH-1 Huey and our Viking UH-1B gunship platoon was formed.[20] The 13th CAB is under the command of the 164th Combat Aviation Group,[21] which is headquartered in Can Tho.

The 121st mainly supports the 7th, 9th, and 21st ARVN Infantry Divisions, the ARVN 44th Rangers, the 9th US Infantry Division, the 5th Vietnamese Marine Battalion, and a multitude of other organizations in IV Corps like the Military Advisory Group, some Special Forces Teams, some Navy Sea Air Land guys (SEALs), the Brown Water Navy units here, defoliation missions, and others. The food here is not that great. I am eating C-rations a lot, but otherwise I am doing fine. I was also unpleasantly surprised to find out that officers had to pay for their meals—including C-rations in Vietnam. I am glad you and I tried to drink all the beer and eat all the steaks in San Francisco before we shipped out—as it seems that we may never get such good food again. That movie we saw, 2001 Space Odyssey was far out. I wonder if we will ever have such space flights and such computers as Hal in our lifetimes.

I have completed my in-country check ride with the Unit Instructor Pilot (IP) and have already flown over 100 hours in the 20 days since my arrival. I still hope I don't have to have anything to do with killing anyone. I prefer to fly troops, cargo, and medical evacuation over here , go home to be an Army flight instructor, and then out of the Army to hopefully fly as a civilian for the airlines, air cargo, Petroleum Helicopters in the Gulf, hospital air ambulance, police helicopters, or some other civilian flight job.

The one thing that troubles me over here is the high risk of continuously flying so close to each other, performing so many "acrobatic maneuvers—like high over head approaches," and almost always being over maximum safe gross weight. We spent so much time practicing safe distances, not exceeding weight limitations, and such in flight school. Now every day we are going balls to the walls with high-speed approaches, high rates of descent, heavy-heavy loads, "nap of the earth" tree trimming flights, and close-quarters flying of every kind—all while dog tired and dehydrated too.

My 2nd World War Veteran Marine Sergeant stepdad always said there are facts and lessons about war that cannot be taught in training—no matter how good the training is. I like the US Marine Corps approach of making every troop a "rifleman first" and every leader a leader, not a manager. I thought our US Army infantry basic training and advanced individual infantry training at Fort Polk, LA was excellent, but now, more than ever, I am firmly convinced that every soldier should go through Advanced Infantry Training (AIT) and get the 11Bush (11Bravo) Infantry Military Occupational Specialty (MOS) before going on to whatever specialty he or she enlisted for—whether it be Aviation, Artillery, Engineer, Signal, Ordnance, Intelligence, Transportation, Medicine, Food Service, Music, or whatever.

Every MOS pulls guard duty here with his rifle and crew served weapons, so why not train us to properly use and care for these weapons and use sound infantry tactics before we are sent into harm's way? I already encountered aviation and combat support troops on guard duty that had no idea how to properly "head space and time" the US 50 caliber M2 Browning machine gun. They also had no head space and timing tool. Some here have forgotten or never knew the immediate action and remedial action for their M14 and M16 rifles.

I could hardly believe I was issued an M14 7.62mm rifle with "only one clip" as my long weapon and a two and one half pound, old M1911A1 Colt 45 automatic pistol for my side arm.

The 45 is heavy, but I slide the holster around between my legs when flying and it offers some good protection for the family jewels. The 45 ammo is heavy also, but the 45 pistol is a darn good side arm, just becomes another thing that helps fatigue a pilot trying to fly a 12 hour day. Wish I had two extra seven round magazines for the pistol, but that is another thing my unit is short of—magazines for 45s! I still smile and sing that song in my head that the drill instructors in basic training made us sing while holding our M14 rifle in our left hand and our private parts in our right hand which went, "This (the M14) is my rifle and this (my Johnson) is my gun, this (the M14) is for shooting and this (Johnson) is for fun!"

As you also probably already found out, the M14 is too long, heavy, and cumbersome for pilots to carry in a helicopter. There is no place to safely secure it in a Huey cockpit, and it would probably fly out of the aircraft in a crash. It would be so nice if we had a secure, crashworthy rifle rack on the back of each of the pilot's seats and a rack over head for each of the two enlisted crew members (gunner and crew chief) rifles in the passenger and cargo compartment.

I also cannot believe we flight crews did not get the new Colt Automatic Rifle (CAR) 15s or at least M16s. I hear the Air Force crews have short CAR15s. The CAR15 would be perfect for us helicopter pilots as it would fit neatly in a Huey or COBRA. The M14 will not fit in a COBRA cockpit at all. I am going to try and find an M2 Carbine, the 30 Caliber WWII and Korean War US carbine, or better a CAR15 to use when I am flying. Some of the South Vietnamese use M2s and I should be able to find one eventually.

I hang my huge M14 across the right side wing (inside wing) of my armored pilot's seat, but sure wish I could get four more 20 round clips for it. Yes, we are also short clips for the M14 here. I also am appalled by the fact that my ceramic chicken plate (bullet resistant up to 7.62mm chest plate) was issued to me without the protective Velcro vest to hold it safely in place. I have to just slip the chicken plate between my shoulder harness and jungle fatigue uniform and hope it does not fall out or fly out in an emergency or crash. I tried on one of those new "ballistic helmets" but the thing is soooooo heavy! I believe it would totally and quickly wear you out wearing it. It would probably break your neck and tear your head off in a crash. I don't think I ever want to use what feels like a ten pound helmet and besides I think there is only one in our entire unit.

Another thing that alarms and disappoints me is only one AN/PRC 90 survival radio is issued to each four man crew here (one radio per aircraft) and there is no special vest or way to safely secure it to any of the crew. So we usually just place the heavy thing on the console between the pilots, where it would fly to who knows where in a crash, or in our jungle fatigue jacket pocket, where it is too large for the pocket and uncomfortable. You would think we would each have a survival radio and some kind of vest for it. I do have my trusty Army issued silk scarf "Blood Chit" telling anyone I show it to in Vietnamese, Chinese, Cambodian, Laotian, and other local languages that I am an American and that if they help me they will be rewarded by my government[22]—that should get me out of a bad situation if I am shot down, and if you believe that I have a bridge to sell you in Brooklyn.

You won't believe who arrived here just a few days ago, "First Lieutenant of Infantry and Army Aviator Bubba Segrest," my old buddy and dear friend from Charleston, SC. As you may recall, Bubba and I lived in the same St. Andrews school district in Charleston but he went to St. Andrews High and I went to the vocational high school, Murray Vocational High School downtown on Chisholm Street. Bubba married the nicest and most lovely "Southern Bell," who ever went to St. Andrews High, Miss Betty Dolan. Bubba and I also played high school football against each other and we went to the Baptist College at Charleston together. Bubba was and still is a much bigger and better football player than my skinny little 5'10"and 140 pound self. Both of us are flying slicks, both missing our families, and both trying to learn how to stay alive in Viet Fu#*ing Nam!

My first impression of the country is it is mostly so very beautiful and green from the air. The farms here remind me of my grandfather Jesse Dandridge and grand ma Letitia Addison Dandridge's farm near Cottageville and Round-O, SC. These Vietnamese farmers grow rice, papayas, pineapples, coconuts, manioc, coffee, rubber, tea, pepper, soybeans, cashews, sugar cane, peanuts, bananas; and other crops and they raise chickens, pigs, water buffalo, and other animals—not all that different from SC farmers, except they do everything by hand or with animal power. Oh how I wish I were on Granddad's farm and not in Vietnam.

I am not so sure about the capability of the South Vietnamese Army. It is so odd to see such small size people carrying the heavy (20 pound) Browning Automatic Rifle (BAR) and that heavy 30 Caliber ammunition and other weapons like the M1 rifle that seem so over sized and ill suited for their small statue. The older guys here don't have much confidence in ARVN. They have warned me to not trust them as they will steal equipment out of our aircraft (like survival radios) and they sometimes misfire their weapons and get their grenades caught on each other and the aircraft seat belts, tie downs, and other equipment. There are few things as exciting and unnerving as hearing a grenade fall on the metal floor of the troop compartment of your helicopter!

Hard to believe there were only 25,000 US troops in Vietnam in 1962 and now there are over half a million of us here. Vietnam reminds me of the 1946 story of old Tar Baby. The Tar-Baby is a fictional character in the second of the Uncle Remus stories published in 1881. It is a doll (the VC in our case) made of tar and turpentine used to entrap Br'er Rabbit (the US Army). The more that Br'er Rabbit fights the Tar-Baby, the more entangled he becomes.[23] Where in the hell is this war going?

I haven't flown any missions yet into the dark and infamous U-Minh Forest that runs along the western boundary of the Delta and IV Corps. The senior guys here tell me the VC own this area of swamps, forests, jungle, canals, rivers, elephant grass, vines, and other dense vegetation. The French caught hell there and the senior guys here say that we can always expect to catch the devil when we operate there. I am sure you have such dreaded places in your operational area. The description of the U-Minh reminds me a little of our biggest and thickest South Carolina Swamps (especially Four Hole Swamp[24] just north of Summerville) and our American Revolutionary War in SC. As American Patriot, Colonel Francis Marion, our beloved SC Revolutionary War hero (The Swamp Fox) could not be followed, found, or defeated by the British Army, in SC's swamps and big forests; it appears the VC may never be defeated in the U-Minh—even with all our fire power and technology.

I am proud of and more appreciative than ever of the good infantry training we got at Fort Polk and the outstanding officer and flight training we went through at Fort Wolters, TX and Hunter Army Airfield, GA. I really feel much more mature and technically competent than when I joined the Army in August of 1967. I also am starting to get a better understanding of the full significance of my wife's and parent's concerns over me going to Vietnam. Just wish I knew more about Vietnam and its' history, people, culture, many religions, language, and counter insurgency.

I have only been flying for two weeks here and already had a close call with death to share with you, a main rotor blade strike with a Dust Off helicopter while landing in a 20 ship formation. I am lucky to be alive and learned that it takes an entire team to fly safely over here and that even our most experienced pilots can make dangerous mistakes, especially when they don't get enough crew rest. Thank goodness that I, nor anyone else, was seriously injured or killed. Attached to this letter is a summary of what happened on October 10, 1968 here at Soc Trang on the yellow squares.

Perhaps we should take a lot of pictures and keep some kind of diary or log of the more exciting, tragic, scary, depressing, bizarre, and funny things that take place over here—in the land of Vietnam. Maybe we could write a book about this war some day. Not sure our children or friends will believe all this stuff we are doing over here. Not sure about everyone in my unit, but I truly believe in this cause of "stopping communism here" and

I am certain we can win this war. The kind of atrocities being committed everyday here by the Viet Cong is proof enough to me that anyone who can butcher their own men, women, and children like the VC does cannot be the kind of people who should be running this country.

Please write me when you have time and take good care of yourself. I am praying for you and all of our classmates to get through this war safely. I know you want to get back to those ski slopes in New Mexico too. We arrived here in good physical condition and I am certain that we shall live through this rotten little war. I cannot wait to get home and go fishing, shrimping, and hunting with my Dad and Stepdad in the low country of SC again!

Your friend,

Larry

Beware of the Yellow Squares at Soc Trang, Vietnam!

"We have met the enemy and he is us."
–Cartoonist Walt Kelly
POGO Comic Strip.

On October 10, 1968, I was assigned to fly as peter pilot under the command of CW2 Bob Hookers, one of the most experienced pilots in the 121st Assault Helicopter Company. Bob had dark hair, a great smile, 1,000 hours of accident free combat flight time, and a black cowboy mustache. I found him to be a rare resource being an experienced Slick Aircraft Commander (AC) and a past UH-1C Gunship Aircraft Commander in a Cavalry unit at Zion. He had been in country for about ten months. Bob was a little older than the rest of the first tour pilots in my unit and he was a Chief Warrant Officer 2, a very rare thing in our unit. He had an air of confidence in his walking, talking, and flying. I felt fortunate to be getting much of my initial in country training from him. He made me feel at ease, but at the same time, since I lived in the same hooch (one story old Japanese and later French barracks), I could not help but notice that he didn't get enough sleep at night.

He had been transferred to the Soc Trang Tigers from another unit, an Air Cavalry Unit, up North about four months before I arrived. Bob was needed to help fill the need for replacements in the 121st and to provide a more experienced pilot to the 121st. The personnel guys called these transfers "infusions." Bob loved to listen to Loretta Lynn music and drink good whiskey, and he was training me to become an aircraft commander and that is what mattered most to me. He even had a rocket box paneled hootch, a fan, and a refrigerator in his room which perhaps only one other guy had in our slick platoon. Bob showed me how to drink the Vietnamese "33" Beer, which was pronounced "Bomb-de-ba." Bob had flown a thousand hours of flight time in the past ten months and had, unfortunately, exceeded any acceptable crew rest standards by flying some 450 plus flight hours for the past three months. He was tired to the bone and letting me, his Peter Pilot, fly much of the morning.

The 121st Assault Helicopter Company's Senior Aircraft Commander, Chief Warrant Officer 2 Robert "Bob" Hookers[25] was leading the second flight of ten UH-1D model Hueys in trail formation returning to Soc Trang to pick up another 240 or so Army of South Vietnam 21st Infantry Division Troops. The D Model Huey was equipped with 220 gallon fuel tank, the 1100 shaft horse power T53-L-11 engine, and 48 foot long and 27 inch wide main rotor blades, which are six inches wider than the old UH-1B Model blades. The D Model also had an enlarged cabin, and a maximum safe gross weight of 9,500 pounds, which was 1,000 more pounds than the B Model Huey. The 121st was equipped with mostly D Model slicks, but we were expecting to receive more and more of the needed new H Model Hueys as time went on. The H Model was really just a D Model, but with a much needed new 1,400 shaft horsepower T53-L-13 engine to cope with the heat, humidity, heavy loads, and mountains in Vietnam.

I was flying as Bob's "Peter Pilot" and known as one of the "Fu#^ing New Guys" or an "FNG." We had been flying troops into a large landing zone (LZ) all morning. Both of us were tired from flying about 36 hours in the past three days. I felt lucky to be flying with one of only three Chief Warrant Officers in the 121st Assault Helicopter Company and Bob and I hit it off quickly. I had only been in county for about 20 days and had been flying

PICTURE 15: WELCOME TO TIGERCOUNTRY 121ST AHC SIGN IN 1968

Picture courtesy of Bill Schmidt.

for only 15 days when we took off on the morning of October 10, 1968. Bob had already shown me that the UH-1D and H Model could carry upwards of 2,100 or more pounds "above maximum published gross weight" in the operator's manual due to the large cabin.

Chief Warrant Officer Hookers shared much of his valuable knowledge and combat experiences with me. He showed me the mangrove swamps, the triple canopy jungle, the black as night heavy forests, the myriads of canals and bunkers built into the canal banks, the dozens of rivers, the vast numbers of palm trees, the coconut trees, the elephant grass, and the utterly destroyed and pulverized areas where B52 strikes had eliminated temporarily all vegetation. He pointed out the thousands of square miles of rice fields and paddies, the pagodas, the graveyards, the ferns of all sizes, the water buffalo at work, and cities, towns, hamlets, and triangular shaped Regional Force and Popular Force (referred to as RUFF PUFF) forts.

Picture 16: 1ˢᵀ Lt. Bubba Segrest & WO1 Larry Dandridge On An Old Bunker At Soc Trang Near Dandridge's Hootch

Picture courtesy of Larry Dandridge.

1. First Lieutenant Laurie O. (Bubba) Segrest.

2. Warrant Officer Larry Dandridge.

3. With rotten timbers and rotten sandbags, this old bunker was more dangerous than staying flat on the ground or under your bunk. The bunker was full of rats, spiders, and worse.

This picture was taken in November 1968. Both pilots were Tiger slick pilots at the time. Both would be wounded flying "Viking" gunships in 1969. Both are from Charleston, SC, and had played high school football against each other. Both attended the Baptist College at Charleston together and both had gone through flight school together (Segrest as a 2nd Lt. and Dandridge as a Warrant Officer Candidate [WOC]). Both were assigned to the 121st Assault Helicopter Company in Vietnam.

He told me to answer "I do not know," rather than, "I will not tell you," if I ever became a POW. He also told me about the patience of the Vietnamese—especially the patience of the North Vietnamese Army (NVA) and Viet Cong (VC) to be willing to evidently fight any invading enemy, whether they are Chinese, French, Japanese, or American. He told me that it is obvious that the Viet Cong and NVA will fight us for however long it takes, to wear us down, and have our citizens and politicians at home tire of the huge expense in dollars and lives it takes to fight a war so far from home. This was unsettling to me.

Bob also shared with me some of the great innovations that the US Army had come up with to do our jobs better and easier in Vietnam. He showed me the 55 gallon drums that some smart enlisted guy had cut in half and attached to the sides of a Huey to hold and then drop Mark 24 Flares when we needed to use them to support night missions. He also told me about the great ways we were collecting intelligence about the enemy including, but not limited to Long Range Recon Patrols (called LRRPs), pattern analysis, acoustic sensors, magnetic sensors, seismic sensors, Mohawk airplane airborne reconnaissance (side looking radar and infrared), infrared lighting, xenon lighting, and night light enhancing (starlight scopes) equipment.[26]

I also learned quickly how to safely "hot refuel" the Huey while the engine was running and rotors turning, by stationing one pilot or the crew chief or door gunner outside, with a fire extinguisher, having one crew member ground the aircraft and refuel line, and then refuel the aircraft. No one could stay inside the aircraft while hot refueling, but one pilot. While hot refueling all crew members wore their gloves and their helmets with the visor down, and kept their jungle fatigue jacket's sleeves rolled down. As a matter of standard operating procedure, we always hot refueled in Vietnam, unless we were somewhere that hot refueling was not available and trucks were being used or unless we were going to shut down and go somewhere away from the aircraft. The Air Force thought we were crazy hot refueling and they may have been right some of the time, but we were always ready to take off quickly and get back to business by using hot refueling and there were very, very few Army hot refueling accidents or fires in Vietnam.

Bob, with all his ten months of experience in Vietnam, told me about how the VC planned their operations in great detail, prepositioned their supplies and ammunition before each battle, rehearsed their attack and ambush plans before executing them, and quickly disengaged and avoided contact with our forces unless they had a significant advantage. He reminded me that the enemy would use delaying forces to ambush and harass our pursuing troops and allow the main VC body to retreat and hide. Bob said the enemy frequently disperses their troops into small bands and rendezvous later at a predestinated point, all in an effort to disengage and avoid a face-to-face fight with US and allied forces. Bob also told me the VC and NVA feared our helicopters, especially our UH-1B and C Model gunships and AH-1G Cobras. The VC and NVA were acutely aware that we would bring our superior firepower of gunships, mortars, artillery, naval gun fire, and tactical air (fighters and bombers) to bear on them quickly once we discovered them, Bob told me.

It meant very little to Bob or me that the political power in the Government of Vietnam was concentrated at the national level and that most important decisions and major programs originated and were directed from Saigon. The fact that South Vietnamese national policies, decisions, and programs were passed to lower echelons of the government at the province, district, village, and hamlet levels for execution was not all that interesting or even useful to a 20 year old Warrant Officer. Bob and I did know that the South Vietnamese had divided South Vietnam into four tactical corps or zones. We also knew that we were going to be primarily supporting South Vietnamese units and the US 9th Infantry Division in the 4rth Corps Tactical Zone most of the time during our tour in the Delta region of Vietnam.[27] What was important to us was doing a good and safe job flying the many types of missions we were responsible for without getting ourselves, our crew members, or passengers injured or killed.

I was in awe of the ability of our crew chiefs and our other 121st AHC maintenance folk's ability to keep all the thousands of helicopter parts cooperating so that we could fly the hell out of these birds day and night, seven days per week. The power plant (engine), avionics, power train, sheet metal, armament, rotor, and other mechanics and the maintenance officers, test pilots, and technical inspectors had a very hot, difficult, and much less glamorous job than us fly boys. The biggest advantage to these professionals was that they did not have to go out and face the enemy and the flying risk day after day. All of us flight crews admired the maintenance guys' perseverance and dedication.

Chief Warrant Officer Bob Hookers had reminded me over the past few days that South Vietnam has 43 provinces and below the provinces are districts that are much like our US counties. He had mentioned that the districts were divided into villages, with an average of 8 to 12 villages per district. Bob told me that South Vietnamese villages normally consisted of four to six hamlets and that historically the villages had been the most important organizations for local government. The hamlets performed all essential legal and tax collecting functions.[28]

Bob told me that this military contest between North Vietnam, with a population of some 17.5 million, and South Vietnam, with a population of almost 16 million, was a dirty war—both sides were killing civilians at an alarming rate. He also took the time between landings and takeoffs and in-country flight training to tell me about the South Vietnamese Armed Forces. Between Bob's explanations and my copy of the Handbook for US Forces in Vietnam, I knew that the Republic of Vietnam Armed Forces consisted of the Army of the Republic of Vietnam (ARVN), the Vietnamese Air Force (VNAF), the Vietnamese Navy (VNN), and the Regional and Popular Forces (RF and PF). What was important to me was that each of these Vietnamese military elements had a specific and important role in the overall strategy for defeating the Viet Cong and North Vietnamese Army main force units, the VC local force units, and the VC guerrillas.[29] What alarmed me as a new guy was that almost no one in the US Army seemed to have any confidence or respect for the South Vietnamese Army (ARVNs as we called them).

The fact that we frequently took small arms fire from ARVN units and outposts did not build much good will in Americans towards ARVNs. It was obvious that some ARVNs had to be VC and it was obvious that many ARVN soldiers' hearts were not in this war. At the same time I had also heard from some of the US Army advisors who worked daily with the ARVNs that many of the ARVNs were good soldiers and many of their junior leaders were highly motivated and professional. I would just have to watch and see for myself over the next 11 months and form my own opinion of them. At the moment I felt sorry for them having to "schlep" (Yiddish for carry a heavy load) those over sized US steel helmets, huge Browning Automatic Rifle and other over sized US weapons, grenades, and gear on long walks in deep water, mud, and jungle in such God-awful heat!

Chief Warrant Officer Bob Hookers had told me that the Army of the Republic of South Vietnam is primarily an infantry force consisting of 10 infantry divisions, plus separate infantry, airborne, ranger, and armor units. Bob explained that ARVN is normally committed against the NVA and VC main force units in search and destroy and clearing operations. He also mentioned that ARVN units, when not on the offensive, are supposed to be committed to securing areas where civilian police or pacification teams are operating and defending key installations, supply routes, and communications facilities. He also said that many of the US guys say the ARVNs go on search and avoid missions and would prefer to leave the fighting to us Americans. I would witness many examples of the incompetency, lack of motivation, and sometimes disloyalty in ARVN forces in my tour of duty in Vietnam.

Hookers said that South Vietnamese Army operations are supposed to be closely coordinated with local Vietnamese Government province officials to ensure those military operations support local efforts and do not endanger South Vietnamese RF-PF local forces. Bob also reminded me that US Military Assistance Command, Vietnam (MACV) advisory teams work with all South Vietnamese Army forces, normally down to battalion level, but sometimes to company level. These US Army advisors provide a ready point of contact in coordinating combined US, South Vietnamese Army, and allied operations. Bob said it all sounds good on paper, but in practice it seems as though the South Vietnamese right hand does not know what the left hand is doing much of the time[30]. Again I was uneasy with this early indoctrination in the alleged short comings of the ARVN troops.

Picture 18: Tiger Crew Chief Mike Dewey With "His" Slick

Picture courtesy of Larry Dandridge.

Specialist 5 Mike Dewey with his "Huey" tail number 890. WO1 Joe Casanova was his slick AC and Specialist (Infantryman extraordinaire) John Romero was his door gunner. After working 3 to 4 months as an aircraft mechanic in the hangar, Dewey volunteered for slicks. A year later he volunteered to fly as a door gunner and crew chief on a Viking gunship. An armor piercing round later hit one of his ACs and himself. That round shot Dewey's helmet off and went out through the aircraft roof and rotor blade. He was terrific training new pilots and door gunners. The author greatly appreciates the training that Mike Dewey gave him as a new peter pilot. His tour ended when he was shot through the back and almost killed. He earned his wings!

Tiger 99[31] was Bob's call sign, and it was about 1100 hours in the morning on a bright, sunny day as Bob took the controls, stating, "I have the controls." I replied, "Yes Sir, you have the controls." Bob corrected me for the fourth or so time in the past three days, telling me, "My name is Bob, please do not call me "sir" again! My dad was Mr. Hookers, and sir, and my name is Bob. Larry, you are out of flight school and officer training now, and I prefer you address me as Bob." Having "Sir" and "Ma'am" drilled into my head as a kid growing up in the deep south, as a cadet at the Citadel, as the step-son of a great marine, and as an army-enlisted recruit and warrant officer candidate it would be a hard habit for me to break.

Bob asked me, "Have you heard the joke about the soldier, marine, sailor, coast guardsman, and an airmen arguing over, which branch of the US military service is the best?" I replied, "No, I don't think so."

Bob proceeded to tell me the joke:

Which US Military Service is the Best?

A soldier, a sailor, an airman and a marine got into an argument about which branch of the service was "The Best." The argument became so heated that the four service men failed to see an oncoming truck as they crossed the street. They were hit by the truck and killed instantly.

Soon, the four servicemen found themselves at the pearly gates of Heaven. There they met Saint Peter and decided that he was the ultimate source of truth and honesty. So, the four servicemen asked him, what he thought. "Saint Peter," they said. "Which branch of the United States Armed Forces is the best?" Saint Peter replied, "I can't answer that. However, I will ask God what He thinks the next time I see Him. Meanwhile, thank you for your service on Earth and welcome to Heaven."

Sometime later, the four servicemen saw Saint Peter and reminded him of the question they had asked when they first entered Heaven. The four servicemen asked Saint Peter if he was able to find the answer. Suddenly, a sparkling white dove landed on Saint Peter's shoulder.

In the dove's beak, was a note glistening with gold dust. Saint Peter opened the note, trumpets blared, gold dust drifted into the air, harps played crescendos and Saint Peter began to read the note aloud to the four servicemen...

MEMORANDUM FROM THE DESK OF THE ALMIGHTY ONE

TO: All Former Soldiers, Sailors, Airmen, Coast Guardsmen, and Marines

SUBJECT: Which Military Service Is the Best

1. All branches of the United States Armed Forces are honorable and noble.

2. Each serves America well and with distinction.

3. Serving in the United States military represents a great honor warranting special respect, tribute, and dedication from your fellow man.

4. Always be proud of that.

Warm regards, GOD, US Army Aviation (Retired)[32]

This story helped take some of the edge off of the stress of flying in combat, and I burst out laughing. "How true that is," I said and promised to remember the story.

Bob and I had just flown three long 12 to 14-hour days performing "ash and trash" transport missions flying water, food, ammunition, spare parts, troops, chaplains, farm animals, and other cargo and passengers all over IV Corps and the Delta region of Vietnam. We had been hauling stuff to dozens of different small and larger bases, towns, forts, and hamlets for the previous three days. Now Bob was teaching me how to fly on a combat assault. This was my 15th day of flying in Vietnam and I was enjoying the training, but also already tired and full of apprehension about the unknown year ahead of me.

Bob pointed out to me on our map that IV Corps consists of the following 17 provinces: Chau Doc, Kien Tuong, Kien Phong,

Hau Nghia, Kien Giang, An Giang, Vinh Long, Dinh Tuong, Long An, Chuong Thien, Phong Dinh, Vinh Binh, Kien Hoa, An Xuyen, Go Cong, Bac Lieu, and Ba Xuyen. He also told me that the Viet Cong dressed in the same black pajamas that all Vietnamese wear. He also told me that they hid easily among the common Vietnamese people, a people so intimidated that they were proved to be an unreliable source of information to the South Vietnamese Army and US military.

I was learning quickly that the 7th, 9th, and 21st Army of the Republic of Vietnam (ARVN) Infantry Divisions played major roles in IV Corps military planning and operations. Bob had already told me and shown me that the US Army's 9th Infantry Division is stationed at Dong Tam and the 9th Infantry Division operates throughout IV Corps. The 9th US Army Division attacks Viet Cong units in their strongholds in the Plain of Reeds, the U-Minh Forest[33], and the Seven Mountains areas. I had already flown to Dong Tam with Bob and had done some close support of the US Army 9th Division's troops. Chief Warrant Officer Hookers explained that the US Army 9th Division is a "Riverine Division." He explained that they used special shallow draft gun boats, floating artillery, armored transports, and helicopters to fight the firmly entrenched Viet Cong in the Delta's flat rice paddies, swamps, canals, streams, forests, and jungles.

CW2 Hookers explained to me that the South Vietnamese District Forces were called Regional Forces (RF) and the South Vietnamese Village Forces were called Popular Forces (PF). He said the RF are a nationally administered military force assigned to and under the operational control of the province chief. The basic combat RF unit is the light infantry company—with some provinces having some mechanized platoons, intelligence platoons, and river patrol companies. PF forces are also nationally administered and operate at the village level, and are made up of light infantry squads and platoons. PF units are commanded by their own noncommissioned officers (NCOs) who are responsible through their village chief to the district (province) chief. PFs are full-time volunteers recruited from their own villages and hamlets to protect those villages and hamlets. PF units are lightly armed, small in size, and have limited training.[34]

Bob had shown me how to help avoid ground fire when ever "low level" or "nap-of-the earth" approaches were not available or too dangerous. He told me to always contact the ground unit or camp on our Frequency Modulated (FM) radio and to get them to pop smoke before we landed. White smoke meant a cold landing zone and red smoke meant the landing zone is hot and under enemy fire.

He demonstrated for me how to make a rapid descending, high overhead approach into the wind and into small areas earlier this week. It seems to me he can do just about anything humanly possible with a Huey. His demonstration of a combat high overhead approach far exceeded the modest rates of descent I had used for making such practice approaches in flight school. I was a little unnerved on my first real combat high overhead approach, riding down in Huey turned on its' side and falling like a rock at over 4,500 feet per minute!

Bob Hookers was truly one with his aircraft and his flying skills were second to none, as with all aircraft commanders in the 121st. I found that I had a lot to learn before I would become an AC. For instance I found that it was easy to get behind when landing in V formation and Trail formation if you did not immediately begin your descent when the lead ship started his descent and then stay on top of the aircraft's rate of descent and avoid the rotor wash in front of you.

Many of the approaches and rapid descents we performed were so steep that they were really almost out of trim auto rotations with a power recovery at the bottom of the approach. I also learned it was easy to overshoot the aircraft in front of you, especially if flight lead chose a step approach angle. Pilota had to stay on top of things like sink rate, trim, closure speed, rotor and engine revolutions per minute (RPM), wind direction, and other factors every second. Getting shot at added to some of the anxiety of flying, but every hour that I flew and my comrades flew built tremendous skill and confidence in me and the other Army pilots flying in Vietnam. We young aviators believed we would live forever.

Chief Warrant Officer Hookers taught me that the Viet Cong and North Vietnamese Army like to place stakes, holes, mines, wires, and other booby traps in potential LZs. Our enemies also liked to place three well-camouflaged 51 caliber anti aircraft weapons in a triangle formation around potential LZs. The VC's and NVA's goal is to ambush helicopters at close range with many weapons from multiple directions. He told me that the Viet Cong are trained to lead aircraft by aiming and firing two to three helicopter lengths in front of the aircraft. They also were taught to fire into the cockpit and engine areas of helicopters on final approach.

It is obvious that the most vulnerable time for a helicopter is when it is landing and transitioning from forward flight to a hover or to the ground. Landings and takeoffs are the most dangerous times for us, as we should not individually leave the formation—no matter how bad things get. Last but not least, Bob cautioned me about stumps, holes, uneven ground, mud, water, vines, small trees, and other obstacles hidden in landing zones. Each of these hazards was waiting to tear the tail rotor off, knock a hole in the bottom of the aircraft, or catch a skid and possibly cause an aircraft to snap-roll over.

I had learned from Bob and other aircraft commanders I had flown with that ground troops loading onto our slicks were taught to approach our helicopter from the nose of our aircraft so that we pilots had a clear view of them and what they were doing. Sometimes troops had to load from one side or another, and then send half of the squad around the nose of the aircraft to load from the other side, if possible. All helicopter crew members, especially the crew chief and door gunner, had to constantly watch and be on guard to make certain troops did not go near to our tail rotor and did not walk from upslope down into our main rotor. They also had to be sure that the troops soft caps were removed and radio antennas were retracted or tied down and secured so as not to fly off and up into the main rotor blades.

Troops *did not use aircraft seat belts* and usually sat on the floor to allow for more troops and to facilitate rapid loading and unloading. Our crew chief and door gunner always checked to make sure troop weapons were pointing muzzle down or at least not pointing at anyone else, with safeties on, and that hand grenades did not get caught on anything in the aircraft. Our wonderful crew chiefs always supervised loading and unloading. The crew chief would hit troops on their steel helmet (called a pot) with something to get their attention, as the thunder of our rotor blades and scream

PICTURE 19: TIGER SLICK LOADED WITH 15 ARVN TROOPS LANDING IN THE DELTA

Picture courtesy of Bill Schmidt.

The tree lined (and bunker lined) canals in the Delta are where most enemy fire originated. It took a lot of discipline and courage for US Army helicopter crews to maintain formation while landing next to these tree lines. Sitting within point-blank range of enemy weapons while troops loaded or unloaded was most exciting to say the least. Made your liver quiver. Thus the legacy of the US Army helicopter pilot in Vietnam!

of our turbine engines made talking and hearing very difficult, if not impossible. The crew chief and door gunner also made sure the troops we were transporting knew not to fire out of the aircraft and accidentally shoot a hole in a rotor blade, another slick, or a covering gunship, even if the door gunners were firing. More than one Tiger crew member had been shot by accidental discharges of friendly troop weapons while boarding, riding, exiting, and standing around helicopters.

There is so much for a new pilot to learn in Vietnam. I thanked the Lord that US Army aviation units in Vietnam had excellent on-the-job (OJT) training programs for all new pilots. The training normally lasted from two to three months before any pilot was made a pilot-in-command (PIC) or aircraft commander. And if a slick pilot wanted to be a loach (scout) or gunship pilot, he would start at the bottom again and learn the necessary new skills. Gunship training included three phases. First phase was learning to be the peter pilot (and gunner) in a gunship. Second phase was learning to be an aircraft commander in a wing ship, covering the fire team leader's aircraft. The third phase included training to become a fire team leader.

No matter what your rank when you arrived, you had to go through the rigorous training on the following:

- the area of operations, navigation, slick and gunship tactics,and weapons,

- standard operating procedures (SOPs), how to check artillery before departing and en route,

- how to direct artillery, naval gunfire, and US Navy and US Air Force and Vietnamese Air Force tactical air support,

- how to use Paddy Control's radar assistance, when, where, why, how, and what formations to be used, and how to use the secret Signal Operating Instructions (SOI),

- weather, where the hospitals and aid stations were, how and where to fly in each type of formation, how to use smoke and what the colors meant, Jack Benny's age (39)[35], and much more.

As we flew this October 10, 1968, day, I was awe struck by the fact that my army had a lot of new equipment to use against our enemies in Vietnam. The light weight M16A1 rifle was rapidly replacing the M14 and M1 rifles and the Browning Automatic Rifle (BAR). The M79 grenade launcher and the M60 machine gun were in use along with the light antitank weapon (LAW), Star Light Scope, and the Claymore mine. Each increased our infantry's fire power and capabilities.

We also had many other innovations, that were helping us to lick the North Vietnamese Army and Viet Cong, most of which I knew very little about as a new guy. Innovations included the armored personnel carrier (APC) and for the first time used it as an infantry fighting vehicle. More innovations included, the supplemental armor kits for the APCs, rifle fired grenade (RPG) screens made of chain-linked fence used to protect and detonate RPGs before they hit the hull of a vehicle, and the combat engineer vehicle (CEV) which was a modified M60 tank with bulldozer blade, a turret mounted A-frame and winch, and a 165mm demolition gun.

The US Army in Vietnam also had the new armored cavalry assault vehicle (ACAV); the Sheridan tank; and the armored vehicle launched assault bridge (AVLBV). Another innovation was the herringbone convoy tactic and process, which required even-numbered vehicles to fire right (vehicles 2, 4, 6, 8, etc. in line) and odd-numbered vehicles (vehicles 1, 3, 5, 7, etc.) to fire left in an ambush. Our grunts also used the herringbone infantry formations, which required the lead to cover forward while troops behind covered left and right and trail covered the rear. We also used a new checkerboard search method that searched an area by covering alternate squares on the map with small units, the artillery ambush, the one-day fire support base kits and construction process, defoliation chemicals and clearing methods, people sniffers (airborne personnel detectors), great snipers, CS gas, the YO3A Quiet Aircraft, AN/VSS Xenon Search Lights, white and infrared searchlights, 17-pound war heads on the 2.75 inch folding fin aerial rockets, and the electric minigun systems. To add to our list of US Army innovations we had mine-detecting dogs, people-detecting scout dogs, Rome plows, and so much more. How could we lose?

And, of course, we had the now famous Huey, Cobra, LOH (armed scout), Crane, and Chinook helicopters. These aircraft provided us with observation, reconnaissance, troop transport and assault, cargo, medical evacuation, gunship, convoy escort, smoke ship, night fire fly, aerial rocket artillery, heavy lift, and unprecedented mobility capabilities. The new Huey Cobra was introduced in 1968 with 75 percent more ordnance, more fuel and time on station, and 30 percent more speed than any of the older Huey UH-B and C model gunships.[36] As we were flying; I thought *Damn! I am so lucky to be flying one of these new Huey helicopters. Flying is fun and it is certainly the most fun you can have with your pants on—it is the combat that sucks!*

I also noticed another field innovation: Each of our slick helicopter door gunners had attached a C-ration can under the M60 machine gun feed slot of his troop transport (slick) door guns. Bob explained that because the door guns were mounted on a pintle post outside of each of the Huey's main cabin doors, when we flew, the ammo belt to the gun was blown flat against the gun, thereby interfering with and inhibiting the smooth feeding of ammunition to the gun. The C-ration can snapped right into place, as if it were made to solve the problem. The C-ration can on door guns was a true "field modification and soldier's innovation" and one of hundreds of innovative G.I.[37] ideas in Vietnam.

Tiger 99 had turned to the final approach phase of landing. We were behind the lead formation of ten slicks. Bob and I noted that it was very unusual to fly 20 aircraft into an LZ or PZ, as the assaults, even in the open Delta, were usually limited to ten or less troop transport aircraft. This was a big operation and many LZs and PZs were large enough to handle 20 troop transport aircraft and their covering gunships. Soc Trang was a major airfield with one 3,000 foot-long, north-south, and hard-cover runway. It was a base with two assault helicopter companies, a bird dog fixed wing (airplane) unit, a medical evacuation detachment, and all the supporting stuff including a combat engineer company and an artillery unit.

The Japanese had built Soc Trang Airfield during the 2nd World War in the shape of an aircraft carrier to practice for the surprise attack on Pearl Harbor. All in all it was a good place to be stationed with an elevation of two feet above sea level which was relatively high ground for the mostly below sea level Delta. Soc Trang had old but sound cement and wooden buildings, sandbagged hootches (barracks) with tin and wooden roofs, an officers' club, mess hall, an asphalt runway, revetments, concrete pill boxes, wooden guard towers, airfield control tower, showers that worked most of the time, indoor latrines with a real underground and working sewage system, potable (safe drinking) water most of the time, and even a hangar for maintenance.

Bob and I lived in the same barracks, and each of us officers had a small room with a cot. We had each placed Perforated Steel

Planking, fondly called PSP and used by the Army to rapidly build runways, under our cot's thin mattress. We also placed sandbags around the building to window level and around our beds to the height of the cot frame, thus providing a miniature but not very substantial bunker that we could crawl into during rocket, mortar, sapper, and ground attacks.

Bob told me about how very important it was to keep up with where artillery (arty) and mortars were being fired before and during flight and he explained how quickly an arty unit could be deployed to a new area. He explained that our Army Chinook (CH-47A) helicopters could carry 33 combat troops and internal cargo up to 78 inches high, 90 inches wide, and 366 inches long or an external cargo of 6,000 to 8,000 pounds, depending on the heat, moisture, and altitude (density altitude). And he stated that a 105 mm howitzer battery and its basic load of ammunition could be moved in as few as 11 Chinook sorties, thus making every arty unit in Vietnam essentially an airmobile artillery unit. Bob went on to say that the Army's CH-54A "Crane" helicopter could lift up to 18,000 pounds, either by sling or an attachable pod, and could lift and transport a 155 mm-towed howitzer without breaking it down into two separate loads—as was required for the Chinook helicopter. He even pointed out the 9th Division's floating Riverine Artillery Batteries along the Mekong River when we flew single-ship missions in the Dong Tam and Ben Tre areas of IV Corps.

Both of us pilots, and our door gunner and crew chief, wore standard-issue, flammable 100 percent rip-stop cotton poplin, green, jungle-fatigue uniforms (jungle utilities) and standard issue leather black boots. The jungle fatigue jacket had four large bellows pockets. The jacket's top two pockets slanted inwards for easy access under web gear and the pockets closed and secured with buttons and slanted flaps. All buttons were covered to prevent catching on things in the jungle. The jungle fatigue shirt (jacket) had shirt-type cuffs and the trousers had seven pockets: two side pockets, two rear pockets, and two bellows-type cargo pockets on the legs. A seventh pocket was located within the left cargo pocket. We pilots all wondered why we didn't wear the Army's cotton flight suit or the new Nomex flight suits that were being tested, instead of standard jungle fatigues. The common answer to

PICTURE 20: TIGER MAINTENANCE HUEY NOSE COVER

Picture courtesy of Bill Schmidt.

The maintenance platoon's aircraft was the "Wrecker" with the nose art shown above. The "Wrecker" recovered aircraft and hauled parts and maintenance teams all over III and IV Corps. The "Wrecker" also served as an emergency medical evacuation helicopter and an emergency slick transport helicopter, and it was used to rig downed aircraft for sling loading by Chinooks. Captain Sam Brackens was our maintenance officer, and he and his maintenance warrant officer, sergeants, and technicians worked day and night, 24/7 trying to keep as many aircraft flyable and mission capable as possible. These Army maintenance professionals were and still are the unsung heroes of Army Aviation.

Sam Bracken walked into a tail rotor one night after getting almost no rest for months on end, trying to keep up with the demand for flyable aircraft. All of us Vikings and Tigers thank the good Lord for allowing Sam to live and recover from his serious head injuries and to return to us. Doing dangerous maintenance test flights at night, working endless hours without sleep, Sam and his wrench-turning troops never stopped working!

that question was that flight suits did not look military enough for the top brass stationed in Vietnam.

Unknowingly at the time, we would soon make the same mistake that other aviators and enlisted flight crew members would make in Vietnam by trading our leather boots for "jungle boots." Jungle boots were made of mostly nylon mesh and would, unknowingly to us, melt quickly at relatively low temperatures in an aircraft fire. Some helicopter crew members had their feet and ankles severally burned and some had to have their feet amputated from the nylon melting into their feet, ankles, and lower legs due to post crash fires during this God forsaken war.

Prior to around 1971, the Hueys also did not have crash-worthy fuel systems, with quick break- away fuel line joints that self sealed in a crash. They also did not have fuel bladders that reliably self-sealed if shot with small arms fire until after the Vietnam War was nearly over. Everyone knew that if the crash did not get you, it was highly probable that the fire would. Although the Army's Vietnam jungle boot, formally named the "hot weather tropical boot," was a great improvement over the Army's standard-issue leather boots for ground troops, with punji-spike resistant aluminum insole, ankle reinforcement, and cooler material, it was a serious safety hazard due to melting in fires for aviation crews.

Standard tactical separation between slicks in flight formation during a combat assault was two rotor widths (about 100 feet of separation). Flying closely in formation kept the formation as small as possible, allowed the troops to disperse in a tighter grouping, and, more importantly, provided a smaller area for the gunships to cover. Flying too close together was dangerous due to the possibility of a mid-air collision. Flying to far apart required the gunships covering the assault to have to cover a much larger area, spread the troops to far apart during landing, and gave the VC and NVA opportunities to exploit. Although some small LZs required a closer formation, two rotor lengths of distance was SOP in the 121st. On this tenth day of October 1968, our 20-ship formation of two flights of ten aircraft was flying with only an approximate two rotor blade distance between each aircraft as we flew back to Soc Trang to refuel and pickup another battalion of ARVN troops.

Because of his seniority, Bob was flying the lead ship of the second flight of ten. He made an appropriate shallow approach, of about five to six degrees, from the cruise altitude of 2,000 feet above ground level, into Soc Trang. He was closely following the last aircraft (trail aircraft) of the first flight of ten aircraft. Bob knew it was much easier on the trailing aircraft if the approach was at a low angle and not steep, and with a slow rate of descent, rather than high rate of descent. He also knew that daylight landings at Soc Trang seldom drew enemy fire in the fall of 1968. High rates of descent were frequently required and desired going into a hot landing zone, but were almost never appropriate for such approaches and landings at an Army major airfield.

Only a few days before this mission, the Soc Trang air field commander ordered high-visibility day-glow yellow squares to be painted, each approximately one foot in diameter, along the east side of the runway and very close to the 121st aircraft parking revetments. The yellow squares left barely enough room for a Huey to safely land and park on the squares but only as long as the aircraft in revetments on the east side of the runway were not running! The only way the yellow squares provided safe distance between an aircraft in the revetment and an aircraft parking on the yellow square was if the aircraft in the revetment was shut down with its main rotor blades tied down parallel to the length of the aircraft. These lovely, new yellow squares were apparently put there for this particular combat mission.

Unfortunately and unbeknownst to Bob and his crew (and probably anyone else), the yellow squares would not allow a Huey to "safely" land on the yellow squares next to an outside revetment with a Huey running in the revetment, with its' rotor blades turning. The Dust Off aircraft next to Bob's yellow square was with engine-running and rotors-turning! On the morning of October the tenth, 1968, as fate would have it, Bob and his flight and the flight of ten aircraft in front of them were instructed to "park on the yellow squares." For 19 of the 20 aircraft landing and parking on the yellow squares, this would be no problem, because 19 aircraft would be parking by revetments that were either empty or with an aircraft tied down and not running.

Picture 21: Soc trang Concrete Bunker With Sandbagged Fighting Position On Top Along The East Perimeter Fence

Picture courtesy of Bill Schmidt.

1. Firing slit. Noise inside the bunker was deafening and instantly damaged hearing. These bunkers were hot, musky smelling, and no fun to occupy.

2. Steel CONEX containers became the backbone of logistics support for Vietnam, and nearly every major Army unit moving into the theater carried their spare parts and supplies in containers. Many containers never made it back from the theater; they were employed as command posts, dispensaries, portable stores, bunkers, and more. The containers provided millions of square feet of covered storage that the Vietnam theater of operations lacked. Commercial industry began to develop methods of moving containers. During the Vietnam conflict, Sea-Land Container Services, Inc first introduced containerships designed only to carry containers.

It was to be that only Bob's yellow square was painted in such a hazardous location that could cause his retreating main rotor blade to overlap with a Dust Off (Medical Evacuation) Huey's turning and advancing main rotor blade. The Dust Off Huey to the left of Bob's aircraft was running and having its tail rotor tracked in the revetment next to our directed yellow spot.

To make the situation more hazardous, the squares were very close (really too close) to each other, in a North-South line, and leaving only about two or three feet of clearance between Bob's main rotor blade and the tail rotor of the aircraft that was parking in front of us. And only the same small separation of two to three feet was all there was from the aircraft behind us. The situation was a classic accident waiting to happen! The only good thing about this mass aircraft landing was that there was only one aircraft on the East side of the runway, in an outside revetment, that was running—or more aircraft would have faced this dangerous situation.

Twenty aircraft were now on the ground or hovering and about to land with all 20 creating their own wind and sand storm. Each pilot was trying to park on the yellow squares, without colliding with the aircraft in front of them or in back of them, and without hitting anything on either side of them. Each aircraft would have to operate at less than six feet of separation. Once again, the airfield tower instructed all aircraft to quickly park on the yellow squares. To make things worse, that day an unqualified tower operator and senior officer was giving directions to the aircraft landing and trying to park. Like in all aircraft accidents, it usually takes a string of things to go wrong, or to be done wrong to produce an accident. We now had six things adding to the risk of an accident:

1. The yellow squares were painted by someone totally unfamiliar with airport obstruction safety distances and the yellow squares were too close to the outside revetments and the aircraft parked in them, and too close to each other in nose-to-tail trail formation,

2. The pilots and enlisted crew on our aircraft had far exceeded crew rest standards and the aircraft commander was exhausted and suffering from sleep deprivation (and probably PTSD, too),

3. The tower operator was untrained and unqualified, and pressuring the pilots to hurry and land "on the yellow squares,"

4. As was the custom of many aviators in those days, the aircraft commander had consumed alcohol the night before and most nights before that for months,

5. The aircraft in front of us and behind us were very close and the aircraft commander was having to deal with their rotor wash and also make sure he did not get too close to the aircraft directly in front of us, and

6. No human parking guides were used to ensure safe distances between aircrafts.

Bob asked the left-side door gunner, who was also the crew chief, and me, the peter pilot, and seated on the left side of the aircraft, "Are we clear of the Dust Off so I can set the aircraft down?" Both the crew chief and I replied immediately with some anxiety, "No sir, looks like we are over-lapped main rotor blades by about a foot and the unhappy Dust Off pilot in the right seat is waving frantically to us to back away and his eyes are as big as saucers." I also said, "Sir, we are dangerously close to the Huey's rotating tail rotor blades in front of us." The Gunner also confirmed that we were very close to the aircraft behind us. The aircraft commander moved Tiger 99 slightly to the rear, perhaps six inches, and slightly to the right, perhaps six inches, and without any warning and to my horror he set the aircraft down.

KaBoom!!!! Crash!!!!!! BAM!!!!! The Dust Off's advancing main rotor blade slammed and crashed into our retreating main rotor blade with the force of two locomotives colliding head on at 200 miles per hour. Rotor blades, aircraft parts, dust, and debris flew in every direction! The collision resulted in a horrific crash and deafening loud bang. The violent crash instantly tore the one thousand pound main transmissions out of both aircrafts breaking their hard steel mounting points and retaining bolts like twigs. The main rotor system of the Dust Off broke off and flew about 200 yards away, and the main rotor system of Tiger 99's slammed into the ground, on the left front of our aircraft. Tiger 99's mast that connected the rotor system to the transmission snapped in

PICTURE 22: WARRANT OFFICER JOE CASANOVA'S CREW IN FRONT OF "DOUBLE OR NOTHING"

Picture courtesy of Larry Dandridge.

1. The outstanding Crew Chief Mike Dewey. A wise young soldier was he. He took great care of his ship and crew, and later volunteered to fly with the Vikings. He was seriously wounded in 1969. He was a terrific warrior and leader!

2. WO1 Pilot Larry Dandridge listening, watching, and learning from these two brave, enlisted veterans.

3. An exceptionally skilled infantryman and door gunner was Joe Romero. He was a great soldier!

half, and then its main rotor system crashed into the ground by our aircraft still spinning.

The Dust Off's main rotor flew about 200 yards in the air almost hitting the hootch that the 121st Assault Helicopter Company Commander lived in and landing right by, but not hurting a group of Vietnamese hootch maids (the old ladies who did our laundry). Our main rotor crushed in the left side of the cockpit and jammed my pilot door shut. The main rotor to main transmission's steel

Picture 23: The Results Of The Yellow Squares, Bad Tower Directions, And Pilot Fatigue!

Picture courtesy of Larry Dandridge.

1. Pilot Larry Dandridge was hit in the head by this "main rotor mast" and the enormous weight of the main transmission. The back of his armored seat and his flight helmet saved his life. He was back flying two days later with a mild headache, sore neck, and minor burns on his wrists and face. No x-rays or CAT scans were taken, but this was the first of his two significant head injuries in Vietnam. Some folks today say it is obvious that he has had serious head injuries! The aircraft commander was flying when this happened and his only injuries were minor burns to his face and wrists.

2. The main transmission ripped out of its mounts. Luckily it fell between the crew chief and door gunner and not on them and was stopped by the pilot's armored seat.

connecting mast slammed down on my flight helmet and my armored seat, giving me a mild concussion and severe forward neck whip lash injury. The head strike knocked me semi-conscious for about three seconds.

The aircraft hydraulic reservoir poured hydraulic fluid all over the aircraft commander and a flash fire started inside the cockpit area of our aircraft and then quickly went out. The AC was in shock, but otherwise unhurt, except for mild burns on his wrists. Both of us pilots had mild burns on our wrists, because we foolishly had our jungle fatigue, long sleeve jackets rolled up about six inches above where our leather gloves ended. Although this looked macho, was a common practice, and helped with keeping pilots cool on hot days, the rolling up of sleeves and the rolling down of the tops of the gloves was quite dumb. I suspect this dumb practice caused many burn, bruise, and laceration injuries in Vietnam helicopter crashes and flying-debris incidents and injuries from bullet damage, crashes, and resultant fragments. I could not open my left side door, which had been smashed and jammed by our main rotor. Therefore, I exited the AC's open door on the right side of the Huey before the AC himself could exit by stepping on his lap. I wanted out of the destroyed aircraft and fire and now!

The flying debris from the Dust off and Tiger 99 struck two other aircraft and seriously damaged them. In a few seconds, due to the tower operator's erred instructions, the fool who ordered the painting of the yellow squares, the lack of crew rest, and the diminished judgment of the sleep deprived aircraft commander, we had done more damage to our unit than the enemy had done in the preceding two months. Unbelievably, the only other injury was a broken foot that was caused by the Dust Off aircraft rocking back and the tail stinger crushing the foot of a maintenance soldier who was helping to track the tail rotor. Luckily, both of us pilots had our helmet visors down and we were wearing safety sun glasses under our visors, thereby preventing any facial burns or flying Plexiglas and other debris injuries above our cheeks. The wearing of helmets with dark-colored sun visors (because that is the only visor that the helmets came with) resulted in the crew members wearing their visors up at night and during times of low visibility. This resulted in many otherwise preventable facial burns, eye injuries, and other injuries.

Within hours, Bob and I were standing before our 13th Aviation Battalion Commander and our 164th Group Commander in Can Tho, answering questions and being shouted at. Both of us pilots were chewed out for causing an aircraft accident. Bob had his aircraft commander orders threatened, and I was told that I may never be an aircraft commander. Both of us were demoralized and admitted partial responsibility, but argued the yellow square parking instructions, unqualified controller in the tower, instructions to expedite parking, lack of crew rest, and placement of the squares (especially the unsafe location of the newly painted squares) were equally if not more so to blame. Of course we did not say anything about how many alcoholic drinks we may have had the night before, but drinking was the culture of Army aviation in the 1960s.

Luckily for Bob and me, my father in law, a retired Navy chief petty officer and great guy, worked for a contractor who installed and maintained tower communications equipment in Vietnam. It just happened that my father-in-law came to Soc Trang the day after the accident. My father-in-law was able to get quickly a recording of the tower instructions and to confirm that the tower operator was not qualified to be directing aircraft operations when our accident took place, thus proving that many more things contributed to the accident than pilot error. Besides, the Army in Vietnam was always short of pilots, aircraft commanders, crew chiefs, and door gunners, and there were always more missions than there were aircrews and available aircraft.

Both of us took a check ride with the unit instructor pilot, were cleared for flight, and returned to combat flying within two days. I made aircraft commander after two months in country and Bob returned to flying as an aircraft commander within a few days. The lessons we learned that day raised our level of awareness of accident prevention to such a height that we never had another accident or incident. Needless to say, I felt like a real schmuck[38] for somehow not preventing this accident, but I, as a fu#8ing new guy could not see how I could have.

Although Bob and I both had to visit the flight surgeon after the accident, we were immediately cleared by the flying doctor for

PICTURE 24: ANOTHER VIEW OF TIGER SLICK DESTROYED IN YELLOW SQUARES SCREW UP

1. Main rotor mast struck the pilot in the head. Helmet and armored seat saved his life. Mild concussion, neck pain, and headaches ignored and back flying two days later.

2. Army Caribou in background.

3. All that is remaining of the Dust Off main rotor system. We have found the enemy and they are us!

flight duty, even though I complained of a mild headache, neck pain, and had some minor burns. No one had heard of Traumatic Brain Injuries (TBIs), Magnetic Resonance Imaging (MRIs), or Computed Tomography (CT) Scans back then, at least not in Vietnam, and crew rest was of little priority. The yellow squares were quickly painted over. Bob and I went on to successfully fly as aircraft commanders, instructor pilots, maintenance test pilots, safety officers, and flight examiners for more than 50 years of combined flight duty without another accident. Army aviation went on to become one of the safest forms of flying today (except when under intense enemy fire).

CHAPTER 4: OCTOBER 20, 1968 ◄

"Nui Co To—An Evil Mountain."

Letter from Warrant Officer Larry Dandridge to
WO1 Jerry Markland 20 October 1968

Date: 20 October 1968

From: Warrant Officer W. Larry Dandridge,
121st Assault Helicopter Company (Airmobile Light),
13th CAB, 1st Aviation Brigade, APO 96296

TO: Warrant Officer Gerald David Markland
187th AHC, 11th AVN BN, 12th AVN GRP, 1 AVN BDE
APO SF 01213

Dear Jerry,

It is hard to believe that the USA now has over 536,000 of us troops in Vietnam. Our operations and intelligence officer told me recently that over 30,000 Americans have been killed in this war and that 1968 is going to be, by far, the worst year yet in killed and wounded Americans. Sure hope those peace talks in Paris amount to something soon. Still have not seen many Snakes (Cobra Attack Helicopters) in the Delta, but I would like to fly one of those someday. I am now able to decipher incoming mortars from the outgoing artillery fire at Soc Trang, but both still scare me out of my sleep.

I am also now realizing the large tail-to-tooth ratio of support troops to us warriors in Vietnam. Until now, I had never really

95

understood that it takes about ten support troops of cooks, mechanics, signal guys, doctors, nurses, administrative specialists, and other combat support and combat service support guys to support one of us war fighters. The war figters included gunship pilots, door gunners, infantryman, artilleryman, and other combat arms warriors. If that ratio of ten to one is accurate, and I think it is, then of the 536,000 US troops over here, about 56,000 are carrying the sword and fight to the enemy, and over 500,000 are carrying the ammo, spare parts, food, fuel, medical supplies, water, and other support stuff and services.

This week, I saw the only mountains in the Vietnam Delta, called the "Seven Sisters." It wasn't a sightseeing trip, but rather a huge heli-borne assault of the largest of the seven mountains from the top and an infantry assault from the bottom. I attached to this letter the details of that mission and the close calls I survived. We went through much enemy ground fire, very small and rough landing zones, much turbulence and cross wind, an overloaded aircraft, high - density altitude, and my own fear. I am amazed at how calm I can be at times under fire, especially if I am the one flying, and yet, at other times, I am in a controlled state of fear—like when I am just riding the controls as peter pilot backup, with little to do but watch people shoot at me.

Since my beloved marine stepdad always seemed so brave and a role model to me, I was sure I would be brave too, but it is not that simple, is it? The huge role that courage plays in a soldier's life and, for that matter, a man's life simply cannot be overstated. A man's and a soldier's self - esteem and self-worth seem to be measured greatly by courage. Do you remember how in our high school and college US history classes the large number of dying soldiers last words were frequently something like, "Tell my wife, parents, and family that I did my duty and died an honorable soldier's death" or something along those lines? I assumed because my dad and stepdad always displayed courage during times of stress back home and because I was a good athlete, boxer, and first kid to do many things like swim, kill my first deer, and other things that boys do, I just assumed I would be calm and brave in combat. How wrong that assumption turned out to be!

I am certain our parents', teachers', and coaches' examples; our minister's, rabbi's, and priest's tutoring; our military training; the fine example of senior officers here; and our on-the-job training has helped to give us the mental and physical strength to get the tough jobs done. However, none of these things guarantee that each and every time we go into battle we will be clearheaded, aggressive, tactically brilliant, and fearless. To be honest, the Army's good training has helped, but there is no way I could ever become totally fearless. So far what I have been able to do is "stay focused on the task at hand and not completely crap my pants every time I am shot at." I have learned to control my fear by staying busy.

I met Warrant Officer 1 Jim Noblin, call sign "Tiger 29er" and his aircraft nicknamed Silver Eagle a few days ago. He flies the ARVN senior advisor around and is in the Blue Tiger Platoon. Specialist 4 Perry is the 29er crew chief. Noblin is also our company motor pool officer, but he has had so few days down from flying that he says he has only been to the motor pool a few times.

The young warrant officer I have met that I really like and am impressed by is WO1 Joe Casanova. Joe is an "aircraft commander extraordinaire" and he is a great teacher and mentor to us new pilots. Joe's Tiger UH-1D slick aircraft is named "Double or Nothing," and he has two fantastic enlisted men serving as his crew: Specialist 5 Mike Dewey and Specialist 4 John Romero. Both have distinguished themselves repeatedly as brave, clear thinking, and always on or ahead of their game. Of course, my best friend over here is 1st Lt. Bubba Segrest, my ole college pal from the Baptist College in Charleston and my ole high school football adversary.

The noncommissioned officers and enlisted men in the 121st, especially the young crew chiefs, who serve and wear three hats as the aircraft mechanic, crew chief, and left-side door gunner on "their aircraft." The crew chiefs and door gunners amaze me daily with their dedication, hard work, positive attitude, sense of humor, and bravery. The crew chiefs and door gunners are all Specialist (Spec) 5s and Spec 4s, except for a few Buck Sergeants (E5s). I have met some of them and they are from all over this country. For example Viking Sergeant and Crew Chief and Gunner George Quackenbush[v] was born in Tacoma, WA, but raised in Miramonte and Dunlap, CA, and he went to high school and college in Reedley, CA.

Some of the other enlisted men I have met so far are Spec 5 Viking Crew Chief and Gunner Jim Saunders from Colorado[vi], Spec 5 Viking Daniel Eismann[vii] from Idaho, Spec 5 Viking Door Gunner Jim Zeitler[viii] from Yonkers, NY, Spec 5 Crew Chief and Gunner Viking Keith Brinnon[ix] from Ohio, Spec 5 and Tiger and Viking Crew Chief Michael Dewey[x], Spec 4 Tiger Gunner John Romero, Spec 5 Operations NCO and Viking Crew Chief Malcolm Rose, Specialist Kenny Rois, Specialist Charvis Morse, Armorer and Spec 4 Fuji (forgot his last name) from Hawaii, Viking Crew Chief Larry Gray[xi], and Viking Sergeant Crew Chief and Gunner Wayne Zander[xii] from North Dakota.

I am sure you have already heard incoming fire while flying. I now know that enemy small arms rounds make "popcorn popping" sounds when they pass our aircraft in flight. It must be the shock wave of the round breaking the sound barrier that you hear, but believe me, when you hear it over the aircraft noise, it gets your attention. I have been lucky so far and have heard only a few rounds, and I am hoping my luck holds out.

A lot of hype has been put into the phrase "follow me," but as my old friend SC Army National Guard Infantry Company Commander and three time Silver Star recipient Major Bill Whatley has said, "Follow my orders is perhaps far more important (than follow me) in winning battles and keeping our troops alive."

Bill Whatley always knew it was what you did before the battle in taking care of your troops needs for water, food, medical, ammunition, showers, rest, and mail that made a good leader. He knew that empowering junior leaders with the training, authority, responsibility, and accountability to do their job was how to ensure they were successful. I was most impressed with how Bill prepared a detailed and flexible battle plan and operations order.

Bill Whatley came up through the ranks as an enlisted man, junior and senior non commissioned officer (NCO). He then attended Officer Candidate School (OCS). Bill's example and the three silver stars he was awarded in Vietnam has reinforced how powerful walking-the-walk of an enlisted man and NCO is to becoming a better officer and leader.

My US Marine Papa (stepdad) always told me to listen to my sergeants, learn to do everything well, don't volunteer for anything, and keep my head down. Unfortunately, we don't have many senior NCOs over here and it is hard not to volunteer when it really is your turn. There is also no place to hide my head in a Huey! I sure hope this "Vietnamization" program is going to work quickly and these ARVN units learn to fight their own war.

Bubba Segrest says to tell you hello and to keep your seat belt and shoulder harness tight. I enjoyed your last letter and was happy to hear you are doing well and like your unit. Sounds like you guys are in action a lot so please don't take any chances that you don't have to. Other than to fly missions, I haven't been off of the Soc Trang Army Airfield since my arrival here. I see no reason to go off this base for anything that I don't have to go off for.

I am disappointed in the number of guys who visit the brothels in Soc Trang. Now I can see clearly what Sun Tzu, the ancient Chinese Military theorist had to say about the use and effectiveness of using prostitutes to spy on and erode the morality and health of the enemy. In our case the spying on and slow degradation of our moral, mental, ethical, and physical health of our US Army, is for sure partially the result of prostitution.

Bubba told me a funny joke this past week and I have to share it with you.

The French General Story

The French and Italians had allied themselves in a joint war against the Russians back when Napoleon was the Emperor of France. The French Army was the senior army and the senior French general had command of the combined French and Italian armies that were encamped in an open area near the Fulda Gap in Germany. The Russian army was arriving on the battlefield and deploying soldiers.

The French general called a meeting of all French and Italian commanders and their staffs on the night before the battle that was to take place the next morning at daylight. The French general, in his strong French accent, told his French and Italian subordinate commanders and staff: At 0430 hours vee shall deploy our troops into le-battle formation and form le-fighting square directly in front of le-Russian guns and strongest point. I will send le-order to our French and Italian artillery to begin bombardment on the head of les Russian swine at 0445 hours. I will have my best French cavalry protect both the right and left flanks of our armies. At 0500 hours vee shall then order the fix bayonet and position ourselves ten meters in front of our fighting unit, draw le-sword, and attack.

All leaders will follow my example by slowly walking across the 1,000 meters of open ground and hold le-fire until we are 25 meters from the Ruskie's front rank. As our soldiers fall the man behind will fill the holes. As les officers fall they will be replaced by les junior officers and as les NCOs fall they will be replaced by les junior NCOs or senior soldier. At 25 meters vee shall halt and fire two volleys of musket into les enemy ranks and then bayonet and sword charge les ranks as mad men, driving le-Ruske from the battlefield. The French General then turned to his aide-de-camp, Second Lt. Leon Del-O-Shay and said, "Mon Cape, s'il vous plait." The French lieutenant then grabbed a beautiful red silk cape and draped it over the French general's shoulders. The French general then said, "Are there any questions?"

The Italian General Antonio Cappella stood and said, "Yes, Whasa disa red acape?" The French general replied, "Le-

Cape is red so that if I am wounded my men they will not see this wound or le-blood and they will not lose their courage and continue le-attack. More important, le-Ruske cannot see my wound or le-blood and they will think I am invincible and they will lose le-courage and flee from the le-battlefield.

The Italian General then turned with a very worried look on his face and to his aide-de-camp, Lt. Alfonso Vino and said, "Alfonso, bringa me minea browna trousers!"[39]

I have been given an additional duty as company education officer, and I have contacted the battalion, group, brigade, and corps education officers and gotten a lot of help. I have thus far set up a classroom, built an education bulletin board and hung it on the outside of the company headquarters building. I also ordered end-of-course tests for some soldiers, scheduled College Level Examination Program (CLEP) Tests for some of our troops, helped get a couple of college courses started here, and personally enrolled in an "Introduction to Management" correspondence course with Texas Christian University. I am hoping to complete my undergraduate schooling within two years of returning to the good old US of A.

The older guys here, including the senior warrant officers, commissioned officers, and noncommissioned officers, and these great crew chiefs and door gunners, have taken me under their wings. I am learning fast the dos and don'ts of Vietnam and combat. Another thing that many guys do here that I am not at all interested in is gambling. Some big-time poker games go on here at night. With a wife and daughter to support back home, I cannot afford to lose one penny gambling. I also believe it can be destructive to troop morale and unit cohesion. I did try playing twenty-one much of my last night as a civilian at the "Merchants Seaman Club" on East Bay Street in my hometown of Charleston, SC. I won $700.00 that night, but it was the only time I ever won anything gambling, the only time I think I ever gambled at all, and I refuse to tempt fate and the odds again.

I was discussing the history of the French efforts here with some of the other pilots, and I keep wondering how the French could have had such a huge military and yet have been beaten so badly by the Viet Minh (now Viet Cong) at the Battle of Diem Bien Phu in 1954 and others. Too bad the French didn't use more helicopters in Vietnam. The French really drew the world's interest, especially the US Army's interest, in military rotary wing operations when they developed a fleet of 600 helicopters in their war in Algeria.

If the French used their helicopters so successfully in Algeria for troop and supply transport, medical evacuation, reconnaissance, and fire support, and we used them so successfully in Korea for medical evacuation and rescue, then surely we will be able to use our modern helicopters to bring this mess under control soon in Southeast Asia. Still, it worries me that the French, with 400,000 troops and 600 helicopters, lost control of Algeria. They also had their asses handed to them on a plate by the Viet Minh (VC) here in Vietnam, even with the USA paying the hundreds of millions for their war here.

This war is like hunting chiggers (we call them "mean ass little biting red bugs" in South Carolina). As you cannot see the chiggers in SC, we almost never see the enemy here in Vietnam's IV Corps. Many of the ground guys we haul around say the same thing. I heard that over 50 percent of our ground troop casualties are from small arms, booby traps, snipers, and mines. This place is so frustrating for us and so frustrating and deadly for our poor infantryman. I heard a 9th Division soldier recently say, "We search and destroy the enemy and the ARVN searches and avoids the enemy." The ground guys also keep saying that this war "don't mean nothing!" but all of this suffering does mean something! The very soul and reputation of the USA, and the lives and limbs of our best and brightest young men, are at stake here.

The infantry guys also tell me that because of our air superiority, they know when they hear the thunder of helicopter blades in Vietnam that it has to be one of ours. I know you will agree, Jerry, that the joy on those grunt's faces, when we pick them up from a hot LZ, is the best medal and reward we pilots and flight crews can get. Here we are fighting a limited war against the NVA and VC, and they are fighting a total war against us![40]

Our Handbook for US Forces in Vietnam and my limited experience here are confirming that when we (the US and ARVN) advance, the Viet Cong withdraw; when we defend, the VC harass; when we are tired, the VC attacks; when we withdraw, the VC pursues. The Viet Cong places great emphasis on speed, security, practice and more practice, surprise, and deception, and he makes the most of the South Vietnamese military's and our weaknesses. The VC and NVA forces do hate and fear our artillery, tactical air, helicopter mobility, and gunships. The VC's survival on the battlefield depends on their uncanny ability to disengage from and avoid contact with our forces—and they seem to perform this feat of escaping far too often.

My wife, dad, and mom say in their letters that the gory details of this ugly war are all over the TV on the evening news. Could you imagine if the losses we went through in our revolution, the War Between the States, 1st World War, 2nd World War, and Korea had been on the front pages of every news paper and TV every day and night—what a disastrous result would have become of those just causes? They also say that there are more and more people joining the anti-war movement. Not so many in South Carolina, but out West in Washington State and California, and in the Northeast. People are burning draft cards, rioting, marching, and moving to Canada to avoid the military service, and they are refusing to answer the draft. My marine stepdad must be furious with the cowards who refuse to answer the call to serve this great nation.

Even the great heavy weight fighter Cassius Clay (Mohammad Ali) refused to answer the draft last year and was found guilty of draft evasion. He says he is a "conscientious war objector." I have no problem with anyone objecting to war based on his or her religion, but such individuals should have to serve in some other way, for instance, as a volunteer helping the poor or working in schools or on public projects like roads. Freedom and our citizenship benefits should not be totally free. Perhaps those who serve in harm's way should have a Class A citizenship and those who do not serve should have a so-called Class B citizenship with no right to vote or some other restriction. Draft evasion is a felony punishable by five years in prison and a fine of $10,000, not something I would ever dream of doing and is not the answer to not wanting to serve.

In many ways, I am glad our flight officer class missed the Tet 1968 (January and February 1968) VC Offensive. I was talking with one of our most experienced slick and gunship ACs, WO1 Rick Thomas, recently and he told me that he was "scared to death during TET of 68 when Soc Trang was surrounded by the Viet Cong and we (the 121st AHC and the 336th AHC) did a night assault on Vinh Long's US Army airfield and base runway." Flying copilot in chalk 3, he still remembers the orange (51 caliber) basketballs coming up at them as they made their approach to the landing zone, which was the centerline of Vinh Long's runway. The Viet Cong had broken through Vinh Long's perimeter and were actually inside the fences and occupying part of the airfield itself!"

In the words of Rick Thomas, "During Tet 1968 the 121st, 336th, and other Soc Trang base units were completely surrounded by the VC for several days whereby very few aircraft were coming in or out of Soc Trang. Vinh Long was, of course, in worse shape than Soc Trang. Soc Trang held their perimeters, but Vinh Long had a breach where the VC got all the way to the inner compound. The rumor was that the base headquarters area was overrun."

Rick remembered someone saying that all the command and control for Vinh Long was coming out of one of the aviation company's operations room. Anyway, the word came down to save Vinh Long, so the 121st and 336th mustered all available personnel. Then the Tigers and Warriors flew them to Can Tho, where they picked up more people and aircraft, and then they assaulted Vinh Longs runway at night, providing much needed reinforcements.

Rick also told me that during Tet of 1968, "An Air Force C-130, carrying fuel bladders for Soc Trang, refused to land due to receiving heavy ground fire on their approach. The Vikings flew cover for the C-130 on short final, but the AF guys didn't want to chance getting hit by ground fire, so they flew home. They did not return until a couple of days later—they could never have made it as Army helicopter pilots."

Oh well, how we win this war is far above my pay grade. I am no fan of this war either and just want to learn to fly everything I can, as fast as I can, and get back home in one piece. I also hope I can show the kind of courage, wisdom, and toughness that our fathers and uncles showed in the Second World War. Just wish these VC wore fancy Nazi or similar uniforms so we could find them more often and so that they would stand out from the population. The VC Tet Offensive was the only time, thus far, in this entire war that the VC did come out and fight us toe-to-toe—and we kicked their asses all over Vietnam. They suffered devastating losses. I just do not understand why the US media did not tell this good news story.

I am beat so will end this letter here. I will write you again soon. Hope you are enjoying some great flying, good health, and good spirits. Write me again soon and take care of yourself, old pal.

Best regards,

Larry

Picture 25: The Real Heroes of Army Aviation!

Courtesy of George Quackenbush.

1. Viking Door Gunner Jim Zeitler.
2. Viking Crew Chief and Gunner Keith Brinnon.
3. Viking Armorer "Fuji."
4. Viking Crew Chief Jim Saunders. Specialist 5 Jim Saunders is from Colorado went back to Colorado and ended up spending 42 years in law enforcement. He retired as a Lieutenant for a large sheriff's office and was the Chief of Police for two smaller agencies and finally was the Undersheriff for a mid-sized county. He and his wife retired and live in California today.

These guys, the brave enlisted men and noncommissioned officers (NCOs), were the real heroes of army aviation in Vietnam. They flew all day in combat and worked most of the night fixing aircraft, cleaning aircraft, and cleaning and loading weapons. Then they flew all day again. The war for them was 24 hours a day and 365 days a year.

Helicopter Crews Contributed Much Blood and Sweat

Based on Pentagon records, the Vietnam Helicopter Pilots Association (VHPA) estimate that over 40,000 helicopter pilots served in the Vietnam War. According to the VHPA website, total helicopter pilots killed in the Vietnam War was 2,202 and the total non-pilot crew members killed was 2,704. The number of Vietnamese killed in Army helicopters is unknown, but it had to be in the thousands.[41] The author's, LTC (Ret) Larry Dandridge's flight class, Army Warrant Officer Rotary Wing Primary Class 68-13 and Advanced Class 68-21 suffered 42 killed in action (KIA) in Vietnam.[42] The author estimates that approximately half of the flight class was wounded or injured or became seriously ill in their first year in Vietnam. The peak year for helicopter losses was 1969, with over 450 lost to enemy action and almost 600 lost to accidents, weather, friendly fire, and other causes that year alone. In 1969, *3,400 helicopters flew some 8.4 million sorties* (a sortie is one aircraft on one mission), with only one helicopter being shot down per 20,600 sorties and only one aircraft hit per 1,300 sorties. To the astonishment of our sister services fighter and bomber pilots, US Army helicopter pilots and their crews flew as many as *14 missions per day*, seven days per week in Vietnam! VHPA records show that 7,013 UH-1 Hueys served in the Vietnam War. Almost all were Army. Total helicopters destroyed in the Vietnam War were **5,086** out of 11,827. An estimated **22,000** were hit by enemy fire and many were hit more than once.[43]

Nui Co To—an Evil Mountain!

"If the enemy is in range, so are you."

—Infantry Journal

Flying as a pilot with my White Tiger Slick Platoon Leader, First Lieutenant and Aircraft Commander Claude Stanley, my heart was racing a little and my eyes were wide open. I was looking at the 765-foot-high Nui Co To Mountain, which had been a killing field for US Special Forces Advisors and ARVN troops for the past five years and others centuries before.

Nui Co To is riddled with caves and fortified Viet Cong (VC) and North Vietnamese Army (NVA) positions. "Seven Mountains" is at the end of the Ho Chi Minh Trail. Located in IV Corps, near the Cambodian border, Nui Co To Mountain is one of seven mountains referred to by the Vietnamese as the Bay Nui (That Son Range) or translated "Seven Sisters." The names of the Seven Sisters are: Nui Cam, Nui Co To, Nui Dai Nam Gieng, Nui Dai, Nui Turong, Nui Ket, and Nui Nuoc.

The individual peaks of the Seven Mountains rise beyond the western edge of the Plain of Reeds, a few klicks[44] (1,000 meters is equal to one klick) southwest of where the mighty Mekong River flowed from Cambodia into Vietnam. Five of the seven mountains are located in the Tri Ton and Tinh Bien districts in Vietnam's An Giang province, very close to the Cambodian border. The other two mountains are in Cambodia. From the peaks of the mountains, the Viet Cong and North Vietnamese Army can view the vast plain and rivers. The Seven Mountains rise abruptly from the surrounding flat mangrove-covered plain. These seven mountains are possibly volcanic in origin or were large bodies of intrusive igneous rock that resisted the forces of erosion that wore down the surrounding plain. The Seven Sisters serve as prominent landmarks for ground and aerial navigation. They are notorious for Viet Cong and North Vietnamese Army ambushes of our ground troops in the area.[45]

Nui Co To is a mountain in Tinh An Giang (An Giang), Vietnam. It is located at an elevation of 233 meters or 757 feet above sea level. Nui Co To is also known as Nui Kto and Phnom Kto. This mountain had dozens, if not hundreds of caves and the US and South Vietnamese Army ground units and helicopter gunships fired directly into the mouths of VC caves on an almost daily basis.

The highest mountain in the Seven Mountains is 2,300-feet-high Nui Cam Mountain, The Forbidden Mountain. Vietnamese history explains how Prince Nguyen Anh, who later proclaimed himself the first emperor of the Nguyen Dynasty from 1802–1945, sought refuge on the mountain from the Tay Son insurgents. Nguyen Anh forbade anyone to come to the mountain, hence its Vietnamese name meaning forbidden mountain. With all the enemy fire coming from the mountain and leaping up towards the helicopters assaulting two separate landing zones there, no one had to convince me that all of these seven mountains, especially Nui Co To, were (and still are) truly forbidden places for US Army helicopters and our troops.[46]

I had no idea who the commander of this mountain assault operation was and really did not care. My job was to fly the Army of the Republic of Vietnam troops and their US Army advisors in and fly them out safely. I knew that airmobile operations in Vietnam were planned in inverse order with the ground tactical plan prepared first, then the helicopter landing plan, then an air movement of troops-equipment-supplies plan, then the loading plan, the reinforcements plan, and everything being prepared to change on a moment's notice. But none of that meant much to me at this moment. I was focused on our mission, doing most of the flying, and ready to follow my aircraft commander's orders, or whatever orders we would receive by radio, flares, or colored smoke.

Lt. Stanley, a very polite and brave officer, had a very difficult job keeping a flight platoon of young officers, warrant officers, noncommissioned officers, enlisted men, contractors, and Vietnamese employees out of trouble. Not an easy task with the heavy workload, the stress of combat, the Post Traumatic Stress Disorder (PTSD) many of the older guys were exhibiting, and the fact that most guys would drink far too much alcohol whenever and wherever they had the opportunity. Like most of us 20-year-olds, he was slim and had a baby-looking face and some in our unit mistook his size and look for softness, weakness, and lack of maturity. He reminded me a little, but only a little, of the Australian-born famous American film actor Peter Lorre[47]. To me, he was a young and brave officer, a skilled pilot and good listener, who was making the most of his limited leadership experience. Still, I was apprehensive about my ability to successfully fly an overloaded Huey and conduct safe approaches, landings, and takeoffs in mountains, crosswinds, turbulence, and down drafts—and under the most heavy enemy fire I had seen thus far in my short time in the country.

I met a lot of fine young lieutenants and captains while in country. One of them was CPT Sam Brackin; others were 1st Lt. Hugh Adams, 1st Lt. Tom Jameson, 1st Lt. Jim Ellis,[xiii] 1st Lt.. Jeff

Picture 26: "Two Of Our Best" 121st Commander Major Harold Ramey And Instructor Pilot 1st Lt. Bill Schmidt Awarded Vietnamese Air Force Training Medals

Picture courtesy of Bill Schmidt.

1. Major Harold Ramey, the beloved 121st Commanding Officer.

2. Combat Arms Infantry Branch Insignia

3. 1st Lt. Bill Schmidt, our terrific Unit IP.

4. Combat Arms Air Defense Artillery Branch Insignia.

5. 121st Assault Helicopter Company Unit Patch. Both officers are wearing the standard uniform of army aviators in 1968, the jungle fatigue uniform. It was not until the 1980s that the US Army formed the combat arms "Aviation Branch" and put aviators on an equal footing for career advancement and promotion.

Neale, 1st Lt. John Dane, and 1st Lt. Bill (Fergie) Ferguson. Our new company commander, Major Harold Ramey, proved to be a fantastic pilot, leader, and commander. They all were quite patient and helpful to me. 1st Lt. Bill Schmidt, who gave me my in-country check ride, was and still is quite a nice guy. He did a fine job training us new guys as well as the Vietnamese pilots he was responsible for training. Some of the more experienced warrant officers present included WO1 Joe Casanova, WO1 Jim Preston[xiv], CW2 Jerry Lynn, WO1 Rick Thomas[xv], WO1 Mike Sherman, CW2 Mike Shakocius (Shaky)[xvi], WO1 Jim Noblins[xvii], WO1 Randy Roe, WO1 Albert Kovatch, WO1 Vic Noe, WO1 Brian Riess, WO1 Rick Bente, WO1 Mike McNellis and so many more that I'd never know all of their names.

When I first arrived in Vietnam, Stanley took the time to explain our parent 13th Combat Aviation Battalion (CAB), 164th Group, and 1st Aviation Brigade missions and locations. My 13th battalion was called the "Guardians of the Delta." He told me that the First Aviation Brigade is headquartered at Long Bin, which is just north of Saigon, and that the 164th Aviation Group is headquartered in IV Corps, at Can Tho and Soc Trang. He further explained that, not only my 13th Aviation Battalion, but also the 214th and 307th Aviation Battalions and the 7th Squadron, 1st Cavalry fall under the 164th Group. He explained that the 13th Battalion commands the 121st Assault Helicopter Company and numerous other aviation companies in the Delta, including the 114th, 175th, 221st, 235th, 271st, and 336th.

That morning in Soc Trang, at 0430 hours, Stanley briefed me on the huge combat air assault we'd take part in on Nui Co To mountain. He explained that there would be every assault helicopter company in our battalion and other IV Corps' US Army Aviation and Special Forces units involved in this massive attack. The operations plan required a mechanized Vietnamese infantry battalion size force and 21st Army of Vietnam Infantry Division forces to attack from the bottom of the mountain on the south and east side. We helicopter guys would be simultaneously airlifting 21st ARVN infantry into two separate LZs near the top of the mountain and on a southern ridge line.

PICTURE 27: 121ST WHITE TIGER PLATOON LEADER 1ST LT. CLAUDE STANLEY

Picture courtesy of Bill Schmidt.

1. Standard Army fatigue (work) uniform.
2. Maintenance hangar in background.

Lt. Stanley mentioned that the seven mountains region was part of D Company 5th Special Forces Group's area of operations, and it was the scene of some of the fiercest fighting of the war. In the next six months I would fly missions to the seven sisters and all around them. I would learn that it was a place of death for many Viet Cong, North Vietnamese Army, US, and South Vietnamese Army soldiers, including US Army helicopter crews. It was a place all Tigers and Vikings would learn to hate!

I could not help but wonder what the Peoples Liberation Armed Forces (PLAF), or as we called them, the Viet Cong, had in store for us today. The old timers in my unit had told me that the Viet Cong spent most of their time controlling or trying to control the local population, training, gathering intelligence, spreading propaganda, and constructing fortifications, and they fought us only when they wanted to fight us. The Viet Cong seemed to have an endless supply of troops. The tremendous losses in manpower they suffered in their Tet Offensive earlier in 1968 had already been made up through the infiltration of North Vietnamese regular army soldiers and their relentless recruitment of Viet Cong in South Vietnam. I wondered if today would be like so many others thus far where the Viet Cong would just do some harassing shooting of a few mortar and small arms at us and then disappear. Would we be chasing our tails again today? Or would this be one of those few times these little bastards would stand and fight and try to bloody our noses?

These mountains were infamous for VC and NVA ambushes. The enemy would let Army of the Republic of South Vietnam soldiers pass so that a sniper could get a good shot at a US advisor. The Special Forces guys had lost people this way recently on Nui Co To Mountain. The Viet Cong were masters at drawing our superior firepower of artillery, helicopter gunships, and tactical air into the civilian population, thus further alienating the Vietnamese people from the South Vietnamese government and the United States. Today I did not expect the Viet Cong to be able to do this since there were no villages, hamlets, or populated areas on Nui Co To. Three things were certain to me: One, the Viet Cong and North Vietnamese Army (NVA) are on, in, under, and around Seven Mountains. Two, these mountains are honeycombed with tunnels dug by the Viet Cong and NVA. And three, this area of the Delta is a major Viet Cong stronghold and the end of the Ho Chi Minh trail, where supplies and replacements poured into South Vietnam.

I did most of the flying this day, as Lt. Stanley was busy being a leader and trying to train me at the same time. Like 99.9 percent of all Army helicopter flight school graduates, I could fly the UH-1 with considerable skill but not with the kind of advanced skill the veteran pilots had here in Vietnam. If they survived those first three or four months in country, these US Army aircraft commanders will have been through the most intensive combat flying challenge in US military history, and they had become truly "one with their aircraft." Today there would be no practice approaches, no go-arounds, and no instructor to catch any little mistake. Today was the day I would have to get it right each and every time, for to miss one of those tiny landing zones (LZs) was to roll to your death down the ragged rocks on the steep slopes surrounding those rugged and unforgiving LZs.

I tried to break the ice with Lt. Stanley by asking if he had heard the story of the blind man walking into Sears with his "Seeing Eye Dog." Lt. Claude Stanley told me, "No, I have not heard that one." I then said:

Blind Man and Seeing Eye Dog Story

"A blind man walked into Sears with his Seeing Eye dog on a leash leading him. When he got to the middle of the hardware and tools section, the blind man picked up his dog and commenced to rapidly whirl the dog over his head, holding him tightly by the leash. The other patrons and salespeople were alarmed and shocked by this sight, and the Sears manager ran over to the blind man and said in an astonished voice, "Can I help you sir?"

The blind man quickly and calmly replied, "No, thanks, I'm just having a look around."

Claude laughed out loud but quickly resumed his review of the tactical map of the Nui Co To area and his flight lead duties. This would be the last humor of the day. Lt. Stanley had reminded me that the Viet Cong are well trained, organized, and equipped for their missions. Stanley told me that the VC employ tactics of the guerrilla because they suit their means. Although most of the Viet Cong lack formal uniforms, their weapons are modern and effective, and they are prepared to fight—and if they have good reason they will stay and fight. However, frequently, if the Viet Cong are hit hard, they will break into small groups and melt away. The VC dig in well and use concealed tunnels and bunkers extensively. The Viet Cong move at night and prefer to fight under cover of darkness. Normally the VC will not attack unless they have great superiority and have carefully recon'ed, planned, practiced, and prepared for the attack and quick withdrawal. The Viet Cong are smart and well trained, but far from unbeatable.[48]

We arrived at Nui Co To at daybreak and loaded our 12 South Vietnamese Army troops onboard and took off in trail formation. There were about 50 or more slicks involved in this mission and dozens of gunships covering them. At any one time there would be 25 or more slicks flying into, off of, and holding around the mountain. Our flight climbed to about 2,500 feet and we circled out of small arms range East of the Mountain as each helicopter was called in one at a time to make an approach into the highest LZ on the mountain. The landing zone had been blasted and cut out of the trees and rocks there, and was barely large enough to land on. The mountain had been struck by B52 bombers many times, but the Viet Cong were always there—always determined to draw our blood and try to break our national will to go on aiding and supporting the South Vietnamese.

I listened to the Ultra High Frequency (UHF), Very High Frequency (VHF), and Frequency Modulated (FM) radios, as one aircraft after another made its approach into the LZ. The US helicopter crews were taking intense ground fire even though the gunships were blasting the area around the slicks' flight path with rockets, miniguns, 40mm grenades, and door gun suppressive fire, and even though US Air Force Fighters were dropping napalm and 500-pound bombs on suspected enemy positions.

The first couple of aircraft tried to approach the mountain from high altitude. Each aircraft called out taking fire, nine o'clock, three o'clock, twelve o'clock, six o'clock, and from every other direction. A couple of our ships took hits and had to make precautionary landings. It was soon evident that a low-level, nap-of-the-earth, and tree-hugging approach from the plains and up a long ridgeline would be a safer way into the LZ.

By the time it was our turn to start our approach, we had figured out with the other aircraft that we would make our "balls to the walls" approach up a ridgeline from the valley running in a southwest direction with winds mostly off our nose. We always tried to land into the wind, especially at high-density altitudes and with heavy loads. We had watched two aircraft before us do this, and they literally appeared to run through a tunnel of enemy small arms fire. Most of the enemy gunners could not get a clear shot at a helicopter going 100 to 120 knots, hugging the trees and rocks, and they were firing over and behind the aircraft.

With the crew listening, Stanley told me, "OK, Larry you got this. You fly; I will stay lightly on the controls with you in case you get hit. I will call out enemy fire by the clock location[49]. Fly in there as fast and low as you can, keep your skids in the treetops, make a quick deceleration, and stick this thing on that landing zone—and don't miss the LZ or we all will be dead. These troops must get off of our aircraft in three seconds or the crew chief and door gunner will throw them off[50]. When I tell you to go, take off straight ahead, use every ounce of engine power, and drop and blast us out of there as fast as you can to the southwest. If any of these South Vietnamese Army guys lose their cool and refuse to get off, crew chief and door gunner you are to throw them off!"

I started the approach run in from the valley floor at 115 to 120 knots, as fast as we could go and maintain our approximate 1-foot distance from the treetops and rocks flashing by underneath us. As soon as we started up the ridgeline, all hell broke loose. Pop, pop, pop, pop. The sound of enemy small arms was coming from all sides of our aircraft, and some of the time it looked like a basketball would pass by! Stanley and the crew in back were calling fire from every direction. The door gunners were firing back at the enemy, and enemy tracers were racing by in front of us, under us, and thank God mostly over and behind us. I was 100 percent focused on flying and that meant not hitting any trees, rocks, or anything else, as we raced upwards and towards the LZ. When we got close enough, I pulled the aircraft's nose up rapidly and executed the fastest deceleration I had ever performed. At altitude, with a heavy load of fuel and troops, on this very hot and humid day, the aircraft did not have the power to hover out of ground effect, so I had to shoot my landing to the ground—Oh God, I prayed, please let me get this landing right!

I was thinking how nice it was to have an armored seat, but I kept imaging that my head and fragile flight helmet had a big "zero shaped target" painted on it. I was also painfully aware that my legs were only protected by 1/8-inch Plexiglas and sheet metal that was even less thick. I could not help but think that helicopter pilots and crew members were twice as likely to die in Vietnam as the ordinary soldier. I knew the seat would probably stop an AK-47's 7.62mm round, but a 51 caliber[51] round would go through the aircraft, the seat, me, and anything else in its way! I had to stop thinking about that and just concentrate on flying us safely in and out of this landing zone.

PICTURE 28: WO1 LARRY DANDRIDGE BY HIS HUEY IN JANUARY 1969

Photo courtesy of Larry Dandridge.

1. Ceramic armored plate that was slid forward and locked during flight and slid back when pilots exited the aircraft. Only the pilots' heads, arms, and legs were vulnerable to small arms fire.

2. Coolers like the galvanized Igloo cooler that Larry's dad sent him were more cherished than money or food. Cold water (or at least clean water) is more important to troops than anything else in combat. Hot meals, cold, clean drinking water, clean clothes, real latrines, and warm showers are highly motivating, and not having them is one large cause of disease, depression, heat injuries, and low morale in all troops.

3. Famous Soc Trang Tiger logo.

The landing zone (LZ) came into view with lightening speed, and it was so small, so terribly small! The landing zone was just a roughly hacked out, crude, uneven, unlevel, and odd-shaped clearing, not more than a few feet longer than and hardly as wide as my Huey. Watching my engine and rotor revolutions per

Picture 29: First Lt. Thomas Jameson Preparing To Fly "Tiger 6's Bird"

Photo courtesy of Tom Jameson.

Combat Engineer Branch insignia. Until the Army formed the Aviation Branch as a separate combat arms branch in the 1980s, commissioned Army aviators were assigned to either armor, infantry, artillery, engineers, military intelligence, transportation corps, chemical corps, medical services corps, ordnance corps, and had to dual track as aviators and officers in their non-aviation branch. This placed aviation officers at a great disadvantage when they competed for promotions, assignments, and schools. Back then, the best branch for aviators was either the Transportation Corps (who owned all aircraft logistics/maintenance back then) or Armor (who owned the air and ground cavalry units). However, only the Transportation Corps treated their aviators equally with their non aviation rated officers.

minute (RPM) at first race above the over speed limit and then rapidly decay, I knew it was my "come to Jesus" time. The low RPM alarm sounded and the low RPM warning light shined a bright and ominous red, and we would lose tail rotor control and basically stop flying in about another two seconds if I did not stick the aircraft on the ground. I pulled in my final little bit of power and pitch, and we hit the ground at zero forward airspeed, bounced around more than a little, and with the grace of God stuck. I was looking directly down the northwest side of the mountain, the tips of our aircraft landing skids were at the edge of cliff that we were sitting on, and I was drenched in sweat. A few feet more forward in our landing and it would have been my first and last landing on Nui Co To Mountain.

The troops got off as Lt. Stanley counted three, and I pulled in maximum power and made a diving airspeed-over-altitude takeoff straight ahead. Straining to get as much airspeed as fast as possible in a dive, and using every inch of power the engine and rotor would give us, we "De De Mau'ed" (exited with great haste) the place. The enemy fire resumed, but this time it was less intense and I had time to notice a totally destroyed aircraft down the slope, someone else's unfortunate mission. I thought, *Man, the guys who rolled down the mountain in that aircraft could not have survived that crash.*

As scary as the approach, landing, and takeoff had been, I knew I was lucky not to be an infantryman trying to climb, crawl, walk, and navigate through all that vegetation and rock covering Nui Co To Mountain. Those poor infantry guys had to not only fight the heat, humidity, fatigue, thirst, insects, sharp rocks, snakes, and the enemy down there, they also had to cope with booby traps, mines, and other traps laid all over the place by the Viet Cong and North Vietnamese Army. My wonderful step-dad, World War II USMC Sergeant Robert Lee Lightle, had told me about the hell he and his fellow marines went through in the South Pacific in WWII under very similar conditions and facing an equally, if not more fanatical, and determined enemy—and I wanted no part of the face-to-face ground war in Vietnam. This helicopter flying may be extremely dangerous, but my clothes are not soaking wet all of the time, I am not dying of thirst and heatstroke, and I am not continuously exhausted to the bone. I am usually not cold at night, I do get some sleep every night, the disease-filled mosquitoes are not swarming around me, and my clothes are not rotting off of me.

Within less than 30 seconds, we were away from the mountain, moving quickly and safely out of small arms range, and returning to the pickup zone (PZ) for fuel and another load of troops. We were all lathered in sweat, and there was no time to celebrate. Lt. Stanley told his crew, "You did good, guys, and, Larry, that was a very good approach." I did not have the courage to tell him that I never felt comfortable for a moment during the entire approach, landing, and takeoff and was convinced there was a huge amount of luck involved and only some skill. But I did thank the heavens above for getting us safely through mission one. Within a few minutes, we had picked up another load of troops and were back in line to make an approach to a lower landing zone on another smaller ridge line running off the mountain. The rest of the day's approaches were also exciting, but I learned to be a little slower and more controlled on each final approach. I did 90 percent of the flying that day, and it was truly my baptism by fire in mountain flying in IV Corps.

Some of our landings that scary day were to a mountain side of boulders, which had been blown around by US Air Force 15,000 pound bombs called "daisy cutters." One of our Tiger pilots, Jim Noblins, called those LZs "pick-your-boulder LZs." We had to put the right skid on a cliff edge or boulder on insertion, taking care not to hit the upward slope with our main rotor and not to strike our tail rotor on rocks or busted trees or more boulders. The troops had to jump out the right side of the aircraft and avoid the main rotor blade—as the main rotor would decapitate or cut anyone in half who ran into it. Always conscious that the tail rotor is the Achilles heel of the Huey and any strike of the tail rotor on "anything" meant a spinning and very likely unsurvivable crash on the mountain. To depart that LZ we had to just drop off to the left and dive for airspeed.

Some aircraft were landing at an LZ where the nose of the aircraft was facing straight into the upward slope and the pilots had to again be very careful not to strike the upward slope. They

120

dropped their load of troops, then backed out, pedal turned and fell down the mountain to gain airspeed and race out of there at 120 knots. The pucker factor on the asses of the Tiger crews on all of those landings was very high.

It seemed we were fighting ghosts and phantoms all day, as I did not see a single Viet Cong or North Vietnamese Army soldier all day. All we saw was our wounded and injured Army of the Republic of South Vietnam and Special Forces troops and a lot of enemy fire. Needless to say, all the Vikings, Outlaws, Tigers, Warriors, Tee Birds, and many other 13th Combat Aviation Battalion crews earned their pay at Seven Mountains. When we flew back to Soc Trang that night we were all exhausted and glad to be alive.

The fighting on October 20, 1968 made it more than ever clear to me why I am in Vietnam and why I am fighting the VC and NVA. Although I love this great nation of ours and although I took an oath to defend the USA, the real reason I fight is to stay alive, to keep my fellow soldiers alive, and to survive to get back home to beautiful South Carolina. Oh how I long for those majestic Piedmont Mountains, black water rivers, pristine white beaches, blue skies, clean drinking water, flowering scents, pinesap and a thousand different flower smells, grand live oak trees, sea birds, and waiving brown and green marsh grass. Yes, I want to help the South Vietnamese to defeat communism, but that means much less to me than seeing the good ole USA and South Carolina again!

Tigers and Vikings Would Fly Many More
Dangerous Missions Around Nui Co To!

I would fly many more missions in, around, and on Seven Mountains over the next six months as a slick AC, a Cobra front seat pilot and gunner, and as a gunship pilot, but none were any more intense or exciting as this day with Lt. Stanley. I hauled troops, wounded, ammunition, explosives, supplies, teargas, gasoline, acetylene, and CS gas through smoke, clouds, and rain onto and off of Seven Mountains, and never felt completely safe on any of those flights.

I spent several gunship mission nights on the ground with our two gunship helicopters parked and ready to crank, with no

Picture 30: Viking Crew Chiefs and Door Gunners

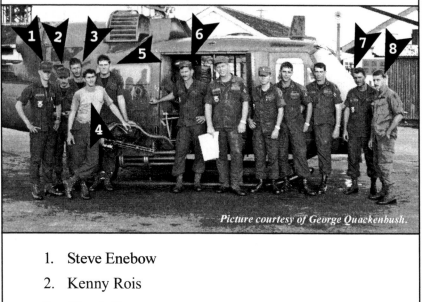

Picture courtesy of George Quackenbush.

1. Steve Enebow
2. Kenny Rois
3. Chuck Burns
4. Richard Stallcop
5. Jim Saunders
6. George Quackenbush
7. Tony Thorton
8. Carl Andrews

other Americans or ARVNs for miles in the area around Nui Co To. We had to furnish our own security on those overnight adventures, and slept on the cold and hard ground. On one such overnight mission at seven mountains, one of our slick aircraft commanders, Rick Thomas, was sleeping on the ground under his slick, "Good Widow Mrs. Jones," stripped down to the waist cooling off. He woke up with something on his belly. Looking down, without moving his body, he was terrorized to see a damn snake, probably the deadly "two-step" snake[52], crawling across his stomach. The snake scared him nearly to death. He froze, and it continued off to the other side. He did not sleep on the ground after that—and that night he got no sleep at all.

Later in the 1968-1969 tour in Vietnam, my Viking Platoon Leader Captain Gene Booth[xviii] told me that he had three memorable and downright scary missions in the Seven Mountains area that he would never forget. The first mission occurred when the Vikings had a light fire team remain overnight (RON) at the Special Forces outpost on the Cambodian border, along with a few slicks and a Dust Off. They were supporting a Special Forces operation that was starting at the top of Nui Co To and working its way down. Evidently the ground guys had been on the top of the mountain for a while since they had constructed a level landing pad area with sandbags. It was large enough to hold the skids of one Huey. They called for a Medivac (Dust Off) helicopter late one night. The Dust Off pilot agreed to go if the Vikings would fly cover for him. Warrant Officer Brian King was the light fire team lead for this mission and Captain Booth was flying wing.

Even though the weather was appalling, the Vikings agreed to try to insert the Dust Off. This was during the rainy season with total cloud cover, no moon, no stars. It was pitch black. The crews could not see any of the mountains; it was like flying into black space. The Dust Off pilot radioed that he could not see anything. Brian King said he would talk him down and proceeded to give him a GCA-type of approach. Captain Booth kept asking his crew if they could see anything other than the running lights on Brian's gunship and the Dust Off. No one could see anything. Anyway, Brian King gave the Dust Off instructions about his air speed, glide path, and rough distance and then told the Dust Off to hover and turn on his landing light. Brian had talked him down to a hover three feet above the landing pad! It was the most amazing thing Captain Booth had ever witnessed. The Dust Off pilot must have had a pair the size of a pair of hot air balloons— or more blind faith than anyone should have.

The second Seven Mountains hairy mission that Captain Booth recalled happened with Viking Warrant Officer Mike Sherman flying lead and Booth flying his wing. They were supporting some ground troops on top of one of the mountains when Mike's

PICTURE 31: CAVALRY COBRA AND TIGER SLICK WITH ONE OF SEVEN MOUNTAINS IN BACKGROUND

Picture courtesy of Mike Shakocius

1. Tiger Slick (perhaps The Good Widow Mrs. Jones" at That Son Airport, South Vietnam. That Son was an Army of the Republic of South Vietnam (ARVN) camp between the mountains and the border to Cambodia. One of Seven Mountains is in the background.

2. Red and white flag Air Cavalry designation. The CAV guys had a saying: "If you ain't CAV—you ain't shit!" Oh course, Vikings and Tigers disputed such claims.

UH-1B gunship was shot down. Mr. Sherman was able to make a pretty darn good auto-rotation into a fairly level clearing on top of the mountain. The crew scrambled out of the aircraft and took cover in some rocks. Charlie was shooting at them. All Captain Booth could do was call the mission commander, who was flying command and control, to come back and pick up the downed crew. The commander would not do it until he flew back to the Special Forces outpost to let off his "back seat passenger." The

Viet Cong never exposed themselves as Captain Booth saturated the area with suppressing minigun, door gun, and rocket fire until the C&C aircraft returned. Fortunately, the C&C aircraft was able to land and get Mike Sherman and his crew out safely.

The third mission that Captain Booth recalled was tragic. Captain Booth said that he never liked the Seven Mountains area because bad things always seemed to happen there. The Vikings were flying air support for an ARVN ground unit working its way between the mountains. A US Army Lieutenant was the ARVN advisor and leading the patrol. The lieutenant was near the end of his combat tour of duty and scheduled to return to the US the following week. Charlie hid out in caves on the face of two of the mountains, looking into the valley between them. The lieutenant was shot, and the South Vietnamese troops pulled back and left him out in the open. The Vikings kept shooting at what they thought were the cave openings, but Charlie just kept shooting the lieutenant. It was like they were using him for target practice. Nothing Gene Booth and the rest of the Vikings did could stop them. Finally, some jets arrived, dropped napalm on the face of the mountain, and the enemy fire stopped. Captain Booth really felt badly about the lieutenant and wondered why he was leading a patrol when he was scheduled to go home the next week.

CHAPTER 5: NOVEMBER 16, 1968 ◄
"51 Cal Kills a Tiger Slick Near Rach Gia."

Letter from First Lieutenant Laurie O. "Bubba" Segrest
to WO1 Sam DeLoach

Date: 16 November 1968

From: First Lieutenant Laurie O. "Bubba" Segrest, 121st Assault Helicopter Company (Airmobile Light), 13th CAB, 1st Aviation Brigade, APO SF 96296

TO: Warrant Officer Sam DeLoach, 498th Medical Evacuation Company (AA), APO SF 01214

Dear Sam,

Hey pal. We have come a long way since we went to St. Andrews High School together and drove school buses there. I hope you are enjoying good health and spirits. Beautiful Charleston, SC and the low country seem like a million miles away these days. Would be nice to take Betty for a walk on the Battery or Folly Beach. It would also be so good to drink clear water again and not have to eat C-rations[53] so often.

Fortunately our good friend, Larry Dandridge, and I are assigned to the 121st together. He told me he wrote you and told you about the "yellow squares" blade strike in early October 1968, before I got here, that destroyed two helicopters. He and his AC and the others involved were lucky they were not injured worse in that crash. Larry and I get together and share war stories when we are not too exhausted from flying all day.

My wife, you remember my girlfriend throughout high school, Betty Dolan? Well, she is now Mrs. Betty Dolan Segrest and she has already sent me a care package of cookies and other good stuff. I miss her dearly. Larry and I have met some great guys (officers, warrant officers, NCOs, and enlisted men) here ,and they include WO1 Brian King, 1st Lieutenant Bill Schmidt[xix] WO1 Jim Preston, 1st Lt. Thomas Jameson[xx], 1st Lt. Jeff O'Neal, WO1 Joe Casanova, 1st Lt. Bob Snider, Captain Bill Risner, WO1 Rick Thomas, WO1 Jim Noblin, 1st Lt. George Taylor, 1st Lt. Gene Booth, CW2 Brian Reiss, WO1 Jim Ellis, WO1 Bob Ennis[xxi], WO1 Mike Shakocius, WO1 Al (short round) Kovatch, and WO1 Jim Noblin.

I also have met WO1 Mike Sherman, CW2 Jerry Lynn, WO1 Randy Roe, WO1 Jim Lucking, CPT Sam Kitchen, Major Saindon (our Company Commander), Pilot Clifford Hineman, Pilot Norman Lille, Pilot Mike Bennett, Sergeant George Quackenbush, Specialist 5 Mike Dewey, Specialist 5 Malcolm Rose, Specialist 5 Dan Eismann, Specialist 5 John Romero, Specialist 5 Jim Saunders, Specialist 5 Wayne Zander, Specialist Forest Webb, Specialist Joel Wood, Specialist Brian Warrilow, Specialist James Mathias, Specialist Robert McDonald, Specialist Charois Morse, Technical Inspector Raymond Christensen, Door Gunner Roger Fox, Specialist Mike Romaniak, Door Gunner John Feathe, and so many others I cannot remember all their names.

We have very little time to enjoy music here, but everyone has bought a new stereo tape deck reel-to-reel system to listen to music when we are back at Soc Trang. Armed Forces Radio and radio Hanoi are the only two radio stations to listen to over here. Since Radio Hanoi is propaganda and music broad cast in Vietnamese for the NVA and VC, we don't listen to anything but the US Armed Forces Radio. There is an outdoor theater here to watch old movies, but the mosquitoes make that recreational facility a seldom used option for entertainment. The one thing that is better in Vietnam than in the states is that the really important things, the important things to staying alive and defeating the enemy, are all that matters over here. Most of the peacetime bullshit like painting rocks, kitchen police, marching in parades, Saturday morning inspections, and spit-shined boots, just do not exist over here. However, our hooch maids do shine our boots for us.

I have been assigned as the civic actions officer for the Soc Trang orphanage near our base. My duties are to solicit donations and support of food, medicine, medical care, funding, and clothing from US corporations and other businesses for the orphanage. I also am tasked to create a good relationship with the orphanage and the US military, and to plan and hold functions from time to time for the kids, such as an Easter egg hunt and holiday parties. The flight surgeons here, with great support from patriotic organizations at home, soldiers families, and patriotic businesses at home, have done a wonderful job making this orphanage the best-equipped, best-fed, and best health-care facility for orphan children in all of Vietnam. I am getting a lot of help from my fellow Tigers and Vikings and it is giving me a good feeling that we are doing some very worthwhile things for the Vietnamese people and not just destroying things and killing people. This is a poor country and the average span of life here is only 35 years—mainly because the Viet Cong take the food from the poor farmers here.

By the way, I got a chance to try the local "33" Beer when I was in Soc Trang recently. It was served "warm in a dirty glass"; that is, with a huge chunk of dirty ice and some straw frozen inside the one large chunk of ice. I only had one. It did not taste bad, but I worried about getting sick from the ice. Ba Moi Ba is the Vietnamese word for 33 (Ba Moi means 30 and Ba means three. Moi counts tens). Some of the guys here call it "tiger piss." I am glad that there is no incentive to drink 33 because there is plenty of US beer in Vietnam.

The Mekong Delta is that area of the Republic of Vietnam that is south of Saigon. It is bordered on the east by the South China Sea and on the west by the Gulf of Siam and the Cambodian border. The Delta area is about 175 nautical miles long on a northeast-southwest line and varies in width from 150 nautical miles at its widest point to about 20 nautical miles as it tapers to a point at its southernmost end. With the exception of five mountains in IV Corps and two sister mountains in Cambodia, referred to collectively as the "Seven Sisters," the Delta is on almost absolutely flat stretch of land, having a mean elevation of less than 20 feet Mean Sea Level (MSL). Soc Trang is only two feet above sea level and that is because the Japanese filled in the rice paddies with fill dirt. Most of the DELTA is flooded in the rainy season. These seven sisters rise abruptly from the flat mangrove-covered plain and are used by all of us helicopter and fixed wing pilots here to help us navigate.

Much of the Delta's shoreline has a narrow strip of dense foliage and trees extending in places as much as two to three miles inland. Other shoreline areas are characterized by swamps and marshes. Large rice fields are found inland, and they cover almost the entire region. Numerous canals, streams, and rivers mark the countryside and along the streams and rivers are tree lines and small villages and hamlets—and Viet Cong bunkers!

The Mekong Delta is crossed by two huge rivers, the Bassac and the Mekong. The Bassac is the most southerly of the two rivers. The Bassac River comes down from Laos through Cambodia and enters Vietnam just north of Chou Doc, flowing southeast past Long Xuyen and then it empties into the South China Sea. Long Xuyen is the site of the Australian Medical Team that we always have in the back of our minds in case one of us is wounded. Can Tho has a major US hospital and is our first choice if wounded.

The three cities of Chou Doc, Long Xuyen, and Can Tho are major cities in the Delta region and they share in importance with So Dec, Vinh Long, and My Tho, which are located on the Mekong River. The Mekong River runs generally parallel and to the northeast of the Bassac River. Rach Gia is a large city where the US brown water Navy and Navy surgical team are located on the coast of the Gulf of Siam. I have every medical team's location and every hospital site carefully plotted on my flight map. Another major city in the delta, which is located on the southern tip of the country, is Cao Mau—a Viet Cong (VC) strong hold and the suspected location of VC Delta Headquarters. My base camp and a major Army Airfield is Soc Trang and is located just south of the Bassac near the eastern coast line. All of these cities are in our area of operations.

I have flown on some operations around the delta city of Bac Lie, which has a US Military Assistance Command (MACV) Compound and was the last city attacked by VC in Tet of January 1968. Another Delta city is Tra Vinh, which has many Cambodian descendants living there. Ben Tre is a major city in the Delta area where we frequently work with the 9th US Infantry Division. Another interesting and important city in the Delta is Go Cong, which is supposed to have an Australian Army unit operated near there.

The Mekong River divides into three branches just southeast of Sa Dec near the US Navy Patrol Boat River (PBR) and Swift Boat base and Vinh Long. Each branch of the major rivers contains numerous small islands. The rivers together with the numerous streams and canals and the flooded rice paddies in the wet season give the impression from the air that the country is predominantly under water. This effect is minimized during the dry season, which lasts from December to late May, when the smaller streams and canals dry up along with the rice paddies.

The Mekong Delta is a rice-growing region, producing over two-thirds of the food produced in Vietnam and housing over half of the country's population. The Delta is an area rich in natural resources, which is tremendously important to the Vietnamese people and the prize the Viet Cong and North Vietnamese Army want to capture and control. The delta and all of IV Corps are the operating territory of the 121st Assault Helicopter Company, "The Famed Soc Trang Tigers." The Viet Cong are firmly embedded here and are resisting all of our efforts with great vigor, skill, and determination.

If you have to be in Vietnam, Soc Trang is not that bad. There is another Assault Helicopter Company based here, the 336th Assault Helicopter Company, and there is a Bird

Dog outfit here too, the 221st Recon Airplane Company. The 221st Recon flies Cessna L19s, which are now called O-1s, and they use "Shot Gun" as their call sign. The 336th slicks use Warrior call signs and their UH-1C gunships use the call sign T-Birds. We are part of the 13th Combat Aviation Battalion (CAB).

The 13th CAB has four Assault Helicopter Companies in it: the 121st, the 336th, the 114th, and the 175th. We conduct joint operations with the other three companies frequently. The 175th AHC slicks are the Outlaws, and their gunships are called Mavericks. The 114th slicks are the Knights, and their gunships use Cobra as their call signs. The 13th Combat Aviation Battalion is part of the 164th Combat Aviation Group, under command of the 1st Aviation Brigade. All the 13th's units use standardized tactics and we all work well together on frequent combined unit missions.

So we September 10, 1968 graduates of the Army's Rotary Wing Flight Class have now had time to figure out who the National Liberation Front (NLF), or as we call them "Viet Cong and Charlie and Chuck," is in Vietnam. We are painfully aware that these VC and NVA fighters are a determined, skilled, embedded, and ruthless group who kicked the French Army soundly. Since the 1968 VC and NVA Tet (Lunar New Year) violent and surprise offensive, no one here takes victory over these little devils for granted.

The good news is the Viet Cong lost half of their forces in their Tet Offensive of 1968. More good news is that the Viet Cong have lost a lot of their influence over the local people of the Mekong Delta, due to the VC and NVA violation of the sacred Tet holiday, the hundreds of executions and atrocities the VC and NVA committed during Tet, and the tremendous destruction of property that resulted. The bad news is the VC ranks have now apparently been augmented with NVA regulars to retrain and rebuild their forces. I don't know how we are going to win this war if we continue to hop around all over the place and never occupy any place long enough to ensure the South Vietnamese Army and government really have control over the area. The Vietnamese people are painfully aware that when we leave an area, they are totally at the mercy of the VC!

On the other hand, 1968 has turned out to be one hell of a year for the USA. LBJ says he will not seek reelection; Martin Luther King and Robert Francis (Bobby) Kennedy were assassinated; race riots highlighted that the USA still has a long way to go before we truly are the land of the free; war protests almost shut down the Democratic National Convention in Chicago; Walter Cronkite said we are "... mired in a stalemate (war) and our only way out is to negotiate a peace"; Defense Secretary McNamara resigned, and over 14,500 US troops were killed thus far this year! With all that negativity, I still see great courage and conviction in the troops of the 121st. I just wish the ARVNs had more spunk and that our civilian leaders would give our top military brass the authority, responsibility, tools, and accountability to conduct this war in a way we could quickly destroy the Viet Cong and North Vietnamese Army.

I also wish the US Army had given us more training on the country of Vietnam and its culture, customs, religions, language, history, climate, military, and geography. All I really know about Vietnam is that our politicians are convinced that if Vietnam falls to the communists, the other countries in this region will fall to communism like "dominoes in a line." I do know most of these Vietnamese are Buddhists and that the leaders seem to all be Catholics—what the hell is that all about? It is already obvious to me that these folks over here are as different from us Westerners as they could be, and few of us know much about this country.

I also see where the so-called "Strategic Hamlet Program" is failing in its attempt to resettle the rural population here into little forts. Resettlement has not worked that well and if I was a Vietnamese farmer I would be extremely pissed off to have to leave my ancestral home and move into one of these dirty little muddy triangular-shaped forts. The older guys here say the Army of the Republic of South Vietnam and its Air Force and Navy military forces are so badly led, so corrupt, so poorly trained, and so unmotivated that they are having very little positive effect on helping us to help them win this war. It looks to me like we are fighting this war while the South Vietnamese Army is watching from the grand stands.

I am hoping the 121st will get the Cobra attack helicopter to replace our aging UH-1B Model gunships soon. With Cobra's ability to carry 75 percent more ordnance, a stabilization system that allows for really accurate rocket fire, and 30 percent more speed, we could pack much more punch in all of our operations over here. We now have five types of US Army units operating in South Vietnam using armed helicopters: nondivisional assault helicopter companies like the 121st; airmobile division and nondivisional attack helicopter companies; infantry division general support companies; airmobile division aerial rocket artillery battalions; and nondivisional, divisional, and armored cavalry regiments' cavalry troops.

I would like to fly gunships as soon as I can get this slick training behind me. I have been in training for three weeks now and have been flying about 9 to 14 hours every day since I arrived here. I like the 121st and have great confidence in our company commander, Major Harold Ramey. I flew with Major Ramey already. He is a highly skilled combat aviator and a courageous, officer and leader. I would follow that guy anywhere. Yes, I am taking my malaria pills like a good soldier and no dysentery—yet.

Larry says to tell you hello and that he wants to teach you how to fish when we get back stateside. So there it is—I have gone from a St. Andrews "Rock" to a Soc Trang "Tiger." It is quite disturbing to me to have been told by the senior aircraft commanders here that the Viet Cong do not recognize the Geneva Convention and that they consider the US troops "War Criminals." On top of that troubling information, the Viet Cong offer a large bounty for helicopter pilots, and they believe the Red Cross is a corrupt partner and tool of us United States imperialist aggressors.

I am converting from my Protestant religious roots to Catholicism to be able to join my wife in church and because

I get more out of my wife's form of Christianity. I have an interest in the religions of Vietnam and am disappointed that the Army failed to provide my fellow officers and me with any real cultural or religious training on this beautiful country. It appears the Special Forces (SF) officers and NCOs have been given some training on this country's religions. One of those SF guys showed me a pamphlet titled "The Religions of Vietnam," Command Information Pamphlet 11-67, published by MACV the other day. The pamphlet is less than 30 pages long and it emphasizes the importance of us not offending a people with traditions older than ours.

The pamphlet also says that we US troops need to develop understanding and tolerance of the Vietnamese religions, values, and their way of thinking and acting. How do we do that when we US soldiers know almost nothing about Buddhism, Animism, Taoism, Confucianism, the Hoa Hao, and Cao Dao, which are, in addition to Christianity, the major religions of Vietnam? Our soldiers here become cynical quickly and everyone refers to the Vietnamese as gooks, dinks, slopes, and worse.

I fear this lack of sensitivity is very bad for our cause. According to MACV Pamphlet 11-67, Vietnam has no state religion and is estimated to be 20 percent Buddhists, 20 percent non-Buddhist, and about 60 percent non-practicing Buddhist, which adds up to a mainly Buddhist (80 percent) country. The Viet Cong are aware of the tremendous importance religion plays in the lives of the Vietnamese people, and they use it in any way they can. However, the SF guys (and the pamphlet) say that the goal of the Viet Cong and North Vietnamese Army is to show the people that there is "no God," "no afterlife," and "no reason to follow any church or religion."

US troops see the Vietnamese as uneducated and religious illiterates. To us Westerners, the swastika is a symbol of the worst man can do to man, but to many Vietnamese, a similar sign (the Buddhist symbol "Chu Van," which is the symbol of enlightenment) is one of their most sacred of religious symbols."[54] I am just trying to make the best of my stay here and trying to be polite to the few Vietnamese we interact with. I have enclosed a picture of the aircraft I was shot down in last week. One hit, from a 51 caliber round through the engine. How unlucky can that be?

The sad news is that the aircraft commander (AC) in that "shoot down and crash" was medical evacuated with a broken back and head injuries, both the enlisted crew were also seriously injured, and several ground troops were killed. I have also attached the story of the crash, the bad fall I took injuring my neck when I released my seat belt, and my close call with the Grim Reaper—this place is dangerous! Write me a note sometime and God bless and stay safe Sam.

Sincerely,

Bubba

51 Cal Kills a Tiger Slick Near Rach Gia!

*"There are few things in life worse than war,
all of which come from defeat."*

—Winston Churchill

It was November 16, 1968, and a ceiling and visibility unlimited (CAVU) day with just a few scattered clouds in the sky. Chief Warrant Officer Connelly, call sign Tiger 88[55] was the AC and I, First Lieutenant Laurie "Bubba" Segrest, was his pilot. I had been in country for only 27 days and had just completed flight school in September of 1968. The UH1-D Huey we were flying that day was soon to take off on a combat assault mission from Rach Gia (pronounced Rock Jaw), South Vietnam to a landing zone about 15 miles northeast.

The aircraft commander and I, and our "dual hated" crew chief, who also served as our left door gunner and our right door gunner, made up the slick's four crew members. We were parked at Rach Gia in the Vietnam Delta with nine other Tiger helicopters after refueling and catching a quick lunch of C-rations. I was new in country but had picked up an immense amount of knowledge and skill flying "ash and trash" and combat assault missions with various senior pilots over the past three weeks. I was learning fast and beginning to feel comfortable in my role in the 121st Assault Helicopter Company.

I saw a US Army helicopter crew throwing heavy and unopened C-ration cans at some local Vietnamese children. I stopped them and scolded them, telling them, "How are we going to pacify this country and win the hearts and minds of these people if you mistreat and hurt their children? If I see you doing that again I will bring you up on charges." I already knew that in combat, troops often become callused and lose some of their otherwise strong moral and ethical upbringing and training. And I knew that it was up to us Army leaders to remind troops of the "Code of Conduct" and the high standards expected of them by the Army and our citizens back home. This was my Army and I intended to keep its reputation and standards high!

Although flying slicks was very challenging and sometimes too exciting, I already knew that I wanted to fly gunships as soon as an opportunity arose. There were seven categories of armed helicopter/gunship (later called "attack helicopter") missions in which armed helicopters (UH-1B and C Model gunships and Cobras) commonly flew in Vietnam, and I wanted to fly those more colorful and offensive missions, some of which included:

1. The armed escort of other aircraft, ground vehicles, surface water craft, and troops on the ground.

2. Security for an observation helicopter (OH-6, OH-23, and OH-13, etc.), performing the high risk, but high reward low-level and nap-of-the-earth reconnaissance.

3. Direct fire support of targets designated by a ground maneuver commander.

4. Smoke ship application and cover operations.

5. Aerial rocket artillery against targets assigned by a fire support center, forward observer, or airborne commander.

6. Night flight find-and-destroy missions, using Lightning Bug-Firefly or white light (Xenon) searchlight and infrared

searchlight systems covered by Cobras or UH-1B or C Model gunships.

7. Hunter—killer tactics to provide security for an observation helicopter and delivering firepower on targets of opportunity.

My flight leader called the aircraft commanders together for a mission briefing. He told us aircrews that we would be loading about 14 Army of South Vietnam's 21st Infantry Division troops onto each helicopter and taking off in 20 minutes. He went on to say we would insert those Army of the Republic of South Vietnam troops in a combat assault on a known enemy location and expect to take fire going in and out of the landing zone. Our Tiger slick was parked in trail, on a dirt road, with the other nine Hueys that would transport these troops to a landing zone.

The Flight Leader warned the ten crews that each aircraft would be loaded above maximum safe gross weight and that heavy weight, combined with the hot temperature and high-density altitude (DA),[56] would make hovering out of ground effect impossible and even hovering in ground effect (close to the ground) difficult at best and perhaps impossible. High-density altitude means high ambient air temperature, high humidity, and high-altitude conditions equate to thinner air and greatly reduced engine, rotor, and wing efficiency—making it much harder for an aircraft to fly. High DA lowers the amount of weight a helicopter is able to carry. It also makes less power available, and reduces climbing ability and stall speeds.

Because of the high-density altitude conditions and the large number of troops on each aircraft, each helicopter would have to use maximum available power and strain to take off and climb out. We pilots would literally have to bounce the helicopter along the road until it hit translational lift (higher lift conditions created by forward flight) and then slowly climb out to a cruise altitude of 2,000 feet. The efficiency of the hovering rotor system is improved with each knot of incoming wind gained by horizontal movement or surface wind until the aircraft transitions (goes through translational lift) to nonhovering flight. The high-density altitude conditions would also mean we would have to land to the ground in the landing zone—as we would not have the power to hover with these large loads. We hoped that the landing zone would be clear of stumps, mines, booby traps, or other enemy or natural hazards.

Flying in another helicopter on this mission was our old friend and flight classmate, Warrant Officer Larry Dandridge from the same hometown, Charleston, SC. We had played high school football against each other (I was a much bigger and better football player). We had also attended the Baptist College at Charleston, now Charleston Southern University, together. We used to play ping-pong together during breaks in college. We both were glad to have someone in the unit with us that we knew and trusted, as we were fire hosed with a myriad of new information and training. To be honest, when I signed in and saw Larry Dandridge, a great deal of the feeling of unknown and the craving for something and someone familiar went away. Larry and I both knew that this LZ could be hot with Viet Cong or North Vietnamese Army small arms fire. We knew it would be dangerous.

It was time to go, so we Tiger crews completed our preflight checks, loaded up, and started our aircraft. We went rapidly but thoroughly through the combat "through flight" checks and start-up procedures, which consisted primarily of battery switch on, main fuel switch on, rotor blade untied, and pulling the start trigger. The flight crews only did one full, by-the-book, complete set of some 75 pre-start, start, and run-up procedures and checks, and that was before the first start and takeoff of the day, normally done about 0430 to 0500 hours each morning.

After each landing during the day, the pilots would set the fuel control to the On position, set the throttle to the Start (flight idle detent) position and have everything ready for a quick combat start for their next flight. That way, the pilot would be starting the aircraft while the aircraft commander put on his helmet, chicken plate (ceramic and bullet-resistant vest/plate), and seat belts. Then the aircraft commander would take over and complete the start while the pilot would put on his helmet, chicken plate, and seat belts. The pilot would double-check that engine and transmission instruments were in the green; all cockpit switches were in the proper position; crew, passengers, and cargo were secured; weapons were safe; and that there was ample fuel quantity as required for the mission, while the AC hovered out for takeoff or took off from where they were parked.

One of the many life critical survival checks of which all of us crew members were acutely aware was the fact that every centimeter of slack in our seat belt tripled the g-force we'd experience in a crash, so we "wise ones" kept our seat belts and shoulder harnesses snug! We also pushed our snug seat belt down as low over our pelvis as possible. I knew that I should be able to feel the upper ridge of my pelvis above the upper edge of my belt if my seat belt was properly fastened. Flight physiology training and other classes taught us that the pelvis is a very strong structure that handles force well. We also knew that if our seat belt was to slide up into our stomach, we had a much greater chance of sustaining dangerous internal injuries and that our entire body could even hydroplane out from under the seat belt thus breaking our backs and necks—and, yes, even decapitating a pilot.

Our crew chief and the door gunner checked their M-60 machine guns and prepared to lock and load those weapons as soon as they cleared the takeoff area. Our crew chief (CE) was seated on the left side of our cargo and troop compartment so that he could see the cockpit engine and transmission instruments. Our door gunner was on the right side. The AC wanted me to fly so he had me take the controls. The 14 fully combat-equipped Army of the Republic of South Vietnam (ARVN) troops loaded into our aircraft and it took all of the Lycoming L-11 engine's power and my flight skill to get the Huey to a low hover and to perform an "airspeed over altitude" low climb out angle, slow rate of climb takeoff.

A new warrant officer and friend of mine had just transmitted what he thought was a funny message on the Frequency Modulated (FM) radio, telling me, "You better be careful Bubba—as you might crash today." The new warrant officer would never pull that stupid stunt again. I saw the farmers working below, as we rapidly passed over them. Water buffalo, coconut trees, bamboo, and palm trees flew quickly by as I nursed the heavy Huey into a 500 feet per minute climb in the steaming hot, moisture-saturated Vietnam sky. I glanced back quickly to see the heavily loaded ARVN troops, some smiling, some looking full of tension, but all enjoying the cooler air passing through our aircraft which was now holding 80 knots.

We were about two miles northeast of Rach Gia, and there was a heavily forested, triple-canopy jungle under us as we passed through 1,000 feet above ground level during a slow and cumbersome climb out. I was flying and feeling good about my safely executed, highly skilled takeoff. I had placed my new Zippo cigarette lighter on the counsel by my right side when I first got in the aircraft. The new cigarette lighter had engraved on it, "Yea though I fly through the Valley of the shadow of death, I shall fear no evil, because I am the meanest son-of bitch in the valley!"

Then, just as we climbed through 1,000 feet above ground level, and without any warning, there were dozens of 51 caliber tracers racing past our aircraft at the one o'clock and three o'clock positions. The enemy tracers seemed to me to be as big as basketballs as they rapidly climbed into the sky around our helicopter. Then there was a bang and the helicopter's engine flamed out. Shit!!!! Suddenly it became eerily quiet. In an instant our helicopter had become the worst glider on earth!

The engine's caution light came on and the low engine RPM and low rotor RPM warning alarms sounded "an impending and damnable song of tragedy" in my ears. The loud noise of the engine was replaced by the almost silent flight of a tragic helicopter and crew with no engine. The aircraft began an immediate and rapid descent. The nose of the aircraft yawed to the left.

As trained in flight school, I entered auto-rotation by lowering the collective pitch control (which reduces the pitch in the rotor blades, allowing the main rotor to spin from the air rushing up through the rotor blades), added right pedal to trim the aircraft, and looked for a forced landing area. There was none, just triple canopy jungle below us! I asked the aircraft commander to turn off the fuel control switch. I adjusted the rotor RPM to 294 and my airspeed to 84 knots, (the best combination for maximum glide) in an attempt to stretch our glide to the open rice paddies ahead, but the paddies were too far ahead to reach from this low altitude.

The aircraft commander confirmed that our flame (engine) was out and that we were going down. I noticed that this auto-rotation

Picture 32: Viking Gunship with Crew Chief on Rocket Pod

Picture courtesy of Jim Saunders and George Quackenbush.

1. UH-1B Model Huey Gunship en route at 1500 altitude, where it is cooler and out of small arms range. 51 caliber enemy weapons could shoot down aircraft up to 3,000 feet or more. Later in the war, 37mm enemy antiaircraft weapons and shoulder-fired heat-seeking missiles shot down aircraft at much higher altitudes. We owned the daytime hours in Vietnam, but the VC and NVA owned the night. The picture was taken by the wing ship door gunner.

2. Specialist 5 Crew Chief Jim Saunders sitting on rocket pod for a picture. Yes, he is wearing his safety strap. No, commanders don't like these kinds of pictures, but soldiers did all kinds of things in combat to break the stress and boredom.

was different from the many I had successfully done in flight school—for some reason it just didn't feel right. Instead of going into a controlled and smooth auto-rotation, the aircraft felt like a heavy ball of rapidly falling mush. The aircraft was so overloaded that the handling characteristics of this over gross weight Huey were quite different and more difficult than all those lightly and moderately loaded Hueys I had flown at Hunter Army Airfield, GA, during flight training. The aircraft was falling like a rock and descending faster than any I had ever flown during auto-rotation previously.

The aircraft commander said, "I have the controls," and I confirmed that this was so and I gave up control of the helicopter by stating, "Roger you have the controls." I completed the engine failure emergency procedures by confirming the main fuel switch was off and by turning the transponder to the emergency code "7700." I then switched the Ultra High Frequency (UHF) radio to 243.0 megahertz, the international emergency frequency, and made a distress call "Mayday, Mayday, Mayday—Tiger 88 is going down 4 miles northeast of Rach Gia." This radio call later seemed stupid to me, as we were in the middle of a flight of ten aircraft and everybody in the formation could see our aircraft take the enemy's 51 caliber hit and that we were going to crash. However, Army pilots are trained over and over to make a Mayday call in this kind of emergency and the training just kicked in. The aircraft was now in trimmed flight but falling out of the sky at a dangerously high rate of descent, and we were seconds from impact.

It was then that I realized that the aircraft commander was using some of his rotor Revolutions Per Minute (RPM) to try and extend our glide past the tree line we were falling towards. The AC wanted desperately to make it into the water-filled rice paddies just east of the forest we were still over. He was trading rotor RPM for distance, rotor RPM we would need to cushion our landing. I realized in horror that this was a gutsy move by the AC and actually not recommended in the emergency procedures part of the operator's manual, but the AC had to make a split-second decision and there was no time to discuss or argue the matter now. The emergency procedures recommend a controlled tree landing with maximum rotor RPM available, rather than using rotor RPM to make a clear area. I realized that we probably would not recover enough rotor RPM when the AC brought the nose of the helicopter up and flared to land. Without a high rotor RPM the AC would not be able to prevent a violent impact and crash landing in the rice paddies and dikes around the paddies. I said to myself, "Oh Hell, we are going to die." I then locked my shoulder harness, pulled my helmet chin strap tighter, and put my helmet visor down. I had always known that life makes no promises and I was ready, for the worst to happen.

There was nothing further that I could do except call out airspeed and rotor RPM for the aircraft commander. I needed to decide whether I was going to watch the crash or close my eyes just before impact? I decided to watch! It wasn't going to take long to hit the ground—only about 45 seconds from when the engine was shot out and failed. I was amazed that everything around me appeared to be in slow motion. I knew we were not in slow motion, as I had learned in flight physiology about how people in high-stress situations focus on the emergency, get tunnel vision, and lose some high motor skills thus giving the illusion of slow motion. The huge amount of adrenalin pumping through my arteries was giving me this slow-motion sensation.

I folded my arms across my chest, told the Lord I had done my best, and waited for impact. We hit the water in a rice paddy with so much force that the aircraft rolled several times, slid about 100 feet, and flipped upside down on the east side of a rice paddy dike. The crash tore the main and tail rotor systems off of the aircraft and ripped the tail boom off, too. I could see flying objects pass my head. A main rotor blade came through the cabin, tore the left door (my door) off, ripped the cabin front roof off from over my head, smashed both windshields out, and nicked my flight helmet. When the aircraft stopped flipping, it was upside down. I wondered if I was dead and thought, "Is this the way being dead feels?" Soon I realized that I was very much alive and covered with mud, soaked with water, and bruised from head to toe. I was also dazed from the main rotor nicking my helmet, high g-forces of the crash, severe neck whip lash, and spinal compression. I did *not* even realize the aircraft and I were upside down!

I released my seat belt and fell headfirst into the wreckage beneath me. Fortunately I did not break my neck or severe my spinal cord, but I did further injure my neck and gash my leg by falling upside down from about four feet up. The water and mud below probably saved my life and kept me from breaking my neck. Amazingly the gash in my leg, painful neck whiplash, and many bruises were the only injuries I suffered. I then climbed out of the wreckage and looked back in the cabin and saw my aircraft commander, Mr. Connelly, upside down with his head submerged in muddy water. I didn't know if he was dead or alive, but I knew I had to act quickly, so I pulled the aircraft commander out of the aircraft, gently placed him safely on the dike, and checked and confirmed that he was breathing and that his pulse was strong.

I then looked inside the upside down and mangled cargo area and saw some troops moving around and some *not* moving at all. Eight Tiger aircraft in the flight of ten were still flying above us and one of the other Tigers landed by our crashed aircraft. Gunships (attack helicopters) from our Viking gun platoon circled above, providing protection. Another slick landed shortly after, and the crews began helping extract the injured and dead from our crashed Huey.

Still in somewhat of a daze, I was standing next to the aircraft and could see the fuel bladder totally exposed and bulging. I realized that we had just fueled up, and I knew that about 1,400 pounds of fuel was in our destroyed Huey's fuel cells. If the fuel cell had burst, as normally happened in such a violent crash, all onboard probably would have perished in the post-crash fire. I retrieved the fire extinguisher and shot its suppressant into the red-hot exhaust of the engine to cool it down.

One of the rescuing Tiger crew members helped the AC, the other survivors, and me into another helicopter and took us to the Can Tho (pronounced Can Toe) US medical facility. Two Army of the Republic of South Vietnam troops were killed, and our door gunner and crew chief were critically injured. The aircraft commander had a broken back, concussion, severe whiplash and many bruises. Later inspection determined that the engine failed from a single 50 caliber round that went through the combustion chamber.

I would fly in the great 121st Assault Helicopter Company for another eight months as a slick and gunship (attack) helicopter pilot, aircraft commander, gunship wing aircraft commander, and fire team leader. My combat tour ended abruptly when I was shot through the right knee and hand on a gunship mission covering another helicopter that was spraying Agent Orange. Agent

Picture 33: 1st Lt. Bubba Segrest's and CW2 Jim Connelly's Crashed Huey

Picture courtesy of Bubba Segrest.

1. This aircraft crashed very hard into a rice field that was full of water about two feet deep and ended up upside down next to a large dike. Three ARVN soldiers were killed in this crash. The Air Craft Commander (AC) elected to use rotor RPM to get his aircraft over trees resulting in a very hard and fast crash landing. This picture was taken after the hulk was recovered to Soc Trang. CW2 Jim Connelly was strapped in this seat, unconscious, and under water after the crash. Bubba Segrest saved his life by pulling him out of the water and getting him breathing again.

2. 1st Lt. Segrest was in this seat, hanging upside down, and dazed after the crash. He released his seat belt and fell about four feet onto his head, seriously injuring his neck. Therefore Bubba was credited with two crashes on this fateful and tragic day!

3. Miraculously, the transmission and main rotor mast did not come out of the aircraft.

.

Orange is a very hazardous chemical used to defoliate jungle. Agent Orange caused many diseases, injuries, and deaths to Vietnam Veterans and Vietnamese over the next 47 years. I would be medically discharged due to my serious wounds and one total finger amputation and two partial amputations. My wife and I had two beautiful daughters, and I have owned several successful businesses. Today I live and work in Charleston, SC, my beloved hometown where I see my old friends Larry Dandridge and Sam DeLoach and their families frequently.

Unfortunately my November 1968 neck injuries from the slick crash and my falling out of my seat upside down and onto my head were not recorded in my medical records. I now suffer extensive and debilitating neck and arm pain from those neck injuries. Because my combat-related and military service connected neck injuries were not recorded in my medical records or personnel records, and because those neck injuries were not x-rayed and not properly investigated, diagnosed, or documented in 1968, I had to obtain lay witness statements and my personal doctor's statements and records to prove to the Veterans Administration (VA) that my serious neck injuries and worsening conditions are military service connected. The morale of this story is fourfold for today's troops:

1. Always report and record in detail all injuries, wounds, illnesses, and hazardous material (HAZMAT) contamination and exposure to your chain of command and to your medical team.

2. Always and as soon as possible obtain and keep copies of all medical records for any service connected injury, wound, disease, and HAZMAT exposure and contamination.

3. Always take (or have taken) pictures of any wounds, injuries, burns, or disease symptoms that are service connected. Write on the backs of those photographs the time, place, witness names, and brief summary of what happened. Keep those pictures in a safe place to be used later when filing your disability claims to the Army and VA.

4. Record all witness names, addresses, phone numbers, and e-mail addresses, and keep them in a safe place.

5. If no medical records are made or available, as soon as possible after any wounds, injuries, illnesses, or HAZMAT contamination, obtain detailed "lay witness" (eyewitness) statements that are notarized, if possible, from witnesses to your wounds, injuries, illnesses, and HAZMAT contamination and exposure. Make certain that those witness statements explain the who, what, when, where, and how of the incident and the extent of injuries, illnesses, wounds, and contamination. Include in the last line of each statement, "I swear that the information provided in this lay witness statement is true to the best of my knowledge."

CHAPTER 6: NOVEMBER 26, 1968 ◄

"Tiger Slick Shoot Down in
Ben Tri Province."

Letter from WO1 Larry Dandridge
to WO1 Jerry Markland

Date: 26 November 1968

From: Warrant Officer W. Larry Dandridge,
121st Assault Helicopter Company (Airmobile Light),
13th CAB, 1st Aviation Brigade, APO 96296

TO: Warrant Officer Gerald David Markland
187th AHC, 11th AVN BN, 12th AVN GRP, 1 AVN BDE
APO SF 01213

Dear Jerry,

Thanks for your recent letter. Letters do help my morale and attitude a great deal. I try to write my folks every week and my wife every day; and I write you and other friends often, as well. I believe writing about this war helps me to cope with what I am experiencing and it proves that I am alive to the people I care most about. My wife writes about twice a week and my dad has been great about writing me a long letter every month or so. I even received letters from my Aunt Nita and my older sister Barbara, this week. My older brother "Skipper" is not a big writer, but Dad always passes on his best wishes. My seven-year-old little sister "Tami" sends me a note inside my Mom's letters and also draws me a funny picture or two.

The last thing I did before shipping out to the land of jungle, bugs, heat, rain, mud, snakes, exotic diseases, and Viet Cong was go dove hunting with my dad. Even though I loved to hunt and fish with my dad, grandfather, uncles, stepfather, and friends all of my childhood, I am not sure if I will ever want to kill any kind of animal again after this experience with war. Seems to me that the only animals deserving to be killed are some of the evil people and hardened criminals who populate this earth—everything else should be left alone.

Now that the famous General Creighton Abrams has replaced General Westmoreland as the commander of Military Assistance Command Vietnam, perhaps the new blood will bring more progress to our fight over here. It worries me, though, that President Nixon has ended "Rolling Thunder," the sustained US Air Force, US Navy, and Republic of Vietnam Air Force (VNAF) aerial bombardment campaign of North Vietnam that took place between March 2, 1965 and November 2, 1968.

Thank goodness that no one has been killed in my unit since my arrival but several US troops have been seriously wounded in combat and others severely injured in accidents. However, many ARVNs and Vietnamese civilians have been killed. Sadly, our sister assault helicopter companies have had several killed in action and accidents. I also have not had dysentery "yet" and hope I don't get that problem.

I had never seen anyone have a fever, chills, and simultaneously vomit and have uncontrollable diarrhea with mucus and blood until I got here. No wonder entire armies in ancient times were decimated by amebic and other forms of dysentery. One of the guys with amebic dysentery told me that the medicine (Flagyl or metronidizole) he takes for dysentery tastes much worse than shit. I wonder how he knows what shit tastes like!

The medics are right—dysentery destroys livers and colons and kills! Disease really is a problem over here. Even our flight surgeon was medically evacuated recently to Japan with hepatitis. His skin and eyes were yellow, and he looked like death warmed over the day he left here. I also medical evacuated a poor infantry soldier from a remote base camp last week with cerebral malaria. He had a temperature of over 106 degrees—the poor soul was already dead, but still breathing. I am taking my malaria (prevention) pills faithfully!

This Mekong Delta seems to be covered with tens of thousands of mines and booby traps. I really don't want to have to walk anywhere, at least not anymore than I have to. Thankfully, we are flying and not humping an M60 or rifle in that heat and misery on the ground. I did have to guard a Province Chief as we walked to several small villages and some forest between Vinh Long and Chau Doc a few weeks back. I was nervous as hell the entire time. I left my pilot, crew chief, and door gunner back at the aircraft with the blades untied, and the aircraft in the quick start mode, in case they had to exit the area quickly.

The Viet Cong are hiding among the locals in the daytime and then raising hell all night. The VC and NVA are picking when and where they want to fight. I haven't seen but a couple of captured and dead bad guys so far. Just as the British could not defeat Colonel Francis Marion (The SC Patriot Swamp Fox) and his troops in the swamps and deep forests of the low country of SC in the 1770s, it is going to be damn hard to defeat a determined VC and NVA foe in their own swamps, jungles, forests, rice paddies, and mountains of Vietnam.

The morale of our 121st troops is high, but we all feel uneasy about serving so far from home against such a determined foe who has outlasted so many invaders, including the Japanese and French of late, and the Chinese before them. I feel like—actually, I am convinced that man is a very weak and insignificant species. We are just not capable it seems of living peaceably with others. We humans are constantly destroying and unable to stop what seems like endless warring and killing.

There are 3,000 miles of twisting rivers and canals in the Delta and the Viet Cong seem to be everywhere. It is hard to believe our total US Force in Vietnam is now approaching one half million troops. I heard recently in the news that the US Army has purchased more than 6,500 UH-1 helicopters since 1958. My commander says the Army now has some 10,000 aircraft in our inventory. Can you believe it? The US Army now has far more aircraft than the Air Force, Navy, Coast Guard, and Marine Corps combined! It is also ironic that the Army also has more ships (the Army calls them vessels) than the Navy, because we have so many liberty ships and other Army vessels in long-term storage.

I now know what real fear feels and smells like, and what death looks and smells like, and it is revolting. A rotting human corpse has to be the most offensive, demoralizing, and disgusting smell on earth. I also now know what the sight of horrific wounds and injuries look like, and I don't like it. I suppose these awful experiences are making me tougher, but I don't feel tough and, if anything, I feel more vulnerable to death, injury, accidents, and disease.

I flew cooked turkeys into our troops in the field all day on Thanksgiving Day, while flying on a single-ship mission that turned out to be a pretty hairy day due to bad weather and so many troops in contact in the Ben Trie Province area. The ceiling was very low, it was raining hard, and visibility was only about one quarter of a mile. On one supply run, we (Warrant Officer McKeatch and I) had to make several approaches and abort the first two approaches due to heavy small arms fire on Turkey Day. Eventually we had to just fly in as fast and low as we could, do a quick stop and high hover maneuver, at about 10 feet above tree top level, and then drop the turkeys into an old blown-up church, with no roof, to the poor grunts held up in there. Those grunts were under continuous fire from the bad guys all around them. I felt good about bringing them some hot chow on Thanksgiving, but thought how hard it must have been to try and eat under such stress, filth, heat, rain, bugs, and constant fire from the bad guys.

Now that we have some in-country help from Australia, New Zealand, Korea, the Philippines, and Thailand, perhaps we will make more progress against the Viet Cong and North Vietnamese Army. The scuttlebutt is that the South Koreans have 50,000 troops here and that their area of operations is the safest place in Vietnam. Unfortunately, I haven't seen any of these allies in the parts of the Delta that I have been flying in. It also makes me nervous to know the Soviets, Chinese, North Korea, Cuba, and God knows who else is helping the VC and North Vietnam.

The news from the states is so disturbing: anti-war demonstrators, men burning their draft cards, race riots, people spitting on troops, and so many congressional leaders condemning the war. How do people expect us to keep up our motivation and willingness to serve in uniform? It seems like the right thing to do to help this poor country to determine its own destiny—free from the ruthless, barbaric, and cruel interference of the VC and NVA. If the demonstrators could just see how scared the Vietnamese are of the VC and their daily and nightly executions and torture of so many of these poor people, I think they would understand.

I ate lunch with, and was talking with, some Special Forces guys last week who are here on their second tour. One of them has a BS in history and is an expert in Vietnamese history. He told me that the North Vietnamese are a tenacious group, and they have not been successfully invaded or defeated by anyone in ancient or modern history—not the Mongols, not the Japanese, not the French, and not the USA. The Special Forces captain told me that a famous and legendary Vietnamese military leader, named Tran Hung Dao, who was born around 1229 and died in 1300, wrote the book on Vietnamese-style guerrilla and conventional warfare that is still used so successfully today by the Viet Cong and NVA.

Tran Hung Dao's book actually shows the Viet Cong troops and civilian sympathizers how to build many different types of bobby traps, especially bobby trap holes in the ground using bamboo spears, bamboo rollers with spikes, and human feces to infect the horrendous wounds they inflict. Evidently "Tran" was a brilliant military strategist, the so-called "father of the VC fighting methods," and he defeated two Mongol invasions using a defensive strategy, guerrilla warfare, and scorched-earth tactics.

He "avoided pitched battles just like the Viet Cong and North Vietnamese Army do today," and he even lured a huge fleet of some 600 ships into the Bach Dang River, where he had placed tens of thousands of iron-tipped bamboo spears beneath the water. At low tide the ships ran aground on these spears and were sunk and firebombed. The fleet and the Mongol troops on board were destroyed. I hope someone told the US Brown Water Navy guys about this![57]

I am going to follow Bubba Segrest's example and try and help the locals here by volunteering to assist with an orphanage near our base, if I can get a minute off to do something like that. I have been appointed the "Class A Pay Agent" for my unit as an additional duty. I took over this nauseating and nerve-racking pay agent job from Warrant Officer Brian King. I'll do it only for three months, but each month I have to fly to Can Tho (pronounced Can Toe), pick up a briefcase full of money and stay up all night dividing the money into piles from which to pay the soldiers in cash the next morning. What a nightmare! Last time, I couldn't get the pay to add up and was short several hundred dollars the first four times I counted all that money. Finally, thanks to the help of my company first sergeant, I discovered where I was about to overpay one trooper.

I feel like I am aging at an accelerated rate. I seem to look older, too. The medical guys say the average US civilian male lives to be about 70 these days, but at the rate we are aging, I don't know if I can make it to 40. Guys over here can fly off the handle into a rage over small things, and I know it is because of stress. I could see in my stepdad's eyes the sadness, grief, guilt, and torment he brought home from those damned island campaigns he fought in the Pacific during World War II. God forbid any of us see so much hell in Vietnam! I fear the ground guys are going through the same, if not more of that hell, here in Vietnam.

A man does not have to be physically wounded, contract cerebral malaria, or be killed here to become a casualty—he can lose his sanity here quickly and without having the slightest hint of a mental health problem before arriving here. I find myself waking up at night thinking things like: "I cannot find myself. What is my real self? What is my purpose in life? Can it be I am destroying my mental health by killing people; worrying about being injured, killed, or captured; and stressing over the fear of Bubba, you, or one of my other friends over here getting seriously wounded or killed."

Best not to think too much over here. I just need to stay busy and focused on our mission. There is never a shortage of work to be done here at Soc Trang, nor while flying. I guess it is quite a blessing to be flying, as there is no time to over think things and no opportunity to be bored. Unlike the ground pounders, we aviators have no mud to suck you into the bowels of the earth; no mosquitoes, ticks, or ants to bite and chew on you; no unrelenting heat (thanks to the cooler temperatures/breeze in flight); and no long-lasting cold due to our enclosed cockpits. We have no immersion foot from the relentless rain and swamps below; no punji sticks covered with feces to cripple us pilots and give us gangrene; and no forty to one hundred extra pounds of weapons and gear to hump mile after mile. I know that while I am flying Hueys I will at least be mostly comfortable 90 percent of the time. Just wish I could eat better chow and more often. I seem to be hungry and thirsty more often than not.

By the way, the good Lord was looking out for my crew and me again last week when we were shot down trying to resupply troops in heavy contact in dense jungle, in Ben Tre province, not far southeast of Dong Tam (the 9th US Infantry division main base). Dong Tam is where our dear friend and classmate WO1 Danny Hickman is stationed in B Troop, 3rd of the 17th Air Cavalry Squadron. Bravo troop is organic to the 1st Aviation Brigade, and they stay in almost constant contact with the enemy around here. I have attached the story of that close call mission to this letter. Too tired to write more tonight and still picking slivers of Plexiglas out of my face and metal shards from my knee from the bullets that passed through our cockpit today. Take care and God bless.

Sincerely,

Larry

Tiger Shoot Down in Ben Tre Province

*"If your attack is going too well,
you're walking (or flying) into an ambush."*

—*Infantry Journal*[58]

Aircraft Commander and Warrant Officer Harry Skelly was one of the most respected and highly skilled slick pilots in the 121st Assault Helicopter Company. I believe he was an ex-noncommissioned officer (NCO), and he was a few years older and wiser than us younger warrant officers. He was training me. I had been in country only about two months, and I would soon be appointed as an aircraft commander. Harry and I had flown many successful missions together. Harry was a legend at Soc Trang. I really admired and respected him. He had successfully handled one of the most difficult in-flight emergencies for a helicopter pilot: a tail rotor failure (tail rotor stopped turning, but no loss of components) in bad weather. Harry had the misfortune of the tail rotor failure about four months previously. He had flown back to Soc Trang in rain, clouds, low ceilings, and poor visibility and made a successful emergency running landing without further damage to the UH-1D helicopter he was commanding. Harry is a genuine hero, and flying with him was a real joy.

On this day, Harry and I were flying a single ship "ash and trash" mission all over the delta region of Vietnam, but mainly in Ben Tre Province. We were hauling supplies, ammunition, and food and water to various fire bases, South Vietnam Regional Forces and Provincial Forces (RFPF which we pronounced "Rough Puff"), triangular-shaped forts, Military Assistance Command Vietnam (MACV) Adviser locations, and Special Forces (SF) locations throughout Ben Tre and other provinces. It was early afternoon, and we had just had lunch with a Special Forces team not far from the city of Ben Tre. Those SF guys really displayed the strength, confidence, professionalism, dignity, stamina, loyalty, and tremendous pride the Green Beret represents.

During the lunch I had scrounged two quart bottles of Beck's German Beer from the Special Forces guys. The day had been so routine and unexciting that we pilots had taken off our heavy, hot, and uncomfortable chicken plates, and set them down between the seats and the aircraft center console. Neither Harry nor I had the special made cloth and Velcro vest that held the chicken plate safely to the wearer. The vests were in short supply in our unit. We had not been shot at all day as far as we could tell, and we had already flown about 8 hours of what was supposed to be a 12- to 14-hour flight day. I placed the bottles of Beck's Beer in each of my pockets on my jungle fatigue olive-drab-colored top jacket. I looked forward to icing them down back at Soc Trang and drinking them the next chance I had to drink a beer.

Harry was letting me do most of the flying, and he was pointing out various locations in Ben Tre Province, including the US 9th Infantry Division's large 2nd brigade base camp in IV Corps at Dong Tam. Activated February 1, 1966, for service in Vietnam and sent there December 1966, the 9th Infantry Division served in III Corps and IV Corps, and its second brigade was the Army component of the Mobile Riverine Force. Ninth Division headquarters was at Bear Cat from December 1966 through July 1968 and Dong Tam from August 1968 until now.[59]

The VC and NVA had their own Psychological Operations (PSY OPS) and propaganda steadily in progress in Vietnam. They continually spread pamphlets directed at and focused on the US units operating in the area. Hanoi had its own "Tokyo Rose" named "Hanoi Hannah,"[60] who was most effective when she told the truth and US Armed Forces Radio was exaggerating or fudging on the facts.

Geographically, the city of Ben Tre was wedged between the two main branches of the Tien Giang River, which is itself one of the two main branches of the Mekong River. The province's northern boundary was formed by the Tien Giang's main course. The province's southern boundary was formed by the Tien Giang's largest branch, which broke away from the Tien Giang just upriver from Ben Tre. Between the Tien Giang and its main branch were two smaller branches, passing through the middle of Ben Tre. The entire province was crisscrossed with a network of smaller rivers and canals. The extensive irrigation that this provided made Ben Tre a major producer of rice, but it also means that the area was prone to flooding. If sea levels were to have risen by one meter, 51 percent of Ben Tre province would have been below sea level and flooded. Ben Tre Province was, on average, only 49.2 inches above sea level.[61]

Both Harry and I had seen South Vietnamese troops and US troops jump out of the Hueys on previous combat assaults in this heavily flooded area, only to go completely out of sight in water over their heads. Sometimes and sadly they drowned quickly due to the combination of their being weighted down with their heavy helmets, ammunition, grenades, canteens, first aid packs, entrenching tool, and backpacks full of food and other personal items, and the dirty, dark, and deep water in many parts of this province. At one time I thought all that hunting and fishing in the swamps and forests of SC would make me a good infantryman, and it probably would help, but I did not want any part of the infantry mission and war in Vietnam!

As we were flying that day, I was thinking how often US Army troops would listen to and sing along with the 1965 hit song recorded by the Animals, "We Gotta Get Out of This Place."[62] And at the same time, I was now convinced after being in Vietnam for two months that the VC and NVA had to be singing, "Time, time, time is on my side, yes it is," recorded in 1964 by the Rolling Stones. Yes, these two songs told the story of the US Soldier's attitude and the VC and NVA's attitude and commitment to this godforsaken war.[63]

The 21st Army of South Vietnam Infantry Division and the US 9th Infantry Division were the two main friendly forces trying to deal with the Viet Cong and North Vietnamese Army in this hot, wet, muddy, and bug- and snake-infested part of Vietnam. At one location in Ben Tre, both of us pilots had come under mortar fire almost every time we had previously landed there. Ben Tre Province was not an area that either of us liked to fly in.

Ben Tre city had been almost totally destroyed during the VC Tet Offensive of January and February 1968. That is where some

Army major had supposedly told a reporter something like, "We had to destroy the place to save it."[64] Old-timers say the river that passes Ben Tre city was full of bodies, both Viet Cong and South Vietnamese, in January 1968, as a result of the Viet Cong's Tet offensive and the US and South Vietnamese campaign to retake the city. I always felt like there were more Viet Cong in Ben Tre Province than there were South Vietnamese government and Army sympathizers. This part of IV Corps was real Indian Country and to get shot down there or to have an engine fail on a single-ship mission was high risk for death or capture. Although flying close formation on combat assaults had proven to be very stressful, dangerous, and fatiguing, it was always a good feeling to know if you got shot down, you would most likely be quickly rescued by the other aircraft involved in such multi-aircraft operations.

As we were returning to refuel at a tactical airstrip near Ben Tre, we were called and given an emergency mission to resupply troops in heavy contact in triple canopy, dense, and flooded jungle about 10 miles east of Ben Tre city. We were to pick up small arms ammunition and a South Vietnamese senior noncommissioned officer, and drop them off in a supposedly secure area behind the frontlines of the ongoing battle. The ARVN unit and its advisors were supposed to be heavily engaged with a large enemy unit, and were taking heavy casualties and running out of ammunition. The VC and NVA were smart cookies, and they were masters of camouflage. They baited US and ARVN ground units into pursuing what appeared to be a small unit, and then ambushed the pursuers with a larger unit—only to disengage completely and quickly, dragging their dead underground or under water, before US and ARVN superior artillery, gunship, and tactical air and reinforcements could be brought to bear on them.

Harry had kidded me earlier this day for fast becoming what we called a "magnet ass" for frequently attracting enemy fire whenever and wherever I flew. Some of my Catholic family's older Charleston Jewish friends, Mr. and Mrs. Dubrow, had called this kind of bad luck person a "schlimazel."[65] I did not want to earn such a reputation, for my own longevity, and for the sake of the fine soldiers that I flew with. However, a cold shiver ran down my back as I thought how often the ARVNs reports of a cold LZ had been wrong. Maybe we should put on our uncomfortable chicken

PICTURE 34: 13ᵀᴴ CAB HUEYs NEAR BA XOAI SPECIAL FORCES CAMP IN SEVEN MOUNTAINS AREA OF THE MEKONG DELTA

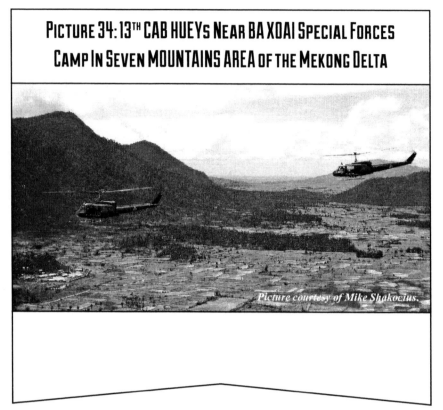

Picture courtesy of Mike Shakocius.

plates, which we had stowed besides our seats after flying such low risk missions all morning. However, since Harry, my AC, was not wearing his body armor, I wasn't going to show my concerns by putting mine on.

We flew our Tiger slick into a South Vietnamese Army compound in Ben Tre City and picked up the Vietnamese Army NCO and a maximum load of ammunition, and took off for the map coordinates given to us. When we approached the landing zone (LZ) we contacted the Cavalry Squadron Cobra Attack helicopters and the Light Observation helicopters supporting us on the Ultra High Frequency (UHF) supporting the battle. The Cobra fire team leader gave us the Frequency Modulated (FM) radio frequency that the infantry advisors were using to support the battle, but unfortunately our FM radio was not working.

Since our FM radio was inoperative, the Cobra fire team leader covering our landing and takeoff offered to relay messages from the ground troops to us. Landing without radio contact with the ground troops is normally a big no-no in combat, but the unit on the ground was in heavy contact, suffering casualties, and running critically low on small arms ammunition and grenades. We requested that the ground troops pop smoke, and white smoke (which should have meant a cold LZ) quickly appeared at "two separate locations" about 300 yards from each other.

There should have been only one smoke signal. Two smokes probably meant the VC were monitoring our radios and they had popped smoke at the same time the ARVN unit's US adviser had popped smoke. The enemy was trying to lure us into landing at their location!

This white smoke response from two locations alarmed the attack, scout, and utility helicopters supporting this mission, and the two white smokes were especially unnerving to me. The last thing that Harry Skelly and I wanted to do was to land at an enemy location and be shot down at close range in an enemy ambush. Harry asked for another smoke to be popped. This time only one green smoke was popped, in heavily flooded jungle and swamp.

Harry took control of the aircraft and began a high over-head approach into a very small opening in the jungle where the smoke was popped—and in the excitement "we both forgot to put our chicken plates on!" Two Cobras and two armed LOHs (pronounced Loaches) provided cover. The Cobras were armed with 2.75-inch folding fin rockets and 7.62mm miniguns, and the loaches had a one minigun and an observer/gunner with AR15 and many hand grenades. The LZ was such a small opening that our Huey had great difficulty landing without striking trees with the main rotor blades and tail rotor blades. We did cut down some smaller tree branches on the way down, and immediately our aircraft came under heavy fire from the ground.

Harry was landing to the west and when he reached the water-flooded small area below where the smoke grenade was still smoldering, there were four or five South Vietnamese troops lying dead in the water around the dissipating smoke grenade. Enemy AK47 and SKS rounds were streaking by and through our aircraft. One round went through the battery compartment in the nose of the aircraft just inches from both of us. The battery exploded and began smoking heavily.

It was at this time that both of us pilots realized we were not wearing chicken plates, and we were both very chicken at this moment! There was no time to put on a chicken plate now. Since our aircraft was mostly facing the direction in which much of the enemy fire was coming, I imagined I was about to watch as bullets came through the one-sixteenth-of-an-inch-thick Plexiglas windshields and rip into my upper torso, legs, arms, and head. I, as the peter pilot, had been calling out on the UHF radio all the way down, taking fire 11 o'clock, taking fire 9 o'clock, taking fire 12 o'clock! Another round went through the battery compartment and hit the air inlet warning light in the center of the console in front of me and then zipped between us two pilots. In the meantime, the crew chief, the door gunner, and the Vietnamese noncommissioned officer were throwing ammo boxes out of the aircraft at warp speed. We were trapped in this deep hole in the jungle and could not take off until most of the ammo was unloaded, as our UH-1D did not have the power to take off vertically with such a heavy load and under such high-density altitude conditions.

Then several rounds went through the tail boom and through the helicopter's main transmission, beginning the sequence of fast overheating and destruction of the many gears in our flight critical main transmission. Oil was pouring out of the transmission; sweat was pouring out of my body; and the aircraft only had a few minutes of flight left in it before the transmission would overheat and seize, thus sending us to our death if we were airborne at the time of seizure. A round came through Harry's Plexiglas windshield on the right side of the aircraft and dozens of shards of Plexiglas struck my face. Blood oozed out of dozens of tiny cuts in my face, but by the grace of God the glass shards did not hit my eyes due to the protection of my sun glasses.

Harry was not so lucky! A long shard of Plexiglas broke off the windshield and flew into his chest almost pinning him to his seat. The shard that struck Harry was about 15 inches long and about 3/8 inch in diameter. Harry looked like he had been shot with a hunting arrow high in the chest near his left shoulder. He flinched as the shard cut through his jungle fatigue jacket and shoulder. He then looked at me quickly and said, "I am OK, stay on the controls with me," and he kept hovering the aircraft and waiting for enough ammunition to be kicked out so he could take off and escape the Viet Cong hornets' nest we had landed in.

I was following my unit's standard operating procedure (SOP) and Harry's instructions, and had been lightly on the controls with Harry, in case he was wounded too seriously to keep flying. Since Harry told me he was OK, he kept control of the aircraft. Just as both of us pilots, our crew chief, and our door gunner were about convinced it was only seconds before we would be shot down, or each of us shot through the front and right side of the aircraft, two OH-6 armed Light Observation Helicopters hovered down through the small jungle opening and got between our Tiger slick and the enemy. They were olive drab colored angels from heaven and they came in with their minigun (each LOH had one mini-gun) and observer's door gun blasting. Throwing hand grenades and firing thousands of rounds from their miniguns, they had their CAR15 rifles point-blank into the enemy positions. It was then I knew there is a God, and that he was protecting us!

The Loach (OH-6) crews had saved the day for us as we had finally unloaded the ammunition we were carrying. Now we had the power to take off. Harry took the aircraft almost straight up and actually cut down some more small trees and limbs off of larger trees while exiting the LZ. Harry was bleeding, but not in much pain, as adrenalin was flooding his veins. Harry was pulling maximum power trying to get that UH-1D up to 120 knots and out of the area as quickly as possible. I am sure he exceeded the engine torque limit, but it did not matter as this aircraft only had a few more minutes or less of life in it anyway! The crew was exuberant and telling Harry, "Great job, sir! You are the man, Harry! Are you OK Harry?"

We were each relieved and happy that we were on the way to safety. Unfortunately the aircraft's nose battery compartment poured smoke into the cockpit and the main transmission made terrible loud noises, noises of gears grinding and bearings failing, noises of a dying Huey, and we knew the transmission would soon overheat and seize. We could not chance flying the aircraft much further, for if the main transmission seized, the main rotor would stop turning and we would crash at hundreds of miles per hour into the jungle or one of the rice paddies we were now flying over. We now knew we would not make it back to Dong Tam or any other friendly location!

I made mayday calls on UHF frequency 243.0 and VHF frequency 121.5, and gave our location and call for help. I also set our transponder to the emergency frequency of 7700. Paddy Control was no real help as we were too low to be picked up on radar. Harry picked out a rice paddy ahead and, about two miles from a tactical US airstrip and set the Huey down in water and mud about four feet deep. Just as we sat down, the transmission completely overheated and seized. Harry had made the right call again and saved his crew—at least for now.

I got the Secret KY-28 black box and radio scrambler out from under my side of the dashboard and grabbed my new M2 Carbine with five extra 30-round clips. Then I helped Harry half walk and half swim to a rice dike about 25 yards away. It was a slow and tiring pull through mud a foot deep and water three feet deep to the dike. The two door gunners pulled and swam to the dike also. Harry was now in some pain, and no one dared pull the Plexiglas arrow out of Harry's chest, as he might bleed to death quickly or collapse his left lung.

I helped tend to Harry's wound and helped the rest of the crew set up a hasty defensive perimeter, and waited for someone to rescue us. Harry turned on the handheld emergency radio and made another mayday call. It was about this time that I noted in horror that our door guns, two M-60 machine guns, were still on the aircraft and that the crew chief and door gunner brought with them only their M14 rifles. To make matters worse, they did not have magazines for their M14 rifles! All they had was a belt of about 100 rounds of 7.62mm door gun ammo. That meant they were each limited to loading one round at a time and firing and reloading after each single shot.

Damn nation, I thought. How could these two soldiers be so untrained as to leave their door guns and bring their rifles with no magazines at a time like this? Then I said to myself, Hell, these enlisted guys are working for two officers and neither of us had thought about checking the enlisted crews' weapons before we left, so we officers were as much to blame if not more so than the enlisted guys for launching without M14 magazines and without going over exactly what we would do if we were shot down. My

World War II vintage 30 caliber M2 Carbine with five total 30 round clips (150 rounds) and a 38 caliber pistol with 18 rounds were my personal weapons this day. Harry only had his 38 caliber revolver. Unfortunately, my rifle and our two revolvers a sound defense would not make!

I test fired my carbine into the closest tree line and it fired only three rounds when the bolt broke. Now all I had for a weapon was my 38 caliber pistol and 30-inch-long club shaped like an M2 automatic carbine. I was preparing to go get a door gun and box of ammo off the dead Huey, when a 9th Division Brigade Commander landed his UH-1 and picked us up. Harry was flown straight to the US Hospital at Dong Tam, which was only about a 10-minute flight away. My crew chief, door gunner, and I were taken to a tactical airfield to await a maintenance recovery Chinook helicopter to pick us up and recover our downed and nonflyable UH-1. As soon as we got out of the brigade commander's ship, the tactical airfield where he dropped us off at came under mortar fire. The mortars exploding near us further unnerved the door gunner, crew chief, and me, and required us to low crawl rapidly about 50 feet into a bunker. Lying in that old crumbling bunker, I finished pulling Plexiglas fragments out of my face and waited for the Chinook cargo and recovery helicopter to arrive.

A twin-rotor Chinook arrived about two hours later. We got on the Chinook and guided the pilots to our downed aircraft. We helped the maintenance guys put a sling on our shot-up Tiger Huey, and we headed back to Soc Trang. I hated Chinooks as it was the only US Army helicopter that could have a mid-air collision with itself (because the front and rear rotors were timed and geared by a combining transmission to allow the rotor blades to rotate overlapping and intermeshing with each other, and, if the combining transmission failed, the huge rotor systems would crash into each other resulting in a catastrophic crash). To add to my anxiety, the Chinook pilots climbed up to about 6,000 feet on their way back to Soc Trang, and because of a mild cold I had, I could not clear my ears. Sitting in that Chinook, worn out, soaking wet, sweated out, with dozens of facial cuts (and still pulling Plexiglas out of my face), and now an ear ache to boot, I thought, *Damn, how many things can go wrong in one day?*

Picture 36: CH-47A Chinook Recovering A Downed Viking Gunship

Picture courtesy of Mike Shakocius.

UH-1B Huey being recovered by CH-47B..

I was so tired—no I was more than tired and more like a fish that had fought an angler with all his strength and soul for eight hours and could no longer move. I did not eat supper, and I just collapsed in my bunk and thanked the Lord for getting me through another day in Viet Fu#*ing Nam. I quietly thought about what the scientist said in the 1955 movie Rebel Without a Cause: *"The universe will be little moved by our demise. We will disappear, destroyed as we began in a burst of gas and fire. In all the immensity of the galaxy and beyond, the earth will not be missed. The problems of man seem trivial and naive indeed, and man, existing alone, seems himself a thing of little consequence."*[66]

My luck quickly changed as I was taking my wet and muddy jungle fatigues off. I was pleasantly surprised and chuckled when I found two unbroken quart-size full bottles of Beck's beer in my jungle fatigue shirt! Harry Skelly returned to our unit a day later and was flying again in a few days. We never knew who those brave CAV scout pilots were, but I suspect they were part of Danny Hickman's B Troop, 3/17th Air Cavalry Squadron. We never had a chance to thank them. So if they are still out there somewhere today, thanks a million, guys, from my children, grandchildren, and me!

CHAPTER 7: DECEMBER 14, 1968 ◄
"Dust Off Mountain Medical Evacuation at Night Under Fire!"

Letter from Warrant Officer 1 Sam DeLoach
to 1st Lt. Bubba Segrest[67]

Date: 14 December 1968[68]

From: Warrant Officer Sam DeLoach, 498th Medical Evacuation Company (AA), APO SF 01214

TO: First Lieutenant Laurie O. "Bubba" Segrest, 121st Assault Helicopter Company (Airmobile Light), 13th CAB, 1st Aviation Brigade, APO SF 96296

Dear Bubba,

Got your most recent letter. You guys in the 121st sound busy. I am very pleased to be assigned to this "Dust Off" unit in II Corps and with so many fine men assigned here. I bet you did not know that Dust Off has its own acronym: "Dedicated Unhesitating Service To Our Fighting Forces." Like you, I sure miss my family in Charleston and all the great hunting, shrimping, crabbing, and fishing.

When I first got here, I read the history of this unit. It has been around since the early days of World War (WW) II. The 498th Medical Company (AA) was constituted in the regular Army as Company C, 57th Medical Battalion, on January 13, 1941, and activated on February 10, 1941 at Fort Ord, California. On September 10, 1941, the unit was reorganized and re-designated as the 498th Collecting Company, and after serving with distinction in WWII, was inactivated at Camp Shanks, NY, on 24 October 1945. The 498th was re-designated as the 498th Preventive Medicine Company on 11 September 1950 and activated on 2 October of that year at Fort Sam Houston, TX. The unit was reorganized and rededicated the 498th Medical Company on June 19, 1953, only to be inactivated on September 24, 1956, at Fort Meade, MD. On September 23, 1964, the unit was activated as an "air ambulance company" at Fort Sam Houston, TX and deployed to Vietnam.

Getting the casualty and the physician together as soon as possible is our number one priority. I am seeing this pay off daily in saved lives and reduced suffering. Unfortunately we don't always get the wounded in time, and sometimes we cannot get to the wounded at all due to weather and enemy fire—and sometimes the wounds are too serious to save them no matter how fast we are. To be honest, I have seen more tragedy since I have been here than I ever could have imagined. I hope this pain and suffering and loss of life and limb is worth all of this effort to stop communism.

I am learning fast to fly safely in mountains. Mountain flying can be hairy at best and downright dangerous at worst. My in-country 498th Dust Off welcome briefing said the following: "MEDIVAC helicopters transport six to nine patients at a time, depending upon the number of litter cases. Medical evacuation flights averaged only about 35 minutes each. Short flight times often mean the difference between life and death for patients. The more seriously wounded usually reach a hospital within 1 to 2 hours after they are wounded or injured."

This war is so frustrating and appears to be so confusing to our leaders back in DC. If they would just come over to the Nam and ride along with us a few days, things would get real clear real fast. These Viet Cong and North Vietnamese Army mean bastards are determined and only total war in the north and south of Vietnam, Cambodia, and Laos will have any chance of breaking their iron will to defeat us!

Like you, I am disgusted with all these men back home burning their draft cards, some soldiers refusing to go to Vietnam, and young men going to Canada and Sweden and other places to avoid serving in our armed forces. What if our fathers had done this in 1941? Don't these guys have any honor? Don't these fools have any sense of duty for this great nation of ours? Don't they know how ruthless, brutal, lethal, beastly, inhumane, and insidious communism is? Yes, we have a long way to go towards erasing inequality, bigotry, racism, unemployment, discrimination, and poverty in the United States. If those draft dodgers could just see the exponential level of cruelty, fanaticism, lies, murder, mutilation, starvation, half-truths, and torture that the VC and NVA are imposing on the Vietnamese peasants here—surely their hearts and minds would support our efforts to help the South Vietnamese to determine their own destiny.

How can so many young people believe they can enjoy the great and many privileges of being an American citizen without having to carry some of the load of the cost of our freedoms? Don't those young men know that the worst thing that we soldiers could feel is the feeling that the folks back home are betraying us and not supporting us? Oh well, those draft-dodging bastards back home don't deserve their US citizenship. I hope all of the spineless SOBs are deported. Don't they know that the most privileged communists have less of everything (money, shelter, education, medical care, religious freedom, political freedom, freedom of speech, freedom of choice, opportunity) than the poorest Americans?

I was re-reading our "Code of Conduct for Members of the US Armed Forces" tonight. I pray that we can live up to its high standard should we get (God forbid) captured. As you and I know so well it says:

- In Article I, "I am an American fighting man. I serve in the forces which guard my country and our way of life. I am prepared to give my life in their defense."

- In Article II, "I will never surrender of my own free will. If in command, I will never surrender my men while they still have the means to resist."

- In Article III, "If I am captured I will continue to resist by all means available. I will make every effort to escape and aid others to escape. I will accept neither parole nor special favors from the enemy."

- In Article IV, "If I become a prisoner of war, I will keep faith with my fellow prisoners. I will give no information or take part in any action which might be harmful to my comrades. If I am senior, I will take command. If not, I will obey the lawful orders of those appointed over me and will back them up in every way."

- In Article V, "When questioned, should I become a prisoner of war, I am bound to give only name, rank, service number, and date of birth. I will evade answering further questions to the utmost of my ability. I will make no oral or written statements disloyal to my country and its allies or harmful to their cause."

- In Article VI, "I will never forget that I am an American fighting man, responsible for my actions, and dedicated to the principles which made my country free. I will trust in my God and in the United States of America."

Of all the fears we face as soldiers, this fear of becoming a POW must be at the top of the list for most of us—it for sure is the one thing I want to avoid at all costs. I read recently that Ho Chi Minh means "He who enlightens" and that his real name is Nguyen Ai Quoc. I wonder who started calling him "Uncle Ho?"

The enemy here seems to be everywhere, but nowhere. The VC and NVA are much better at using camouflage than us and they seem to emerge, attack, and then vanish back into the jungle, mountains, and Cambodia and Laos. It is uncanny how the VC and NVA are able to hide their activity and then suddenly mass, attack, or ambush and then retreat and disperse before we can engage them and destroy them. We keep killing them and the north keeps sending more to replace the ones we have killed. One of my friends here is a history buff and he told me that the term "VC or Viet Cong" means Vietnamese Communist and was first used in 1958 by then South Vietnamese President

Ngo Dinh Diem. This country of South Vietnam is 80% Buddhist and is mostly being led by Catholics—doesn't that sound a little screwy to you? That is like electing General William T. Sherman to be the South Carolina governor in 1865.

You guys have it easy in the Delta flying at sea level and being able to haul 12 to 14 ARVNs around. I am lucky to be able to hover out of ground effect and haul five or six US troops in these mountains up north. The Army was smart to send their best pilots up north with me and to send amateur pilots like Larry, Danny, and you down south to get more practice before daring to send you to I or II Corps. Like you and Larry, I have already flown several exciting and in some cases "scary as hell" missions. One of those scary ones was this month near Dak To. It is that mission that made me review the Code of Conduct, as that night I had an opportunity to have become a POW or dead soldier and I thank God for bringing my crew and me home alive that dark night. I have attached the story of that mission. By the way, please tell Larry Dandridge that he cannot teach "something he knows nothing about—fishing that is!"

Best regards,

Sam

Dust Off Mountain Medical Evacuation
Under Heavy Enemy Fire at Night

"Every citizen (should) be a soldier. This was the case with the Greeks and the Romans and must be that of every free state."

–Thomas Jefferson, 1813

My call sign is Dust Off 22. I arrived in the republic of Vietnam in May and was, like most other Army Aviation new warrant officers at the ripe old age of 20, a newly appointed Warrant Officer 1. I was assigned to 2nd platoon, 498th Medical Evacuation (Medivac or more frequently called "Dust Off") Company, 44th Medical Brigade. The experienced aviators of that highly decorated unit took me under their wing as a "peter pilot" (as opposed to an aircraft commander) and taught me how to really fly a UH-1. That meant learning how to navigate single ship, communicate via radio with the myriad of activities and agencies the Medivac needed to talk to, ensure I was not flying through an active "gun-target line" (azimuth direction and altitude of artillery firing in my flight area), control a flight crew, and generally do all the things necessary to execute a "Dust Off" and survive.

The first days as a Medivac pilot in Vietnam I thought to myself, *Sure, I and every other Wobbly One had successfully completed flight school. But this was a whole nother game!* To complicate matters for me, I had a six-week layoff between flight school and arrival in RVN. If I knew how to do anything when they pinned my wings on at the completion of flight school, I thought surely I had forgotten it by the time I was signed in to the 498th.

When I found out that 99 percent of the Medivac missions were single ship, I became acutely aware that one of the most dangerous missions we would execute was a hoist rescue. Hoist rescues were required when there was no LZ available near the person needing evacuation. All other things being equal (weather, enemy fire, aircraft condition, patient condition, crew condition), it was easier and faster (hence safer) to land, get the patient, and bug out. Hovering above 100-to150-foot-tall trees while the crew chief or medic lowered the cable with jungle penetrator or litter on it was damn uncomfortable, sometimes terrifying, and always presented the aircraft as a large, fragile, and stationary target.

As any helicopter pilot can tell you, high hover in a single engine helicopter is way on the wrong side of the dead man's curve.[69] Toss in a little crosswind, darkness, some enemy fire, friendly fire, and bad weather, and things could get sketchy (damn dangerous) fast. I had survived for several months in Vietnam, was deemed competent, and eventually elevated to aircraft commander. In the 498th, the aircraft commander (AC) was in charge of his aircraft and crew wherever they were. Aircraft and their crews frequently operated detached from their platoon and company headquarters for weeks at a time.

I had learned a great deal about mountain flying and its many hazards. I knew, for instance, that dangerous turbulence frequently lies in wait in mountains for unsuspecting aircrews and is down-right dangerous. I knew that mountain turbulence is the kind that rips wings off of airplanes and smacks aircraft of all kinds, including helicopters, against the ground below.

I had also learned the clues to the existence of this bad turbulence, such as the existence of lenticular (lens-shaped) clouds or a forecasted strong wind blowing across a ridge, but I had also learned that mountain flying was as much "art" as science and that clouds don't always form to warn the pilot, and winds are unpredictable much of the time. Perhaps the most important thing I had learned was that I would have to go when my crew and I were called, whether it was night or day, good weather or bad, enemy fire or none, and that I would be called on time and time again to fly in conditions no civilian pilot would think of braving. Like my fellow Army bird men, I knew my job and I would do it!

This particular mission took place just west of Dak To, near the tri-border area of South Vietnam, Laos, and Cambodia. The countryside was absolutely beautiful. The mountains were lush and green, with an occasional waterfall spewing water over the side. These waterfalls were white in color and made a stark contrast to the dark green canopy as they fell hundreds of feet to rejoin the green. However, this was very much "Indian country," and I knew the enemy were always here and in large numbers.

My Dust Off 22 aircraft and crew were collocated with the 173rd Airborne Infantry Brigade, along with elements of the 4th Infantry Division. These two US combat units were waging pitched battle with four North Vietnamese Army (NVA) regiments of about 6,000 troops. Most of the action was to the west of Dak To, toward the tri-borders, and in severe mountainous terrain, mostly covered in triple canopy jungle.

My three fellow crewmen and I had been there nearly a week, successfully executing 8 to10 medivac missions. Most of the wounded we had been evacuating had gunshot or shrapnel wounds. Up until this mission, we had been fortunate in that we were able to use landing zones (LZs) that were blown or cut for insertions, evacuations, or resupply. None of these missions were especially hairy, although I had to hover-down into some LZs where the area was too small to allow any sort of angle of approach other than vertical. One LZ was so tight; the tie-down bracket on the end of the main rotor blade was actually slicing into trees as Dust Off 22 hovered down.

About midnight the field phone rang alerting me to an urgent mission. I hustled to operations while the pilot and crew got the aircraft ready. The patient was wounded and needed medical evacuation now. The severely wounded soldier's unit had broken contact but was unable to construct an LZ and unable to move to one. The wounded troop and his unit were about five miles west, on the eastern slope of a mountain. The mountains topped out about 4,500 feet around there, and I determined that it would be difficult, but we could hover to pull a hoist out.

While I had not pulled any hoist missions on this particular operation, I had been involved in about half a dozen of them since arriving in country. They had all been a little exciting, just because of the flying involved, but all had gone well. Well, maybe one patient would disagree with that thought, as he'd become stuck about 50 feet down. I had to use the aircraft to pull him free of the forest canopy and then fly a short way to an opening where I could land and bring both the patient and the cable into the aircraft.

I got airborne and began FM homing to the hoist site. It was cool and clear. My crew and I were amazed and somewhat alarmed by the number of fires burning below us. It looked like the stars of the sky were reflecting off the jungle canopy. One of the enlisted crew members said they were North Vietnamese Army cooking fires. I hoped not!

As we closed in on the hoist site, the ground unit said they had a secure perimeter, but it wasn't very big. The NVA were west of the friendlies. That was not ideal, as I had to hover nose in or parallel to the slope. Dust Off crews preferred to turn our aircrafts' tail to the most likely enemy fire, but in this case it needed to be left side to us. In other words, we would be parallel to the enemy and their fire power!

When I arrived in the area, I asked them to pop a smoke grenade. A short while later I identified white or yellow, something light colored—too hard to tell at night. I could not see any way this task was going to get easier, so I just shot my approach to the smoke. I, the AC, was flying. My pilot was handling the radios and watching torque and RPM. The peter pilot was a Medical Service Corps first lieutenant and had not been in country very long. He clearly recognized the many dangers associated with this night mission. This was the pilot's first field deployment and he was wide eyed and anxious like all new guys. The crew chief was clearing the tail out the left door, and the medic was clearing the tail out the right door. I had just about come to a hover in the smoke when I called for the searchlight to be turned on. I needed to see the treetops a little better to be able to hold a stable hover.

The search light came on and instantly the whole left side of the aircraft lit up from enemy ground fire. The area around the aircraft looked like a cross between a pinball machine and a disco dance floor as North Vietnamese Army bullets slammed into our aircraft. The enemy fire was very close and I heard a steady stream of "pop-pop-pop" and the loud "bam, bam, bam" of enemy rounds hitting our rotor blades, skids, tail boom, and my armored seat." I held my hover for about three more seconds. When the aircraft had taken more than 30 hits and my crew chief was shot and wounded, I decided our aircraft would be shot down and crew lost, if I did not peel out of there. I sucked up some collective (added power by increasing collective pitch) and started an evasive diving fall off the mountainside to the right.

The next few minutes were nerve-racking as my crew and I assessed damage while getting our helicopter and crew headed back to Dak To. I was surprised that my aircraft was still airborne and I expected to see oil pressures dropping, flight controls stiffening, smoke pouring out of the engine, and RPM plummeting. I could not see squat on the ground so a successful auto-rotation was out of the question, if our engine was to fail. There are no emergency parachutes in Army helicopters as it would be impossible to avoid being struck by the main rotor in an auto-rotation and most flight operations are too close to the ground for a chute to deploy.

The crew chief's wound was assessed and treated by the on-board Medic and it turned out the wound was not life-threatening, but his blood and pain added significantly to the crew's stress. The crew chief had returned fire during the brief time we were in

Picture 36: Warrant Officer 1 Sam DeLoach at Fire Support Base Oasis in the Central Highlands

Picture courtesy of Sam DeLoach.

The above picture was taken in II Corps, where Sam and his crew were supporting the 4th Infantry Division. Sam was within a month or two of becoming 20 years old. Warrant Officer 1 Sam DeLoach was a new aircraft commander and shortly after this picture was taken, he and his crew made a running takeoff down a dirt road with 22 US troops on board. It was a personal best for him and an unofficial record. He could not remember what the rush was, but he had to get all the sick and wounded off the Fire Support base (FSB) right then. His tent was next to the graves registration unit—a memory of sadness and stress.

contact. The aircraft held together, and we made it to Dak To. The wounded crew chief was taken to the aid station and was shortly after evacuated further to Plieku. My crew and I did a post-flight inspection of the aircraft by flashlight, finding a couple of dozen bullet holes along the left side, including some strike points on the bottom of my armored seat. Those bullets that struck my seat may have fragmented when passing through the helicopter's skid shoes and skids because they did not penetrate the seat. The crew also found some holes in the main rotor blades. My crew and I will never understand how - with all the hits we took - nothing vital to flight was damaged.

My team was a little shook up, and a man short in our crew, so the company replaced the crew and the aircraft the next day. My pilot was so unsettled by this mission that he stopped flying altogether and requested and was given a ground job after this mission. He volunteered for every ground job in the unit after that, doing a great job in each, thus freeing those who wanted to fly more hours. The four of the crew that replaced us were killed several days later when they hit a mountain on a night mission in the same area as the Dust Off 22 near-disaster. No one will ever know for sure, but the pilots who saw the debris path from the crash indicated the aircraft must have been going 80 to 90 knots at impact. Mountain flying is totally unforgiving of the smallest mistakes.

I do not know why we were spared that night. If the NVA shooters had waited five more seconds until we had settled into the treetops, they probably would have blasted Dust Off 22 to pieces. Or if they had used a Rifle Fired Grenade (RPG), they would certainly have destroyed Dust Off 22, my crew, and me. I also did not ever find out what happened to the patient we were trying to evacuate. I would like to believe that he was pulled out the next day by another aircraft.[70]

CHAPTER 8: DECEMBER 20, 1968 ◄
"Night Flying, Flares, and Wire Strikes."

Letter from WO1 Larry Dandridge
to WO1 Jerry Markland

Date: 20 December 1968

From: Warrant Officer W. Larry Dandridge,
121st Assault Helicopter Company (Airmobile Light), 13th CAB,
1st Aviation Brigade, APO SF 96296

TO: Warrant Officer Gerald David Markland
87TH AHC, 11TH AVN BN, 12TH AVN GRP, 1 AVN BDE
APO SF 01213

Dear Jerry,

Hooray! I was approved and certified as a slick aircraft commander this month and in less than three months after my arrival in Vietnam. I have really enjoyed being in charge of my own aircraft and crew and have been flying everyday for three weeks now.

121st Operations put me to work right away flying and training South Vietnamese Pilots and several new US Army warrant officers and lieutenants. I like teaching and hope I will like becoming an Instructor Pilot (IP) at Fort Rucker, AL or Fort Stewart, GA's Hunter Army Airfield after I return to the USA in September, 1969. I have less than nine months until my tour is over and time is passing quickly—but of course not quickly enough.

The South Vietnamese pilots I have been teaching to fly Hueys and conduct combat "ash and trash" missions and assaults here have been very nice guys, but their English is awful. And of course all I know to say in Vietnamese is

181

"Chow men yeo" (How are you?) and "Di Di Mau" (Get out of here) and "Chung Wee" (warrant officer)—so we have a hard time communicating sometimes. Two of the Vietnamese took me to dinner at their air base near Can Tau. I ate some kind of chicken dish that had the bones smashed and cut up into small pieces, all stirred together with the rice, meat, and vegetables. It was tasty, but the bones were a nuisance and scary, as they were splintered and I assume dangerous to eat without grinding them up well in your mouth first. All I could think about while eating the stuff was how my dad had warned me not to give our hunting dogs or pet dogs chicken bones because they could splinter and puncture the dogs' intestines!

Does your unit let the crews paint the nose cones of their aircraft? The 121st allows the naming of aircraft and painting symbols and pictures on our Huey nose cones (the battery compartment door). Our UH-1Ds' names of our slicks include "Double or Nothing," "Little Annie Fanny," "Passionate Rebel," "Captain Klutz," "Buzz Off," "Mad Tom," "Beer Bullet & Blood," "Harvy," "Peg of My Heart," "The Good Widow Mrs. Jones," "The In Crowd," "The Questionable Mad," "Tiger Lady," "Tin Bin," "We Buy US Bonds," "What Me Worry," "Blow Your Mind," "Soot Em Up Babe," "The Passionate Killer," and "Tiger Surprise," and others. And our UH-1B Gunshipss have names like "Birth Control," "Till Death Do Us Part," and "Cherry Buster."

Enclosed is a picture of WO1 and Aircraft Commander Joe Casanova's, Specialist 5 Crew Chief Mike Dewey's, and Specialist 4 Door Gunner Joe Romero's UH-1D slick "Double or Nothing"—an aircraft I have flown frequently as the peter pilot with Joe.

The other interesting thing I have been doing is some night flying and flying under, around, and almost through flares being dropped from other helicopters and fired by artillery. I do not like flying a flare Huey. Those damn MK-24 flares used in helicopter flare drops are so dangerous to handle in a helicopter. Our pal Danny Hickman wrote me recently and told me that there have been at least four

1st Aviation Brigade Hueys and the crews lost due to flare accidents in flight.

Danny said his CAV unit crews were issued parachutes for M-24 flare drop missions. The huge flares would sometimes ignite inside the aircraft and blind and burn the crew—resulting in catastrophic crashes. So they issued the parachutes, which turned out to be standard paratroop reserve chutes that fit in your lap and a harness so tightly binding as to make you want to sing soprano and very difficult to fly with.

Danny also said that like most things in Vietnam, there were no instructions for how to use the parachutes, so he and his crews had many discussions on how to jump from a perfectly flyable aircraft in a situation where the helicopter was on fire and untenable and outside visibility was zero. The CAV finally decided that the gunners would jump immediately, and then the pilots would jettison doors, though they always flew night missions without doors and that the AC would bail out his door right behind the gunners, leaving the peter pilot for last (man out).

Danny said the reason the peter pilot was last to bail out was he had the best instrument panel in order to keep the aircraft straight and level, could turn on the force trim with slight left stick, and then roll out the right door with the least amount of obstruction. The pilot would necessarily have to go over the collective or go back between the seats into the burning cargo compartment—both difficult on force trim with perhaps only three to four seconds of exit time once the stick was released to force trim only. So the co-pilot (peter pilot) was left holding the bag. Danny went on to say that his CAV unit's pilots accidentally popped all of their parachutes one-by-one until there were only three left. Danny said he volunteered to fly without one until his unit finally stopped using them altogether.

The two flare ship missions I went on were right before I made AC. We flew with the doors on, we had no parachutes, and I was the peter pilot. We were given a minimal safety briefing before we took off. The AC, crew chief, and gunner seemed to know what they were doing and luckily nothing happened that was exciting or risky except that about two out of every three flares we dropped did not ignite. As you probably well know an unlit flare and its parachute is awfully large and hazardous in this pitch black Vietnam sky. The flares we dropped were not hazardous to us, but any aircraft flying below us could fly into an unlit flare and that would be the end of that crew and aircraft.

I believe there are two fuse settings on the MK-24; one for the parachute ejection and another setting for the flare itself to ignite. They had to be set in sequence. Perhaps the flares that were not igniting were from an old or defective lot of flares, or maybe the flare crew was not setting the second trigger. I know the flares were very old. Danny Hickman told me that his unit had a MK-24 go off (stage one/parachute ejection) on the ground and it broke the crew chief's arm when the parachute blew out. But thankfully the second trigger was not set and it didn't ignite.

Danny said that his unit finally figured out that wearing a parachute inside a windswept helicopter with no doors could be as lethal as burning to death, should the chute accidentally pop open inside the aircraft the way it had on the ground. A crew member could only hope to be dragged out cleanly without hitting or hanging on the door gun. Fat chance of that and look out tail rotor! Danny and I agreed that we hate flare drop missions. Cold, dark, boring, and stressful.

As aircraft Commanders, both Danny and I (and every other Army pilot in Vietnam) can relate to flying slicks on combat assault missions, through the night sky with hidden parachutes suddenly appearing out of the darkness right in front of us, causing several narrow misses from MK-24s and from 155 artillery flares that had burned out too high. Nerve-racking!

By the way, I nearly busted my ass and my crews' asses by hitting a wire while flying low level out of the center of a village earlier this week. Attached is the story. Hope to hear from you soon.

Your friend,

Larry

Night Flying, Flares, and Wire Strike

"Everything depends on the Americans. If they want to make war for 20 years then we shall make war for 20 years.
If they want to make peace, we shall make peace and invite them to tea afterwards."

–North Vietnamese leader Ho Chi Minh
December 1966

I was flying an "ash and trash" mission in the plain of reeds and thinking about a recurring dream that had been bothering me for a month now. I dreamed there was a hierarchy of hell on earth that soldiers had to (or might) endure concerning military service in combat. The dream tormented me. The levels of hell on earth for a warrior would include:

Levels of Hell on Earth and in Hades for a Warrior and the Hierarchy of Evil Things that Could Happen Matrix

Level*	Description of Choices	Consequences
1. (worse than horrible)	Avoid the draft or not join when your country needs you and many of your friends are serving and need you.	Must live outside your country or face criminal prosecution. Despised by family, friends, and comrades. When you get older and wiser, plagued by the guilt of not serving and bringing great shame on your family. Turned on a rotisserie by the world's most infamous criminals (Adolf Hitler, Joseph Stalin, etc.).
2. (horrible)	Being a coward in combat when my buddies needed me and causing them to be killed or wounded.	Court-martialed and shamed for life or shot by a fellow soldier. Committed to hell upon death with no chance of parole. Scorned by all.

185

3. (terrible)	Being a Rear Echelon Mother Fu#@er (REMF) when the Army needed me as a combat trooper.	Scorned by the real warriors for my avoiding serving in a combat capacity—especially when I knew I could be a good combat soldier. Immediate acceptance in hell upon death.
4. (revolting)	Be severely wounded or injured in combat and come home blind, legless, and with brain damage.	Be a helpless invalid, ridiculed by war protesters, never to marry and have children, never to be able to support myself, becoming a terrible burden on my family.
5. (real bad)	Be severely wounded and captured by the VC or NVA.	Be tortured by the VC or NVA and later executed or dying of starvation and disease in a POW camp.
6. (nightmare)	Being captured by the VC or NVA.	Being tortured, starved, and kept in a POW camp for decades or executed as a war criminal.
7. (cowards' way out)	Committing suicide to escape all other choices.	Burning in hell's hottest fires on rotisseries turned by the VC.

*Level 1 being worst level of hell and 7 being the least painful.

The dream, or perhaps it's better described, as a nightmare was somewhat ridiculous, but it summarized my thoughts about serving in Vietnam and the bad things that could happen to me over here and after. I had already been injured seriously in a crash, wounded slightly from bullet fragments, and cut in dozens of places in my face from shards of plexiglas that exploded from a bullet shattering my windshield. I did join the Army voluntarily, but I was highly vulnerable to Level 4, 5, and 6 catastrophic events (or levels of hell). Luckily I never let such thoughts trouble me for very long, as I almost always had something important to concentrate on—like flying and staying alive. Even if I was somewhere that I could day dream, for example when they grounded me for crew rest for a day after flying too many hours, I would just do like Scarlett O'Hara in *Gone With The Wind* and tell myself, "I am not going to think about that (shit) today."

Today I was an aircraft commander flying a UH-D Huey, taking everything from people to pigs all over IV Corps and the areas along the Cambodian border of the Delta region. I was training a new peter pilot and the day had been uneventful as far as getting shot at or suffering any kind of in-flight emergency.

The pilot had made the landing to a village to deliver supplies to some unit there and we had landed to the south and into the wind fully loaded and dropped off the supplies. The troops on the ground told us to take off to the north or northwest to avoid overflying the heavy tree line immediately to the south and east of the village, where they had been receiving fire from on an off all morning. Since we needed to make a downwind takeoff, which was always a last resort decision, I took the controls, did a quick hover check and took off straight down the center street of this village of no more than five or six streets. As we passed through translational lift and got up to about 40 knots, I turned left down a side street, still flying below the tops of the small buildings in this village. I was preparing to make a cyclic climb as soon as the helicopter reached 80 knots, when a wire suddenly appeared directly in front of us. This was a huge surprise, as we did not think this place had any electrical power, certainly no phones. We hadn't seen any wires while landing.

My pilot saw the wire the same time I did, but there was no time to climb and the wire was too low to go under and no way to turn left or right due to buildings and trees, so we took the wire right below the chin bubble where it caught the skids and thank God immediately broke. We both had such a pucker factor that our buttocks could have bit a hole in the seat cover. I did everything but crap my pants. It happened so fast that we had no time to react. The wire was evidently a communications wire, for if it had been any larger, we could have been killed. Much of my confidence as an AC had dissolved for a few minutes, but I learned another lesson that day in Vietnam. That lesson was to look for wires going in, while you are on the ground, and coming out and to expect the Viet Cong, North

Vietnamese Army, South Vietnamese Army, and US Forces to put wires anywhere and everywhere.

As all Army helicopter pilots in Vietnam, I had to learn so many things so quickly to stay alive. Now I had wires and other things like poles, concertina wire, punji, antennas, and all sorts of other obstacles in my reservoir of dangers. Such things would come in again during a night mission.

A flight of five Hueys (one of them mine) on a combat assault carried a reactionary force to an Army of the Republic of South Vietnam Regional Force and Popular Force (RF/PF) Triangular Fort with several US Army advisors stationed there. The little fort, stationed not many miles from Soc Trang, was lightly armed with only a couple of heavy machine guns and a mortar pit manned by South Vietnamese poorly trained militia. It was being overrun. The US advisers were in a bad way, screaming for help over their radio.

Night flying in Vietnam, with no moon light, is the darkest kind of night flying there is—a total lack of light and almost no way to see the horizon, clouds, or any ground references. Safe visual flying depends on the pilot being able to see the horizon and ground references (like trees, buildings, mountains, towers, lights, etc.) to judge the attitude of the aircraft (nose low, nose high, banking right, banking left, etc.), how high the helicopter is off the ground, the speed at which you are flying, and the rate at which you are climbing or descending or turning. So flying this very dark night was a major task for both pilots. We worked together: one of us watched the instruments, the other flew and tried to keep us in formation without having a midair collision with the aircraft in front or behind us.

All of a sudden these millions of candle power of flares lit right over us and we instantly lost all of our night vision. It takes a good 30 minutes for a pilot's eyes to adjust to low light conditions and to fly from total darkness into the brightest light one could imagine was unnerving, shocking, and dangerous. To add to our blast of light glare and partial blindness, the flare showed us we were flying through a mine field of flares that did not ignite and that until now we did not see. A collision with one of these huge metal flares

PICTURE 37: 121ST SMOKE SHIP TURNED INTO NIGHT GUNSHIP AND RECONNAISSANCE HELICOPTER

Picture courtesy of Bill Schmidt.

Chief Warrant Officer Jim Preston was the aircraft commander of Viking Surprise when they changed the name to Tiger Surprise. Viking/Tiger Surprise became a legend in the Delta, first as a smoke ship laying smoke screens during combat assaults and later as a "night fighter" equipped with a cluster of landing lights, twin electric M60 machine guns (and later a minigun and 40mm cannon), and a 50 caliber heavy machine gun. Surprise had an XM-52 Integral Smoke Generator system installed that produced a dense cloud of smoke by injecting atomized fog oil into the hot gasses of the turbine engine. After "Viking Surprise" became a night fighter, the VC could no longer claim they alone owned the night—as "Surprise" would frequently and fatally surprise enemy troops, sampans (flat bottom boats), and their equipment in the open. Surprise and the other Viking gunships answered many calls for help at night, thus placing a higher price on the heads of these brave Viking air crews. Surprise was hit mid-air by a VC B-40 rocket in May of 1970 and destroyed, but another aircraft took its place. The stories of the night fighter and smoke-spewing Huey and its Tiger and Viking crews will live forever in all Vikings' and Tigers' hearts!

hanging under a rather large parachute would have destroyed our aircraft and killed everyone on board.

Then to add to the danger and just as our eyes had somewhat adjusted to the bright flare illumination, the flare would go out and without another flare to keep the landscape and sky lit. Now we were really in a mess with our pupils constricted for bright light and now trying to adjust and widen for the total darkness we were in. Now we were flying in and among unlit flares again. And again we could not see them. Now it was back to instruments and the 23rd Psalm, "The Lord is my Shepherd; I shall not be in want. He maketh me lie down in green pastures; He leadeth me besides still waters; He restoreth my soul; He leadeth me in the paths of rightness for his name sake; Yea though I walk (fly in this case) through the valley of the shadow of death, I will fear no evil, for thou are with me; your rod and staff, they comfort me. You prepare a table before me in the presence of my enemies. You anoint my head with oil; my cup runneth over. Surely goodness, mercy, and love will follow me all the days of my life, and I will dwell in the house of the Lord forever!"[71]

It took the powers to be too long to react with the rescue force and by the time we got there, the fort had been taken by the VC and our American comrades were nowhere to be found. We flew around the Fort for an hour, dodging flares, and returned to Soc Trang. The next morning, after only two hours of sleep, we were back out looking for the MACV advisers. We did not find them but our gunships did find some VC in the area and they extracted as much revenge on them as possible.

CHAPTER 9: JANUARY 11, 1969 ◄

"Sad Day—
187th Smokey is Shot Down and Two Killed!"

*Letter from the 187th Adjutant and Personnel Officer
to Warrant Officer WO1 Larry Dandridge*

Date: 11 January 1969

From: Captain Alvin A. Siegel, The Adjutant, 187TH AHC, 269th AVN BN, 12th AVN GROUP, 1 AVN BRIGADE, APO SF 01213

TO: Warrant Officer W. Larry Dandridge, 121st Assault Helicopter Company (Airmobile Light), 13th CAB, 1st Aviation Brigade, APO SF 96296

Dear Larry,

I regret to inform you that your friend and mine, Warrant Officer 1 Gerald (Jerry) David Markland, was killed in action (KIA) on 28 December 1968. It was a very sad day for the Crusaders of the 187th Assault Helicopter Company, 1st Aviation Brigade. Jerry and the Aircraft Commander Warrant Officer Roger Howell were flying "Smokey," our 187th UH-1C smoke ship, and they were shot down while on a run putting down a smoke screen so the command and control (C&C) aircraft could land in and take off from the hot LZ safely.

Two of the smoke ship's crew, SP4 Stephen C. Ponty Jr. and WO1 Gerald David Markland were killed and Aircraft Commander WO Roger Howell, Crusader "25" and Sp5 Marshall were wounded. Another Rat Pack ship was also shot down at the same time resulting in the pilot and aircraft commander receiving slight wounds. The shoot down took place in III Corps in Binh Duong Province. As you know Jerry was only 21 years old and from Albuquerque, New Mexico. One of your and Jerry's flight classmates and another dear friend of Jerry's is accompanying his remains home. His family has been notified. Jerry had mentioned you to me as one of his close friends. I regret to have to be the one to notify you of his death. Enclosed is your last unopened letter to Jerry.

I would hate to have to be the one who tells Jerry's mother that all the years of loving and raising Jerry were for nothing! The woefully inadequate $10,000 of Army life insurance will never replace Jerry's smile, touch, and voice, and his family and friends shall forever live with a black hole in their/our hearts. Memories are nice, but they do not go far towards replacing a son. It is like a part of us dies every time one of our dear comrades dies over here. Jerry was so intelligent, such a talented pilot, a fine officer, a natural leader, a terrific athlete, and such a great American. I will add Jerry to a list that is getting longer by the day of those who have fought by us and who died over here. I pray that God will forgive Jerry of his sins, make him "His" own personal pilot in heaven, and make him an angel first class.

1968 was a tough year for the US Army in Vietnam, with almost 16,000 troops killed here in the past 12 months. Headquarters says that one in every ten soldiers that have been sent to Vietnam have been either killed or wounded, or has become seriously ill. Again, I am very sorry to have to tell you about our tragic loss. May God, in our time of bereavement, comfort his family, you, and all of us who served with Jerry, and may all of us find some small comfort in the knowledge that Jerry died doing what all birdmen love most—flying.

I pray that you will have a safe tour here and get home soon. The attached story of this awful day was told by the Aircraft Commander Roger Howell, who was flying with Jerry on the 28th of December 1968.

Sincerely and respectfully,

Alvin A. Siegel

Adjutant, CPT US Army Aviation

Sad Day: 187th Assault Helicopter Company
Smokey is Shot Down and Two Killed[72]

"And He will raise you up on eagle's wings,
hear you on the breath of dawn,
make you shine like the sun,
and hold you in the palm of His hand."[73]

−From the First chorus of
***"On Eagles' Wings"** by Father Michael Jonas*

I, WO1 Roger Howell[xxii], arrived in Vietnam in early 1968, after graduating from flight school and a short leave (vacation). I loved flying and was happy to be assigned to the heralded Crusaders of 187th Assault Helicopter Company, in Ta Nien. The 187th was based in III Corps and assigned to the 269th Aviation Battalion, 12th Aviation Group, 1st Aviation Brigade. We supported the US Army and ARVN 25th Infantry Divisions and everyone else in the area. Like all new guys, I served my time in one of the 187th's slick platoons, flying troops, ammunition, and all kinds of other things in and out of landing zones (LZs) and pickup zones (PZs). Flying slicks taught me how to fly the UH-1 helicopter with great skill, but I always wanted to be a gun pilot.

I knew the gun pilots were hand selected from the best slick pilots. I also knew I would get to kill anyone who shot at me or the slicks and troops that I was covering, if I could find them. I was tired of flying low and slow into and out of LZs, and having no real way to shoot back at them. Luckily for me, I was soon picked to fly in the gun platoon, which also had a smoke gunship assigned to it.

A great and talented senior gunship pilot named Dave Searle provided most of my gunship training, and within six weeks I was appointed a wing gunship aircraft commander (AC). Within another month I was cleared as a fire team leader and smoke ship AC. All of us gun pilots liked flying "Smokey," because of the great autonomy we had with deciding who, what, when, where, and how we deployed that smoke ship. My gunship call sign was Rat Pack 37.

On the 28th of December 1968, I was assigned to fly the Rat Pack's "Smokey" with my pilot, Warrant Officer Jerry Markland. Our enlisted crew included Crew Chief Specialist 5 Marshall and Door Gunner Specialist 4 Stephen C. Ponty Jr. Jerry was a new guy in gunships. He was an outstanding pilot who had been selected very early on to fly gunships. Markland had already proven to be one of the best pilots in the gun platoon.

Just three days after Christmas, our 187th Assault Helicopter Company was supporting the US Army's 25th Infantry Division, conducting an air assault at a nearby Michelin Rubber Tree Plantation. We were operating northwest of Ta Nien in an area thick with North Vietnamese troops and tunnels. The tunnels played a major role in the North Vietnamese winning the war against the South Vietnamese. Frustrating both our aviation efforts and the US troops' ground efforts to assault a heavy jungle and bunkered tree line was the fact that headquarters would not allow much-needed tactical air and artillery fire on and near the plantation. The ground troops were pinned down, unable to advance, and taking casualties.

This particular day, my pilot was training to shortly become an aircraft commander (AC), so he was flying in the left seat, which is normally where I, the AC would sit. I was flying in the pilot's seat, the right-hand seat, and training Jerry for his upcoming role as a smoke ship AC. We made our initial smoke run covering the first insertion of troops and received what I would call moderate small arms ground fire but took no hits.

The ground commander in the C&C ship over head was frustrated with the progress his troops were making on the ground and asked the C&C aircraft to take him into the LZ so he could personally take over the fight on the ground. The C&C ship requested smoke on the enemy tree line and directly in front of the tree line to cover his approach and landing in the LZ. One of the first rules in combat flying is never fly the same path twice in a hot area, if at all possible.

I brought the aircraft down to nap of the earth, just clearing brush and trees and averaging about ten feet above ground level. We were flying "balls to the walls," pulling max power and leaning into 120 knots. Jerry was dispensing the smoke, and I was flying. The wood line was on our left side, Jerry's side, and our crew chief was firing his M60 trying to suppress the now-heavy enemy fire coming from the tree line. We were in a hornet's nest!

Enemy rounds began slamming into our aircraft and coming through the door gunner and pilot compartments. A dozen or so rounds tore through the floor and one round struck our door gunner and crew chief Specialist 5 Marshall in the leg. A second later, several rounds struck the mixing lever controls between the pilots' seats and severed the flight control linkage! Jerry and I looked at each other in horror and realized our world was about to come to an end. We were helpless as the aircraft did not respond to any cyclic control movements. We were now a low-level, unguided missile bearing down on the rubber trees directly in front of us. Jerry was then shot through the head by enemy fire.

The aircraft's advancing main rotor blade struck a tree with such force it ripped the transmission and main rotor system out and off of the aircraft and flipped the aircraft upside down. The aircraft impacted the ground like a runaway freight train and slid upside down for about 100 yards, bursting into flames as it slid to a stop. I was critically injured and unconscious, and Jerry and our Door Gunner, Specialist 4 Stephen C. Ponty Jr. were killed by their gunshot wounds and crash injuries.

Both Jerry and I were hanging upside down in the destroyed aircraft cockpit. Ground troops rushed to our aide and two other aircraft landed to assist. They pulled us out before the aircraft's blazing fire could consume us. My jaw was broken in two places, every bone in my face was fractured, and I had a serious and life-threatening Traumatic Brain Injury (TBI). To add to my misery, my right upper arm bone (humerus) was shattered and my back was broken.

We pilots of the Rat Pack wore our chicken plates under our flak jackets, but not in the cloth vest that was issued to some of us. It had not occurred to us that this heavy ceramic plate would become a deadly airborne missile in a crash. Army Aviation safety still had a ways to go back in 1968. I was rushed onto a slick and whooshed to a major field hospital at the US Base at Cu Chi (pronounced Coo Chee). When I woke at the hospital several days later, I found my battalion commander there standing over me, wanting to award me with a Purple Heart. I was only interested in finding out how my men were, and I was devastated to hear that Jerry and Stephen were dead. God had two more rotary wing qualified angels to help "Him" and his assistants get around heaven.

I spent two months in hospitals in Vietnam and Japan. I was in the orthopedic ward (also the amputee ward) in the 249th General Hospital at Camp Zama, Japan. Like the author of this book's experience there, it was an awfully sad place to be. The buildings and other facilities, doctors, medics, nurses, and care were terrific, but to have to see so many gravely and in some cases terminally wounded soldiers and marines there was a truly "significant emotional event" that has added to my grief and post traumatic stress disorder (PTSD).

Across from me in my ward at camp Zama was a poor young soldier who had lost his body and legs from the hips down. He was at that time one of the only troops to ever survive for a few days such a horrific wound. He died the day after my arrival. At Camp Zama I had to suffer with wired jaws, a body cast, and from a pinned elbow under traction. The traction was so great; it kept pulling me out of my bed.

After two months in Japan, I was sent to Fort Belvoir still in a body cast and with jaws wired. I spent two more months at Fort Belvoir on convalescent leave. After I recovered mostly from my physical injuries, I was given orders to go to Hunter Army Airfield, GA, to become a flight instructor, but my dad, who was an FBI Agent, was able to get my orders changed to Fort Eustis, VA to be closer to my family. I did get back on flight status for the rest of my two years in the Army, but mainly flew OH-13 observation helicopters and never got back into my beloved Huey again. I should have stayed in the Army or at least asked for a medical discharge, but young guys don't want to think that far ahead. I was honorably discharged from the Army on October 8, 1970. The VA initially gave me 30 percent disability for my wounds and injuries, but as I got older and my injuries and Post Traumatic Stress Disorder (PTSD) worsened and bothered me more and more, I eventually became 100 percent disabled.

I became a commercial helicopter pilot and certified flight instructor for a short while after leaving the Army, but the pay was so bad I soon abandoned all attempts to make a living flying. The commercial aviation market was flooded with tens of thousands of Vietnam and Korean War military aviators and it was a terrible time to try and get a job as a commercial pilot.

I did want to join the Army National Guard and fly helicopters for them, but I could not make time for that with my demanding heating and air-conditioning business, which I'd started soon after I married and became a dad to two terrific children. I trained myself to block out mental and physical pain, but as I got older, I had to get help from the Veterans Administration for my PTSD. I relive the 28th of December 1968 everyday in my thoughts and every night in my dreams. I retired from my business in 2010, and my wife and I have moved to Orlando, FL.

I shall never forget my brothers in Vietnam and I pray for them every-day. I pray daily for Jerry Markland and Stephen Ponty, Jr., who gave their last full measure to my comrades, their country, and me. I offer this prayer and devotional song[74] written by Father Michael Joncas in 1979 to my dead friends:

You who dwell in the shelter of the Lord, Who abide in His shadow for life,

Say to the Lord, "My Refuge, My Rock in Whom I trust.

CHORUS:
And He will raise you up on eagle's wings,
Bear you on the breath of dawn,
Make you shine like the sun,

And hold you in the palm of His Hand.
The snare of the fowler will never capture you,
And famine will bring you no fear;Under His Wings your refuge,
His faithfulness your shield.

CHORUS

You need not fear the terror of the night,
Nor the arrow that flies by day,
Though thousands fall about you,
Near you it shall not come.

CHORUS

For to His angels He's given a command,
To guard you in all of your ways,
Upon their hands they will bear you up,
Lest you dash your foot against a stone.

CHORUS

And hold you in the palm of His Hand.

Picture 39: 121st AHC Blue Tiger CW2 Mike Shakocius (Shaky) Outside Soc Trang Command Bunker

Picture courtesy of Mike Shakocius.

1. Steel pot with camouflage cover.

2. 1st Aviation Brigade Patch.

3. 121st pilots were initially issued the M1911 45caliber pistol, holster, and magazine pouches. Everything fit as it should. Later pilots were issued the 38 cal revolver, but without a holster or ammo pouches. Shoving the 38 into the 45 holster did not work at all so Mike had a local shop in Soc Trang make him a special holster with slots for extra 38cal rounds. It worked nicely, but he took some criticism from the RLOs for not using standard Army-issue equipment. The bandoleers over his shoulder held extra 7.62mm rounds that served him well when shot down in Tieu Can near seven mountains.

CHAPTER 10: JANUARY 30, 1969 ◄
"Attempted Surprise Capture of VC and NVA Generals."

Letter from Warrant Officer Larry Dandridge
to WO1 Sam DeLoach

Date: 30 January 1969

From: Warrant Officer W. Larry Dandridge, 121st Assault Helicopter Company (Airmobile Light), 13th CAB, 1st Aviation Brigade, APO SF 96296

TO: Warrant Officer Sam DeLoach, 498th Medical Evacuation Company (AA), APO SF 01214

Dear Sam,

Hey pal. Hope you Dust Off pilots are enjoying good weather and safe flying in the north. I am glad I am in III and IV Corps where there does not seem to be as many North Vietnamese Army (NVA) units as you guys face in I Corps and II Corps. We mainly encounter Viet Cong units, but more and more we are seeing NVA units and advisers in the Delta.

I am very sorry to tell you that our dear friend WO1 Jerry Markland was killed on 28 March 1968 flying a smoke ship. He was a great pilot and friend and his death has left me with a feeling of emptiness, rage, and grief. Like the black nights here, his death is a black hole in my heart. I really never imagined that such a smart, athletic, and talented guy like Jerry could be killed. He and I tried to eat all the steaks and drink all the beer in San Francisco on the way over here. I am glad we did, as Jerry will be having no more steaks or beer. I still cannot believe he is gone.

199

Of all the dangers we face over here, it seems to me that the idiots in Washington, DC, are by far our worst and most serious enemy. The thought of dying, or worse, becoming a Prisoner of War (POW) or paraplegic or brain-dead vegetable run through my subconscious thought too frequently these days. I am still flying slicks and have been an aircraft commander (AC) for about three weeks now. However, since the death of Jerry, I want to fly gunships. I have not received much mail from the states other than from my wife, dad, mom, sister Barbara, and my aunt Nita. I guess the rest of the family has no idea how tough things can be over here and how much the mail means to us—especially for those poor infantry guys. Jerry Markland and I had written each other every month up until his death and I shall miss his correspondence, good wishes, and humor.

I had to fly 12 hours on Christmas day with an Air America[75] Huey. We were flying some Special Forces guys who were intercepting sampans that were bringing weapons, ammunition, supplies, and reinforcements into Vietnam via Cambodia. I was a little nervous with "the Truce" being in effect and all that. I did not think we would be doing a lot of combat stuff on December 25, 1968, but as frequently is the case I was wrong! I guess there is nothing wrong with us catching them violating the truce and killing some of them while they are doing the violating.

I do have some good news: On December 31, 1968; my unit and I were privileged to fly on a mission that supported the rescue of Major James N. Rowe in the U-Minh Forest. I got the hell scared out of me thanks to a machine gun that almost shot us down on our short final approach into a very hot landing zone while we inserted Vietnamese troops and their US advisors. I personally had nothing to do with saving Major Rowe.

However, my company and I helped to insert the troops that were applying great pressure on the VC prison guards and other Viet Cong forces in the area. More significantly, the B52 Arc light strike (saturation bombing) just prior to our heli-borne operations had made all the VC "shit their pants and panic" just a few minutes before our air assaults and our hunter-killer teams (two OH-6 Light Observation Helicopters low and one Cobra high) swarmed the area. One of my good friends and fellow 121st Assault Helicopter Company Warrant Officer pilots, WO1 Bob Croghan and one of our Door Gunners/Crew Chiefs Ken Roies had the honor of flying Major Rowe back to Can Tho.

Major Rowe was captured in the fall of 1963, when he was an Army Special Forces first lieutenant. I had been on several other attempts to find and rescue him and other US Prisoners of War (POWs) in October, November, and December, 1968. B Troop, 7th Armored Regiment, 1st Air Cavalry "Dutch Masters" is the unit that saw Major Rowe and saved him. Until the rescue helicopter got really close to him, Major Rowe was thought to be a VC.

It was a miracle that the Cobras or LOHs (OH-6s) that spotted him did not accidentally kill him. All helicopters in the area were taking heavy fire from the trapped and frantic VC, and the attack helicopters and heavily armed LOHs were having a field day killing dozens of VC in the area. Major Rowe was in black pajamas like the VC. He had lost so much weight, he looked much smaller and lighter than his once tall and ample frame. The only reason he was not killed by the helicopter hunter-killer teams that first spotted him was that the flight commander of the group of Dutch Masters wanted to capture the Viet Cong who was standing and waving his white mosquito net in the open area in the reeds below.[36]

First Lieutenant, now Major James Rowe, was being led by a small band of VC guards to his execution when a US B-52 strike on the U-Minh forest forced them into an attempt to flee. Major Rowe killed the guard leading him through the heavy reeds and foliage. That is when an Army multi-unit, multi-assault, multi-reconnaissance, and multi-hunter-killer helicopter task force found Major Rowe waving his white mosquito net. Rowe was never broken, and he is now exposing firsthand the communist blue print of tyranny, execution, torture, brainwashing, intimidation, and destruction of religion, freedom of choice, and peace in South Vietnam, Cambodia, and Laos.

We had a Korean Band at our little O-Club for "New Years Eve," and Bubba Segrest and I had great fun over drinking, singing along with them, and trying to copy their strong and funny dialect. They were singing "Hang on Sloopy," the 1964 song recorded by The Vibrations and originally titled "My Girl Sloopy." They could not pronounce "Sloopy" or "on" or "hang" so when they sang they were saying "HUNG WON SUEFEE—SUEFEE HUNG WON!"—and Bubba and I were singing with them in the same hilarious dialect! It was so funny I could hardly catch my breath, and we being half drunk added to the humor. I haven't laughed that much in Vietnam before or since.

I finally got to use the Military Auxiliary Radio System (MARS)[77] station here about two weeks ago, but the phone call was only about two minutes long and it was so ridiculous saying, "Hello, I miss you guys. OVER. How is our dog Maggie? OVER. I love you. OVER." No privacy and so awkward that I was stressed before, during, and after the call, but it was better than not being able to call that one time during my tour in Vietnam.

I spent a few nights so far on the ground in remote parts of IV Corps, away from our home base at Soc Trang, and I hated each night out there alone except for a couple of other flight crews. Bugs, heat, sand, mud, endless crushing humidity, snakes, and the fear of the enemy make for light sleeping and sore backs. Some of those nights were on mountains with "no notice sleep overs with no infantry protection" and without a poncho, blanket, sleeping bag, or jacket, and it was cold at night to add to the discomfort. This war without fronts is enough to drive a guy to drink.

I had another very close call with death yesterday and shed a little blood for Uncle Sam for the second time, and do not intend to "volunteer" for anymore missions anytime soon. It was a traumatic and emotional event for my crew and me. We were supposed to take three slicks full of Army of the Republic of Vietnam Rangers and their one US Advisor, with six gunships covering us, into a VC stronghold, and capture some VC and perhaps NVA Generals. It did not work out as well as we hoped.

Attached is the story.

Best regards,

Larry

Attempted Surprise Capture of VC and NVA Generals

"Leadership looks you in the eye, kicks you in the ass, covers your flank, and takes your place on the most dangerous mission."

– Homeland Defense Journal December 2007
by W.L. Dandridge

My 121st Assault Helicopter Company's Tiger "Slick" Platoon Leader had just asked for volunteers to go on a high-priority, three-helicopter, short notice, combat assault, and high risk mission. We would be taking three Tiger UH-1D Model Huey (slick) helicopters, with six UH-1C Model gunships from another unit to try to capture a North Vietnamese Army (NVA) general and several Viet Cong (VC) high ranking officers, who planned to meet deep in the rain forest and delta region of South Vietnam— deep in some of the worst "Indian country" in IV Corps. This is some of the area where Major James Rowe and other US Prisoners of War (POWs) were so easily hidden from tens of thousands of Army of the Republic of South Vietnam troops and thousands of US troops.

As a new slick aircraft commander (AC), I had a temporary call sign of Tiger 191 (the last three of the aircraft tail number). I couldn't wait to show off my new flying skills and knowledge so I volunteered— something I would later regret. After only 31/2 months in Vietnam, I had learned to hate the Viet Cong and the North Vietnamese Army (NVA) and all they stood for. I had adopted what appeared to be a country-wide US military attitude and code that "A dead Vietnamese was a dead Viet Cong, and the only good VC was a dead VC." I was also more comfortable volunteering because one of the best senior aircraft commanders in the 121st and one of the excellent combat pilots in the unit, Warrant Officer Joe Casanova, call sign for this mission of Tiger Lead,[78] had also volunteered.

A picture of Joe is on the following page You can see he is lucky to have been issued one of the new two-piece jacket and trouser Nomex fire proof flight uniforms that doesn't burn but instead just turns to beads of material after prolonged exposure to high temperatures. Nomex survives long after the occupant is barbecued and disintegrated. In the picture, Joe is wearing his 45 caliber automatic pistol in a shoulder holster, and he has his SECRET Signal Operating Instruction (SOI)[79] in his left breast pocket with the safety lanyard hanging down.

The mission sounded exciting and, according to intelligence, it had a high probability of success. Besides the slick pilots and their crews had been sitting around for more than two hours at a stinking and filthy forward rearming and refueling point, on standby, with nothing to do. We pilots and crews were hot, sweating, dirty, bored, and tired of the sticky, foul-smelling, and slippery mud we were parked in, and a chance to fly and cool off was inviting.

The pilots, door gunners, and crew chiefs who volunteered for this mission suspected from the start that it could be a bad one. Much of the time "intelligence was not accurate" and our combat assaults went unrewarded with an elusive enemy that moved frequently. The VC did not pick any fights that were not heavily in their favor. The enemy was a master at ambushing and then quickly escaping the area before the full force of the US combined arms team could be brought to bear on them.

The young US Army adviser, to the Vietnamese Rangers, briefed the three UH-1D helicopter aircraft commanders and the fire team leader of the six gunships and their pilots. The flight of three slicks and six guns would fly in, nap-of-the-earth (as close to tree top and other terrain features as safely possible), from about 30 miles out. They would be vectored into their small landing zone by a command and control aircraft and the overall mission commander, an Army aviator captain.

The command and control (C and C) aircraft would be at 3,000 feet high above the target area. The three slicks would carry 31 troops, including the US Army adviser and the 30 Army of Vietnam Rangers. The US Army ground adviser showed us a tactical map of the area that we would be assaulting. It was basically an island, in heavy jungle and a small area of tall elephant grass, with one

PICTURE 48: WO1 JOE CASANOVA "AN EXTRAORDINARY FINE AVIATOR, OFFICER, SOLDIER, LEADER, AND GENTLEMAN!"

Picture courtesy of Larry Dandridge.

1. Warrant Officer Insignia. Joe is wearing Army's new two piece NOMEX fire resistant flight suit and standing by his slick "Double or Nothing."
2. Paper SECRET Signal Operating Instructions (SOI) lanyard. SOI is inside his left shirt pocket.
3. 45 Caliber pistol.

small open area hopefully large enough for three Hueys to land. The adviser told us that intelligence estimated there would be a platoon-size force protecting the enemy senior officers that we planned to capture or kill. We would have very little room for three aircraft and would be in danger of striking stumps, small trees, booby-traps, and elephant grass with our tail rotors in the LZ.

The 31 troops we would be carrying included a Vietnamese Ranger who also was the radio operator and bi-lingual interpreter. With the usual warning to not shoot down their own gunship cover, the slick door gunners were cleared to engage the enemy as soon as they were in range and targets were identified, but they must cease fire whenever a gunship, the C&C, or another slick came into the door gunner's gun target line. This meant that the slick door gunners would not have much opportunity to fire in the LZ, as the six gunships would be circling low level and nap-of-the-earth, very close to us, in a tight circle, and firing constantly. The gunships would begin suppressive fire with their folding fin 2.75-inch aerial rockets, 7.62mm minigun, 7.62mm door gun, and 40mm cannon fire as soon as they reached the LZ, which would only be seconds before we landed.

The UH-1B model gunships in the 121st Assault Helicopter Company Viking gun platoon's 7.62mm minigun basic load (the electric minigun ammo carried on board the aircraft) was about 7,600 rounds, with 3,600 rounds in the ammo trays and about 200 rounds in the chutes for each gun. The miniguns fired 2,000 rounds per minute each, unless the gun hit the inboard stop and then the opposite gun picked up to 4,000 rounds a minute.

The gunships also had two highly qualified door gunners on each helicopter. Door gunners brought to the pilots great comfort because the door gunners provided effective suppressive fire in an almost 360-degree area around the gunship and were the only weapon system on board able to bring rounds on target when the gunship turned away from the target. Many Cobra attack helicopter pilots missed being able to see under and behind them. Cobro pilots also missed being able to easily hear enemy fire because unlike the gunships, the Cobra cockpits were enclosed and suppressed the sound of ground fire. But what Cobra pilots missed the most was the great comfort of door gunners suppressing enemy fire when they were breaking away from the target.

In addition to the minigun capability, each of the gunships carried 14 rockets, seven on each side of the aircraft in a seven-shot rocket pod. Two of the gunships covering on this day also had a belt-fed 40mm grenade launcher mounted in a turret on the nose of the aircraft. To top off the fire power of the UH-1C gunships, the crew chiefs and door gunners were all master gunners with the M60 machine gun they carried. Our 121st Viking door gunners never used a bungee cord. Each door gunner had 2,200 rounds of 7.62mm ammunition on board and in 11 boxes of 200 rounds each. The Viking gunships used only 2,000 rounds of door gun ammunition maximum on any mission and saved the last 200 rounds in case the aircraft went down on the way home.

The typical M60 fired 550 rounds per minute with a hydraulic buffer. The M60s used on the XM-16 system flex guns, with two M60s on each side of the aircraft, used a mechanical buffer and boasted the rate of fire of up to 750 rounds a minute. Viking crew chiefs and gunners, being smart about these matters, put the mechanical buffers in their door guns. This was really impressive when they used solid tracers on night fire fly missions. The problem was that after a few hundred rounds of tracer firing, the M60 barrels "carboned up"; that is, the residue built up in the barrel rapidly and almost made them useless. The gunship door gunners and crew chiefs spent hundreds of hours cleaning their guns.

The young US Army adviser, who was also the mission ground commander, was the picture of an American warrior: healthy, well-muscled, tanned to deep brown, and bright blue eyes. He was, thoroughly skilled in his trade and brimming with confidence and enthusiasm. He also was wearing a large, handsome gold ring with a huge blue sapphire on his left hand and brown leather, hush puppy type brown boots.

The ranger's US adviser told us Tigers and our gunship pilots that he had "high confidence intelligence." He told us that the odds were in our favor that we would surprise and capture or kill several very high ranking North Vietnamese and Viet Cong Officers on this mission. The adviser's best friend, an older Army Special Forces sergeant first class (SFC), probably 29 or 30 years old, also listened to the briefing. He would not go on the flight, but would be waiting for his friend and brother warrior to return safely with the prizes.

The air crews could tell the Rangers' adviser and the sergeant first class had formed a close bond comprised of trust, deep respect, codependency, and comradeship during the many months they had depended on each other to stay alive in a deadly part of Vietnam. This kind of selfless love bond, created by the suffering and trauma of war, is unknown to other professions, except perhaps in a smaller way by police officers and firemen. The tactical map used to brief the pilots showed an island in the middle of what we troops called "Indian country," or areas controlled by the North Vietnamese Army and Viet Cong. The French had lost large numbers of troops in this area a decade earlier. There were rumors that they'd lost an entire airborne battalion not far from where this impromptu attack force was going.

The three Tiger slicks (Tiger Lead, Tiger 24, and Tiger 191[80]) would be landing in V formation to the southwest, with the objective—the heavily camouflaged huts and bunkers used as the meeting area by the enemy—to our left and south upon landing. I was flying on the left of the lead aircraft in *V* formation, in the "chalk 3" position, with only one to two rotor blades of distance separating each aircraft. The other Tiger aircraft commander was in the "chalk 2" position on the lead's right side.

The little Assault Force of 31 troops surprise should be overwhelming to the enemy protecting force and the North Vietnamese Army and Viet Cong Generals they were guarding. The battle was expected to be short and violent, and to result in a great victory and prize for our US and South Vietnamese mini Task Force. For some crazy reason, I was trying to remember what I would say if captured: name, rank, and serial number (Wayne Larry Dandridge, warrant officer, W3161984). But that was silly because the Viet Cong and NVA usually executed helicopter pilots that they captured. I would have much more to worry about if we were shot down this day.

The pilots briefed the door gunners and crew chiefs on each of the Tiger slicks. Within 15 minutes the Tigers lifted off in "V" formation and started flying into the unknown, at 90 knots, with their six gunships on both sides and Joe Casanova leading the assault formation. The C&C ship kept giving the Assault Force small heading corrections to turn left 210, turn right 215, turn left 212, and telling them how far the aircraft were out from the LZ. The closer the flight got to the Landing Zone, the tighter the pucker factor, or in other words, the amount of compression in pounds per square inch between the buttocks of the crew members became. All of the crews had been in tight spots before, and all knew the unknown was always one of the hardest parts of each combat mission.

I felt good and very grateful that the veteran Tiger aircraft commander Joe Casanova and his famously brave Crew Chief Mike Dewey and courageous Door Gunner John Romero were on this mission, as they had saved wounded Lt. Tom Jameson, wounded Warrant Officer Michael Sherman, and their crew when they were shot down in the U-Minh Forest a few months earlier under intense enemy fire. I respected and admired Joe for his coolness under fire and his outstanding flying skills. Joe and his enlisted crew were truly brave and extraordinary fighting men and the best examples of all that is good about our country and our soldiers.

The slick crews were painfully aware that the UH-1 was a fragile bird. The pilots were the only crew members with armored seats and a ceramic bullet resistant chest (chicken) plate. We were also aware that sheet metal a few thousandths of an inch thick and fragile Plexiglas windows that produced hundreds of dangerous shards were all that was between us and the enemy's guns. Door gunners and crew chiefs had a ceramic chicken plate, but no armor seats and the vests that held the chicken plates were in short supply. Some crew members simply slide the chicken plate between the two shoulder straps with the bottom of the chicken plate resting on the lap belt, which proved to be potentially dangerous and even lethal in a crash.

As was the case of Specialist 4 John Romero, Warrant Officer Joe Casanova's gunner, many door gunners in Army helicopter units, especially in gunship units, in Vietnam were battle hardened infantryman, with a Military Occupational Specialty (MOS) 11B – Infantry. These gunship door gunners and slick door gunners were frequently on extended tours of duty in Vietnam and volunteered to serve in aviation units as door gunners after having served from six months to a year in the infantry. These *seasoned in blood* foot soldiers were not only of great benefit to the aircraft while flying, but in case of an emergency landing or shoot down, these brave soldiers and skilled fighters could organize a credible, hasty defense of the landing site and make maximum use of their door guns on the ground. The door gunners and crew chiefs are some of the unsung heroes of the Vietnam helicopter war. I always knew I could count on these *"flying Infantryman"* to take charge of our ground defense tactics if we were shot down.

As the assault force closed in on its LZ, all weapons were made ready and placed in the hot mode with safeties off, ready to fire.

I instructed my Tiger 191 slick crew to get ready, keep their eyes open, put their visors down to prevent Plexiglas and fragments from injuring their eyes, and call out enemy fire and movement. I also instructed my pilot, a green first lieutenant, to get on the controls with me, to call out rotor and engine RPM every few seconds, and to be prepared to take over should I be shot or otherwise injured during the landing. The pilot called out the prelanding check: "RPM 6,600, fuel quantity 1,260 pounds, engine and transmission instruments are in the green, bleed air is off, pilot and copilot armor plates in forward position, troops in the back are ready to disembark upon landing, and door guns are hot."

It crossed my mind how strange and unfair it was that during the Vietnam War era commissioned officers (lieutenants, captains, majors, lieutenant colonels, and colonels) were paid so much more flight pay, basic pay, and other pays for doing the same thing warrant officers were doing flying helicopters in Vietnam. Warrant officers frequently were acting as aircraft commanders, slick flight leaders, fire team leaders, pink team leaders, and wing ship commanders with higher ranking officers (normally captains and lieutenants) flying as their copilot. Warrant officers were inexpensive pilots compared to their commissioned counter parts and a bargain for the taxpayers. I then refocused totally on flying and the upcoming and most likely hot LZ that I would be landing at in less than two minutes.

The slick pilots were flying the D model Huey, but we would have been better off with the newer H Model with a more powerful Lycoming L13 engine, which was sorely needed in the high density altitude caused by hot, moist, and thin air coupled with higher altitudes, and heavy combat load conditions of Vietnam. The H Model engine allowed pilots to hover out of ground effect under much heavier loads and at higher altitudes, except when flying fully loaded and fully fueled in the mountains of Vietnam. But this was no time to worry about that, today we would make do with our older D Models.

I knew what it was like to be shot at and shot down, as Warrant Officer Harry Skelly and I had been shot down and suffered minor wounds recently. It happened in Ben-Tri province, only a month before, while trying to resupply troops in heavy contact, and in triple-canopy, flooded jungle. We had been flying an underpowered D Model slick that day.

My crew and all of the pilots and crews on this mission were already very aware of the thing that Harry Reasoner, would say later in the war during his February 16, 1971, commentary: "... *helicopters are different from airplanes in that helicopter crews know that if something bad has not happened, it is about to!*"

The command and control officer said that we were on course and one-half mile from touchdown, and that we should prepare to decelerate rapidly and disembark troops. The C&C ship also instructed our door gunners to refrain from firing unless they had a clear and close target, as the gunships covering us would be flying low level, just inches above the trees. He did not want a gunship to be hit by friendly fire. "You are now one quarter mile from touchdown," called out the command and control ship.

The mission commander then said, "You are approaching the LZ. We have troops running in the area. Begin decelerating, but remain as close as possible to the tree tops to avoid early detection and ground fire. You are now 200 yards from touchdown; gunships begin firing and landing zone preparation."

As the landing zone came rapidly into sight, I along with the other two aircraft in "V" formation performed a rapid deceleration with the aircraft nose high, collective pitch control down, and rotor RPM climbing into the red area (too high) on the rotor tachometer. Immediately the LZ was alive with enemy fire from the south, which was our left (9 o'clock) side. The left-side door gunner, who was also our crew chief yelled into his mouth microphone, "Taking fire 8, 9, and 10 o'clock!" Most of the LZ was full of elephant grass about five feet tall and the landing zone was "too small for all three aircraft to land in formation!" I would have to land about 40 meters away from the other two helicopters, with a small tree line separating us, or risk having a midair collision with flight lead. Tiger Lead and his aircraft on his right (Chock 2) had a clearer and larger area to land in, and they had shot their approach to the ground due to their heavy loads. I would have to land further to the southeast and partially out of sight of the other two aircraft or crash in trees to the left of the other two aircraft!

I quickly maneuvered my Huey, now out of transitional lift, losing RPM, and straining under such a heavy load, into a small opening in the LZ area away from the other two slicks. My initial planned landing area was too filled with trees to land safely. I was bringing the aircraft to a low hover in very high elephant grass, when disaster struck my aircraft and the troops on board. The brave adviser was standing behind my left side seat, barking orders, and just jumping out of the aircraft, when an AK47 round hit him square in the face and blew the top and back of his head and soft cap off. The luckless adviser died instantly and his brains, skull fragments, and hair went all over the aircraft. The unfortunate Adviser's lifeless body tumbled out of the aircraft. It happened so fast that later no one was sure what they had seen or who had been head shot.

The right side door gunner yelled, "Taking fire 3 O'clock!" and the Vietnamese radio man and interpreter was shot through the stomach as he jumped off our helicopter. Another Vietnamese Ranger was shot and killed and two others were wounded jumping out of the helicopter and, in three seconds, the aircraft was empty and I was taking off. The Vietnamese Rangers were now assaulting a very hot LZ with no US adviser, no US leadership on the ground, and a critically wounded radio operator /interpreter. It was the OK Corral and Wyatt Earp was dead and Doc Holliday was badly wounded!

I was taking off at maximum power. The gunships were firing six 7.62mm miniguns (each gunship firing approximately 2,000 rounds of minigun per minute [one gun at a time]), 2.75-inch rockets, 550 rounds per minute of door gun, and 40mm cannon into the areas where the enemy fire was coming from. Over 14,000 rounds per minute of suppressing fire shredded the foliage surrounding the landing zone.

The enemy fire was coming from bunkers, spider holes, and numerous other fighting positions, mostly where our aircraft had just landed to a hover and taken off from. No enemy troops were visible, but it was now apparent that there was a very strong, well-prepared, highly skilled, and perhaps tipped-off and highly pissed-off, company size enemy force on the ground. There are approximately 120 troops in a company, and even the ARVN 44rth rangers cannot survive long with such bad odds.

Remarkably, all three Tiger helicopters flew out of the LZ with only minor damage and a few hits from the ground fire. *I thought, God if only I could get out of this damned place alive today, and I had a place to go, I would leave Vietnam now.* And then we were clear of the enemy fire and climbing to a safe altitude. Each of us Tiger slick crewmen began to relax as we climbed to 1,500 feet. We each thanked the Lord that we got out of that death trap in one piece. We were also glad to know that we would not have to go back in there anytime soon. Then the C&C ships ultra-high frequency (UHF) radio crackled to life with the overall mission commander's message to the Tigers and gunships:

"The rangers are being slaughtered! We have no contact with the US Army adviser and the radio man is severely wounded. You Tigers are going to have to go back into the LZ now and extract the remaining Rangers—before they are overrun, captured, or killed! Form up in V formation and land to the northeast (NE) this time and make room for all three aircraft on the southwest (SW) end of the LZ. Gunships, I want that LZ leveled and the gooks (NVA and Viet Cong) kept in their holes and bunkers until the Tigers get in, load, and get out. And don't leave anyone in that LZ!"

Shocked and now alarmed, we Tigers formed up about one mile south of the LZ and began our approach at 100 knots and flying low level to avoid ground fire. Our approach would be from the opposite direction, from the south to the north, of our original landing direction. This time flying empty of troops, with less fuel, we had plenty of power available. We three Tigers found room to land our slicks together with no more than a foot or two between our main rotor blades.

The South Vietnamese Rangers were laying along a skirmish line from north to south. The South Vietnamese Rangers were between the Viet Cong and our three slicks. The enemy was trying their best to press into the LZ, and not only kill the Rangers, but also destroy our aircraft, which were now on the ground like *sitting ducks*. The Rangers had dragged their wounded and dead back to the edge of the LZ. All of us Tigers and Rangers were in high grass of varying heights. The panicked South Vietnamese troops would not get up and get onto the aircraft for fear of being shot. All of the

Rangers' leaders had been killed or wounded, and the stench of death and fear permeated the air.

Seconds turned into a minute. A US Army door gunner tried to get them up, but they would not get into our slicks. The Rangers were frozen with fear. Then the US Army captain mission commander did one of the bravest things any of the troops in that formation and on the ground had ever seen. He landed his C&C ship behind our aircraft, jumped out of his helicopter, dashed through the murderous gunfire that came from both sides. He ran into the center of the Rangers defensive line and ordered them up. When they still remained locked in terror, he started pulling and jerking them up by the shirt collar, one by one, and pushing them into the three slicks. For the moment, Tigers and their gunships had superior firepower with the gunships pouring thousands of rounds of minigun, hundreds of 40mm grenades, and dozens of 2.75-inch rockets into the enemy positions.

Months later, one of the reasons I would accept an invitation to volunteer for gunships was to avoid ever again having to fly slowly in formation, into a landing zone, under intense enemy fire, and then have to *sit there* and get shot at from point-blank range. We Tiger crews felt like we had been on the ground for an eternity, when a Viet Cong soldier stood up in the elephant grass only about 20 meters in front of Tiger lead's aircraft and was about to hose the entire formation with his AK47 when the gunships blew him to pieces with their miniguns.

The courage that the mission commander instilled in the rangers and everyone on that mission was something to behold. The mission commander, along with the help of a crew chief and door gunner, had saved many lives and got everyone of the rangers and their wounded and dead into the slicks in less than two minutes. We four Tiger aircraft then took off and flew straight for Vi Thanh, South Vietnam, in the Delta region of IV Corps. As we flew back, the mission commander asked over the UHF radio, if anyone had the US adviser on their aircraft? Tiger Lead replied *"negative."* Chock 1 and Chock 2 replied *"negative."* I asked my crew chief and door gunner if the US adviser was among the three dead, three wounded, and four uninjured troops on board of my blood filled aircraft. The crew replied, "No Americans back here sir, but one body is missing most of his head."

All of the rangers and the US adviser had been wearing tiger striped camouflage uniforms, so they all looked alike in most ways. I told the crew to look on the headless troopers hand for his sapphire ring, and they replied, "No rings on the headless guy." I then made one last quick look and saw the hush *puppy-like, soft brown leather, non regulation boots* that the adviser had been wearing in the briefing only an hour before. The Vietnamese Rangers were wearing tennis shoes or US jungle boots.

To this day I am shocked and angered because one of the Vietnamese Rangers had probably taken the adviser's ring soon after he was killed, even as the combat was underway in the LZ. I landed at Vi Thanh and the Army sergeant first class, the dead adviser's close friend and comrade in arms, ran to the Huey. He grabbed the young lifeless officer in his arms and screamed the *cries of grief and morbid sounds* only mothers and fathers of dead children and we band of combat brothers know. The sergeant was inconsolable and fell to the ground, and his face contorted with despair and sadness, sobbing, screaming, wailing, and holding the brave lad's still, bloated, and already stiff body in his embrace. I wanted to vomit and scream, but this was no place for that reaction. My future nightmares would force me to relive this sad scene and the gray distorted face of the dead US Army adviser for the rest of my life.

Our mission was over and we flew home to Soc Trang to wash the blood from our aircraft floors, clean up our bird, and clean our weapons for the next day's mission. The blood, brains, and other body fluids in the aircraft stank and made us sick to our stomachs. We all wanted to get away from that smell as soon as possible. Upon arrival at Soc Trang, my pilot and I helped the crew chief and door gunner to clean the aircraft and guns. We silently assisted the crew chief and gunner with their post-flight maintenance checks and services. We were still in shock from the day's emotional events. We hardly said a word to each other. I prayed silently for the dead American and told myself, "I am not going to think about this shit anymore today! It don't mean nothing."

My crew and I then stumbled in for chow and some beers, and then hit the rack to prepare for another day in Vietnam. I wondered how my fellow warrant officer and commissioned officer rotary wing class flight graduates and friends were doing in their particular part of this hell called Vietnam.

I cannot remember the name of the mission commander. He was an Army aviator captain and he should have been put in for the Silver or Bronze Star for his heroism that day. I also do not remember who was flying the third Tiger slick (Chock 2) on the mission.

Seeing, hearing, smelling, and touching death on this mission and my repeated nightmares since then seeing that poor, headless lieutenant adviser has reinforced my admiration for our ground troops. The ground troops' almost mission impossible to find and get these Viet Cong and North Vietnamese Army troops to fight is a mission I am glad I do not have. I want to kill all of these communist sons of bitches! In response, I have come up with what I call the "Ing Definition of US Army Infantry in Vietnam." Here is the definition:

Dandridge's " - - - - ING" Definition
of US Army Infantry in Vietnam

Enlisting, training, and learning; deploying, landing, and assigning; training, recon-ing, and patrolling; sweating, hoping, wishing, and praying; planning, coordinating, following, and leading; running and waiting; flying, fearing, missing, and taking and retaking; anticipating; shaking, locking, and loading; jumping, assaulting, shooting, taking, and retaking; crawling, sweating, listening, scratching, sneaking, taking and retaking; searching, attacking, bayoneting, taking, and retaking; resting, recuperating, firing, throwing, suffocating, slogging, mortaring, cursing, and swimming; fainting, fumbling, cutting, and sliding; climbing, observing, carrying, shelling, and loving; crying, infiltrating, slogging, ambushing, searching, and destroying; yearning, coughing, craving, taking, and retaking; complaining, begging, blasting, smoking, resupplying, and fighting; falling, swearing, drinking, directing, and blasting; digging, building, grieving, praying, yelling, taking, and retaking; inserting, bleeding, reckoning, blessing, toking, and extracting; thanking, humping, wailing, winning, losing, taking, and retaking; vomiting, securing, slapping, pulling, observing, releasing, tapping, and shooting; dragging, lacking, lobbing, loathing, hating, and vietnamizing; farting, foaming, frothing, fortifying, fumbling, taking and retaking; evacuating, extracting, excruciating, advancing, and retreating, wading, wobbling, wanting, washing, and never drying; voiding, vomiting, mourning, exhilarating, and suppressing; surprising, confusing, drenching, taking, and retaking; digging, dogging, remembering, and forgetting; breathing, blowing, surviving, taking, and retaking; chilling, falling, peeing, day dreaming, binging, breaking, taking, and retaking; worrying, wounding, hurting, and dying; bloating, bagging, and draping; wailing, sobbing, saluting, honoring, folding, and presenting; and burying, suffering, mourning, and grieving!

CHAPTER 11: FEBRUARY 4, 1969 ◄
"A Day in the Life of a Crew Chief and Door Gunner."

Letter from Warrant Officer 1 Larry Dandridge
to WO1 Danny Hickman

Date: 4 February 1969

From: Warrant Officer W. Larry Dandridge, 121st Assault Helicopter Company (Airmobile Light), 13th CAB, 1st Aviation Brigade, APO SF 96296

TO: Warrant Officer Danny Hickman B Troop, 3rd/17th Air Cavalry, Squadron, 1st Aviation Brigade, APO SF 01210

Dear Danny,

I am happy to tell you that I have been selected to fly UH-1B gunships in our Viking gun platoon. Our friend Bubba Segrest has been in the Vikings for about three months already and he asked me a month ago if I ever thought about flying guns instead of slicks. I told Bubba, I not only have been thinking about it, I was about to ask Captain Gene Booth, the Viking platoon leader to please nominate me for the next gunship pilot slot to come open in the Vikings.

I met two new warrant officers this week, WO1 Rick Bente and WO1 Paul McClymonds[xxiii]. Both are nice guys and good pilots. There is just so little time and energy for socializing here. It is all I can do after flying all day to help the crew chief and door gunner, then eat something, then write a letter home. Sergeant George Quackenbush is one of the senior Viking crew chiefs here and is on his second tour. He is a master maintenance mechanic and was the second shift maintenance supervisor before volunteering and getting selected to fly for the Vikings

219

as a crew chief and door gunner. He greeted me into the gun platoon and told me his friends call him George, but I, as a new guy, should address him as Sergeant—and he made it clear that these gunships were the crew chiefs' aircrafts and the flight line was their domain. It is clear that, as a new and unproven gun pilot, I was there to listen and learn.

George also told me that he had fired more than 500,000 rounds of door gun ammunition and that he and his fellow crew chiefs (CEs) and door gunners were darn good at spotting the enemy and hitting very small targets at several hundred yards and at 90 to 95 knots, and with first shots. George made it crystal clear that the enlisted men and aircraft commanders did not care much about what I, the new guy, thought about anything I had done before joining the Vikings. They only cared about how I would act in the future, under fire, and the only thing that really mattered to any of these combat veterans was would I add value to the Viking gun team!

As I mentioned in previous letters, I am tired of landing on top of and near these VC and NVA ass holes and getting the crap shot out of my aircraft without having any real fire power (other than my two door gunners) to shoot back with. Ever since Jerry Markland was killed by these slope communist, mud-and-blood-sucking, bottom-dwelling, garbage-eating VC and NVA bastards—I have wanted to go into the gunship business and kill as many of them as I can!

So here I am back in the left seat, flying as a peter pilot, and learning how to fly an over loaded and older-model Huey B-Model gunship, so that I can find and kill our enemies. I did love having my slick aircraft commander orders and being able to plan, fly, and lead both single-ship and multi-ship combat missions, but I am sure that learning to be a gunship wing ship commander and after that a fire team leader will be even more rewarding—and, at times, probably more exciting, too. My business is now killing people, and business is good.

I am already impressed with the comradeship, respect, and devotion that these Viking officers, warrant officers, non-commissioned officers, and enlisted men show each other daily and nightly. As gunship pilots, crew chiefs, or door gunners we are basically on 24-hour standby for immediate response to any emergency mission that might come up. That might be our own airfield being mortared or rocketed, or the need to prevent the VC or NVA from overrunning one of our (US or ARVN or Allied) units or outposts.

My hooch is right next to our Viking flight line and revetments, so I have to run only about 30 yards to the nearest armed, fueled, and ready-to-start aircraft. When the first Viking pilot reaches an aircraft, he jerks off the main rotor tie-down, pulls the starter trigger, and gets the aircraft up to operating RPM within seconds as the other pilot, the crew chief, and door gunner also mount up. If another pilot does not show up in time, he is left behind or occasionally replaced by a crew chief.

I have to tell you a funny story: One night we were mortared and Bubba Segrest was in the showers, which is one of the closest buildings to our gunships. Meanwhile some VC mortars started dropping and exploding on our airfield. Bubba dashed to the flight line, losing his towel en route, arriving at the gunship in his birthday suit, and jumped in one of our ready gunships and took off. After a record response and aircraft start and takeoff, Bubba, wearing only his skin and shivering in the cool night air, looked over to the left and to the rear of the aircraft and to his somewhat semi-inebriated surprise he realized that the peter pilot, crew chief, and door gunner had not made it to the aircraft! He spent an hour flying naked, wet, and freezing his ass off, doing what he could with the other fully manned gunships that had responded to this attack. He used the call sign "Lone Viking" that night!

Bubba and I have had a lot of fun at the O-Club together and just hanging out when we had some time off, which is seldom. I put a whole canister of talcum powder (baby powder) in his cot one night when he was especially inebriated. When he laid down in bed it looked like a smoke grenade went off in his room. It was one of the funniest things to see him choking in talcum dust and bewildered.

I have come to admire the field artillery guys and their "easy to man handle" 105 mm howitzers. With the 105 being helicopter transportable and quick to get set up and fire, and because it offers a high rate of fire, it is certainly a key weapon in this war. One of the artillery guys showed me his new M102 105mm howitzer a month ago, and he explained that it weighed only 1.5 tons, had a range of over 11,000 meters (about seven miles) and could fire in any direction. Those "arty" guys are shooting in 360 degrees day and night (they use mils and call their firing a 6,400 mil environment). It is a good feeling to know we can call in arty fire almost anywhere and anytime though it sometimes takes too long to get it firing before the bad guys disperse and disappear.[81]

Of course, our Viking gunships are a form of aerial artillery. I understand that our airmobile divisions further north have entire aerial rocket artillery (ARA) helicopter units assigned to them to help augment and extend the range of the cannon artillery in I, II, and III Corps. They have B and C Model gunships carrying 48 rockets and Cobras carrying 76 rockets to the enemy. We now have the equivalent of over ten US Army divisions (two Marine divisions, seven Army divisions, three separate brigades, an armored cavalry regiment plus all kinds of headquarters and support units) helping the Army of the Republic of South Vietnam.

It is hard to believe the North Vietnamese and the Viet Cong have not given up this fight. The terrain and the tactics used by the VC and NVA so favor them, that it seems that they are dictating how this war is fought far more often than we are. We cannot seem to contain the enemy here. He operates mostly in small units and masses only when everything favors him, then disbanding and rejoining the population or going underground before we can bring our superior fire power and troops to bear on him. Very frustrating!

We somehow have to win the support of the people of South Vietnam for their government and us, if we have any chance of winning this damn war. And I see no hope of the ARVN or us winning the "hearts and minds" of the poor Vietnamese people with all the corruption and incompetence of the South Vietnamese government and their poorly led, trained, and unmotivated army.

One of our Viking crew chiefs, Sergeant George Quackenbush, jotted down for me what a day in the life of a Viking crew chief was like. After reading his notes, I had Crew Chiefs Mike Dewey, Dan Eismann, Ken Roies[xxiv], and Wayne Zander and Door Gunner Jim Zeitler tell me what they thought a "crew chief's and door gunner's typical day in Vietnam" was like also. I have attached their explanation of the tough and relatively thankless job these flying aircraft mechanics, crew chiefs, door gunners, and great sky soldiers have to do seven days a week and 15 to 20 hours per day.

Keep your powder dry and your eyes, ears, and nose open, old pal. Please write me when you have a free minute—as you know as well as I, letters are our life line over here.

Best wishes,

Larry

A Day in the Life of a Viking Crew Chief and Door Gunner

"Army Hueys flew a total of seven and one half million flight hours in the Vietnam War. The Huey, including the AH-1G Cobra gunship, which flew 1,038,969 flight hours in Vietnam, have more combat flight time than any other aircraft in the history of warfare!"[82]

– Vietnam Helicopter Pilots Association (VHPA)

To become a member of the "Viking Team" you had to want to be a Viking and you had to have proven yourself in Vietnam to be trustworthy and steady in battle and aircraft emergencies to other Tigers and Vikings in Vietnam. You also had to: have enough in-country experience to learn a new and demanding job, show qualities of confidence and wisdom and others (see list below), and be voted in by your Viking peers. This made for a cohesive platoon filled with the best available flying troops. Facing danger daily as a team and knowing we could count on each other created a bond that cannot be broken even after a lifetime (47 years now) of separation. We are a true band of brothers.

Other Viking enlisted crew member qualities required included:

1. Willing to work very long hours and go weeks or months without a day off.

2. Committing to team work and an unwavering loyalty to the Vikings and the gunship mission.

3. Confronting and controlling your fears (staying cool under enemy fire).

4. Demonstrating fearlessness of heights and speed or at least not showing fear.

5. Being an adrenaline junkie and loving to blow stuff up.

6. Being almost certifiably crazy.

A crew chief's and door gunner's typical day included a wake up between 04:30 and 06:00 hours, followed by a quick breakfast of rubbery scrambled eggs, coffee, and a glass of juice, if the mess hall was open and you had time. Most of the time the mess hall was closed, because we always left so early, so we defaulted to eating a can of fruit from a C-rations pack and drank some water, coffee, or a soda. Next we grabbed our flight helmets, camera, and personal weapons,[83] and a case of C-rations, and filled the water cooler with ice, if the mess hall ice machine was working, and headed out to the flight line. We sometimes stuffed several beers into the very bottom of the cooler and covered the beer with many cans of soda and ice, making sure the officers couldn't see the beer. We prayed that someday, someone would bottle water for soldiers.

We then performed a quick but thorough preflight inspection of both helicopter and armament systems to see if anything was missed the night before when we were finishing up maintenance in the poor lighting of the flight line. Next we would wipe the dew from the helicopter's windows and check what C-rations were left for lunch or later and flip a coin for the best C-rations and relax a few minutes while awaiting the pilots. The peter pilot would arrive before the AC and do his meticulous preflight inspection and the crew chief and door gunner would help train the pilot with their advanced skill and knowledge of the aircraft systems and weapon systems. The pilot would hang his M14 rifle, or whatever long gun he carried (sometimes an M16, sometimes a shotgun, or other weapon) over the inboard rear-side wing of his armored seat, beside the crew chief and gunner's M14s. He would hang his helmet over his seat from the overhead hook.

Most days the operational area was not near Soc Trang, so Tigers and Vikings would saddle up and ferry to a staging zone, each flying in our separate formations. Sometimes we would operate out of Rach Gia, Bac Lieu, Vinh Long, Can Tho, Tri Ton, Moc Hoa, Ben Tre, Dong Tam, Vi Thanh, Chau Doc, Go Cong, or one of the dozens of other locations in IV Corps and once in a while in III Corps. Upon arrival, the helicopters would be refueled and thoroughly inspected, and the aircraft commanders would attend a mission briefing.

The briefing would cover such things as the mission objective; map coordinates; friendly units involved; enemy situation (including the enemy units we expected to attack); weather and other hazards like tall grass, trees, and booby traps; planned heading into and out of the landing zone or pickup zone; key terrain features; escape and evasion procedures; door gun firing restrictions; artillery activity and firing lines; US Air Force and South Vietnamese Air Force tactical air support; frequencies to use for slicks, guns, ground units, and C&C, and other participating units and their locations. While the AC was briefed, the rest of the crew, the pilot, crew chief, and door gunner, checked everything again and relaxed.

We kept an eye on local civilians and tried to keep children away from our aircraft, unless we wanted to give them some canned food and candy from our C-rations. It was not unusual to find a grenade or other unused live ordnance laying on the ground in our staging areas. All of us enlisted crewmembers liked the M14 rifle, in spite of its length and limited numbers of available magazines, because it fired the "same 7.62mm caliber ammunition" as our M60 machine guns. Many of our gunships had an M79 grenade launcher on board for extra firepower and to shoot when we were reconing by fire. Some of our Viking crews had an ammo can full of loaded M14 rifle magazines on board.

Standard operating procedure (SOP) dictated that no one saluted anyone else, as we were all paranoid of being shot at by snipers.

Rank meant almost nothing on the flight line. Everyone pitched in to get the job done. If we found anything wrong with our aircraft at Soc Trang, we would call a technical inspector (TI) over to check the problem out closely and make a call on what needed to be done to correct the fault or problem. When we were in the field, the crew chief was the TI, mechanic, and master of all work done on the aircraft, unless the world famous 121st UH-1D Tiger *Wrecker* (our unit's maintenance aircraft) was on station for technical and logistic support.

The aircraft were inspected to death, with pilots performing preflight and post-flight inspections; crew chiefs and door gunners performing daily inspections, preflight inspections, post-flight inspections, and inspections of all work done on the aircraft; and major 25-hour and 100-hour inspections; and inspections before and after every test flight. The crew chief, door gunner, and aircraft commander crew assigned to each aircraft were stable for long periods of time, but peter pilots in training came and went every three months and sometimes sooner if wounded, injured, killed, or they became sick. The Vikings did a dangerous job, and most were injured or wounded at one time or another during their tour of duty in Vietnam. Some were wounded more than once. Many gun pilots and enlisted crew members extended their tours and ultimately were wounded, injured, or killed for their trouble.

The Viking fire team would then recon by flying low level and nap-of-the-earth in search of enemy troop movement or anything out of the ordinary. In this way, they also baited the enemy to give their positions away by firing at the gunships. The Vikings also found an appropriate landing area for the transport helicopters to insert the Army of the Republic of Vietnam or US troops to make their sweep. After the gunship attacks, if the recon encountered significant enemy presence or resistance, the troop insertion would be delayed while the Vikings softened up the area with rockets, miniguns and M60 door guns. If there was still significant resistance, artillery, A-1 Sky Raiders, or F-4 Phantoms (tactical air support) would be called in for additional support.

When the LZ was as safe as was possible, the Viking fire team would coordinate with the troop transport helicopters and mark the LZ with smoke. The Vikings would then meet with the slicks and escort them in, protect them while on the ground, and escort them out until they reached 1,500 feet of altitude (the maximum effective range of small arms). The Vikings would then return to the operational area and support the troops during their sweep of an area, attacking any points of resistance, and returning to hot refuel and rearm. Usually one fire team would be on-station (flying cover over the troops on the ground), while another fire team was refueling and rearming.

The extraction of troops from a pick-up zone (PZ) was accomplished by escorting the troop helicopters in; protecting them with rocket, minigun, 40mm grenade, and door gun fire while they loaded; and escorting them out again. The Vikings escorted the slicks back to an unloading and refuel location and headed for the barn, where on short final all guns were unloaded and weapon circuit breakers were pulled. Upon arrival at home base, the work was just beginning. Upon shutdown, the pilot would immediately do a prestart check up to the point in the checklist where all the pilot had to do to start the aircraft was turn the battery on and pull the start trigger. After shutdown, the gunner double checked to make darn certain the battery switch was off, and then he carefully rearmed the helicopter, while the crew chief refueled it. These actions made the gunship ready to respond to an emergency within minutes. After the helicopter was ready to scramble, the gunner would remove one gun for cleaning then reinstall that gun and remove another. We never had more than one minigun off at a time, in case the helicopter had to be scrambled at a moment's notice.

The crew chief would start his daily or 25-hour inspection but, like the gunner, would only open up one area of the helicopter to be inspected at a time in case he had to close up the area and scramble quickly. Readying the helicopter for the next day's flight typically required two to three hours. The gunner had his hands submerged in jet fuel most of that time, and his hands would burn and much of his skin on his hands would peel off every three weeks. This was before the days of proper Hazardous Material (HAZMAT) handling training, protective safety equipment, and Material Safety Data Sheets (MSDSs). Every door gunner and crew chief who served in Vietnam and still alive today could put in a claim to the Veterans Administration (VA) for HAZMAT (agent orange, solvents, oil, hydraulic fluid, grease, fuel, and other chemicals) caused injuries, diseases, and illnesses. It is sad that they did not know back in 1968 and 1969 about the terrible long- and short-term effects of defoliants, solvents, and other HAZMATs.

The crew chiefs also experienced constant skin irritation from a mixture of jet fuel from fuel samples, grease, oil and hydraulic fluid samples and fluid spills they worked with. They also suffered from a continuous variety of safety wire and cotter pin cuts. By the time the door gunner and crew chief had finished their end-of-day maintenance and other duties, the mess hall was usually closed and the movie half over. However there always was just enough time to get a snack at the enlisted club and have a couple of *brewskies* (beers) to counteract the adrenaline so the crew chief and door gunner could get a good night's sleep—if the base was not mortared. Anytime Soc Trang was mortared or rocketed, or a sapper tried to get in, the Vikings would scramble into the gunships and have them in the air within a couple of minutes. The Vikings frequently flew barefoot and wearing only under shorts, a chicken plate, and a helmet, and we had to be very careful about where the hot brass landed!

That is a description of as normal a day as possible, but very few days went as planned and those days that are "off script and unplanned" are the days of which memories are made. They are the days that bonded the Vikings tight and kept boredom to a minimum. Those who have never experienced successive "normal" combat days, even though they would *not seem normal to most*, would not comprehend how it could get to be boring in Vietnam. Adrenaline can be, and is, addictive, and living on the edge is why a normal person exceeds the speed limit, surfs big waves, skis freestyle, skydives, climbs mountains, deep sea dives, explores caves, or races cars. We didn't have a car, surfboard, snow, parachutes, diving gear, or a race car at Soc Trang, but we went hunting in very fragile flying machines for people who wanted to kill us. We felt cheated if contact with the enemy was not made. We had scores to settle, friends to avenge, shit to blow up, and a war to win!

The Viking platoon was always voluntary. One could always return to the Tigers[84] or maintenance, where much safer and shorter working hours awaited, but no one even contemplated leaving an elite unit like our beloved Viking gun platoon. Every Viking (and Tiger) was your brother, especially after so many close calls with the grim reaper or being shot. Everyone was constantly aware that if you flew guns long enough in Vietnam, you would almost surely get injured, wounded, or killed. But it was the other days, the *non-typical days* and *non-typical nights* that made things interesting and memorable...

Non-typical Days and Nights Were Filled with Typical Dangerous Events!

Being chased around the airfield by a main rotor after a blade strike, flying through thousands of ducks blasting the windshields out of your aircraft, flying into thousands of bats, accidentally shooting holes in your own main rotor blades, accidentally shooting cannon plugs (electrical connections) off your miniguns, capturing an NVA soldier, an inadvertent electronic triggered mass rocket launch on the ground, being mortared while trying to pick up an ARVN soldier that didn't catch his ride out, having to save other downed aircrews under intense fire and the most hazardous flying conditions, or watching The Good Bad and Ugly movie all night because of mortar attack interruptions. These were the kinds of things that were "not normal" and "not typical," but frequent in the life of a crew chief and door gunner.

Flying three times into the U-Minh forest to save a crew and the troops on board an aircraft that was just shot down by the enemy is one of those not normal events in the daily life of our outstanding crew chiefs and door gunners. On that day in 1968, Warrant Officer Aircraft Commander Joe Casanova and his peter pilot, Crew Chief Mike Dewey, and Door Gunner John Romero bravely, without hesitation, and under intense enemy fire, chopped their way down through small trees far enough for door gunner John Romero to courageous hang down below the hovering, out-of-ground-effect Huey to pull up the wounded and injured crew and troops. The rescued would surely have been killed or captured without his help. Romero, a fearless door gunner and fine young man, handed the wounded up to crew chief Mike Dewey who was lying flat on the floor of the hovering slick. This harrowing rescue had to be completed three times, as the aircraft could not lift more than three of the soldiers needing rescue at a time without itself crashing. All of this while the tail rotor was perilously close to hitting the trees and other vegetation, and while enemy fire sprayed the jungle all around the hovering Huey. As was almost always the case, no award nominations were submitted for Dewey or Romero or Casanova that day. It was a non-typical day in the life of a crew chief and door gunner. We had more to do than write award nominations.

The day our wonderful Viking Crew Chief Dan Eismann[84] was wounded seriously twice in the time span of just a few minutes was another *non-typical day.* In a heated battle, he suffered shrapnel wounds to the lower leg and side, and he never stopped firing his door gun. Dan did not tell his aircraft commander and fellow crewmen of his injuries until they returned to Soc Trang hours later, and then only after he completed his daily maintenance on the aircraft. Thus was another *non-typical day* in the life of a crew chief and door gunner. "I was not incapacitated," Dan said. "I was able to keep shooting and doing my job, so I did not see any need to tell anyone, take them away from their jobs, or terminate our mission when we Vikings were needed on station. I saw no need to complain!" Dan spent two weeks in a hospital recovering and then went right back to crewing and gunning. Dan wrote an interesting book titled *"FREEDOM IS YOUR DESTINY!"* (See footnote 85) about his strong religious beliefs and his combat tour in Vietnam and he and his wife were very kind and helpful with publication advice for *Blades of Thunder* Book I.

Another *non-typical day* in the life of a crew chief or door gunner occurred when Viking AC and Fire Team Leader Bill Ellis, with Crew Chief George Quackenbush, were doing a nap-of-the earth reconnaissance flight. The flight was a light fire team of two Viking B Model gunships, and Jim Ellis was flying the wing ship. The lead ship jumped over a tree line at the edge of a lily-padded swamp that had thousands of ducks sitting on the pond. As they neared what seemed like 10,000 startled ducks, the ducks took off in waves going straight up. The lead gunship just missed the terrified ducks, but the poor unaware wing ship flying at 90 Knots (103.7miles per hour) slammed into dozens of ducks!!!! Splat, splat!, The ear-splitting slam, thump, splat, whomp, boom, and bam reverberated through the wing ship, as the birds knocked out both chin bubbles, smeared windshields, and tore off a minigun ammo chute. Various unrecognizable bird parts flowed through the ventilation system after the multiple duck strikes. There were ducks parts in the vents and in the chin bubbles. There were duck strikes on the mast and, main rotor hub, and multiple strikes on the main rotor blades. Had one of the birds hit a door gunner or crew chief, that fellow easily could have been killed. Just imagine a 10-pound bird hitting you in the head at more than 100 miles per hour! It was another *non-typical day* in the life of an enlisted crew member!

On another *non-typical day*, flying near Ca Mau a command and control lieutenant colonel was concerned about how to return to Soc Trang with an enemy gunner's 51 caliber hole in his helicopter's rotor blade. The hole was causing a lateral vibration. Because of the crew chief's previous experience with rotor-blade repair, he was asked to assist. The crew chief told the lieutenant colonel that he should let the crew fly the helicopter back "as is" and just bear the vibration because there was no field repair immediately available and darkness and the enemy were at hand. The light (lieutenant) colonel refused to accept his advice, so the crew chief borrowed his aircraft commander's 45 caliber pistol, estimated the distance from the tip of the blade to where the hole was, and shot another hole in the opposite blade to equal out the imbalance. The lieutenant colonel was absolutely speechless and trembling from surprise and anger. However, he flew the helicopter back to base (out of fear of what might happen should he not do so) and, yes, the vibration was almost completely eliminated. Everyone worried that the lieutenant colonel would press charges for the destruction of government property, but reason prevailed. Another *non-typical day* in the life of a veteran crew chief!

Other interesting and exciting *non-typical days* in the life of our Viking crew chiefs and door gunners (and pilots) occurred when several crew, while assigned to night airfield security, advised the tower that they were going blackout and would be checking out lights in a nearby tree line. They then went looking for a fight wherever they could find one. They flew at low level in the dark until they were shot at, and then they lit up the target (a hootch) with the searchlight and landing light. They then flew over the hooch within several feet of the roof and dropped a homemade bomb (made from an ammo can, C-4, bolts and nuts, and a hand grenade).

After several weeks of these aggressive (an unauthorized) flights, the Vikings were finally caught when they came upon an ARVN outpost under enemy attack by several hundred Viet Cong. The Vikings were able to break up the attack and destroy many of the attackers with several loads of rockets, minigun and M60 fire, all while supposedly flying airfield security. The outpost called 121st Assault Helicopter Company operations to thank them for their lives and inadvertently let the cat out of the bag. After checking the flight line and finding the helicopter guns filthy and the cabin full of M60 brass and links, there was no doubt who had been flying. The crews were halfheartedly threatened with a court marshal for leaving their posts and flying unauthorized missions. Again, the Vikings escaped jail time, but only because they saved the lives of those at that outpost, and so ended *another non-typical day!*

On another *non-typical day*, one of the Viking crew chiefs spotted a body in the middle of a field outside of the operational area. The body was dressed in the uniform of a North Vietnamese Army (NVA) soldier. Finding a body in the open was highly unusual, as the NVA and VC always hauled their dead and wounded away quickly, before US troops could get to them. With the wing ship providing cover, the fire team leader aircraft commander brought the gunship to a hover over the NVA, and the door gunner kept his M60 trained on the NVA body. He appeared dead until the helicopter's powerful rotor wash hit him. Then the miracle happened—that North Vietnamese soldier became a real and live wide-eyed and scared trooper within two seconds. His eyes were as round and as big as saucers! The crew chief motioned for him to come closer, checked him for weapons, and told him to get in. He motioned for him to sit in front of him, behind the AC on the floor. The crew chief had him covered with his M60 while he sat in back of the pilot's chair. The AC questioned the crew chief's intelligence for letting the NVA soldier sit so close to the pilot who was flying the aircraft.

As the aircraft climbed through 500 feet, the crew chief could see that the NVA was a mere boy of perhaps little more than 12 years old. After a minute or two the Viking crew realized that they would be the laughing stock of Soc Trang if they presented their proud catch (a boy prisoner) to others on base, so they decided to release him. The gunship crew also believed that if this child was turned over to the Army of the Republic of South Vietnam that he would have been tortured and killed. So the aircraft commander landed in another open field to turn him loose, but the poor little soldier was sure they were dropping him off for target practice that he wouldn't go. He was one tough dude and it was hard to get him out of the helicopter without shooting him. The crew chief said it was as hard as trying to stuff a raccoon into a gunnysack. Anyway, the NVA boy finally ran away and lived to either fight another day or perhaps, the crew all prayed, to have second thoughts about how bad his American enemies were. Everyone hoped he would have returned to civilian life and thrown down his fighting days, but the Vikings will never know what happened to that young and frightened NVA boy soldier.

On another *non-typical night* while the Vikings served on airfield standby as the gunship protection, Soc Trang came under mortar attack. The Vikings raced to their gunship and did their standard scramble and lightning start. They tried to take off overloaded as always, but the aircraft commander (AC) couldn't get the aircraft flying as the helicopter would bleed off RPM every time serious collective was pulled. After three attempts to get the gunship flying and most of the runway used up, the AC finally realized that the throttle was not fully on. After hurriedly rolling the throttle all the way on, the gunship just barely made it over the fence with about a foot to spare! The crew chief and door gunner said, "Crazy ass pilots were always trying to kill us!"

On another *non-typical night* while flying gunships on a firefly mission, a Viking light fire team of two gunships found a bunch of enemy soldiers in a tree line, and the crew chief kicked out a big aerial canister of gas that had about 100 little gas grenades in it. The gas was flowing nicely into the tree line while the pilot was working over the area with the miniguns, and the crew chief and door gunner hammered the tree line with their door guns. The miniguns jammed and instead of breaking left, the Fire Team Leader Jim Ellis broke right and flew right through the gas. The thing that saved everyone's asses was the cyclic control[86] forced trim feature being set to automatically pull the cyclic back and cause the aircraft to rapidly climb if the pilot let go of the controls.

For about five minutes nobody could see anything, not the AC, not the peter pilot, not the crew chief, and not the door gunner. They each had burning eyes and tears streaming down their faces. Flying at night and fighting was typical, but flying blind at night was not typical!

Another *non-typical* incident included a South Vietnamese Army fuel truck driver crossing in front of a Viking fire team taking off just after rearming with 17-pound (war head) 2.75-inch rockets. The AC had to do an emergency cyclic climb[87] to get over the bastard and then bleed off rotor RPM to the point that they were then skimming over the paddy dikes at about six inches and about to crash. Meanwhile, Door Gunner Mike Dewey and Crew Chief George Quackenbush pitched ammo out the door to lighten the load and allow the AC to nurse the aircraft back to flying again! "I don't know about the other crew members," said George, "but my ass bit more button holes out of the seat than any other time!"

Then there were *non-typical days* of Crew Chief and Door Gunner Ken Roies who served 18 months in Vietnam, first as a White Tiger flying slicks for about four months and after as a Viking for 14 months. He had many non typical days, as he was with Captain Bill Ferguson when Bill was shot in the chest. He was with Viking Captain Bubba Segrest when Bubba was shot through the knee and hand. And he was flying with Viking Captain George Taylor when Ken was wounded by a bullet and the exploding debris when a Viet Cong AK47 round came through the chin bubble and shot off George Taylor's boot heel and bullet fragments and metal aircraft fragments were blown into Ken's eyes, face, and shoulder.

Ken Roies also helped rescue Major James Rowe on a *non-typical day* by serving as crew chief on the White Tiger aircraft that flew Major Rowe from the U-Minh Forest to safety after Rowe was discovered by Cavalry Cobras waving his arms and frantically signaling for help. Perhaps Ken's most non-typical day was the day he was flying as door gunner with Viking Crew Chief Chuck Barns and their aircraft was hit by numerous small arms rounds and the rocket pod on Ken's side was set ablaze. Ken pulled the emergency jettison handle on the rocket pod but it would not disengage and fall free. So he jumped up and down on the burning and fully loaded rocket pod several times before it broke free and left him dangling outside of the aircraft by only his monkey strap! The rocket pod exploded when it hit the ground. Ken's heroic action and quick thinking had saved his crew, his aircraft, and himself!

On another *non-typical day* Ken was seriously wounded when he was flying as crew chief and gunner with Viking Warrant Officer McKeatch. As their gunship passed low-level over a contested area, a VC in a spider hole popped open his camouflaged cover hatch and shot Ken through the upper leg (near his hip) with an AK-47 at close range. "I saw the VC and had him in my sights and was ready to squeeze the trigger on my M60 when the pilot made a violent evasive maneuver and spoiled my aim. Some days you get the bear and some days the bear gets you!" Ken said. When Ken was told by the doctors at his hospital in Vietnam he was being evacuated to Japan, he refused to be medically evacuated, limped out of the hospital with steel wire stitches in his leg, and caught the first helicopter back to Soc Trang, where he completed his tour of combat duty with the Vikings.

There were so many *non-typical days and nights* that they all blur together, but one incident stands out. As the Vikings were just finished rearming and refueling at Can To, the avionics crew came to check out the radios on one of the gunships. When they were through, they drove off with the power cord still plugged in and when the stretched cord passed in close proximity to the ass end of the rocket pod, it set off a mass launch of all seven rockets from that rocket pod! (Electromagnetic interference was little understood at that time!) The mass launch tore the cowlings off of the parked lead gunship and caused several rockets to punch through the pilot's open door, missing him by inches. The passing seven rockets, which together produced more than 7,000 pounds of thrust, knocked the peter pilot down and rolled him in the gravel into the nearby refueling points. Most, if not all of the rockets went into the nearby town with unknown results. All involved were extremely lucky that the rockets had not flown far enough to arm the war heads when they passed through the peter pilot's open door and when they passed within inches of the cowlings of the aircraft in front. The incident was probably blamed on the VC! The helicopter that was hit flew without crew doors for a month before somebody had a crash and could cannibalize (donate) a door to replace the one damaged by the rockets.

Yes, our Viking and Tiger crew chiefs and door gunners were in a dangerous and stressful business, but they made a difference and they got to blow stuff up too. These young enlisted men and non-commissioned officer soldiers had real *chutzpah*[88]!

PICTURE 41: VIKING GUNSHIP NOSE ART

Picture courtesy of George Quackenbush and Bill Schmidt.

Note all these dozens of screws holding the chin bubble onto the aircraft. As training and punishment to pilots firing rockets and 40mm grenades to close to the aircraft, crew chief's made the pilots change these chin bubbles if they broke them or cracked them. It took two pilots four times as long to change a chin bubble as one crew chief!

CHAPTER 12: MARCH 7, 1969 ◄
"Vipers Intercepting Enemy Troops in the Open."

Letter from Warrant Officer 1 Larry Dandridge
to WO1 Danny Hickman

Date: 7 March 1969

From: Warrant Officer W. Larry Dandridge, 121st Assault Helicopter Company (Airmobile Light), 13th CAB, 1st Aviation Brigade, APO SF 96296

TO: Warrant Officer Danny Hickman, B Troop, 3rd Squadron, 17th Air Cavalry Regiment, APO SF 01915

Dear Danny,

I just recently returned from my two week training with the 235th Aerial Weapons Company (AWC), also called Armed Helicopter Company, in Can Tho. Flying Cobras was much more exciting and eventful than I imagined it would be. The 235th was also a sad experience due to the death of one of our classmates and a collateral damage incident.

I regret to inform you that Warrant Officer 1 Larry Allen Bodell[89] was killed in action flying in the front seat of a 235th AWC Cobra on the 19th of February 1969, during the time I was flying with the 235th. Did you know Larry very well? I had just spoken with him briefly when I first arrived at Can Tho, and although I did not know him well in flight school, he seemed like a very nice guy and sharp pilot. I know his family must be devastated. First Jerry Markland and now Larry Bodell. I sure hope our number does not come up over here. Those guys will never know what it is to live a long and happy life.

237

I am scheduled to go on Rest and Recuperation (R&R) leave on 10 March 1969. My birthday is 11 March. Since this is my seventh month in this beautiful hell hole, I am really ready and excited to be going to meet my lovely wife in Hawaii. My dear friend from Charleston, SC, and our parallel officer classmate First Lt. Bubba Segrest is departing for Hawaii with me on the same flight and so is Captain Bob Snider, who is one of our Tiger Slick Leaders in the 121st. I cannot wait to go swimming in a clear blue ocean again, eat some great food, drink some of those famous Polynesian drinks, lay on the beach, hear Don Ho sing "Tiny Bubbles in the Wine," and of course see my wife.

I am still flying UH-1B Huey gunships and it is, most of the time, quite a lot of fun and, in my opinion, much safer than landing over loaded slicks full of troops, in hot landing zones and picking them up again in hot pickup zones. Getting shot up at close range in a slick, in tight formation, by little guys that we seldom even see is hopefully history for me. It is great to be able to shoot back and kill these dink bastards before they can kill me. Since Jerry Markland's death, I am hell-bent on killing as many of these little Viet Cong and NVA assholes as I can.

Hard to believe that just six months ago I was a real pacifist and wanted nothing to do with killing. This is not my dad's war. No clear-cut Nazis or Japs or North Koreans in uniform to kill. Although these VC and NVA bastards are committing atrocities every day and night, they won't come out and fight, except to ambush and then run. I am frustrated with trying to find them in any numbers where we can engage them and defeat them decisively. We keep taking areas and giving the areas back to them the next day, or even the same day. How will we ever win this mess of a war if they are allowed to go back to their Cambodian and Laotian safe-havens at will?

Congratulations on becoming your unit's UH-1 instructor pilot (IP). I have been on many combined airmobile missions with the 9th Division and a few with your cavalry troop. Your Cobra and LOH guys have saved my buns twice in the past three months. Would love to see you, but have never had a chance to stop long enough at Dong Tam to look for you. We always seem to have just enough time to hot refuel and get right back at it. I know your cavalry troop at Dong Tam has Cobra Attack Helicopters, and I have been told that our unit is in the queue to receive Cobras to replace our older, but beloved B Model Huey gunships.

I know our crew chiefs and door gunners are going to hate it when they can no longer fly with us and play such an important role in our armed helicopter mission. Because we will soon be getting those Cobras (perhaps as soon as July), some of us Viking gunship pilots have been sent to Can Tho to train as front seat pilots (and gunners) in the 235th Aerial Weapons Company. We Vikings are sharing with the 235th our tactics and detailed knowledge of IV Corps' terrain, climate, and enemy threat tactics and the 235th guys are teaching us how to fly (from the front seat), how to best use the XM28E1 armament subsystem chin turret, armed with a 7.62mm minigun and a 40mm M129 automatic grenade launcher located below the front pilot's seat.

As with our Viking UH-1B gunships, the 235th Vipers' turret mounted, Cobra's M134 minigun is an electrically operated, six-barrel Gatling-type gun with rotating barrels. The guns ammunition belts had a tracer round as every fifth round and at 2,000 rounds and 4,000 rounds per minute, the fire from these deadly weapons looked like a continuous red streak aimed at the enemy. Combined with the Cobra's two XM159, 19-shot, 2.75-inch (70mm), folding fin aerial rocket pods (one on each side), the Cobras put the fear of God in every VC and NVA soldier in the Delta.

The stability augmentation system on the Cobra meant an AC could hit a target at about 1,000 meters nearly every time, if the aircraft was in trim. The maximum range of the 2.75-inch rocket was about 8,000 meters. The 2.75-inch rocket came in the standard 10-pound high explosive (HE) war head and a 17-pound HE version that could knock a Russian made tank out of commission if fired on the engine deck. We also had white phosphorous rockets for target marking and incendiary use and an anti-personnel flechette (aerodynamically shaped darts with tailfins) rocket that was devastating to troops in the open. We called the flechette ammunition "nails," as they would nail a man to a tree with the 1,180 darts in each rocket.

As you probably already know, Can Tho is one of the largest cities in Vietnam and is the largest city in the Mekong Delta. It is located on the south bank of the Hau River, a branch of the Mekong River. The name Can Tho means "river of poems". The city of Can Tho is located about 100 miles south of Saigon. It is hot and humid here, and the weather guys say Can Tho gets about 65 inches of rain per year. IV Corps' Headquarters is located here and the Army airfield is a little over one mile northwest of the city.

There are a whole lot of US and South Vietnamese outfits and support organizations here in the Can Tho area, including, but not limited to Eakin Compound, Stateside Lounge, Dempsey Compound, the Pink Palace, the 29th Evacuation Hospital, Company D 5th Special Forces Group C Detachment, 440th and 565th Transportation Companies, Artillery, the 156th Army Security Agency Company, an Air America (CIA) unit, a refueling point, the Navy Brown Water/ SEAL facilities, the 52nd Signal Battalion, a Logistical Support Activity, the 51st Maintenance Company, other transportation units, Binh Thuy Joint USAF and South Vietnamese Air Force Base, and much more.

I have been dodging Vietnamese Air Force (VNAF) A-1h Sky Raiders for the past seven months as they flew reckless penetrations into and out of Binh Thuy Air Base in Can Tho during low ceiling weather, but had only landed there for more than refueling a couple of times to eat lunch with some South Vietnamese helicopter pilots that I was training. I also flew a couple of wounded troops to the hospital there. I have also helped cover some of the VNAF Black Horse (who were stationed at Binh Thuy Air Base) helicopter unit's combat assaults as a gunship pilot, but I knew little about Can Tho and the bases around it until this visit with the 235th.

Attached to this letter is the story of what went on during the two weeks, I flew Cobras out of Can Tho. I am "haunted" by one of those missions with the 235th Aerial Weapons Company during which we killed two Vietnamese farmers, probably man and wife—and they turned out to be friendlies, at least that's what the province chief said. I cannot stop thinking about them and my possibility of going straight to Hell over their deaths. I am also sick of the confusion, frustration, waste of life, free-fire zones, and body counts in this God forsaken place. I am revolted by having to decide who I can legally kill and who might not be a legal kill, with only my map-reading skill determining who is in the free-fire zone and who is outside of it.

More frustrating is having some corrupt South Vietnamese civilian decide who is a VC and who is not. And it is revolting to me to see us give brand new farm tractors to Vietnamese farmers one day and then have to blow up the farmers and tractors a few days later when some Vietnamese politician apparently decides these farmers are now VC or VC sympathizers.

The lines of morality here are so unclear and fluid. Right and wrong seems to be changed daily by the South Vietnamese; and it is all nauseating to me. I was not a saint when I arrived in Vietnam, but I wanted to do the right thing as a warrior and now perhaps I am one of Satan's own?

Take good care of yourself, old friend. We have to survive this mess and go back home to our families and to fishing in South Carolina and North Carolina.

Sincerely,

Larry

Vipers Intercepting Enemy Troops in the Open

"VHPA records show that 7,013 UH-1 Hueys served in the Vietnam War. Almost all were Army. Total helicopters destroyed in the Vietnam War were 5,086 out of 11,827."[90]

One of the Tigers flew me, my duffel bag, my flight helmet, my side arm, and my M16 up to Can Tho and dropped me off. I walked over to the 235th area and reported to headquarters. I was warmly welcomed and escorted to a temporary room where I would be sleeping for the next two weeks. I was shown where the flight line was, where the aircraft were parked in revetments, and where the latrines, mess hall, and showers were located. I ran into one of my warrant officer flight school classmates, WO1 Larry Bodell, that night and talked to him briefly. We promised to have a beer together as soon as we could get back together and catch up on what we had been doing for the past six months. I was not close to Larry Bodell during flight school mainly because he was not in my flight platoon, but he was a nice guy and it was so good to see a familiar face. During flight school and warrant officer training, I seldom was able to talk with or interact with the guys outside of that small group of 39 warrant officer candidates in my flight.

I arrived at Can Tho Army Airfield in mid-February 1969 with mixed emotions. I felt like I was watching my mother-in-law drive off a cliff in my new Mercedes. I was excited and happy to be learning to fly and to use the Army's newest and most-advanced gunship—the AH-1G Cobra! But at the same time, I would be living in temporary quarters, in a strange and new place, away from my unit, trusted friends, the familiarity of Huey gunships, our Huey gunship low-level tactics, and Soc Trang.

I also knew about the VC Sapper (Commando) Team attack on Can Tho and the 235th's Cobras that took place on the early morning hours, during darkness, the night of January 13, 1969— just a month before I arrived. That VC Sapper attack resulted in the destruction of seven Cobras, one Huey, and two Chinooks. More tragically, a 235th Cobra pilot was killed by the sappers while he tried to get to his aircraft from the ready hootch. The 235th aircraft and the ready hootch were near the perimeter. I was told that the VC entered undetected and then raced to the flight line, where they made quick work of those ten helicopters with their AK-47s and their explosives and they killed the poor Cobra pilot in his aircraft's revetment.

My unit's gun platoon, the 121st AHC Vikings was one of the gunship units to respond to that sapper attack and who helped end it. I can't help but wonder if such an attack might take place while I am at Can Tho and so unfamiliar with everything. The Can Tho airfield security was increased after the sapper attack and the 235th now has a Cobra in the air all night long as part of the increased security. To say the least I am anxious and will sleep with my M16 at the ready every night of my short tour of duty with the Vipers.

To add to my worrying about sappers, I need to make new friends, learn a great deal about Cobras in a short time, start out immediately serving as the front seat pilot and gunner, serve as a navigator on most missions, and get use to new tactics. I found it morbid and unsettling that some senior guys referred to Cobra front seat drivers as the "bullet stopper or meat in the seat."

I recently heard the amazing story about the US Army's 235th Cobras saving US Air Force Captain Ronald R. Fogleman, an F-100 Supersabre pilot with the 510th Tactical Fighter Squadron who had been shot down in the Delta in January, 1969—just a month or so ago. Fogleman's F-100 was shot down. The 235th Cobras responded to the area that Fogleman parachuted into. The enemy was closing in rapidly on the downed Air Force pilot and there was no time to wait for a Huey or LOH to arrive and pickup the Air Force pilot. A Cobra piloted by the Fire Team Leader Warrant Officer Charles P. Haney landed while his wing ship covered. The front seat Cobra Pilot and Gunner Warrant Officer Steven Walston got out, under fire, and opened the ammo bay door for the Air Force guy to climb onto. The shook up and grateful Air Force pilot then slid in that 18-inch by 36-inch ammo bay door and they flew him out of harm's way, straight to safety of a major airfield just 20 minutes away. I bet that was the most exciting and cool ride of that USAF Captain's life. Army saves the Air Force again!

I actually had the pleasure of helping save another USAF pilot from the river that same day in January, when I was still flying as an aircraft commander in the Tiger slicks. I assume it was the F-100's other crew member. I responded to the Air Force Mayday call along with every other available Army helicopter in the area, and got there quickly to take over dragging the Air Force guy out of the river. An Army OH-6 light observation

Picture 42: Cobra Attack Helicopter Flying Low Level

Picture courtesy of Bill Schmidt.

1. Rocket pods and 2.75-inch folding fin aerial rockets were operated by the back seat aircraft commander.

2. 7.62mm miniguns on inboard pods were operated by the back seat pilot, who was the aircraft commander.

3. 7.62mm minigun and 40mm grenade launcher turret were operated by the pilot in the front seat. The pilot was referred to affectionately and sadistically as a "bullet catcher," "meat in a seat," and "bullet stopper." My friend and flight classmate, WO1 Larry Bodell was killed in this seat. God please bless his soul and comfort his family.

helicopter (LOH) could not accomplish the rescue due to all the survival gear the Air Force Pilot had with him. He had so much survival and flotation equipment around him that the LOH, which arrived just before we did, simply could not get him out of the water. The LOH backed away and allowed me to move my Huey in, half sinking it in the process of the rescue. With great effort, my crew chief and door gunner dragged him into our slick. I didn't get his name, but he was one happy dude when we dropped him off at Can Tho a few minutes later.

That first night at Can Tho, the chief warrant officer 2, a wing ship commander who would train me that first day, met with me. I am ashamed, that I cannot remember his name. He told me all about the 235th's mission and asked about my experience. He told me that we would be flying wing ship in a light fire team of two Cobras at 0500 hours the next day. I met him at the aircraft the next morning for a more detailed briefing and preflight training. We would fly in the U-Minh Forest. From the start, the wing ship AC let me fly and he showed me how to operate the weapons turret control and sight which was very similar to the Huey gunship flexible minigun sight and control. I also test fired the 40mm and 7.62mm miniguns in a free-fire zone that was en route to the area of our mission. We were to escort the brown water navy along a river and search and destroy enemy targets as well.

I instantly liked almost everything about the Cobra. It was much faster than the Huey, could carry more fuel, could carry much more ordnance (especially rockets), and dive longer and steeper. It also was much more stable and, therefore, if you were in trim (with the ball centered in your turn and slip indicator), your rockets hit what you were aiming at; and it was much quieter inside an enclosed cockpit with tandem seats. On the other hand, my Cobra's shorter cyclic stick was on my right side—not between my legs like it was in every other helicopter I had flown—and the Cobra front seat collective lever and throttle control was also much shorter, than I was accustomed to in the Huey.

Not having the luxury of two door gunners to cover our backsides while we were breaking away (turning away) from targets was a little unnerving at first, but two Cobras in a light fire team or three Cobras in a heavy fire team are an awesome killing team. And if the Cobras were working with OH-6 scouts, their ability to find and destroy the enemy multiplied by roughly ten. Two other things I did not like about Cobras: First and since we were enclosed within the canopy, I could not hear much of the enemy fire we'd be taking; and, second, my M16 rifle would not fit in the cockpit. The M16 is too darn long to be used in a Cobra. In a UH-1 B or C Model gunship with the back doors open and the front windows down, I could hear even a single round fired, if

PICTURE 43: SOC TRANG ARMY AIRFIELD 1968

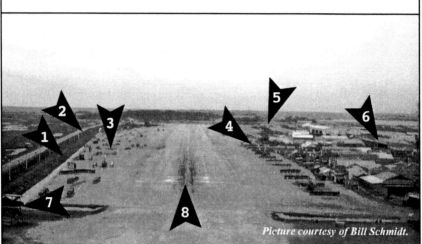

Picture courtesy of Bill Schmidt.

1. Perimeter concrete fighting bunkers, with gun slots and sandbag fighting positions on top.

2. Lighted east perimeter fence.

3. Tiger revetment parking.

4. Viking flight line.

5. Control tower.

6. 121st Maintenance hangar.

7. Guard Tower.

8. Runway 22 (220 degrees). Note the airfield was built in the shape of an aircraft carrier by the Japanese.

it was no more than a couple of hundred yards away and I could sling my M16 over the side of my armored seat—hopefully to still be there in the event of an emergency landing. When LOHs, gunships, and Cobras got shot down or had to make a precautionary landing due to mechanical problems, the crew had to defend itself until rescued.

I was enjoying the Cobra but not enjoying flying in the U-Minh Forest again. Every time I'd flown there previously my aircraft had taken a lot of enemy fire. The U-Minh was almost totally owned and occupied by the VC! The town of Ca Mau borders the U-Minh Forest, which is a huge mangrove forest covering 600 square miles of Ca Mau and Kien Giang provinces. It is the largest mangrove forest in the world outside of the Amazon. US patrol boats are frequently ambushed there, and the VC regularly plant mines in the canals.

I especially hated flying Huey defoliation missions over the U-Minh while spraying Agent Orange. My past experiences flying gunships that covered the defoliation helicopters in the U-Minh were also miserable, as we had to fly below the defoliation ship much of the time to adequately cover it. That meant we would have to fly through the wet and gooey clouds of hazardous chemicals (defoliant). The Agent Orange got all over our aircraft and us, and we had to fly all day with that stinking, hazardous, and slimy defoliant all over our aircraft, clothes, and equipment. Then when we got back to Soc Trang, the Agent Orange was hard to get off of everything, especially the aircraft.

As we approached the dark forest, our fire team leader told us to go hot on our weapons and to fire at anything we want—as the whole area we would be flying in was a free-fire zone. We started flying down a river and I did some recon by fire along both banks with the minigun and the 40mm. There were lots of beautiful birds in the area, and I hated to kill wildlife, but I figured, hell, the Agent Orange must be killing everything there anyway. The place was beautiful in many ways, with so much lush green vegetation, but the water was awful muddy and uninviting. I prayed we would never get shot down in that place because I was sure then as I am sure now that the VC would get me before another US Army helicopter or ground force could.

As we flew, I recalled some of the single-ship missions I had flown in the U-Minh as a Tiger slick pilot, when we would drop off a single Navy Seal just as the night was arriving, at some remote coordinates and would not come back for him until two or three days later at another LZ. They all seemed to be sniper, scout, pathfinder, paratrooper, frogman, and super-secret recon expert, all rolled into one. We frequently conducted combat assaults in areas near where the Seal had been dropped off the very next day or so. My God, those guys had giant balls!

I had gotten pretty good at firing the 40mm and the 7.62mm minigun on our Viking Huey gunships but had not shot enough with the Cobra weapons to know how good I might be with the turret weapons. There were lots of small streams and canals running off to the right and left of the river we were flying over, and some of them had narrow, wooden foot bridges across them. Those narrow foot bridges were built with two supporting approximate 14 feet long bamboo or other wooden poles driven into the mud of the creek bottom and forming an X with the poles. The poles were tied or nailed together where they passed each other at the center of the X that the poles formed. The VC and NVA then laid approximate six inch wide by10 feet to 12 feet long plank or log on top of the X joint formed by the supporting poles. The walking planks overlapped each other. These were similar to the kind of bridges my childhood friends and I had built in and around the rice fields of SC in my pre-teen years. These X shaped supporting pole configuration were sunk into the mud and the crude foot bridges were sturdy and could hold more weight than anyone could imagine. There were also plenty of highly used trails in the area leading to these foot bridges.

Just as we approached a narrow canal, about 40 feet across, running off the left side of the river, an NVA soldier in full uniform, with helmet, backpack, and rifle, burst out of the jungle and ran onto the bridge. Luckily I already had the turret facing to the 10 o'clock position near the bridge. I took quick aim and squeezed off about ten 40mm rounds. Unbelievably four or five of the rounds hit the foot bridge's walking plank, each round bursting behind the running soldier. Although the soldier never slowed and was across the bridge in three seconds—the purely lucky 40mm hits were sights to see. The NVA had to have some hot 40mm shrapnel fragments in his ass. The wing ship commander declared, "Damn Dandridge, you are a dead eye with the 40mm cannon!" I did not tell him it was the first time I was ever sure I had hit an enemy soldier with the 40mm thumper (grenade launcher).

We took a little fire and broke left and came back around, but nothing developed from our reconnaissance by fire so we headed up-river. We passed a graveyard, in the middle of no-where, along the west bank of the river. The wing ship commander told me to shoot up the cemetery, as that was a tactic the Vipers said that they frequently used to draw the enemy out. I fired several hundred rounds all around the area, but again we only took some sporadic fire and then it ceased too. We discovered some sunken and camouflaged sampans in shallow water. We could clearly see there were lead boxes of ammunition in them. We fired a pair of rockets into those boats and then turned north up the river after the US Navy boats we were covering.

We covered the Navy boats up and down the river, rearmed and refueled a couple of times, and then returned to Can Tho with no confirmed kills that day. On the way back to Can Tho my AC told me the definition of a helicopter, "thousands of parts flying in close formation around an oil leak waiting for metal fatigue to set in!"[91] This doomsday definition of a helicopter being an accident ready to happen combined with my thinking about how infuriated I would have been if the VC or NVA had blown up my family's little "Red Oak Cemetery" in Cottageville, SC, sent cold shivers down my spine. If we had been shot down by that cemetery, the VC would have had no mercy on us!

We flew missions all around IV Corps each day and each day I gained more and more admiration of the Cobra and more respect for the 235th pilots who took good care of me. The 235th guys were patient with my many questions about the sleek new attack helicopter and they were eager to show me how terrific their new attack helicopter was. A few days after I arrived, while flying southwest of Can Tho, the Viper fire team I was flying with got word that Larry Bodell had been shot through the head and killed instantly. I was told it was the only hit the aircraft took. Damn! How bad could Larry's luck have been? I silently said a prayer for him and said to myself, "I have got to get back to Soc Trang and then on to Hawaii to see my wife. I have to see my peaceful and wonderful USA."

That day with the 235th I had come to clearly see that Vietnam and this war in general is no place for anyone from the USA, at least no one who was sane would want to be here. Just as I know I could defeat any enemy in the swamps, marshes, mountains, and forests of my beloved South Carolina, I was certain that the VC felt the same about their country. And just as I know that I would resist any invader of US soil, for any length of time, and die if necessary, I have come to realize that Vietnam and these swamps, jungles, forests, rivers, and mountains "are the beloved homes of these VC" and they are not going to give up no matter how many of them we kill! I just do not see where or how we can win the hearts and minds of these people while we kill so many people and destroy so many of the forests, hamlets, animals, people, and other things that they love. More than ever, I really don't think I want to be a career soldier. However, I do love flying, I do like many things about being a soldier, and I certainly love these great men I serve with. No wonder my WWII combat Marine stepdad was such a serious guy, so strict with me, and so protective of me—and so worried when I left for Vietnam.

The 235th AWC missions I flew were generally similar to the ones I had been flying in gunships in the 121st, with the exception of my last two missions. The 235th guys had reinforced my knowledge of aerial fire ballistics and the tactics used to best survive as a helicopter pilot in Vietnam's DELTA region. During my six months in IV Corps, I had become a highly skilled slick aircraft commander and now a novice attack (gunship) helicopter pilot. At least I now understood the basic science that deals with the motion of projectiles (2.75-inch folding fin rockets, 40mm grenade, 50 cal door gun, 7.62-mm door gun, and 7.62-mm minigun). I am now acutely aware of the fact that whenever the bore line axis of the weapon differs from the flight path of the helicopter the velocity of the helicopter causes a change in the direction and velocity of the projectile.

My training and weapons operator experience at the 121st and the 235th had shown me firsthand that there is a lot to flying and shooting accurately. I now know the 2.75-inch folding fin rocket motor burns out approximately 1.7 seconds after launch, and I know that the angle of attack will influence the rocket's warhead fragmentation pattern, with low angles of attack producing an elongated fragmentation pattern and high angles producing a more symmetrical and concentrated pattern. It is also now evident that surface conditions (trees, buildings, bunkers, water, etc.) also greatly affect rocket effectiveness and lethality. My 235th training made me acutely aware of the significant effects the following things have on the accuracy or inaccuracy of my shooting and perhaps my survival:

No.	Ballistic Rules & Effects	Explanation[92]
1.	Port/Starboard Effect on 7.62mm and 40mm Flexible Weapons (and Door guns).	Due to projectile drift and trajectory shift combined, I have to lead fire to the left of the target to hit it, but because projectile drift tends to cancel trajectory shift, little or no correction is needed, depending on range to target.
2.	Firing into the Wind or with a Tail wind.	Requires no compensation laterally, but some adjustment is required for range.
3.	Projectile Drift.	Caused by the horizontal-plane gyroscopic effect. Gyroscopic precession and gravity cause the projectile to drift to the right and the gunner to aim left of target.
4.	Barrel/Tube Wear (and Cleanliness)	Residue and projectile movement results in loss of muzzle velocity and may induce yaw. Frequent cleaning of weapons and barrel changing are necessary.
5.	Wind Drift.	Cross winds cause the projectile to drift/move with the wind. The gunner must aim upwind to compensate.
6.	Projectile Weight.	Heavier projectiles will have lower velocities, if all other factors are the same. I have no control over it.
7.	Propellant Burning.	Is effected by temperature and moisture, but I have no control over it.

8.	Propellant Charge.	The amount of charge is fixed.
9.	Barrel Twist.	Most Army weapons have a right-hand twist. I have no control over this, but most Army weapons generally have projectiles with a clockwise spin.
10.	Drag.	The air resistance between the projectile and the air. Drag reduces velocity and limits effective range.
11.	Gravity.	Causes projectile drop depending on distance to target and muzzle velocity of the projectile, and must be compensated for.
12.	Air Temperature and Density.	Effects drag and propellant burn rate. I have no control over this.
13.	Humidity.	Effects density altitude and drag. I have no control over this.
14.	Yaw of a Projectile in Flight.	Yaw is the angle between the centerline of the projectile and the trajectory. High yaw angles cause trajectory change and increased drag.
15.	Velocity of the Helicopter.	The velocity of the aircraft is added to the muzzle velocity of spin stabilized projectiles to determine projectile (7.62mm bullet or 40mm cannon projectile) speed if the weapon is fired in the stowed (fixed) mode.
16.	2.75-inch Rocket Fins	The primary purpose of the rocket fins is to ensure that the center of pressure on the rocket in flight follows the center of gravity of the rocket (which is forward due to warhead weight).

17.	Aircraft Trim for Rocket Firing	The "relative wind effect (a greater cross wind effect)" causes a rocket to weather vane into the wind if a rocket is fired while the aircraft is out of trim either horizontally or vertically. For rocket fire to be accurate, the pilot must ensure that the aircraft is in "trim." If the tactical situation does not permit aligning the helicopter into the wind, an upwind correction is applied.
18.	In Trim Horizontally for Rocket Firing	If the turn and slip indicators needle and ball are not centered, the aircraft will be out-of-trim and a horizontal relative wind will be induced.
19.	In Trim Vertically and Proper Aircraft Power Setting for Rocket Firing	The proper power setting is needed to maintain a desired rate of descent and airspeed to keep the aircraft moving in a straight line towards the target. If power is too low, rockets will impact short. If power is too high, rockets will impact long.
20.	Hover Rocket Fire	Must adjust fire according to rocket impact. Can be out of trim vertically and horizontally at a hover due to rotor wash—there is no computer, just the pilot's brain.
21.	The Right War Head	Use Flechettes (nails) for troops in open, high explosive for harder targets. Use 17-pound high explosive war heads on the engine deck of enemy tanks.

PICTURE 44: FIRST LT. GENE BOOTH AND SIX OF HIS VIKINGS

Picture courtesy of Bill Schmidt.

1. White Tiger Platoon Leader 1st Lieutenant Claude Stanley.

2. Warrant Officer Randy Roe.

3. * Warrant Officer Jim Castillo.

4. Viking 1st Lieutenant George Taylor.

5. * Warrant Officer Bill Ellis.

6. 1st Lieutenant Gene Booth, Viking 26. Note the big mustache!

7. * Warrant Officer Bob Johnson.

8. CPT Sid Seitz. Vikings wore black tee shirts and black berets (not worn this day to company awards ceremony).

9. * Warrant Officer Mike Sherman.

10. Notice the black tee shirts.

*Note: Not positive identification. Could not confirm with person in the picture.

During my time with the Vikings, I had learned that the impact area of the 2.75-inch flechette rocket depended on the steepness of the angle of attach of the aircraft, and I had learned that the spread of destruction and kill zone was dependent upon the range the rocket was fired from. Rockets are usually fired in pairs and the more armament we carried, the more fuel we had to trade off due to the extreme weight of the 2.75-inch rockets, the 7.62mm, and 40mm ammunition. The flechette rockets would burst just short of the target, and a puff of red smoke would dispense upon rocket detonation. We could not really see the darts, but the red smoke told us if we had hit the area we were shooting at. Some of the Cobras carried two 19-shot and two seven-shot rocket pods in addition to the minigun and 40mm, but their fuel load was limited because of the heavier weight of more armament. Firing rockets accurately was a high-skill task due to so many variables the pilot had to take into account, including the angle of attack, crosswinds, the range estimation (especially difficulty at high speeds), visibility conditions, aircraft vibrations and changes in attitude, the speed of the target, proximity to friendly troops, and enemy ground fire.

The day before my last day with the 235th was my worst day yet in Vietnam other than the days Jerry Markland and Larry Bodell were killed. We Vipers were on IV Corps standby, just sitting by the already fueled, armed, preflight-checked, and ready-to-go Cobras when we got a quick reaction mission to fly about 30 miles or so east and south to intercept enemy troops in open fields and on some canals in sampans. We quickly mounted up, started, and took off. The fire team leader briefed us en route. I had my "one over the world scale map" of Vietnam and plotted the coordinates for the Viet Cong sighting. A small free fire area was designated, perhaps two miles long and one mile wide, and we were cleared to kill and destroy anything we came across that was or looked like, VC.

When we arrived in the area we found several sampans with VC flags flying and armed VC on board. We destroyed these vessels, killed several of the occupants, and continued our search of the area. After a few minutes, and with the death of Larry Bodell still fresh in our minds, we came upon a man and woman, wearing black pajamas and working in a large open and cultivated field. The area was so very green. The crop in the field reminded me of my grandparents' 150-acre farm and my parent's 20-acre farm in lower South Carolina.

I spent the first three years of my life on my dad and mom's tiny farm, and I lived with my grandparents on their farm near Cottageville, SC, about four weeks every year until I was about 14 years old. When I was only about a month old, John Clifton and Dorothy Joyce Dandridge had adopted me out of the Florence Crittenton Home on St. Margaret Street, in Charleston, SC. I have wonderful memories of picking cotton, pulling peanuts, shelling and grinding corn, picking and shelling butter beans, feeding chickens, taking water to cows, taking cows to water, milking cows, caring for infant pigs, throwing corncobs at wasp nests, swimming in ponds and creeks, hunting with BB guns, riding my grandfather's 40 year old mule "Dandy," and doing the hundreds of other chores and fun things on that farm. These two Vietnamese looked like farmers to me, and they eerily reminded me of my Grandfather Jesse and Grandmother Letitia Dandridge, and the farms in lower state South Carolina.

All of us Vipers and Vikings had heard of and some had actually encountered VC armed patrols in open fields that were surprised by the sudden appearance of our gunships. When surprised the VC would stop and start hoeing and digging with their weapons pretending to be farmers. From 1,000 feet they looked like farmers, but to a low-level fire team they looked like Viet Cong trying to fool us. These two people did not have weapons, but why were they working in an open field in a free-fire zone? Many Army pilots were tormented and discouraged at the way we waged this war in Vietnam, one day killing the people in an area and the next month we could not fire at obvious enemy targets in the same area.

This field was on the edge of the free-fire zone and our map was not all that accurate, so the fire team leader radioed in the target and confirmed what he had and where. The headquarters approved us to go ahead and kill the two Vietnamese. I felt terrible, as I got the order from the AC to kill them with the minigun. I discussed the final decision with the AC and went ahead and prepared to shoot these two unfortunate people. We came in low, from the west to east and not more than 50 feet above ground level. The two Vietnamese started running away from our aircraft. My head was about to explode with guilt, doubt, and depression, but I did my duty and shot about 500 rounds or so at these two middle aged people. Each of these Vietnamese was blown across the ground what appeared to be about 10 feet by the multiple 7.62mm rounds that struck and ripped open their bodies. I estimate they were each struck by 40 to 50 rounds. To my horror, they were still crawling on the ground—*really dead, but not knowing it, not wanting to face it*, their adrenalin trying to pull them back to the sunshine and green beauty all around them, while Satan sucked the blood out of their torn open arteries in torrents of crimson.

The fire team leader told us he was going to come around so that I could finish them off, and I said to myself, "I cannot shoot them again. I am going to hell for this!" To my relief the wing ship commander said, "Don't shoot them. I will finish them off with a pair of rockets." We came around, lined up on the two crawling and blood-covered Vietnamese, and he let a pair of rockets into them. They were instantly blown into thousands of pieces by the high explosive rockets. I could not see any obvious large pieces of their bodies as we flew over where two human beings had been crawling moments before, but there was a red mist in the air and one lone foot of the two extinct human beings lay smoldering in the field.

We continued searching the area for another 20 minutes, then returned to Can Tho to rearm and refuel. We four pilots in the two aircraft were unusually quiet going home. Right after we landed, an operations officer came up to us and told us we had killed two friendly Vietnamese civilians. We were each very saddened, but I was mortified. I could not believe I had let myself shoot those two poor souls—whether or not we had clearance to shoot or not. I was sick to my stomach and although not overly religious—I did believe in one supreme God and heaven and hell. I knew from the moment I pulled that minigun trigger that I would have no chance to make it to heaven.

The Viper Fire Team was asked to explain what happened and after our explanation, the incident was closed. There was no further investigation. The good we had done destroying enemy sampans and killing armed VC was, in my opinion, all wiped away by the death of those two poor Vietnamese farmers. Luckily we had no more missions that day, so we had some beers at the bar that night and went to bed and prepared for another day. I tried to put the incident out of my mind and just told myself, "I am not going to think about that today, I have other work to do." The problem is, those two farmers keep coming back in my dreams (nightmares) at night and in my thoughts during the day—I have a guilty conscience and I am not sure how I will handle that incident for the rest of my life.[93]

The next day, I flew one last mission with the Vipers on a quick reaction to a South Vietnamese Mechanized Infantry Battalion that had engaged and partially surrounded a hard-core VC Regimental-size unit between Can Tho and Vinh Long. When we arrived on station, eight or nine Cobras from the B Troop, 3/17th US Air Cavalry stationed at Dong Tam were attacking the well entrenched and bunkered enemy troops in dense jungle. The South Vietnamese tracks were in a semi-circle facing the enemy-hardened locations. Several of the ARVN's tracked vehicles were burning and smoking. Much more firing was coming out of the jungle from the enemy locations than there was South Vietnamese fire going in. The Cavalry Cobras were also taking a beating with several shot up and making emergency landings at Vinh Long. All of us Vipers were still shaken up from Larry Bodell's death and the prior day's mission.

Within five minutes of our arrival, the B Troop Cavalry's Cobras withdrew and returned to Dong Tam, licking their wounds, and we were cleared to attack. My first thought was, *Damn, a whole Air Cavalry Troop's attack fleet could not adequately suppress or slow down that enemy fire and now two little Viper Cobras are going to try to do what the CAV could not do with nine Cobras!* Just as we started to roll in using a high-altitude attack, we were called off and told to orbit a mile southwest while artillery pounded the area. The artillery smashed the area for about five or ten minutes before we were again given the go ahead to attack. The enemy fire returned more intensely than before as soon as the artillery let up.

Again I thought, Artillery and the Air Cavalry haven't slowed these little VC bastards down, why does anyone in IV Corps Headquarters believe two Vipers can get this job done? Just as we prepared to begin our rocket and gun run, we were called off to circle southwest again while US Air Force Tactical Air (fighter bombers) used their 20mm cannons and 500-pound bombs on these VC devils.

Two USA F-100 Super Sabers 4s arrived. They first attacked from south to north and dropped their 500-pound bombs. Then they made a second attack with their cannons, again south to north. Those fast movers took a huge amount of enemy fire on both of their passes and on the second pass the lead aircraft took a number of hits from the ground fire and declared an emergency. The Tactical Air broke off their attacks and limped for home. There was no doubt what would happen next. Our dreaded orders came quickly from the command and control aircraft, "Vipers you are cleared to attack!" Our fire team leader instructed the gunner (peter pilot) in his aircraft to begin firing the minigun as soon as they were within range. He told my aircraft commander, the wing ship commander to have me (the wing ship gunner and peter pilot) do the same thing when we started our attack.

The fire team leader told us that we were going to make one altitude attack from south to north, starting at 2,500 feet, and expend all rockets by 1,500 feet and then head for home. I started lobbing 7.62mm rounds into the enemy positions before we even started our rocket run. I hosed down the approximate 1,000 meter by 500 meter area with my minigun, only stopping when rocket firing activated the minigun interrupter switch (rocket firing automatically interrupts the minigun). I swear the rounds and tracers coming up at us appeared to exceed the 4,000 or so 7.62mm rounds per minute that I was pouring into the VC positions. My AC fired all 52 of our Cobra's 2.75-inch rockets as fast as they could be fired and we headed for Can Tho just as the sun was going down. Thank goodness we were not called out again that day.

Back at Soc Trang, I prepared to go on rest and recuperation (R and R). Each day since the killing of the two Vietnamese farmers I told myself that mistakes happen in war and that I did not intentionally kill the wrong people. This was war and it has happened to many others and will happen again. Every day, I said the same prayer asking for God and these poor dead farmers and their families to forgive me. I asked the good Lord to please take those two poor souls to heaven. When those farmers came into my mind in the daytime and night, I told myself, "I cannot do anything about it now. It was just a mistake. I am *not* going to think about that today. I am tough, I am a warrior, and I am an America Soldier. I just need to stay focused on flying safely, doing my job, and living through these five more months of combat in Vietnam. I am sure my luck will hold out after I return from R and R. It doesn't mean anything!"

CHAPTER 13: JUNE 25, 1969 ◄
"Milk Run."[94]

*Letter from Warrant Officer 1 Danny Hickman
to Warrant Officer 1 Larry Dandridge*

Date: 25 June 1969

From: Warrant Officer Danny H. Hickman,
Troop B, 3rd Squadron, 17th Air Cavalry Regiment, APO SF
01915

TO: Warrant Officer Larry Dandridge
1413 Pooshee Drive
Charleston, SC 29407

Dear Larry,

Got your letter this week and am glad to hear you are on convalescent leave and recovering from your last crash and wounds. I hope the Army doesn't send you a bill for all the helicopters that were shot out from under you. It was especially good to learn that they have "unwired" your jaw, and that things are improving.

From the little news we get here in Vietnam, we have heard that it's the "Summer of Love" in America. If you figure out what a "love-in" is; write and tell us over here in Vietnam. We are not seeing much love here; and frankly, I've heard about but haven't seen any drugs here either.

The war has been heating up for us. Bravo Troop is still based here in Dong Tam where there are no "love-ins," though we did have an adrenaline rush when a VC mortar round blew up our ammo dump. Larger North Vietnamese Units (NVA) are moving south. We are now seeing NVA regulars in regimental strength south of Saigon. Ironically President Nixon is beginning to pull U.S. forces out, with another 25,000 leaving soon. Uncle Ho (Chi Minh) is shrewd to take advantage of the US draw-down. However, those of us left here are fighting shorthanded against increasing numbers of enemy.

Our Cavalry Troop has 26 helicopters (10 Cobras, 10 LOHs, and 6 slicks). Since I've been here, 19 of the original 26 have been destroyed and replaced. Most were lost to battle damage, but we've had a few accidents also. Our flight school buddy, Danny Hamrick, was injured badly and shipped back to the US. Warrant Officer Jim Newman got shot in the neck, but he's OK; and CPT Elmore Jordan got home without a scratch, despite many close calls.

I'm getting nearer to my DEROS (going home date) but just yesterday got into one of the damnedest fights I've been in lately. Warrant Officer Gene Combs and I were flying a milk run (convoy cover) and blundered into a platoon of NVA less than four clicks from the Dong Tam perimeter. We killed several of them and got back with minor damage to our LOH. Anyway, I'll see you in a couple of months. Am looking forward to clean sheets, pretty girls, and Sundays off again. In the meantime, take care of yourself; and I hope to see you back in the cockpit again by the time I get there.

Your friend,

Dan

Milk Run![95]

"Never share a foxhole (or cockpit) with someone braver than you."

– Anonymous

There was a running joke that Bravo Troop's scout platoon had a 100 percent casualty rate. No, not all scout pilots got wounded; but some got wounded twice just to keep up the statistic. My good friend and Scout Pilot Warrant Officer 1 Gene Combs had already been wounded once. He'd been hit in the leg by a grenade fragment during one of his scout training flights. A wiry, plain-talking guy from Arkansas, Gene was fun to be around but took his duty as a scout pilot deadly serious.

To say aero-scouting was routinely dangerous is an understatement. Flying scout missions in the armed OH-6 (Hughes 500) helicopter with its single minigun (Gatling-type gun) was atypical, even in Vietnam. A two-man crew operated this agile helicopter, giving it a huge power reserve. Also unusual, the pilot flew from the right seat, while the observer/co-pilot was in the left seat.

Their low-level missions put them face-to-face with the enemy on a daily basis. In the thick jungle and tall grass, most engagements were mere feet from scout helicopters. The pilot, in the right seat, normally flew most of the time and fired the minigun. The observer/CP in the left seat fired a CAR-15 submachine gun and threw grenades from the open left door. The observer's job was also to report sightings to the pilot and engage "targets of opportunity." The rear compartment was filled with a single 2,000 round belt of ammunition for the minigun.

Scout missions were not just low level; they typically flew low and slow enough to see into houses, bunker doors, and between the trees. Scout crews usually killed as many or more of the enemy than our best Cobra (AH-1G) drivers, who had far more munitions on their heavy attack helicopters.

It was Summer 1969, and today's mission was supposed to be a milk run—just a routine armed reconnaissance for a large truck convoy moving north from the 9th Infantry Division base camp in Dong Tam. The threat of ambush was so rare on this route that a single armed OH-6 would provide security. My friend WO1 Gene Combs drew the assignment; and even though close to becoming a "short-timer" (going home in a few weeks), I got my Command and Control job changed in order to fly this mission as his co-pilot. Flying a route recon with Gene promised to be a fun day of easy flying in a hot-rod helicopter—just a milk run with a good friend.

The day began routinely enough. We got to the flight line before daylight and preflighted and inspected the Scout Bird, which had been pre-armed by the crew chief. We took special care around the loaded minigun and checked pins and loading of the offensive grenades. The armed OH-6 was fully loaded with our standard configuration of 2,000 rounds for the minigun. Thirty loaded magazines for the stubby CAR-15 were crammed into a canvas bag atop the instrument panel, and four cases of assorted grenades were piled between the seats or hanging on taunt safety wires strung around the already cramped cockpit. With a huge power reserve at our disposal, we also carried a full fuel load, which gave us the luxury of almost three hours of flight time.

Wearing our bullet-resistant chicken plates, we slid sideways into the cramped seats and secured ourselves with the aircraft's shoulder harnesses and seat belts. The start-up was routine. Gene and I were joking as he fired up the turbine. We seldom got to fly together so we looked forward to the day. As our small turbine engine began to spin up, the sweet smell of JP-4 jet fuel surrounded us. The fuel odor was soon blown clear by the rotor wash and replaced with whirling bits of fine dust and sand. As our main rotor gained speed, we were quickly enveloped in the world of noise and vibration that is the domain of all helicopter pilots.

With engine RPM rising into the green, I called on the FM radio for artillery clearances to make sure we didn't fly into any friendly fire. Simultaneously, Gene called the tower on the UHF radio and cleared us for takeoff. All instruments were "in the green" and we were soon zooming off the east end of Dong Tam airfield into the early morning ground fog. Gene closed the circuit breaker that armed the minigun. I jammed a loaded magazine into the CAR-15 and jacked the charging handle to chamber a round. We were hot and ready now, though we really didn't expect any action today.

We stayed very low, hooking back to the north across the treetops to intercept Highway One and our convoy, which was exiting the main gate as we were taking off. As soon as we identified the convoy, we tuned to their radio frequency and checked in with the convoy commander. Then we sprinted ahead of the lumbering trucks just beneath us and began checking the roadside ahead. We were looking for trouble, though not expecting any—this was a milk run. We were soon greeted by a brilliant sun rising from the eastern horizon. The ground fog slowly began to burn away. This was going to be a good day.

It was a hoot! After flying overloaded Hueys, zooming around in this nimble OH-6 was like moving from a heavy truck to a sports car. Even fully loaded, we could hover out of ground-effect and accelerate quickly. As we cut tight left-hand circles through the tops of fog-shrouded palm trees, I was awed by the power and responsiveness of our little sportster. In the humid air, water droplets traced tiny trails from our rotor tips. Flying so low and without doors, we could smell the green jungle and even the water buffalos that bolted as we passed just above their broad backs. At times, we literally brushed the palm fronds with our skids, sending showers of silvery dew sparkling into the jungle below.

Gene was jinking the aircraft—never flying in straight lines and changing course rapidly every few seconds. He varied our speed but averaged around 30 knots, occasionally coming to a brief hover in order to take a longer look at something we couldn't identify. We still joked a lot though we had settled into the routine of scouting, looking for any telltale sign of the elusive enemy and checking out every potential ambush site along the route. I test fired the stubby CAR-15 into a rice paddy 10 feet below our skids and was reassured to see a perfect stitch pattern as the bullets impacted the water. Gene joked about the prospect of surprising naked girls showering in the back yard of farmhouses along the route, and we continued our mission—always searching for the enemy.

After about twenty minutes of Gene's erratic flying with me hanging out the left door looking down into the trees, I began feeling queasy. As embarrassing as it was, it was motion sickness. The solution was simple. Without mentioning the nausea, I asked Gene to let me fly the aircraft. I handed him the CAR-15 and took over the flight controls. Our search pattern then changed as we flew right-hand circles to keep Gene (in the right seat) positioned to best observe the ground below. Trimming the aircraft and making gentler turns helped to settle my stomach. Watching the horizon always helps clear the head, and in a few minutes I was feeling much better.

With a settled stomach, flying became enjoyable again. We continued scouting ahead of the convoy. A wide turn took us deeper into the jungle where we passed through the yard of a

Picture 45: Warrant Officer And Aircraft Commander Danny Hickman 1969

Picture courtesy of Dan Hickman.

B Troop 3rd/17th Air Cavalry Squadron red and white scarf.

large tile-roofed farmhouse about 600 meters off the convoy route. As we slowly flew across the dirt yard, we both saw a surprised North Vietnamese Army (NVA) soldier cleaning his AK-47 in the doorway of the house. Though shirtless, he wore the distinctive green trousers of the North Vietnam Army uniform. This NVA soldier was no immediate threat to our convoy, but we had found the enemy. The green uniform and the AK-47 were a death sentence.

"Did you see that? Did you see that NVA?" Gene was shouting over the intercom.

"He's an NVA for sure! Let's call it in," I responded.

"Hell no, let's kill him. It won't take but a minute!" Gene shot back. Gene was the aircraft commander and I was the co-pilot, so I deferred to Gene's decision; even though it seemed unwise and outside the envelope of our primary mission of protecting the convoy.

As soon as we cleared the farmhouse yard, Gene handed me the CAR-15 and took over the controls again. We then began an argument (debate) that would last for the rest of the flight. Since the NVA soldier was obviously no immediate threat to our convoy, it stood to reason that we should report the sighting and call in a gun team, a pair of Cobra attack helicopters that could attack the house with rockets. From hard experience, I knew that NVA soldiers were never alone—there were bound to be more of them nearby. Our primary job was to guard the convoy, which was now moving further away from us. Gene passionately disagreed. Though senior to him, I deferred because this was his mission and he was the AC; and he had the final say. "Well, we should at least report the sighting," I protested.

"Hell no!" Gene said as he circled through the trees about 400 meters from the house. Gene was popping up for quick looks. Now very excited, he said, "There he is again. He's standing just inside the door. We'll have him killed in just a minute, and then we'll get back to our convoy." In brief glimpses of the house, I could see the green-clad NVA soldier's legs as he stood in the shadows inside the doorway. Gene was determined that we were going to kill this man. Until then, our convoy was on its own.

Gene circled to come in from a different direction, bouncing up and down out of the tree tops to keep the house in sight. As we prepared for our attack, Gene began snapping orders, "Get a Willie-Pete (White Phosphorus Grenade) ready. I'm going to make another pass through the yard. When we hover by the door, you throw the grenade into the house." Then Gene banked hard over, dropped down into the yard, and went straight at the house. Gene flew right up to the door, jerked the aircraft right, and yelled, "Throw it now!"

I threw the grenade…and missed! It hit the wooden door frame and dropped onto the threshold near a large crockery urn. Gene pulled full power, and we roller-coastered over the house as the grenade exploded with a burst of fire and white smoke. After bounding over the house, Gene dropped us into the back yard and made a quick 270 degree right-pedal turn. Scarcely hesitating, he accelerated through the back yard and around the left side of the house now just 40 feet outside our open left door. We were flying five or six feet above the hard-packed dirt yard. Rounding the corner and entering the front yard again, there was movement to our front. Green uniformed soldiers, armed with AKs were sprinting across the open yard. Without pause or comment, Gene cut into them with the minigun, slewing the stream of fire left and right with his pedals. To my immediate left, three more NVA burst through the smoke-filled door. A long burst from the CAR-15 sent them tumbling. Gene fired several short bursts with the minigun while I changed magazines. Each time the minigun fired, we gladly suffered ear-splitting pain as hundreds of bullets swept the yard clean to our front. Now flying away from the house, we quickly passed over the enemy and had to pull up to clear the rapidly approaching jungle.

Then the roles switched, and we became the target for a bunch of mad enemy soldiers who now had the advantage of being behind us. Gene anticipated the NVA's next move and skillfully picked the nose up, pulled full power, and kicked in full left pedal. This maneuver made our aircraft appear to be heading left when we were actually turning slightly right. The OH-6 responded quickly; and we lurched upward, flying nose-left but turning to the right. Now vulnerable to enemy fire from behind, the helicopter strained for the safety of the jungle. Gene continued to hold our nose hard left, which allowed me a clear view to the rear. With a fresh magazine in the CAR-15, I leaned out the door and sprayed short bursts at green-clad soldiers while we exited the yard.

With another magazine emptied, I ducked back into the aircraft just as the air outside the left door filled with streams of green and red tracers. They were aiming to our left—the way the aircraft was pointed. Gene had made us a deceptive target - flying out of trim and pointed about 30 degrees left of our actual course which was a right turn. "That's an old scout trick, make em think you're going somewhere you're not!" Gene shouted excitedly. "Reload! We're going back at em!" he added as he doubled back to the right to set up another attack. "Always attack them from different directions." he said as if giving a class.

In the few seconds before the next run, I'm thinking, no one knows where we are or what we are doing. We haven't made a single report. Another concern was that we had completely abandoned the convoy we were supposed to be supporting. I'm also thinking that I'm a short-timer, and what the hell am I doing in a fight like this when I've got just a few weeks to survive before I can get on the freedom bird home?

As we turned inbound for our second run at them, Gene and I were in a non-stop debate about what to do next. I was for calling reinforcements, a gun team at least. Gene's response was, "Hell no! Let's kill as many as we can now. They're afraid of us!"

"They are afraid of us?" I repeated to myself. Now there was a comforting thought as we charged into them again. And I took note of the fact that the enemy's fear didn't seem to have stopped them from trying to shoot us down as we dodged through bursts of rifle fire. Though we had only fleeting glimpses of green clad enemy, they gave away their positions with streams of red and green tracers. Many of the enemy had moved away from the house and were in the brush on the west side of the yard. There were bodies in the yard as we charged through again, minigun blazing.

As we shot our way through the yard again, Gene shouted, "Drop a frag (M-26 fragmentation grenade) into the brush as we clear the yard. That'll help cover our getaway." Overflying the enemy once more, we climbed enough to clear the trees on the edge of the yard. Nearing the tree line, I leaned far out the door again and emptied another magazine in short bursts under our tail and dropped the fragmentation grenade I'd been holding with my left hand. The grenade disappeared into the leafy jungle below and exploded close enough to feel the concussion as we exited the yard. Over the jungle again after the second run, the air cleared of tracers, and we were again circling our prey. We orbited the yard, scanning for another opening. I made several attempts to radio our command and control bird, but got no response. Amazingly, we had little battle damage though tracers had streaked by close enough to reach out and touch. Gene's habit of flying out of trim was paying off—making us appear to be going in directions other than where we were truly headed. Overflying targets was the greatest risk.

Normally a scout was paired with a Cobra attack helicopter circling high above. Whenever the scout bird received ground fire, the Cobra would drop its nose and fire several rockets with high-explosive warheads to suppress the enemy. This tactic usually allowed the scout helicopter to break contact safely. But today, we were on our own. Alone without the Cobra we needed so badly. This wasn't a normal day.

Our lonely battle continued for long uncounted minutes, perhaps another hour. Several more runs through the enemy seemed to diminish their fire, and things became less chaotic. We weren't taking so much fire now and were seeing fewer signs of live NVA.

Circling about for yet another run, I spotted several medium-size 20- to 25-foot sampans hidden in a shallow creek near the house. It was a common technique for the enemy to travel by sampan at night and then remove the outboard engines and submerge the boats during the daylight hours. But by looking straight down into the water, we could see them clearly. We doubled back several times and dropped frag and concussion grenades into each of the boats. The grenade's effects in the shallow water were devastating. The NVA soldiers may have floated in, but any survivors would have to walk out.

We continued to hunt stragglers in the brush, occasionally catching a glimpse of one. As we slowly cruised about looking down into the bushes, I spotted a soldier running underneath our helicopter. I leaned out the door to shoot him with the CAR-15 and was about to pull the trigger when Gene shouted, "Wait Wait! Don't Shoot! I think it's an ARVN (South Vietnamese Army)." In that moment, I recognized the olive drab uniform as a "friendly" and let the lucky South Vietnamese soldier continue to run to the west. Only then did we notice a small ARVN outpost about 800 meters to our west. The ARVN and NVA units were on top of each other. It occurred to me then that our ARVN allies were taking no part in this fight against their and our arch enemy, the NVA. I had often suspected there was collusion between some ARVNs and the NVA, but we didn't have time to sort that out in the middle of this fight.

Gene and I had continued our argument throughout the fight. It was a great relief when I heard MAJ Willard Conklin's voice on the radio saying, "Stogie 13, this is Stogies 6, what the hell are you doing?" Hallelujah! The Calvary was on the way.

"Killing the enemy! We're killing NVA!" Gene answered. The troop commander quickly got a team of cavalry Cobras on the way, and then we began marking targets with colored smoke for the attack helicopters. Smoke grenade after smoke grenade went out the door to mark everything we'd found. The Cobras spewed high explosive rockets and torrents of canon fire into each marked location. In addition, I was still shooting at anything suspected to hold enemy, referring to it as "recon by fire." By now, empty ammo casings littered the cockpit and shiny brass empties rolled across the cockpit floor plates whenever we banked hard.

On one occasion, Gene asked what I was shooting at; and I explained that it was recon-by-fire. "You need to save your ammo." Gene said.

"Save ammo for what?" I asked.

"If we get shot down, we'll need that ammo," Gene shouted.

"Damn it! If we hand-off this mess and get back to our primary convoy mission, we won't get shot down," I said.

We'd been in close combat for about 90 minutes without a break. At that point I realized that I couldn't see clearly from my left eye. Sweat, dripping from my forehead, had completely obscured the left lens of my sunglasses. I ripped the glasses off and stuffed them in a cargo pocket. We were also running low on minigun ammo and were down to our last three grenades. About that time Gene called attention to our instrument panel. The generator wasn't putting out, and the aircraft battery was going down fast. Our turbine aircraft could still fly without electricity; but when the battery died, we'd lose the electrical-powered minigun along with our radios. We hadn't been shot down (yet), but we were soon to be combat-ineffective.

To my relief and Gene's dismay, we had to break off the attack and make the short flight back to base. On the flight back we passed another pair of Cobras on the way out to help us. We flew back

Picture 46: OH-6A Cayuse Light Observation Helicopter "The Famous Loach"

Picture courtesy of Dan Hickman

1. Not shown in picture, but smoke grenades were also carried, normally behind pilot's head.

2. M26 fragmentation, grenades.

3. Concussion grenades for use in bunkers.

4. Non adjustable armored seat wing (side) protection.

5. Green-colored white phosphorous (WP) grenades for burning and smoke.

6. Red-colored "thermite" incendiary grenades for burning hootches.

7. Armored seat bottom.

8. Minigun ammo tray.

9. Black colored throttle control (engine & rotor speed) and collective pitch (climb and descend) control.

10. Pouch for observer/gunner's extra CAR-15 Magazines.

11. Cyclic Control (for maneuvering left, right, forward and back and cyclic climbing) located between the pilot's and gunner's legs.

12. 7.62mm minigun.

into Dong Tam like we went out—low and fast. As we crossed the berm, Gene said, "Let's jump another aircraft and get back out there. We may still find more stragglers." He was in such a hurry that his landing hit the ground hard enough to cause our shoulder harnesses to lock against the strain, and the aircraft skidded forward a few feet before stopping. About that time, we got a radio call that our fight had taken place in an ARVN controlled area-of- operation, and all US forces were to break off the attack and withdraw. The politics of war had stopped our operation and would likely be sorted out slowly enough to allow the surviving NVA to recover their weapons, retrieve their wounded, and escape into the jungle.

During the entire flight, we had never climbed higher than 200 feet and had traveled only four kilometers from our base. On this single mission, Gene and I had fired approximately 2,500 rounds of ammunition and thrown three and one-half cases of hand grenades. The milk run was over.

That evening we enjoyed a beer and joked about the battle and our humorous argument. In our own way, we were letting off some stress and steam. Alive and going home in a few weeks, I wasn't sure whether to thank Gene for keeping me alive or kick his butt for almost getting me killed. His tactics had paid off, though. We'd discovered an NVA platoon, attacked them relentlessly, and probably upset some larger plan by one of the NVA regiments infiltrating our area-of-operation. And, to our great relief, the convoy we'd abandoned made it through just fine. Gene had been right to attack a target of opportunity quickly, and to take advantage of surprise and superior fire power. I didn't agree at the moment; and had our convoy been attacked, Gene would have been wrong. But the fortunes of war were with Gene Combs today. We fought a tough fight together and lived to laugh about it afterwards.

A few weeks later, Gene was shot down and wounded again. I was flying my slick on the same operation that day. Gene had been screening ahead of a US infantry unit when he and his observer/ gunner ran into an enemy light machine gun in the hands of a skilled crew. The infantry company became pinned down in tall elephant grass, and Gene aggressively flew forward to attack the machine gun crew. Problem was, he didn't know exactly where the machine gun was located; and the enemy gunner found Gene first. Gene's OH-6 came under fire from his 8 o'clock (left rear), and above the reeds and six-foot-tall grass there were few trees to duck behind for cover. Unable to turn and use his minigun to suppress the enemy machine gun, Gene's OH-6 was riddled by a single long burst from the enemy machine gun.

The hail of bullets knocked out the engine, and a single bullet wounded both Gene and his observer. A bullet broke Gene's left arm after passing through the observer's hip. With their engine shot out they went down fast. Gene's broken left arm prevented him from pulling up on the collective pitch control to cushion their crash landing. The helicopter hit hard at 40 knots, rolled several times, and caught fire as they came to rest. The burning helicopter was caught in a crossfire between the friendly and enemy lines. Gene was initially pinned in the bottom of the wreckage, but managed to free himself and crawl out through the broken chin bubble. Ignoring his wound and rising flames, Gene climbed back up onto the aircraft. Exposed to enemy fire, Gene used his good arm to unbuckle his wounded observer and pull him over the side of the burning helicopter. They both fell to the ground, where Gene began dragging him toward the friendly line. Gene's war was over for a while.

Within minutes the C and C aircraft was able to call in an air strike. Phantom jets dropped several napalm bombs forcing the enemy to withdraw. The wall of flames and billowing black smoke allowed us to safely extract the wounded. A medical evacuation helicopter whisked Gene and the observer away, heading for the nearest medical facility, the Third Surgical Hospital. As soon as we could break free, I flew my slick to the Third Surg also. After landing, I left the crew with the helicopter and rushed in to check on our wounded. The observer was already in surgery, and Gene was in the triage area lying on a stretcher among several other wounded. Though in significant pain, he was not complaining. His left arm was broken in two places; and according to the x-ray picture hanging over his stretcher, the bullet was still in his arm. We talked for a few minutes as morphine worked its magic. His last whispered words to me were, "I killed six more VC today—be sure and let the commander know." He was evacuated to a medical facility in Japan the next day.

Leaving the hospital, I was carrying Gene's and the Observer's blood spattered gear that they had hung on to throughout the evacuation. Lugging a chicken plate, two sub-machine guns, and two pistols, plus my own pistol must have looked unusual because a nurse turned around to walk beside me in the corridor. "What are you doing with all those guns?" she asked.

The war and my crew were waiting so I answered as we walked. "Ma'am, these are the tools of that war going on out there and I'm putting them back into service." Going home in ten days, there just wasn't time enough for long conversations. I would miss Gene. He was a great warrior, superb pilot, and a good friend.

CHAPTER 14: EPILOGUE ◄

Search and destroy had been abandoned when Army General Abrams took command of US Forces in Vietnam in June of 1968. It was replaced with smaller unit tactics of ambush and withdrawal. US Defense Secretary Melvin Laird's plan of October 1968 to shift the burden of the war to the South Vietnamese, called "Vietnamization," was going too slowly and US units continued to do the vast majority of the fighting and dying in Vietnam.

While Warrant Officers Brian King and I (WO1 Larry Dandridge) recovered in the 249th General Hospital at Camp Zama, Japan, US troop strength in Vietnam peaked at 543,400 on April 30, 1969. In May of 1969, the 101st Airborne Division suffered heavy casualties taking Ap Bia, Hamburger Hill. In May 1969, US Operation Speedy Express, conducted primarily by the US 9th Infantry Division in the Delta, claimed over 10,000 enemy casualties, the highest total for any US combat operation in the Vietnam War. On June 8, 1969, President Richard Nixon announced the withdrawal of 25,000 troops from Vietnam would take place by the end of August 1969.

By May of 1969, the US Army units operating in III and IV Corps were noticing a rebuilding of and more frequent contact with the vicious Viet Cong (VC) units that had been decimated in their failed January and February 1968 Tet Offensive. By June of 1969, North Vietnamese Army (NVA) regular units were being seen and engaged by US forces and South Vietnamese forces more frequently than ever in the Delta region of Vietnam. As Warrant Officer Danny Hickman mentioned in his June 25, 1969, letter to his wounded friend, Larry Dandridge, B Troop, 3rd of the 17th Air Cavalry Squadron and the other Army Aviation units in III and IV Corps were beginning to see more of the enemy, with no increase in help from the South Vietnamese Army.

The anti-war movement in the United States was also strengthening and civil rights injustices in the US were hurting Army morale[96] and cohesion worldwide in 1969. The US military effort in Vietnam was weakening, especially with the beginning of the withdrawal of the US 9th Infantry Division in July of 1969. Even though the vast majority of the South Vietnamese wanted independence from North Vietnam and in spite of the fact that this same vast majority of South Vietnamese wanted a non-communist government, the slide towards a North Vietnamese invasion and takeover of South Vietnam by communist North Vietnam had begun.

Based on Pentagon records, the Vietnam Helicopter Pilots Association (VHPA) estimate that over 40,000 helicopter pilots served in the Vietnam War. According to the VHPA website, total helicopter pilots killed in the Vietnam War was 2,202 and the total non-pilot crew members killed was 2,704. The number of Vietnamese killed in Army helicopters is unknown, but it had to be in the thousands.[97]

Helicopter crews suffered terribly high casualty rates, with approximately 4,906 killed in action (about ten per cent of all US KIAs). Approximately 20,000 more Army aviation warriors were wounded and injured by the enemy and as a result of accidents. However, in the author's opinion, the real heroes of the war were the officers, noncommissioned officers, and enlisted men who served in combat on the ground—Army Aviation's primary customers and comrades. It was our leg infantry, airborne infantry, cavalry and airmobile infantry, armor, combat engineers, and artilleryman who did not have the luxury of riding in helicopters everywhere they went. These ground pounders had little warm food, few showers or baths, no chicken plate (body armor) to wear, no clean uniforms for weeks at a time, and no soft cot and mosquito netting to come back to every night, as we aviators did at Soc Trang, Dong Tam, Can Tho, and other Army aviation major bases.

These earth bound heroes had to spend weeks and months at a time in the bush, the jungles, forests, swamps, plains of reeds, and mountains. The grunts (we called the infantry "grunts") lived in, slept in, and fought in swarms of disease-carrying mosquitoes, leeches, ticks, centipedes, caterpillars, ants, scorpions, and spiders. With deadly snakes[98] everywhere, our ground troops trekked slowly and arduously through some of the harshest terrain on earth. They endured choking smoke, and dust in the rice paddies in the dry season (from November to April in III and IV Corps). The grunts struggled through torrential down pours and water filled rice paddies, canals, streams, swamps, and rivers in the rainy season. They pushed themselves in daytime hellish heat and humidity, and the sticky, stinking mud and more mud. They pulled themselves up and down mountains during cold monsoon rains and they shivered through cold early morning and night helicopter rides.

The real heroes had to live with the constant fear of snipers, booby traps (today called Improvised Explosive Devices—IEDs), dung-covered punji sticks, barbed spike plates, spiked bamboo whip traps, bridge spike traps, spiked trap pits, punji bear traps, mines, and other ingenious VC and NVA killing and maiming devices. They had to cut and thrash and push their way through razor-sharp grass, strangling and exhausting vines, and stinging trees that could prove to be fatal with prolonged contact.[99]

They had to walk through, sit in, eat in, lie in, sleep in, and at times drink polluted water filled with deadly pathogens. They endured vertical rain, horizontal rain, and more rain. Even in the fire bases and base camps, the real heroes frequently lived in muddy, cold, water-filled trenches, bunkers, and foxholes. At best, they got to sleep in a tent or a building only on occasion. A shower and clean uniform and dry socks were nothing less than heaven to our ground combat arms soldiers. These real heroes walked, searched, climbed, swam, ran, and humped (carried) a huge load of equipment that was not limited to:

- An M16 rifle (seven pounds) with M7 bayonet or one of the following weapons: Model 12 Winchester pump shotgun (nine pounds) or M60 machine gun (23 pounds) or M9A1-7 Flame Thrower or M19, the 60 mm mortar (a team weapon) or M67 Recoilless Rifle (a team weapon) or 45 Caliber Pistol (some carried both pistol and rifle), or M79 grenade launcher (with a very heavy 40mm ammunition filled vest).

- Heavy ammunition and magazines for their weapon (troops with the M16 carried three or four bandoleers with seven magazines each with 18 rounds per magazine for a total of 378 to 504 rounds of 5.56mm, plus the clips in the gun and taped to the butt stock) and one bandoleer (100 rounds of 7.62mm) for the squad's machine gun. Each machine gunner carried 300 or more rounds with his heavy gun.

- Individual Load-Carrying Equipment (ILCE), with belt and suspenders, entrenching tool carrier, first aid kit, magnetic compass pouch, small arms ammunition cases, two quart canteen case and covers with two to five canteens, sunglasses, and tropical rucksack.

- A hot, heavy steel pot (M1 Helmet) and helmet liner with nets to pull down to keep mosquitoes from biting their faces and necks.

- A heavy, rubber poncho and jungle boots with steel-reinforced insoles, water drains, and nylon mesh for better ventilation.

- A light anti tank weapon (LAW) and heavy hand grenades and smoke grenades.

- C-rations, shaving kit, extra socks, and a red lens flashlight, stationary, writing pen, knife, and a small bottle of A-1 sauce, a small bottle of Heinz 57 sauce, and a small bottle of hot sauce to help make the C-rations edible (not necessarily all three sauces) and some kind of good luck charm (cross, Star of David, horse shoe, rabbit's foot, four leaf clover, St. George or St. Christopher Medal, family picture, and other good luck devices).

- Claymore mines (anti-personnel mines for night defense and ambushes), an air mattress, and extra mortar rounds.

- An entrenching tool (folding shovel), knife, and a gas mask (which frequently was discarded).

- A lightweight combat jacket and pants (jungle fatigues). The buttons often caught on weeds and branches.

- And other equipment (like the PRC-25 Radio).

Each day and night for a year the grunts carried these heavy tools of war and then they had to sit up part or all of the night on guard duty.[100] The real heroes, the US Army combat soldiers, US Marines, and Navy SEALs on the ground, fell by the thousands from wounds, heat injuries, sleep deprivation, endless walking and crawling and climbing and slipping, and fungal infections, malaria, blackwater fever, hepatitis, immersion foot and trench foot, smoke inhalation, and dysentery and other diseases.

Over 50 percent of US military deaths in Vietnam were caused by *small arms fire* and ambushes and the grunts took it all and kept on going. Mines and booby traps in Vietnam resulted in over *10,000 amputees*! US, ARVN, and allied *ground pounders* were in constant terror of tripping a booby trap or setting off a mine. Our beloved Vietnam-era ground combat troops suffered from a demoralizing loneliness that only the dark day and night jungles, forests, and tunnels in Vietnam could produce. The real heroes did not get enough sleep and withstood hour-after-hour of boring fatigue, never knowing when or where the enemy might make a stand and ambush them. The *grunts* paid more than their dues under fire and, as in most previous wars, too many died of heat exhaustion and heatstroke.

The real heroes of Vietnam learned that happiness was a cold (free of enemy fire and booby traps) landing zone and pick-up zone. A soldier's bliss was the thunder of rotor blades from the helicopters coming to rescue them, medically evacuate them, extract them from pursuit and possible annihilation or capture, move them to another position in the jungle, bring them food-ammo-water-mail, and frequently to just take them back to their base camps to eat, shower, rest, write letters home, and recharge.

Many simultaneously vomited and had uncontrollable, mucus and blood filled, and explosive diarrhea; gut-wrenching stomach cramps; and fever with chills from amebic dysentery. Some troops, especially Prisoners of War (POWs), died of the resulting diarrheic flood and dehydration[101]. They suffered from tropical impetigo[102], dengue fever[103], and battle fatigue (Post Traumatic Stress Disorder [PTSD]), though no one called it PTSD back then. They loathed their loneliness and isolation and developed serious sleep disorders. They learned to eat, sleep, and live among the putrid smell of feces and lime and burning dung, rotting vegetation, and death. They became *paranoid* and *hypervigilant*, many for the rest of their lives! This hypervigilance helped make some of these veterans become outstanding police officers in their future careers and, at the same time, hurt their long-term health and shortened their life span.

Many combat troops experienced anger, grief, guilt, confusion, denial, and fear on a scale unheard of or known to most civilians. They honed their senses of smell, hearing, feeling, sight, and taste to the level of bloodhounds. They craved and cherished C-ration pound cake, canned peaches and pears, beans and weenies, and beef and spices with A-1 sauce and Heinz 57 sauce. These Vietnam combat infantrymen served an average of *240 days in combat per year*, as compared to World War II infantryman who served on average 40 days in combat. That's six times more combat on average!!!

The real heroes, the combat dog faces (grunts) on the ground, had the revolting smell of "rotting and bloated human corpses" burned into their memories and nostrils, a smell so offensive it is *impossible to describe* and depressing to recall. Unfortunately some resorted to alcohol, denial, dirty jokes, cigarettes, whores, pot and other drugs, and work, to dull their senses and distract them from reality. They acquired an unwanted addiction to the large, bitter-tasting, orange colored malaria prevention pills (cloroquine-primiequine-phosphate) and the almost guaranteed dysentery it causes.

A few even became addicted to the horrific and mentally destructive excitement (adrenalin high) of the endless tragedy and stimulation of combat. All were reduced to surviving, fighting for each other, and dreading the next ambush and booby trap. They were conditioned to focus on protecting one another. They became life time members of a unique fraternity of men and a team of *friends for life* who wore the combat infantry badge, combat medics badge, and other distinguished combat insignia.

With the ground guys given their due, few other groups of military men and women have contributed more to this great nation and US military history than US Army helicopter pilots and their brave enlisted and noncommissioned officer (NCO) crew members. In the Vietnam War, many of these young bird-men were just out of high school or perhaps had one year of college under their belt when they graduated as pilots from Army Rotary Wing (Helicopter) Flight School or graduated as enlisted men from their respective enlisted Army military occupational specialty (MOS) school. Almost none of them had previous flight experience prior to the Army's flight training.

Almost all of these helicopter pilots were sent to war within days of graduation, armed with the bare minimum instrument flight training to safely fly through clouds, rain, smoke, dust, snow, and bad weather. In spite of these training and experience limitations, Army Aviation and its crews would evolve during the Vietnam War into one of the **"largest cans of whip ass"** on the modern battlefield. These Army Aviation crews established air-mobility by helicopter as an irreversible part of the combined arms team in the US Army.

The best estimate that the Department of Defense can conclude is that between 2.7 million to 3.2 million troops served in-country and in the waters of Vietnam between 1954 and 1975. Of the 2.7 million Americans who served in Vietnam, approximately 58,220[104] were killed or died. Over 1,700 troops are still missing! One out of every ten soldiers who served in Vietnam was killed, wounded, injured, or became seriously ill. This is in stark contrast to US census figures and Veterans of Foreign Wars magazine polls, which show that 13,853,027 Americans claim (yes, 13.8 million) to be Vietnam Veterans![105] The Veterans Administration and Department of Defense estimate that approximately one-third, 850,000, of those who did serve in Vietnam are alive today and that two-thirds are dead[106]—making it more important than ever for surviving Vietnam Veterans to participate in the "Joint VA and Library of Congress Veterans History Project."[107]

These Vietnam-era service men and women were the sons and daughters of the Greatest Generation, what Brigadier General (Retired) Danny Hickman calls "the John Wayne Generation." Now the sons and daughters of the sons of the John Wayne Generation are serving in Afghanistan and Iraq, and almost every hot spot in the world. Only one third of the troops who served in Vietnam were drafted and two-thirds volunteered. Eleven thousand of those troops who served in Vietnam were women. The average age of troops who served in Vietnam was 21. The troops who served in Vietnam were on average better educated than those who served in previous US wars.

These sons and daughters of the John Wayne Generation had been raised on the stories of their fathers and mothers serving bravely in Europe and the Pacific as soldiers, Army air corps soldiers, marines, sailors, coast guardsmen, and merchant marines in World War II. The sons and daughters who served in Vietnam were less likely to question the motives and justification their civilian leaders gave them for the war in Vietnam. The sons and daughters of the greatest generation who served in Vietnam wanted to honor their parents, coaches, teachers, pastors, priests, rabbis, scout leaders, and the other adults who served so valiantly in WWII and Korea before them.

Army aircrews in Vietnam successfully flew tens of thousands of day, night, and bad weather missions without Global Positioning Systems (GPS), without crash-worthy fuel systems, without radar altimeters, without Very High Frequency Omni Directional Range (VOR) navigation support, without Instrument Landing Systems (ILS), without night vision goggles, and without active or passive protection (until late in the war) from heat-seeking or radar-guided missiles. They flew without fire control computers, without ballistic resistant vital aircraft components, without grease-filled gear boxes (the oil-filled gear boxes in Vietnam were much more vulnerable to bullet damage than the grease-filled ones are today), and without multi-engine redundancy (except for the twin main rotor and twin engine Chinook and the twin engine Crane Helicopters). They also flew without adequate flight training in instrument meteorological conditions (IMC) and with little or no armor. Unfortunately, the time, instructors, and navigation aids necessary to make it possible for Army helicopter pilots to maintain IMC flight proficiency were not available in Vietnam.

In spite of these limitations, the UH-1, AH-1G, OH-6, CH-47A, and the CH-54A Helicopters changed the face of Army Aviation and warfare. The Army started its Aviation Warrant Officer Program in 1951 and the Aviation Warrant Officer proved to be one of the smartest programs ever introduced by the US Army. These Aviation Warrant Officers and their commissioned brothers (mainly lieutenants and captains, some majors and lieutenant colonels, and few colonels) made the Huey, Cobra, Loach (LOH), Chinook, and Crane helicopters a legend in military aviation. Army Aviation crews and their maintenance support soldiers made air mobility work in Vietnam. They overcame the tremendous problems of working in the jungles, swamps, forests, plain of reeds, dust, smoke, rain, high humidity, and mountains of an undeveloped and enemy infested country.

The North Vietnamese Army (NVA), Viet Cong (VC), bad weather, fragile aircraft, artillery and air dropped flares that did not always ignite, and maintenance failures were not the only hazards Army aviators had to cope with in Vietnam. They also had to avoid being shot down by friendly fire (especially artillery fire), poorly trained and poorly motivated South Vietnamese soldiers, and VC and NVA soldiers who had enlisted in the South Vietnamese Army as spies and subversives. American Army helicopters took fire routinely from Army of the Republic of Vietnam bases, camps, forts, and positions throughout the war.

Before every takeoff and throughout their flights, Army pilots called artillery operations and got the current Artillery firing and B52 bombing data. It consisted of: (1) all firing battery locations by grid coordinates, (2) direction of (each) fire, (3) impact areas by grid coordinates, and (4) maximum "ord," which was the maximum altitude of the rounds en route to the target. From those four pieces of data, the pilot had to determine how best to weave through the maze without getting shot down. It was not unusual to have six or eight batteries, plus mortar platoons, firing during a single operation.

To add to aviation crews' hazardous conditions, the pitch black Vietnam night sky often hid flare parachutes and metal flare carcasses that would suddenly appear out of the darkness right in front of an aircraft. The dud MK-24 flares dropped from other helicopters and other aircraft and the 155 mm artillery flares that burned out too high in the sky were nerve-racking and downright dangerous. There were probably more helicopter accidents and mishaps from flares than from getting hit by friendly or enemy artillery, but the author could not substantiate this in his research.

These Army pilots and many enlisted crew members were volunteers before there was a volunteer Army. As a matter of fact, **66** percent of the soldiers who served in Vietnam were volunteers! And the crew members who were drafted served with great distinction and pride, even though many did not agree with the war or the reasons they were in Vietnam. The Warrant Officer Rotary Wing Flight School examination and other requirements were very demanding and only men with high Intelligence Quotient (IQ) scores were accepted to flight and warrant officer training. Perhaps this partially accounts for why many of these young men later became successful senior Army officers or highly successful civilian businessmen, lawyers, state Supreme Court justices, police chiefs, sheriffs, professors, doctors, computer programmers, and more.

The author's, LTC (Ret) Larry Dandridge's flight class, Army Warrant Officer Rotary Wing Primary Class 68-13 and Advanced Class 68-21 suffered 42 killed in action (KIA) in Vietnam.[108] The author estimates that approximately half of the flight class was wounded or injured, or became seriously ill in their first year in Vietnam. Some were injured or wounded more than once.

The peak year for helicopter losses was 1969 with over 450 lost to enemy action and almost 600 lost to accidents, weather, friendly fire, and other causes that year alone. **In 1969, 3,400 helicopters flew some 8.4 million sorties** (a sortie is one aircraft on one mission), with only one helicopter being shot down per 20,600 sorties and only one aircraft hit per 1,300 sorties. To the astonishment of our sister services fighter and bomber pilots, US Army helicopter pilots and their crews flew as many as **14 missions per day**, seven days per week in Vietnam!

Fighting and flying in an unpopular war, insulted and despised by too many US citizens of the time, this group of brave bird men set records in flight hours flown, missions accomplished, and courage demonstrated. Army UH-1 Huey helicopters alone flew a total of 7.5 million (7,531,955) flight hours in the Vietnam War between October 1966 and the end of 1975. The author and the Vietnam Helicopter Pilots Association (VHPA) believe that the Huey, including the AH-1G Cobra gunship, which flew 1,038,969 flight hours in Vietnam, have more combat flight time than any other aircraft in the history of warfare.[109]

There were about 12,000 helicopters, including UH-1 Iroquois helicopters (Hueys), AH-1G Cobra attack helicopters, OH-6 Cayuse scout helicopters (called LOHs and pronounced Loaches), CH-47 Chinook cargo helicopters, CH-46s (US Marine Corps and

Navy Sea Knight Multi-Purpose Helicopters), CH-34 Choctaw cargo and troop carrying helicopters, CH-21 Shawnee multi-purpose helicopters, OH-23 Raven scout helicopters, CH-54 Sky Crane heavy lift helicopters, and others, that served in the Vietnam War.

Dust Off helicopters alone flew some 500,000 missions. The VHPA has specific tail numbers for 11,827 helicopters from all services. VHPA records show that 7,013 UH-1 Hueys served in the Vietnam War. Almost all were Army. All of the Army's Vietnam-era helicopters had American Indian names except for the AH-1G Cobra. The UH-1 was officially designated the Iroquois. It was the first turbine power aircraft purchased by the Army and had the largest numbers produced of any helicopter for that era. Of the 390,000 wounded who were transported by US military helicopters during the Vietnam War, 90 percent of them survived largely due to the speed at which helicopters picked up and transported those wounded to hospitals.

The Huey started out as the civilian model 204 and was designated XH-40 when the first three prototypes were ordered. The first of these was flown by Floyd Carlson at Fort Worth on October 22, 1956. Before this first flight, a service test batch of six YH-40s had been ordered and these were delivered by August 1958. When the YH-40 was ordered into production, it was re-designated HU-1A in the Army category for utility helicopters and officially named the Iroquois. The HU designation gave rise to the ***Huey*** nickname.[110]

The first of nine pre-production HU-1As were made on June 30, 1959. In 1962, the Iroquois became the H-1 in the new tri-service designation system, which changed the HU-1A and HU-1B to UH-1A and UH-1B, with U standing for utility. In Vietnam, the Army had five types of helicopters: (1.) Utility, (2.) Attack/Gunships, (3.) Observation, (4.) Cargo, and (5.) Heavy Lift. Those types included: Utility (UH-1s), Attack (then called gunships: AH1Gs and converted UH-1s), Observation/Scout (OH-6s, OH-58s, OH-23s, and OH-13s), Cargo (CH-47s, CH-34s, and CH-21s), and Heavy Lift (CH-54). UH-1s were used to transport troops, haul cargo, medically evacuate, and, when equipped with extra armament (rockets, miniguns, and 40mm grenades), attack the enemy and provide aerial artillery fires. Bell Helicopter built

10,005 Hueys from 1957 to 1975. Of the 10,005 production Hueys, the first 732 were designated HU-1A and HU-1B and 9,216 of them went to the U.S. Army, 79 to the U.S. Air Force, 42 to the U.S. Navy, and 127 to the U.S. Marine Corps. The rest went to other countries.[111]

According to Wikipedia, the free encyclopedia *http://en.wikipedia. org* and *www.history.com,* the Vietnam War was a military conflict that occurred in Vietnam, Laos, and Cambodia from November 1, 1955, to the fall of Saigon on April 30, 1975. The Viet Cong (also known as the National Liberation Front, or NLF) fought a guerrilla and terror war against anti-communist forces in the region, and during Tet of 1968, the VC and NVA launched a major attack on almost every city and every US and ARVN base in Vietnam. The North Vietnamese Army engaged in a more conventional war, at times committing large units into battle. The US government viewed involvement in the war as a way to prevent a communist takeover of South Vietnam as part of their wider strategy of *containment* of communism.[112]

The North Vietnamese government and Viet Cong viewed the conflict as a colonial war, fought initially against France, backed by the United States, and later against South Vietnam, which it regarded as a U.S. puppet state. American military advisors arrived in what was then called French Indochina beginning in 1950. U.S. involvement escalated in the early 1960s, with troop levels tripling in 1961 and tripling again in 1962. U.S. combat units were deployed beginning in 1965. Operations spanned international borders, with Laos and Cambodia heavily bombed. American involvement in the war peaked in 1968, at the time of the Tet Offensive. After this, U.S. ground forces were gradually withdrawn as part of a policy known as *Vietnamization*. Despite the Paris Peace Accords, signed by all parties in January 1973, fighting continued.[113]

The communist forces in the Vietnam War included North Vietnam, the Viet Cong, Khmer Rouge, and Pathet Lao, which the Soviet Union, China, North Korea, Czechoslovakia, and Cuba supported. The following countries provided troops supporting the South Vietnamese government: The United States of America, South Korea, Australia, the Philippines, New Zealand, Thailand, the Khmer Republic, and the Kingdom of Laos. The South Vietnamese were also supported by Spain and Taiwan.

US military involvement ended on August 15, 1973, as a result of the Case–Church Amendment passed by the US Congress. The capture of Saigon by the Vietnam People's Army in April 1975 marked the end of the war. North and South Vietnam were reunified the following year. The war exacted a huge human and animal cost in terms of fatalities and wounded. Estimates of the number of Vietnamese soldiers and civilians killed vary from fewer than one million to more than three million. From 200,000 to 300,000 Cambodians, 20,000 to 200,000 Laotians, and 58,220 US service members also died in the conflict.

According to a survey by the Veterans Administration (VA), some *500,000* of the approximate three million troops who served in Vietnam suffered from post traumatic stress disorder (PTSD), and rates of divorce, suicide, alcoholism, and drug addiction were markedly higher among veterans. Unfortunately, like WWII and Korean War Veterans, some of these Vietnam War service men and women never were evaluated by the VA and have not received treatment or benefits that many need or needed before they died. Many veterans' confidence in the ability of civilian politicians to make good decisions was shaken to the core by decisions top leaders made during the Vietnam War.

In the United States, the effects of the Vietnam War would linger long after the last troops returned home in 1973. The United States spent more than *"$120 billion dollars"* on the conflict in Vietnam from 1965 to 1973. Accounting for inflation, the cost to the US war in Vietnam between 1965 and 1973 would be *"$641.7 billion in 2014 US dollars"*[114]! This massive spending led to widespread inflation.

The war ended the myth of American invincibility and had bitterly divided the nation. Many returning veterans faced negative reactions from both opponents of the war and its supporters.[115] According to the Department of Veteran Affairs, approximately 70 percent of all veterans who commit suicide are 50 years old or older. This is twice the suicide rate for the nonveterans' in the same age group. The VA estimates that 22 veterans commit suicide each day. This means approximately 8,030 veterans commit suicide every year and more than 5,540 of those who kill themselves are 50 years old or older. The VA estimates that 30 percent of Vietnam veterans suffer from PTSD, compared with 11 to 20 percent of Iraq and Afghanistan veterans.

Millions of gallons of the harmful and hazardous material (HAZMAT), Agent Orange, and other defoliants (*called rainbow defoliants*) were dumped by US planes and helicopters, and sprayed by hand by ground troops upon the dense forests of Vietnam. According to the Department of Veteran Affairs (VA), the VA has recognized certain cancers and other health problems as "presumptive diseases associated with exposure to Agent Orange or other herbicides" during military service. Veterans and their survivors may be eligible for disability compensation or survivors' benefits for these diseases. Without any protective equipment, the author and contributors of this book, and most other Army helicopter crews actually dispensed Agent Orange and other deadly defoliants or flew through them while providing gunship coverage to the aircraft spraying the defoliant.

The US Army learned how to best use helicopters in Vietnam, but at a high price in aircraft destroyed and damaged, and in aircrews and passengers injured and killed. In Vietnam attack helicopters and armed scout helicopters became the best *eyes and ears* on the Vietnam battlefield. In Vietnam, the utility, scout, and cargo helicopters became the fastest way to move on and around the battlefield. Army helicopter crews and their sheet metal iron horses are now legendary.

In summary, the helicopter and the men[116] who flew them were the most significant innovation of the Vietnam war, and they *balanced the odds* with an enemy who used an easily hidden, lightly loaded, highly mobile, highly disciplined, highly motivated, and ruthless team of North Vietnamese Army and Viet Cong soldiers to terrorize South Vietnam, Laotian, and Cambodian civilians. Book II of Blades of Thunder will include war stories from July of 1969 until the end of the war and is scheduled for publication in September of 2016.

APPENDIX A:
A TRIBUTE TO WARRANT OFFICER
GERALD DAVID MARKLAND

Jerry Markland and this author went through flight school together. We were close friends. We spent many of our off-duty hours together. Jerry was an exceptional athlete and downhill ski instructor. He loved to ride his Norton 650cc motorcycle, and he enjoyed the beaches at Tybee Island, near Hunter Army Airfield, Savannah, GA, where we finished the advanced part of flight school together with the rest of our Rotary Wing Warrant Flight Officer Class 68-13 and 68-21. We played together, drank together, and shared dreams of one day flying for the airlines. Neither of us planned to be career soldiers and neither of us wanted to die or become injured in Vietnam.

Jerry and I were in Oakland, CA, together for three days before we shipped out for Vietnam. He and I tried to eat all the steaks and drink all the beer in San Francisco and Oakland before we caught the big Air Force bird to Vietnam. We went to see the "new" movie 2001: A Space Odyssey together and wondered if such computers as Hal, and such spaceflights, would ever be possible. We dreamed of being test pilots and astronauts together someday.

Jerry Markland's name is on the Vietnam Memorial in Washington, DC, at wall coordinate location 36W-083, along with the names of 58,195 other military men and women killed in the Vietnam War. He started his tour of duty in Vietnam on October 1, 1968, and he was killed on December 28, 1968. His call sign was "Rat Pack." Like me, he was a Caucasian of the Methodist faith, but not very outwardly religious. Jerry was a helicopter pilot extraordinaire and the honor graduate of his flight class. His Military Occupational Specialty (MOS) was 062B, Utility and Light Cargo Single Rotor Helicopter Pilot. He had been in combat for 89 days when Smokey was shot down. As I recall from the notification of death letter I received in

Vietnam, Jerry did not die instantly, but mercifully he was with friends when he passed away.

Jerry Markland was my first close friend to be killed in Vietnam. He would be followed by other close friends like Barry Alexander of South Carolina, who was my very first and best Army buddy in basic training and flight school. Each of these deaths was shocking and hurtful. The notification of Jerry's death changed my way of thinking and acting in Vietnam.

For years I have tried to find out how to contact Jerry Markland's family so that I could tell them what a fine young man they raised and what a terrific pilot and officer he was. My research and many phone calls failed to locate them. In March of 2013 I contacted Chief Warrant Officer (Retired) Roger Howell who was with Jerry Markland the day that Jerry was killed. Roger was terribly wounded in the crash with Jerry. Roger told me that he was able to contact Jerry Markland's mother in the 1970s and that he helped her to obtain some closure regarding Jerry's demise. Mrs. Markland was thrilled to hear from Roger and was so happy to get more details regarding that fateful day of December 28, 1968. She told Roger that the grief and stress of Jerry's death had resulted in her and her husband divorcing. She also told Roger that she had not wanted Jerry to join the Army, but her husband had approved his joining because Jerry loved flying so much. Roger also got a letter from Jerry's sister thanking him for contacting the family. Roger was saddened to hear that Jerry's death had stressed the Markland's marriage to the point of divorce, but he felt good that they finally had some missing information they desperately wanted and needed to help ease their pain.

As I do for all my Army comrades, I pray each day for Jerry Markland and his family. I am certain that Jerry knows his life was not given in vain. The domino theory was accurate and the Philippines, Indonesia, Malaysia, Singapore, and Thailand stayed free of communism because of our commitment to Vietnam. The Vietnam War was the beginning of the end for the ruthless form of communism practiced by Vietnam. The US military was not defeated in Vietnam. The American military did not lose a single battle of any consequence in that war. Douglas Pike, a professor at the University of California, Berkley said it best, "The US did not lose the war in Vietnam. The South Vietnamese lost it two years after the US military left Vietnam."

Jerry Markland, like the rest of us who fought in Vietnam was no lover of war. Most of us young army warrant officer aviators saw the Army as a way to serve honorably but for only as long as it took to become highly qualified pilots. The majority of us planned to leave the Army after our obligation was up and to become civilian (and much better paid) pilots, doing much less dangerous flying.

A year or so ago, in a speech to the Association of the US Army, Retired US Marine Corps General Antony Zinni said that considering how many young Americans protested the Vietnam War it was ironic that today some 13.8 million Americans falsely claimed to be Vietnam Veterans. "I have never heard of someone falsely claiming to have attended Woodstock!" he said.[117] We Vietnam Veterans are so grateful that Americans today support our troops.

We troops who survived Vietnam are the lucky ones when so many better men and women gave their lives for us. We Vietnam War survivors owe a sacred debt to those who perished. We are honor bound to live our lives as honorably and as wise, kind, compassionate, constructive, and empathetic as humanly possible. We also owe our support, generosity, volunteer time, and gratitude to those Vietnam veterans and veterans of all US wars who have been wounded, injured, crippled, and disabled by war.

I wish Jerry Markland had been able to have a full and happy life like I have enjoyed. I wish he had the opportunity so many of us had to marry, have children, and experience the tremendous joy of grandchildren. I wish his mom, dad, sister, and family had not lost Jerry. I wish Jerry's family had not had to suffer so much over his loss. Now that two thirds of those of us who served in Vietnam are dead, I know he is joined by many brothers-in-arms in heaven.

I can only hope that the current generation has learned from the things that Jerry Markland and his generation did right and what we did wrong. Until I make it to that big LZ in the sky, I salute you Jerry Markland and the 58,195 United States military troops who lost their lives in Vietnam. My hat is also off to the 304,000 wounded who served in Vietnam, 75,000 of which are severely disabled. I have come to believe the old saying, "Only the good die young!"

If anyone reading this book can help me find one of Jerry's surviving family members, please e-mail me, W. Larry Dandridge, at LDandridge@earthlink.net, or send me a letter to LTC (Ret) W. Larry Dandridge, 236 North Ainsdale Drive, Charleston, SC 29414, or call me at Cell Phone: 843-276-7164 or Office Phone: 843-573-9657 or FAX me at 843-573-9241.

APPENDIX B: DISCLAIMER

All of the combat missions described in this book are true to the best recollection of the pilots, crew chiefs, and door gunners who described these stories to the author or who wrote some of the stories. The aircrews mentioned in this book actually performed these combat assaults, medical evacuations, extractions, fire team missions, aerial gunnery missions, ash and trash missions, cargo missions, pink team missions, rescue missions, convoy escort missions, and other aviation exploits. These Vietnam Army Aviation war stories are all "non-fiction."

Although the core of this book, the War Stories (aerial missions) are true, there is some "fiction" in this book in the letters that begin each chapter. For example, when one of the pilots graduated from flight school, the exact date of each mission, some call signs, the name of the aircraft commander in the "yellow squares" story, the "USAF-Navy-USMC Fighter Pilots Prayer," "God the Retired Army Aviator Story," and "other jokes told by aviators in the book" are fiction. Specifically:

The Letters between Fellow Aviators that Begin Each Chapter: The letters that begin each chapter were fabricated by the author or the author and contributors but these letters are representative of the kinds of letters written by army aviator friends to each other during the Vietnam War. Larry Dandridge, Danny Hickman, Bubba Segrest, Sam DeLoach, and Jerry Markland did make such a promise to write other Army aviator friends often during their first combat tour of duty. They were good about writing letters to their families and friends, unfortunately none of the original letters have survived the past 47 years. The technical information in the letters about locations, climate, distances, aircraft characteristics, tactics, weapons, time frames, and other related technical information are accurate to the best of the author's and contributors' knowledge and research. The pride, joy, sadness, anxiety, fear, grief, guilt, pain, anger, denial, worries, concerns, depression, bravado, elation, pride, passion, love, isolation, dependence, conflict, and close comradeship exhibited in these letters are the kinds of feelings and emotions that soldiers in all wars have talked about in their letters home and to comrades-in-arms. US Army air crews who served in Vietnam are a close knit brotherhood.

Some of the Pilots in this Book Graduated from Flight School before September 1968. Larry Dandridge, Danny Hickman, Jerry Markland, and Bubba Segrest actually graduated in the same flight class or parallel flight class on September 10, 1968. Dandridge , Markland, and Hickman graduated as warrant officers and Segrest as a first lieutenant. Sam DeLoach graduated in an earlier flight class, and not with Dandridge, Hickman, Markland, and Segrest.

The Time-Line. This book states these missions all took place between September 1968 and July 1969. All but one of these missions did take place in that time frame. The story told by COL (Ret) Sam DeLoach in Chapter 8 titled, Dust Off Mountain Medical Evacuation at Night Under Fire! is based on his warrant officer combat tour in Vietnam in 1967. The story date was changed to allow the author to include a medical evacuation mission in the book and to highlight the author's great admiration for his friend, mentor, and comrade-in-arms.

Some Call Signs. Some call signs in the book are fictional only because the actual players' names and call signs could not be remembered. The 121st Assault Helicopter Company Tigers (slick pilots) used the last three tail numbers for their call signs in most cases except for Tiger 6 (the company commander), Tiger 5 (the executive officer - XO), and Tiger Platoon Leaders. Viking 26 was the Viking Gun (attack) Platoon Commander's call sign. As with all war stories, told 47 years after the battles and events took place, they are based on one, two, or in some cases three or four soldiers perspective and memory and are not exactly what another person in the same battle or mission may have recalled. History is truly in the eyes of the beholder.

The Aircraft Commander's (AC's) Name in the "Yellow Squares Story" in chapter 3 is not his real name. The real aircraft commander is a highly decorated retired army aviator and veteran who honorably and voluntarily served his country with great distinction and courage. The name has been changed to protect his privacy. The names of some other key players on some of the missions in other stories have also been left out for the same reason.

USAF, Navy, and USMC Fighter Pilot's Prayer. The origins of this prayer (and joke) in this book are unknown. The author, Larry Dandridge, first heard this prayer at an Apache Action Team Meeting in Mesa, Arizona in 1988. Although this funny story is the kind of joke crews shared with each other to ease stress and to entertain each other, army aviators have the highest respect and regard for their US Marine Corps, US Navy, US Coast Guard, and US Air Force brother and sister bird men and women.

God, US Army Aviation Retired Joke. The funny story about which military service is the best, in Chapter 3's Yellow Squares Story is not the joke that was told 44 years ago, as the author could not remember the actual joke that was told. However, the story is typical of the frequent jokes crew members told each other to break the ice and relieve stress on missions and back at their bases. This particular joke about God signing a letter as US Army Aviation Retired is typical of how very proud army aviators and enlisted and noncommissioned officer (NCO) crew members are of their Army, especially their Aviation branch of the Army, and their flying exploits. Obviously, our beloved United States Marine Corps, Navy, Coast Guard, and Air Force comrades did contribute equally and gallantly in the Vietnam War. It is the Army's and Marine Corps boots on the ground mission that put so many soldiers and marines in harms' way so often that results in higher casualties for these branches of our military services.

The Seeing Eye Dog and Blind Man Joke, the French General Joke, and other jokes. These jokes in Chapter 5 and other chapters are not the jokes that were told 47 years ago, as the author could not remember the actual jokes that were told. However, the jokes are typical of the frequent jokes and funny stories that crew members told.

APPENDIX C: ACKNOWLEDGMENTS

The author of this book wishes to give his sincere appreciation to:

Mr. Jerod Ruleaux, Commercial License Administrator and Oregon Catholic Press (OCP) for giving Tigers, Vikings, and Vipers Publishing LLC and the author permission to print in this book *On Eagles' Wings,* a devotional song composed by Michael Joncas, a priest (c) 1979, Jan <u>Michael Joncas</u>. Published by OCP. 5536 NE Hassalo, Portland, OR 97213 All rights reserved. Used with permission.

US Marine Corps Major General (Retired) James Livingston, Vietnam War Medal of Honor Recipient, for his review of the book and his recommendation of the book and comments.

US Army Major General (Retired) Rudolph Ostovich, past Commander of the US Army Aviation Center, and highly decorated Vietnam War Veteran, for his review of the book and his recommendation of the book and comments.

Mr. Charles Waring, Publisher of the Charleston Mercury for his review of the book and his recommendation of the book and comments.

Vietnam Helicopter Pilots Association (VHPA) for their assistance, advice, and permission to use statistics and information and the Vietnam Helicopter Crew Members Association (VHCMA) for assisting in finding Vikings and Tigers.

US Army Aviation Museum for its historical and technical information and the US Army Transportation Museum for its help with the history of the Conex container.

187th Assault Helicopter Company Association for its help with information on Gerald David Markland and his last mission.

Mr. John Schmied, 121st Aviation Association Board Secretary for reviewing of the book and his recommendation of the book and historical information.

Richard G. Robbins, US ARMY Medical Command (MEDCOM) Armed Forces Pest Management Board (AFPMB) for assistance with information on poisonous snakes in Vietnam.

Mrs. Sheila Eismann, Speaker, Author, Publisher, and Book Writing Coach, Desert Sage Press, *www.desertsagepress.com* for her advice and kind assistance.

Most significantly the author wishes to thank the following Army helicopter pilots, crew chiefs, and door gunners who contributed exciting stories and pictures, served as technical advisers, and served as reviewers of much of the material:

US Army Brigadier General (Ret) Danny Hickman.[xxv] For writing the Milk Run story in chapter 12 and donating it for use in this book (with all rights to the story reserved to Dan Hickman) and serving as a technical adviser. Danny Hickman served in Vietnam as a warrant officer flying slicks, Cobras, and occasionally scouts while in B Troop, 3/17th Air Cavalry Squadron. His mini biography is in the end notes.

US Army Colonel (Ret) Sam DeLoach [xxvi] for writing the Dust Off story in chapter 7, donating it for use in this book, and for acting as a technical editor, reviewing parts of this book, providing one picture, and serving as my mentor and best friend throughout my Army career and after. Sam served in Vietnam as a combat Dust Off and Cobra pilot, maintenance test pilot, and maintenance detachment commander. Sam served two combat tours in Vietnam, one tour with the 498th Medical Evacuation Company and one with the famed 1st of the 9th Air Cavalry Squadron. One of his Cavalry stories "What is a Pink Team" will be in Book II of Blades of Thunder. His mini biography is in the end notes.

US Army Major (Ret) Bill Schmidt for contributing many of the pictures used in this book, providing many helpful suggestions, and reviewing two chapters. He served as a Tiger platoon leader, assistant operations officer, slick pilot, unit instructor pilot, motor officer, and much more in the 121st Assault Helicopter Company. His mini biography is in the end notes.

US Army Ex-Captain Laurie "Bubba" Segrest[xxvii] for allowing the author to tell his combat story in chapter 5 about being shot down. Bubba Segrest flew Tiger slicks and Viking gunships in Vietnam. Today he is the owner and operator of a successful tour business *Charms of Charleston* (reservations phone number 843-762-2294 and email *Charmsofcharleston@gmail.com*) in Charleston, SC. If you ever visit beautiful Charleston, Bubba has a great air conditioned bus and he gives the best tours available! Bubba's mini biography is in the end notes.

US Army Ex-CPT Eugene Booth for donating several pictures and providing some of the short stories in this book. Gene Booth flew Tiger slicks and Viking gunships in Vietnam and was the Viking gun platoon commander. One of his hair raising combat missions, about his aircraft taking over 200 hits, will be in Book II of *Blades of Thunder*! His mini biography is in the end notes.

US Army Chief Warrant Officer 4 (CW4 Ordnance Corps Retired) Jim Zeitler for contributing to and reviewing chapter 11, *A Day in the Life of a Viking Crew Chief and Door Gunner.* Jim Zeitler flew as a door gunner in Tiger slicks and Viking gunships in Vietnam. His mini biography is in the end notes.

US Army Chief Warrant Officer 2 (CW2 Retired) Brian King for donating pictures and reviewing and helping to tell the combat story in Chapter 1 and for saving Larry Dandridge's life in Vietnam. Brian King flew Tiger slicks and Viking gunships in Vietnam. Many of his fellow birdmen called him, "One of the bravest and best helicopter pilots they ever knew!" His mini biography is in the end notes.

US Army CW2 (Ret) Roger Howell for telling and donating the tragic story in chapter 9 of his aircraft's destruction and the loss of two crew members. He served in Vietnam as a slick pilot and an armed smoke ship and gunship aircraft commander and fire team leader, in the 187th Assault Helicopter Company. His mini biography is in the end notes.

US Army Ex-Specialist 5 Michael Dewey for helping to train and keep alive the author of this book in 1968 and 1969. And I thank him for telling the story of a routine day and non-typical day of a Tiger and Viking crew chief and door gunner in Vietnam. Mike Dewey was a Tiger slick and Viking gunship crew chief and door gunner in Vietnam. Many Tigers and Vikings agree that he was one of the bravest and best of the best! His mini biography is in the end notes.

US Army Ex-Specialist 5 George Quackenbush for helping to tell the story of a routine day and non-typical day of a Viking crew chief and door gunner in Vietnam, and for providing many pictures, much advice, and numerous short stories. George Quackenbush was a Tiger slick and Viking gunship maintenance supervisor, aircraft mechanic, crew chief, and door gunner. Many Tigers and Vikings agree that his courage, knowledge, and skill with Hueys are legendary! His mini biography is in the end notes.

US Army Ex-Specialist 5 Jim Saunders for helping to tell the story of a routine day and non-typical day of a Viking crew chief and door gunner in Vietnam. Specialist 5 Jim Saunders served in the 121st AHC as a Viking gunship crew chief and door gunner and in the 7/1st Air Cavalry Squadron as a crew chief and door gunner. His mini biography is in the end notes.

US Army Ex-Sergeant and Chief Warrant Officer (Ret) Wayne Zander for helping to tell the story of a routine day and non-typical day of a Viking crew chief and door gunner in Vietnam. Wayne Zander was a 121st Assault Helicopter Company Tiger slick and Viking gunship crew chief and door gunner. His mini biography is in the end notes.

US Army Chief Warrant Officer 4 (Ret) Mike Shakocius (Shaky), for contributing many of the pictures and short stories used in this book. He was a Blue Tiger from October 1967 to October 1968. His mini biography is in the end notes.

The many other Tigers, Vikings, and other Vietnam Veterans including, but not limited to: Paul Mcclymonds, Rick Thomas, Tom Jameson, Dan Swecker, Bill Ferguson, Keith Brinnon, Bob

Ennis, Dan Eismann, Larry Gray, George Taylor, Jim Preston, Sid Seitz, Jerry Esmay, Jim Ellis, Mike Sherman, Ernie Bartlett, Joe Casanova, Rick Thomas, Ken Roies, Jim Noblin, Wes Komulainen, Fred McCarthy, and others whom I contacted and who contacted me and provided helpful information, pictures, facts, locations, suggestions, and war stories. Wes Komulanien's story of his CH-54 Flying Crane heavy lift helicopter being attacked by two North Vietnamese MIGs in Laos will be in Blades of Thunder Book II. Each of their mini biographies are in the end notes.

Free Lance Editor and Writer Kim Catanzarite for editing and providing outstanding advice. With great appreciation, I sincerely thank my formal editor, Mrs. Kim Catanzarite, for her understanding, support, detailed review, positive comments, book recommendation, and excellent advice. Her advice and editing were instrumental in the successful completion of this work. If you are a writer or business needing writing, editing, or training assistance, go to *www.editandproof.com* or email her at *kimjoec@aol.com* and ask her to fit you in to her busy schedule. Mrs. Catanzarite is a brilliant and terrific editor, writer's adviser, and Writers Digest instructor!

Graphic Artist, Desktop Publisher, and Branding Expert Nora D. Richardson for the complete and beautiful production of this book. My sincere appreciation is given to Ms. Nora Richardson and her SPOT-ON BRANDING company for the beautiful front and back cover art, the set-up and desk-top publishing, fantastic photography enhancement, and helpful advice she and her company provided. If you need the best help available in the full-spectrum of production services she provides, contact her at *nora@spot-onbranding.com* and website *www.Spot-OnBranding.com.*

Judi Dandridge. I also sincerely thank my wife, Judi and my family for putting up with my war stories, Post Traumatic Stress Disorder (PTSD), endless stream of old Army buddies visiting and calling, and over two and one-half years and many hundreds of hours I spent researching and writing this book about my comrades and my days and nights in Vietnam. Although I had an official, helpful, and wonderful editor in Mrs.

Kim Catanzarite, it was my wife who acted as his first editor throughout this writing adventure.

Anyone Missed. Every effort has been made by the publisher and author to secure permissions to use images and information in this publication. If there has been any oversight, Tigers, Vikings, and Vipers Publishing LLC will be happy to rectify the situation and written permission should be sent to:

Tigers, Vikings, and Vipers Publishing LLC, Attention: Larry Dandridge, 236 North Ainsdale Drive, Charleston, SC 29414 or faxed to 843-573-9241 or scanned and emailed to *LDandridge@earthlink.net.*

APPENDIX D:
LESSONS LEARNED AND
LESSONS PERHAPS NOT LEARNED

1. Introduction

2. Document Wounds, Injuries, Illnesses, and HAZMAT Contamination.

3. VA Needed Improving and Enlarging.

4. Don't Base Today's Commitments on Vietnam Alone.

5. All Americans Must Be Treated As Equals.

6. Solve Our Own Domestic Problems First.

7. Terrorists, Fanatics, and Revolutionaries Are Like Fire Ants.

8. Allies Need to be Taught to be Self-Sufficient.

9. Special Forces, Special Operations, CIA, and State Department.

10. VC and NVA Disguised Themselves As ARVNS.

11. The Enemy Must Be Denied Safe Havens.

12. Plan and Carefully Study Enemy Defense Agreements Before Committing Troops.

13. Report Corruption in Governments We Are Supporting.

14. Every Soldier Should Read Five Years to Freedom.

15. The Public Must Know What the Cost of Foreign Wars Will Be.

16. Tactical Flying (Nap-of-the-earth, masking, out of trim, tail to fire, and more).

17. Tactical Flying (Varying routes, avoiding over flying the enemy, and avoiding approaches into the sun).

18. Tactical Flying (Sideways Bad Weather Flying).

19. Making the Most of the Golden Hour.

20. Controlling Troops Approaching and Departing Helicopters, Securing Antennas, Using the Night, and Clear Visors.

21. C-Raton Can on M60 to Prevent Ammo Belt Flopping and Jams.

22. Minigun Bullet Catcher.

23. Hunter-Killer and Pink Teams.

24. Synthetic Materials Melt in Aircraft Fires.

25. Crashworthy Fuel Systems.

26. Nomex.

27. Crashworthy Seats.

28. Secure Everything Before Flight.

29. Maintain a Blood Donor List.

30. Priority Must Be Given to Evacuating the Dead.

31. Smoke Colors Matter.

32. Safety Weapons and Secure Grenades.

33. Mines Kill Troops and Civilians.

34. Essential Information About the Enemy for Pilots.

35. Chieu Hoi Program Worked.

36. Red Cross Gave No Protection.

37. Helicopters Need Rotor Brakes.

38. Attack Helicopters Need Rocket Debris Proof Windshields.

39. Longer Mike Cords and Helmet Mike Hookup Needed at Fuel Port.

40. Fuel Sight Gages Needed.

41. Safer, Faster, and Easier Fuel Sampling Needed.

42. Crew Personal Weapons.

43. Better Hearing Protection and Safer Helmets.

44. Army Aviation in Vietnam Did Have Limitations.

Lessons Learned and Some Not Learned

1. INTRODUCTION.

The Vietnam War remains the United States most controversial war. It was a long and frustrating struggle between the nations allied with South Vietnam and the nations allied with North Vietnam. The war was much more than just a struggle and contest between the armed forces of the NVA and VC and the South Vietnamese and Americans and their allies. The war incorporated military, economic, cultural, political, and social dimensions. Perhaps the three most important lessons learned in the war for the United States was that the US:

- Knew far too little about the political situation.

- Had far too little understanding and appreciation of the determination and appeal of the enemy.

- Paid far too little attention to counterinsurgency and pacification.

The following 43 paragraphs list a few of the lessons learned by the author in Vietnam. The author tried to limit lessons learned to those things learned for the first time in Vietnam, rather than those things we already knew but confirmed in Vietnam. Although the US Army was trying to fight the Vietnam War primarily with conventional forces and tactics, it is now obvious that the foundation of our strategy in Vietnam should have included:

- Understanding that the Vietnam War was primarily a counter insurgency and guerrilla war and that wining the hearts and minds of the Vietnamese people was the prize we should have sought relentlessly.

- Using the minimum force available to deal with the enemy would reduce civilian casualties and property damage. It would help to win the support of the Vietnamese people and give the VC and NVA a reason to desert and come over to the US/South Vietnamese side.

- Making the enemy desert, rather than killing them was far more desirable and productive.

- Treating prisoners of war well and doing everything possible to avoid disrespecting the VC, NVA, and Vietnamese civilian population.

- Understanding that every time the US or South Vietnamese disrespected a VC or NVA prisoner or Vietnamese civilian, we were working for the VC and NVA.

2. DOCUMENT EVERY WOUND, INJURY, ILLNESS, AND ENCOUNTER WITH HAZARDOUS MATERIAL.

Every wound, injury, illness, and encounter with Hazardous Material (HAZMAT) that a US military man or women has may very well cause some kind of service connected long-term disability. Not only immediately, but also as time goes by these wounds, injuries, illnesses, and HAZMAT contaminations may prevent the troop or veteran and his or her family from working and enjoying life. These illnesses, injuries, and contaminations also cause problems, disease, and deformity in offspring. If a veteran or active duty troop cannot show the military service or the VA strong proof that these things happened while on active duty and are military service connected, a military medical board and the VA compensation and pension folks will likely not award a service connected disability benefit for these potentially disabling events! Every active duty troop and every veteran, as time permits, needs to:

1. Report in detail all injuries, wounds, illnesses, and hazardous material (HAZMAT) contamination to his or her chain of command and to their medical team.

2. Make sure these injuries, wounds, illnesses, and HAZMAT contaminations (Agent Orange and other rainbow chemicals, radiation, asbestos, lead, chemicals like solvents, fuel,

lubricants, cleaning materials, etc.) are documented in as much detail as possible in the service person's medical and personnel records. Obviously if proper protective equipment is used, MSDS is followed, and no contamination or injury or illness takes place then you should not document.

3. Always and, as soon as possible, obtain copies of all medical records, personnel records, and line of duty, accident, incident, and other reports for any service connected injury and contamination.

4. Take pictures of any wounds, injuries, burns, disease symptoms, and HAZMAT exposures that are service connected and record all witness names, addresses, phone numbers, and email addresses. If the event is not documented completely in official military records, then get lay witness statements documenting the time, place, and extent of the injury, wound, illness, contamination, and exposure. It is also wise to get a copy of the HAZMAT label, tag, markings, and Material Safety Data Sheet (MSDS).

5. As soon as possible after any wounds, injuries, illnesses, or HAZMAT contamination obtain detailed **"lay witness"** (eye witness) signed and dated statements, from witnesses to the injuries and contamination. These lay witness statements should include the full name, address, email, phone numbers of the witness and explain who, what, when, where, and how of the incident. The lay witness statement should explain the extent of injuries and contamination. The service member should then keep these pictures and lay witness statements in a safe place for the rest of his or her life. The service member should also ensure his or her spouse knows where the lay witness statements are stored. Include in the last line of all lay statements, *"I swear that the information provided in this lay witness statement is true to the best of my knowledge."*

6. Obtain a written and digitized copy of his or her personnel and medical records when he or she is discharged, separated, or retired from the Army.

Young troops, especially Vietnam Veterans, have historically not done a good job of keeping proof of these injuries and contaminations and they live to regret this as they get older. These injuries and exposures frequently cause *worsening* health related conditions. They also cause *secondary* health problems, cause health problems in their children, and result in many premature deaths. Almost every one of the soldiers mentioned in this book have service connected disabilities. Almost everyone of their service connected wounds, illnesses, injuries (including injuries participating in military sports activities, at physical training, at the military gym, and other activities), and HAZMAT exposures have resulted in worsening health conditions, secondary health problems, and loss of quality of life. *Lesson not learned, but due to the computer age and extensive VA and military outreach and training programs, young troops of today and younger veterans are getting better at documenting these things. The Army and VA are getting better at helping troops and Veterans with this documentation!*

3. THE VETERANS ADMINISTRATION (VA) NEEDED TO BE IMPROVED AND ENLARGED.

We learned from the Vietnam War that we must better provide for the readjustment of our fighting men to civilian life. Vietnam Veterans were dumped back on an ungrateful US society with very little assistance in readjustment. This disgraceful situation ruined the lives of thousands of Vietnam Veterans and their families. However, despite what you may hear in the news media and despite what you hear from some of our countries top leaders, the VA has transformed itself from a woefully inadequate, incompetent, underfunded, out dated, and depressing organization. The VA medical centers and their clinics today are, for the most part, high quality medical centers. For example, the Ralph H. Johnson VA Medical Center in Charleston, SC is a high quality hospital, medical center, mental health treatment facility, and long term care facility. Yes, VA claims are back-logged, but primarily because the VA has done an extraordinarily good job the past ten years at going out and advertising VA benefits, and soliciting and encouraging claims.

Today, the Ralph H. Johnson VA Medical Center is ranked in the top 10% of medical centers (not just VA medical centers, but all medical centers in the USA) based on quality of care, access, safety, customer satisfaction, patient and family centered care (PFCC), compassion, kindness, empathy, mail order pharmacy service, and other important metrics. The Ralph H. Johnson VA Medical Center and its outlying clinics are providing outstanding service to over 64,000 patients (mostly veterans but some active duty military also) and their family members. The medical care part of the VA is striving to become a world- class (six sigma level of quality) organization and that is the kind of care we owe our veterans and their families. If you know a Veteran, please encourage him or her to visit the local VA Medical Center and sign up for his or her benefits.

The VA (there are three parts of the VA: 1. The Veterans Health Agency, 2. The Veterans Benefit Agency, and 3. The Cemetery Agency) still has problems with:

1. Human Resources (HR) system and the long lead times to hire and fire exasperate the problem the VA has with retaining staff;

2. Lack of real, skilled, and dedicated employment assistance at each of its medical centers;

3. Lack of affordable places for Veterans families to stay near its medical centers (there is a need for more Fisher Houses);

4. Lack of efficiency and speed in procuring products and services (contracting and buying is pitifully slow and filled with red tape);

5. Too much red tape in the decision making process (leaders need to act quickly on obviously good ideas and not bog down simple decisions, innovations, improvements, and corrective actions down awaiting a quorum to attend a committee meeting);

6. Lack of first line and variety of medications at the VA Pharmacies (must stock more than generics);

7. Many patients still have to travel long distances to get the care they need;

8. Parking at some medical centers;

9. Allowing smoking in designated areas at VA hospitals (VA facilities should be made into smoke free campuses); and

10. The time to process claims for Veterans compensation and pension takes far too long.

Most of the above lessons have finally been learned concerning VA Medical Care and other VA provided services (claims, education, burial, etc.)!

4. DON'T BASE TODAY'S COMMITMENTS AND MILITARY STRATEGIES ON VIETNAM ALONE.

Vietnam and now Iraq and Afghanistan hover over every major foreign policy debate and decision. One major lesson America should have learned from the Vietnam War was to avoid similar situations in the future. That is we should not commit major troop, equipment, and money resources to a low value, high risk, and foreign national revolution. When the US does decide to go to war, the war must be fought properly and with all of America's resources to insure victory. Collateral damage and indiscriminate damage to civilians and their property create hatred of the USA by those we are trying to liberate and protect. Collateral damage and indiscriminate damage to civilians and their property also help to destroy public support in the USA, public support among allies and their citizens, and damage our image worldwide. America's leaders were right to worry about Vietnam causing China or the Soviet Union to enter the war. The US should have been much less willing to try to defeat an enemy that had almost free reign to use Cambodia and Laos as safe havens.

The Vietnam War was not won by the Viet Cong (VC) guerrillas, but by a massive invasion of South Vietnam by a powerful, well trained, well equipped, and highly motivated North Vietnamese military. The French before us and our leaders early on in the war knew that the North Vietnamese and VC were involved in a highly popular nationalist revolution and not so much a march towards international communism. US leaders should have known and did know (at least by February of 1968) that the NVA and VC were prepared to resist indefinitely and bleed us dry of money, troops, and patience. America's leaders should not have involved the USA in Vietnam in a large and protracted war. Therefore, the USA should have learned today to view any future endeavor with great skepticism. The United States of America should have learned from Vietnam that there are real limits to our power and that even the great USA can fail. ***Lessons only partially learned and our invasion of Iraq show we have much yet to learn!***

5. ALL AMERICANS MUST BE TREATED AS EQUALS IN ALL THINGS TO HAVE MOTIVATED SOLDIERS AND AN ARMY THAT WILL WIN WARS.

The US military has lead the way and come farther than any other part of United States society towards promoting equal opportunity and brotherly and sisterly love. However, the entire US civilian populace still has a long way to go before all Americans are treated equally. US citizens and civilian organizations need to follow the military's lead in promoting civil rights, ensuring equal opportunity to education, and love of one's neighbor. The United States of America cannot expect a soldier to be completely dedicated or fight to his full potential if this great nation does not treat everyone of his or her race, color, creed, origin, religion, age, sex, and sexual orientation the same. This is a country created by the people, of the people, and for the people, all people. African Americans and, to a lesser degree, some other individual minority groups of US citizens were treated with prejudice and even hate back home in the USA during the Vietnam War. Therefore, many of our troops of color in Vietnam were not only lowly motivated, but questioned the morality of killing other people of color and race in a foreign country and endangering their health and life at the same time.

To add to racial problems was the fact that the DRAFT imposed most of the burden of the fighting and dying in Vietnam on low income US citizens. Many of the middle and upper classes of Americans escaped military service in Vietnam due to the loopholes in the draft for those in the National Guard and college. The reason the US military had serious racial problems in Vietnam and throughout the uniformed services during the Vietnam War was primarily based on the fact that the US Government and many US citizens treated minorities in and outside the USA with prejudice and unequal opportunities. Civil rights problems in US civilian society were directly reflected into civil rights problems in the military in Vietnam. *Lesson only partially learned but much progress is being made in the US military and to a lesser degree in US civilian sectors!*

6. SOLVE OUR OWN DOMESTIC PROBLEMS BEFORE WE SHOULD TRY TO SOLVE THE REST OF THE WORLD'S PROBLEMS.

The US should have learned from the huge loss of life and loss of national treasure in Vietnam, that it had no business there with a huge military waging a full blown conventional war. America has so much work to do on its tax code and international competitiveness, race relations, equal opportunity, education system, roads and bridges infrastructure, poverty, hunger, crime, curing and preventing diseases, mental health system, legal system, immigration system, and more. America needs to be much more selective in spending its precious resources on any overseas problems. Science, Technology, Engineering, and Math (STEM) education needs to replace invading countries with large Armies and staying there for long periods. War should be avoided, unless it truly cannot be prevented and is absolutely necessary. And when war is necessary it must be waged with all of America's might. Yes, the United States must always have a foreign policy that is constant in purpose and flexible in means. Yes, the US needs to continue to support its allies, like Canada, Mexico, Great Britain, Australia, NATO, South Korea, and Israel, but America must end these huge blunders like sending huge armies to Vietnam, Iraq, and Afghanistan, especially when Special Forces, Special Operations, Central Intelligence Agency (CIA), and State Department efforts are more likely to provide long run favorable results. Yes America must recognize that every hate filled group in the Middle East is seeking to focus their venom on us and the rest of the Western World. *Lessons not learned!*

7. TERRORISTS, FANATICS, AND REVOLUTIONARIES ARE LIKE FIRE ANTS.

For those of us from the south, who have fought fire ants[118], cockroaches[119], water hyacinth[120], and kudzu[121] we know it is impossible or at least economically impossible to totally get rid of these invasive species. In Vietnam we troops learned quickly that the VC and NVA were an invasive and persistent species who could not be totally eradicated, without invading Laos, Cambodia, and North Vietnam. All we did there was 'kill them back" to a degree until they quickly multiplied and reinvaded every part of South Vietnam, just like the fire ants, cockroaches, water hyacinths, and kudzu do in FL, GA, SC, AL, and other southern states. The USA must be much more careful in the future in involving ourselves in foreign conflicts that have no major bearing on our safety, security, or economic well being. And if the US does decide to involve itself in foreign problems, like those in Vietnam, Iraq, Afghanistan, Pakistan, Somalia, Syria, Libya, and Yemen, it is better for America to plan well, solicit help, and carefully devise its options first.

Additionally, USA involvement should have a way of paying for itself if at all possible. In some cases there will be no economic return like oil rights, base rights, mineral rights, land, sea ports, or other treasure. So in those cases where no immediate and tangible economic benefit will come of our involvement, we need to get in quickly and kill back as many of the terrorists, martyrs, revolutionaries, criminals, guerrillas, and fanatics as possible, but not all. The cost of killing all of any evasive species is almost always prohibitive.

Killing poorly trained Iraqi soldiers in open and flat desert is like shooting ducks on a pond. On the other hand, soldiers know that to fight a determined, well armed, zealous, fanatical, and indigenous foe in his crowded cities, rugged mountains, heavy forests, and thick jungles is the US Army's worst nightmare and one of our most difficult of military challenges. These natural strongholds, as the VC and NVA taught us, and as the Japanese taught us in the South Pacific in WWII, and the Russians taught Napoleon at Moscow, and the Russians taught the Nazis at Stalingrad, are almost unconquerable without exhausting every penny of the western world and without wasting thousands of young American lives. The lessons of the Middle East and Far East have been experienced by westerners from the beginning of time. Yet, the US and other western powers keep trying to change a culture that is as large and unconquerable as our own. So the lesson here is to do like the rat killing held on SC farms every few years.

Kill the fanatics back without huge collateral damage, and then leave quickly or plan to stay indefinitely as we have done in South Korea. The US cannot afford to fight a protracted war of attrition with fanatics, unless there is no other choice and, if we do, then we must do it wisely! *Lesson not yet learned!*

8. ALLIES NEED TO BE TAUGHT TO BE SELF SUFFICIENT AND NOT ABRUPTLY ABANDONED.

North Vietnam relentlessly and fanatically conditioned their population and Army to achieve self-sufficiency and to rely on their own resources. The NVA and VC regarded aid from China and Russia as unreliable and supplemental. Unfortunately, the US taught the South Vietnamese government and its military forces to rely on US Aid for almost everything. The US conditioned the Army of the Republic of South Vietnam and its Air Force and Navy to treat US aid as a way of life. South Vietnam expected that the US aid would never end. We were so arrogant and ignorant in Vietnam that we thought we could win the war without the aid of the South Vietnamese. Had we not stayed in Korea after the Korean War, the North Koreans would have reinvaded South Korea. Since we did not stay in Iraq, we now have seen ISIS and other terrorists reinvade and take over much of the country. *Lesson lost and being relearned in current conflicts and wars!*

9. ONE SPECIAL FORCES ADVISER IS MORE EFFECTIVE AT WINNING WARS AGAINST INSURGENCIES AND GUERRILLAS THAN A COMPANY OF COMBAT TROOPS.

Had the US protected the South Vietnamese population, rather than opening up free fire zones; had we armed and supported local forces better, instead of fighting a big Army war; had we concentrated more on pacification efforts, rather than using B52 strikes in the south; and had we used the high impact face-to-face Special Forces troops more, America would have had a much better chance of saving South Vietnam and not killing so many US troops. The combination of US special forces, US special operations forces, limited and better trained in counter insurgency regular forces, and highly trained state department persons, are essential to fighting an asymmetrical war like we faced in Vietnam and we face in Southwest Asia today.

In a war on terrorists, guerrillas, subversives, insurgents, and assassins we have to preserve and win the hearts and minds of the people. In a war by improvised explosive devices, booby traps, mines, and ambush, the US has to pacify, protect, win, and keep the support of the populace, instead of using conventional only military warfare. In a war where the USA is fighting mostly infiltration instead of conventional aggression and in a war where the enemy is seeking victory by eroding and exhausting us instead of engaging and fighting us conventionally, America has to do the same and more so to the enemy. In Vietnam, as today in SW Asia, US enemies prey on unrest and continuous terror; and the US needs to counter that terror by establishing security, safety, and stability for the civilian population. ***Lesson mostly learned by the military but not by politicians!***

10. THE VIET CONG (VC) AND NORTH VIETNAMESE ARMY (NVA) SOLDIERS OFTEN DISGUISED THEMSELVES AS ARMY OF THE REPUBLIC OF SOUTH VIETNAM SOLDIERS.

As we have seen happen too many times in Iraq and Afghanistan today, enemy troops in Vietnam not only dressed as Army of the Republic of Vietnam soldiers but frequently joined the ARVN army and waited to the times of their choice to attack the ARVNs and US units. These kinds of attacks today are called "green (Taliban and other terrorists) on blue (US) attacks" in Afghanistan. The problem of VC and NVA troops disguised as ARVNs and even joining ARVN units in large numbers was never controlled in Vietnam. The control of uniforms and equipment and the screening and background checking of enlistees and draftees by the ARVNs was never adequate in Vietnam and is obviously lacking in SW Asia today. ***Lesson partially learned but counter measures are not nearly adequate yet!***

11. THE ENEMY MUST BE DENIED SAFE HAVENS.

As the Taliban and other terrorists do in Southwest Asia today by attacking targets in Afghanistan and then retreating to the mountains in Pakistan, the communists in Vietnam did the same thing by attacking targets in South Vietnam and then rapidly retreating to safe havens in Cambodia and Laos. Although the US bombed Laos and Cambodia and invaded Cambodia and Laos (February 1971) briefly, the US Presidents did not allow what was needed. That is they did not allow US forces to invade Laos and Cambodia and clean them out of NVA forces there and block the Ho Chi Minh trail. US leaders were always afraid of Chinese and Russian intervention (and rightfully so) and the cost in US lives and dollars of expanding the Vietnam War. These kinds of "no-win" situations should have been better thought out in Vietnam and later in Afghanistan, before we committed to long run support of a war effort in either of these countries. *Lesson not learned.*

12. CAREFULLY STUDY ENEMY DEFENSE AGREEMENTS AND PACTS BEFORE COMMITTING OR NOT COMMITTING US TROOPS IN FOREIGN WARS.

North Vietnam had a mutual defense pact with China. Such defense agreements and pacts could quickly suck the US and its allies into another world war. As Hitler was wrong in thinking the French and British would not come to Poland's aid when he invaded Poland in the Second World War and as the US was wrong in thinking the Chinese would not come to North Korea's aid in the Korean War, the US could have started World War III by fighting in Vietnam. The North Vietnamese and Chinese Defense Pact did prevent the US from whole heartedly invading Laos and Cambodia. The Vietnam War made it more evident than ever that it is vital for our presidents and other top government leaders to be experts in world geography, politics, cultures, religions, history, and military science. *Lesson not learned.*

13. REPORT AND HAVE A CLEAR PLAN TO DEAL SWIFTLY WITH CORRUPTION WITHIN THE GOVERNMENTS WE ARE SUPPORTING.

Of all the things the US did wrong in Vietnam, not helping and requiring ethical, honest, and law abiding behavior from South Vietnam's government (really multiple governments that turned over rapidly) and South Vietnamese armed forces was a guarantee for failure. So many corrupt South Vietnamese governments came and went during our long war there; the US could not keep up with who was in charge. America never really had a plan to require ethical, honest, compassionate, and empathetic behavior from the South Vietnamese government or its armed forces. The US military also allowed our own troops to grow more and more cynical and irresponsible towards the Vietnamese people, its armed forces, their farm animals, their wildlife, and their natural resources. The US was too quick to say things like, "bribes, payoffs, fraud, stealing, and such were just the way of Southeast Asians (and now SW Asians)." The US turned its eyes to such destructive behavior. As cruel as the VC and NVA were, they had a better psychological and day-to-day propaganda warfare program than us. The NVA and VC sold to the North and South Vietnamese populace their program. The US needed to, but failed to convince the Vietnamese, to resist and defeat communism. Today the US military and US State Department have the same mission in SW Asia to convince the Afghanis and Iraqis to resist and defeat Al-Qaida, ISIS, and other radical Islamists. The US should not wait and try to educate our soldiers at the last minute. US children today must become educated world citizens and taught world geography, customs, languages, religions, and politics, along with science, technology, engineering, and math oriented subjects. If the USA is to truly be a world leader in commerce, behavior, peacemaking, and society, it cannot wait and only half-train soldiers in these things, at the last minute, and only right before or after they deploy to war. *Lesson partially learned but today's effort is still far from optimal!*

14. EVERY SOLDIER SHOULD HAVE TO READ (deceased) MAJOR JAMES ROWE's BOOK "FIVE YEARS TO FREEDOM."

How to deal with being captured and tortured is a skill that should be thoroughly taught to US Soldiers. Courage is a process and torture is much harder to withstand than death. Troops should know and expect to be starved, beaten, bound, raped, killed, used, tricked, beheaded, and worse by our enemies. US military troops must continue to be taught not to submit to the temptation to torture or mistreat prisoners for whom they are responsible. US soldiers must be trained in and must be committed to our code of conduct, the Geneva Convention, and US and international law. At the same time, our troops must know that almost every man or women has a breaking point. American troops should act with honor and dignity to the best of their ability, even as POWs. Our troops should also expect to be treated as heroes and heroines when they return home. US leaders, especially since so many of today's Presidents, Vice Presidents, Department Secretaries, Congressman, and Justices have never served in the US military, must continue to be careful to observe the same code, the same Geneva Convention, and the same laws or they can expect our enemies to savage US troops when they are captured! Reading Major James Rowe's book <u>Five Years to Freedom</u> is an education in how to survive and escape as a POW. *Lesson partially learned in Vietnam.*

15. PUBLIC SUPPORT IS ESSENTIAL TO WIN A WAR AND POLITICAL LEADERS MUST TELL THE PUBLIC WHAT THE COSTS OF A FOREIGN WAR WILL BE.

Wars are not cheap. Wars cost lives and cost great amounts of money. Wars divert precious resources that could be used to fight disease, poverty, crime, and ignorance. Wars use up huge quantities of valuable natural resources. Expensive equipment is consumed by wars. The US should not go to war unless the majority of the populace is willing and able to bear all of the costs of war. *Lesson not learned.*

16. TACTICAL FLYING (MAP OF THE EARTH, MASKING, OUT OF TRIM, TAIL TO FIRE, AND MORE).

As the scout pilot did so skillfully in the war story "Milk Run" in Chapter 13 of this book, Army scout, utility, and attack pilots and other pilots learned to fly with great skill nap-of-the-earth and use the terrain to mask (hide) behind anything (trees, buildings, terrain, etc.) available. They learned to point the nose in one direction and fly out of trim in the opposite direction, changing their heading and speed where possible, thus fooling enemy gunners. The Dust Off pilots learned to put their tail into the direction of enemy fire, after landing and while loading and unloading patients thus providing the smallest target and some protection from fire by placing the transmission and other large aircraft components between them and the enemy. Every Army pilot learned to have the ground unit identify where the enemy was and where the enemy fire was coming from before planning their route into and out of the landing zone and pickup zone. *Lessons learned but today's aviators will benefit from reviewing such lessons.*

17. TACTICAL FLYING (VARYING ROUTES, AVOIDING OVERFLYING THE ENEMY, ATTACK FROM DIFFERENT DIRECTIONS, AND AVOIDING APPROACHES INTO THE SUN).

All Army pilots learned to vary their routes and directions into and out of landing areas. Every pilot avoided, when possible, flying directly over the enemy. Attack pilots learned to attack from different directions to avoid enemy ground fire and make maximum use of their wing man and door gunners to suppress enemy fire. Every Army aviator learned to avoid landing into the sun, especially over water to avoid being blinded by the intense sunlight, especially sunlight reflecting off of water. *Lessons learned but today's aviators will benefit from reviewing such lessons.*

18. TACTICAL FLYING (SIDEWAYS BAD WEATHER FLYING).

We learned how to fly (really hover) in less than 200 feet of visibility in day light, up the side of a mountain and down the side of a mountain, by flying sideways, with our heads out of the window, and keeping the ground-trees-foliage in sight and the rotor blade tip in sight, and all crew members looking outside. New night vision and obscuration vision equipment, radar altimeters, and other navigation and sight aids have replaced this type of high risk flying. *Lesson Learned, but lost as no one practices this these days.*

19. MAKING THE MOST OF THE GOLDEN HOUR.

Every Army helicopter pilot made a bee line for anyone wounded or injured to get them to medical attention during that first critical hour, the golden hour. All US Army pilots knew it was best to let Dust Off helicopters evacuate wounded and injured, if time allowed, as they had highly trained medics on board and specialized equipment to save the wounded troops lives. *Lessons learned but today's aviators will benefit from reviewing such lessons.*

20. CONTROLLING TROOPS APPROACHING A HELICOPTER, SECURING ANTENNAS AND HEAD GEAR, USING THE NIGHT, AND CLEAR HELMET VISORS.

Utility (slick) and scout helicopter pilots learned to have troops approach their aircraft from the front or sides of the aircraft to stay clear of the dangerous and fragile tail rotor. Army aviators also knew to require troops to store radio antennas and loose head gear before approaching the main rotor system or aircraft. Pilots, crew chiefs, and door gunners demanded a clear view of troops wanting to approach their aircraft and they needed to control loading so that the troops radio antennas did not strike the main rotor blades and so that head gear did not fly off and into the rotor system. *Lessons learned but today's aviators will benefit from reviewing such lessons.*

Everyone knew that the Viet Cong and NVA owned the night on the ground in Vietnam, but Army aviators learned that the enemy had a terrible time seeing and hitting their helicopters with any non-radar and non-heat seeking weapons at night when aircraft running, landing, and search lights were off and cockpits dimmed. Army Dust Off helicopters did a huge number of medical evacuations at night to take advantage of the cover of darkness. All pilots recognized the need for night vision equipment and Vietnam did accelerate the development of night vision goggles and other night vision equipment. *Lessons learned.*

The Army also learned to provide clear visors for aviation crews and aviators and they learned to install clear visors in their flight helmets. They used sunglasses in the daytime to prevent glare and they used just the clear visor at night to prevent eye and other facial injuries and burns. The US Air Force had a dual visor (tinted and clear) capability in some of their helmets. *Lessons learned but today's aviators will benefit from reviewing such lessons.*

21. C-RATION CAN ON M60 TO PREVENT AMMO BELT FLOPPING AND JAMS.

Army door gunners and machine gunners learned to snap a C Ration can on the side of the M60 gun to prevent the wind from "flopping the ammunition belt around and against the weapon." The can allowed for the ammunition to flow uninterrupted into the gun, prevented the flopping action, and prevented jams. *Lesson Learned in Vietnam but lost after.*

22. MINIGUN BULLET CATCHER.

Army aviation maintenance experts invented a steel bullet catcher to slide on the killing end of our minigun barrels when we were on the ground to prevent an accidentally fired round from wounding or killing someone. All that needed to be done to fire a loaded minigun was to rotate the barrels by hand or by electric motor or by accident. *Lesson Learned but forgotten by some.*

23. HUNTER-KILLER AND PINK TEAMS.

Army aviation learned to use hunter killer teams (frequently called pink teams by our air cavalry units) of scout and attack helicopters backed up with artillery, tactical air support, and naval gunfire to find, attack, and kill the enemy. The pink teams could deploy an infantry platoon to develop what the pink team found. These teams were commanded by company grade officers (1st Lieutenants and Captains and yes, even Warrant Officers) and they had the highest find and kill ratios in Vietnam! The young officers leading these hunter killer teams and pink teams were highly empowered, highly motivated, and well trained. The hunter killer and pink team concept and tactics seem to have somehow been lost by many in today's Army Aviation. Also the empowerment of company grade officers and warrant officers appears to have been removed and replaced with close general officer and even civilian high level supervision for even the most routine of military missions in Southwest Asia. As one general told me a few years ago, "When my unit was looking for Saddam Hussein, had we seen him standing on a corner a block away, we could do nothing until I prepared a power point briefing and explained a detailed operation plan to a three Star General or higher." The US Army seems to be so "risk averse" today that it has, at times, to seem to have difficulty getting the full potential from its young officers. *Empowerment of junior military leaders was a Lesson learned in Vietnam but perhaps partially lost since then!*

24. THE SYNTHETIC MATERIAL IN JUNGLE BOOTS MELTS IN AN AIRCRAFT FIRE.

Army air crews discovered the hard way that the synthetic material in jungle boots melted at low temperatures in a post crash fire and resulted in foot amputations. Therefore air crews went back to all leather boots for flight crew members. *Lesson Learned.*

25. CRASHWORTHY FUEL SYSTEMS.

Army aviation figured out that aircraft needed to be designed and equipped with crashworthy fuel systems with breakaway fittings, self sealing connections, and fuel bladders/tanks, and fire suppression systems to prevent fires. *Lesson Learned.*

26. NOMEX.

Army and industry scientists invented the one piece Nomex (fire resistant) flight suits, gloves, and head covers to prevent air crew burns. Army bird men stopped wearing jungle fatigues and cotton flight suits, but only after hundreds of fire injuries and deaths. *Lesson Learned but painfully and sadly slowly.*

27. CRASHWORTHY SEATS.

The Army and the aviation industry learned to build crashworthy seats for crew members and passengers (troops) that better absorbed crash forces and cut down significantly the crippling compression fractures of air crews' spines and other injuries caused by high rate of descent vertical crashes. Unfortunately, troop seats are sometimes removed to allow for more troops to be carried. ***Lesson Learned by the wisest commanders.***

28. SECURE EVERYTHING IN FLIGHT.

Everything, including, but not limited, to chicken plates (body armor), weapons, coolers, C-Rations, ammo boxes, extra helmets, grenades, flares, emergency radios, and other items, in the cockpit and cargo/troop cabin areas of a moving aircraft or wheeled vehicle becomes an unguided and dangerous missile in a crash. Chicken Plates must be used within the vest holder and not worn lose to prevent them from becoming airborne missiles in a crash. Unfortunately, in Larry Dandridge's and Roger Howell's cases and many other Army aviation crew members' cases that were in crashes in Vietnam, there were not enough chicken plate vests to go around. There was no built-in place to safely secure the crew members rifles, and too many items (coolers, extra ammo, c-rats, etc.) were just placed on the floor of the helicopter. ***Lesson Learned.***

29. MAINTAIN A BLOOD DONOR LIST.

Smart commanders and doctors kept up-to-date lists of each member of their unit and what each of their troopers blood type was. These folks were then called upon when the type of blood needed was not immediately available. ***Lesson learned.***

30. PRIORITY TO EVACUATING THE DEAD.

Army aviation and all Army commanders learned it was very important to remove the dead from the battlefield as soon as possible to prevent the loss of bodies, to prevent disease, and to reduce the grief and demoralization of the troops left alive in the combat area. After the evacuation of wounded and need for resupply, removing the dead by helicopter is a high priority. ***Lesson Learned.***

31. SMOKE COLORS MATTER.

Troops learned that green smoke is harder to see than other colors in green foliage and they learned that red smoke is very hard to see at dusk and during other low light conditions. ***Lesson Learned.***

32. SAFETY WEAPONS AND SECURE GRENADES.

US and ARVN troops had to be taught and disciplined to safety their weapons and keep muzzles pointed away from other troops, crewman, and aircraft vital components. ARVNs frequently dropped grenades in US Army helicopters and at times got their grenades caught on aircraft doors and other items in the aircraft. Army helicopter crew chiefs and door gunners made it Standard Operating Procedure (SOP) to check troops as they boarded, after they boarded, while en route, and as they were leaving the aircraft for all weapons on safe and muzzles pointed either straight up or down or out of the doors. The crew chiefs and door gunners also checked all grenades for secured pins and safety. After the troops departed the aircraft the crew chief and door gunner checked for items, especially checking for dropped grenades, left by troops. *Lesson Learned.*

33. MINES AND CIVILIANS.

The Army learned that war is hard on troops, but hell on the civilians in the war zone. The Army learned that mines are perhaps the worst weapons for civilian populations as they continue to kill for 10 to 50 years and longer after the war is over. *Lesson partly learned.*

34. ENEMY ESSENTIAL INFORMATION ABOUT THE ENEMY FOR PILOTS.

Army aviation learned that pilots needed to know less about whether a landing zone or pickup zone was secure or not and more about: where the enemy was located, what direction fire was coming from, and what kind of weapons (small arms, .51 caliber, shoulder fired missiles, rifle-fired grenades, etc.) the enemy had. *Lessons learned but today's aviators will benefit from reviewing such lessons.*

35. CHIEU HOI PROGRAM WORKED AT ENCOURAGING VC AND NVA TO DEFECT TO SOUTH VIETNAM'S SIDE (EVEN THOUGH PROPAGANDA LEAFLETS WERE POORLY WRITTEN).

American ignorance of Vietnamese culture and language resulted in some very poorly written Chieu Hoi pamphlets which were dropped from 1965 to 1972 throughout Vietnam. Unfortunately the pamphlets were written in high Vietnamese, rather than the common Vietnamese peasant language and style. Chieu Hoi leaflets were delivered by artillery shell or dropped over enemy-controlled areas by aircraft, or messages broadcasted over areas of South Vietnam. Overall, the Chieu Hoi program was considered successful. The program was relatively inexpensive and removed over 100,000 combatants from the field, although some defected back to the VC and NVA. ***Lesson partially learned for later US wars and armed interventions.***

36. COMMAND AND CONTROL.

Besides the highly effective Command & Control (C&C) Helicopter, the US and ARVN forces learned to use: (1.) radios and radio encoded grid coordinates to report their positions; (2.) colored smoke grenades to mark friendly positions, the enemy's positions, and targets; (3.) hand held and fired pop-up flares to show their positions and the enemy's positions; (4.) marker panels to identify landing areas and friendly and enemy locations; and (5.) signal mirrors to relay information and locations. Some commanders in C&C helicopters did lose their appreciation for the great difficulties facing troops on the ground in terms of time and distance. Even moving short distances up and down mountains, through mud sucking rice paddies, and clawing and cutting through thick jungle requires great effort and care. It is easy to forget this in a helicopter gliding effortlessly over the battle area. Only the assault helicopter flight leader and the gunship fire team leader were allowed to communicate with the commander on the ground to cut down on radio traffic and prevent confusion. ***Lessons learned but today's aviators will benefit from reviewing such lessons.***

37. RED CROSS GAVE NO PROTECTION.

Dust Off (medical evacuation) pilots learned that large Red Crosses painted on the sides of their helicopters gave them no protection from enemy fire. ***Lesson learned.***

38. HELICOPTERS NEED ROTOR BRAKES.

Army aviation learned we need rotor brakes on helicopters to accommodate maintenance, high wind shut-downs, and for shutting down on ships, barges, and boats. *Lesson partially learned!*

39. ROCKET DEBRIS-PROOF WINDSHIELDS.

Army aviation learned that gunships and attack helicopters need windows and windshields that are rocket debris-proof (resistant to burns and scratches). The pitting of windshields from hot rocket motor debris is a maintenance headache and a safety issue. *Lessons learned but today's aviators will benefit from reviewing such lessons.*

40. LONGER MIKE CORDS AND HELMET MIKE HOOKUP BY THE REFUEL PORT.

Army aviation learned that it needed a helmet hook-up (female port) by the outside refuel port of its helicopters so that the refueler can hook up his or her mike cord and safely talk to the pilot in the aircraft during hot refueling. Army aviation also learned that crew chiefs and medics needed longer helmet cords so that they could get out of the aircraft and still talk to the Aircraft Commander and pilot. *Lesson partially learned!*

41. SAFER, FASTER, EASIER FUEL SAMPLING.

Army aviation learned that it needed a safer way of doing fuel sample checks. Army aviation needed a way to take fuel samples without having to crawl under an aircraft and risk having a fuel valve stick open and pour fuel all over the place, the person taking the sample, and possibly resulting in a fire or an environmental disaster. Crew chiefs and maintenance officers suggested installing clear sight bowls at the lowest cell points and other key places. *Lesson partially learned!*

42. CREW PERSONAL WEAPONS.

Army aviation learned it needed secure gun racks for crew member long weapons (ideally the short barrel Colt Automatic Rifle 15). In every crash in Vietnam, the crews' long weapons went flying, were damaged frequently or lost, and sometimes injured occupants. No more long rifles for aviators, door gunners, and crew chiefs. They need pistols and short rifles (like the CAR15 or today's other carbine size weapons). *Lesson learned!*

43. BETTER HEARING PROTECTION AND SAFER FLIGHT HELMETS.

Army aviation learned we needed better flight helmets that were more comfortable, safer, and with better hearing protection. Future helmets need to be so secure that they will not fly off in a crash, as all crew members helmets did in the gunship crash in chapter one of this book. Everyone who worked around aircraft in Vietnam, who did not also wear ear plugs in addition to their helmets most likely, has significant hearing loss today. The old helmets caused headaches, had hot spots, and would fly off under high G crashes, no matter how tight the chin strap was. *Lesson learned and helmets are constantly being improved today!*

44. ARMY AVIATION IN VIETNAM DID HAVE LIMITATIONS.

Army Aviation was hampered by night (low light) conditions, low ceilings and bad weather (clouds, smoke, rain, dust), vulnerability to enemy small arms and other ground fire, high vulnerability to anti-aircraft gun fire and heat seeking and radar guided missiles, and fuel and ammunition weight limitations. The Army and civilian aviation industry have overcome many of these obstacles today with much more powerful aircraft engines, dual engines, night (low visibility) vision devices that see through all kinds of obscuration, much more rugged and larger aircraft; active and passive defensive equipment, huge advances in counter-measures, more fire power, fire control computers, improved munitions, better armament, more training, more instrument flight navigation aids, radar altimeters, global positioning systems (GPSs), and all kinds of design improvements and innovations. *Lesson learned.*

APPENDIX E:
US ARMY PRIMARY FLIGHT TRAINING CLASS 68-13 AND ADVANCED CLASS 68-21 MEMBERS WHO WERE KILLED IN ACTION (KIA) OR DIED DURING TRAINING (DDT)[122]

1. Bodell, Larry Allen (KIA)	13. McGrew, Stephen L. (DDT)
2. Bois, Richard Joseph (KIA)	14. Morris, David Michael (KIA)
3. Bonine, Thomas Marvin (KIA)	15. Pannell, Phillip Randall (KIA)
4. Burkhardt, William Harley (KIA)	16. Pearlstein, Jerrold S. (KIA)
5. Crosby, Arthur Allen (KIA)	17. Polak, Peter Paul (KIA)
6. Hearne, Maury William (KIA)	18. Popp, David Fred (KIA)
7. James, Kenneth Bradley (KIA)	19. Roberson, Samuel Albert (KIA)
8. Jelich, John Anthony (KIA)	20. Stacy, Walter Robert (KIA)
9. Jenkins, Bert Mc Cree (KIA)	21. Stuck, Lawrence Milton (KIA)
10. LeMaster, Michael Eugene (KIA)	22. Taber, Martin Lester (KIA)
11. Markland, Gerald David (KIA)	23. Thoman, Theodore Vail (KIA)
12. Mathis, Samuel Judson (KIA)	24. Wright, Clifford Devon (KIA)

25. Zappini Jr. Joseph Vincent (KIA)	35. Harker Jr., Jack Albert (KIA)
26. Brault, Dennis James (KIA)	36. Harris, Edward Lewis (KIA)
27. Breaden, Larry L. (DDT)	37. Kinghorn, Stephen John (KIA)
28. Bridges, Thomas C. (DDT)	38. Mason, Sven Sterling (KIA)
29. Brown, Steven Merle (KIA)	39. Michael, William Frederick (KIA)
30. Bullerdick, Gary Allen (KIA)	40. Niewenhous Jr., Gerald E. (KIA)
31. Chase, Freddie Nicklys (KIA)	41. Sholar, Edwin Franklin (KIA)
32. Clemons, Willard Lee (KIA)	42. Stahlstrom, Allen Emile (KIA)
33. Depaul Sr., Michael Joseph (KIA)	43. Barry Kenneth Alexander (KIA) Class 68-23[123]
34. Donics, William Caldwell (KIA)	

Unfortunately, Larry has been unable to locate Barry Alexander's family. If anyone can help Larry find Barry's parents or other family members, believed to be from the Clemson area of SC, please notify Larry at LDandridge@ earthlink.net or cell phone 843-276-7164.

APPENDIX F: GLOSSARY AND ACRONYMS

Aerial Rocket Artillery (ARA). The UH-1 B/C model Hueys armed with two 24-tube 2.75 inch folding fin aerial rocket (FFAR) pods and door guns. Used as US Army airborne mobile artillery in Vietnam.

Assault Helicopter Company (AHC). The basic war fighting Army Aviation unit in Vietnam's 1st Aviation Brigade helicopter war. The 121st AHC (Airmobile light) was composed of five platoons which included the Viking armed platoon of UH-1B model gunships (attack helicopters), the two transport (slick) helicopter platoons (the Blue and White Tiger platoons), the service platoon (aircraft maintenance), and the headquarters platoon which was responsible for command, control, and administration.

Armored Personnel Carrier (APC). According to Wikipedia, the free encyclopedia, URL *http://en.wikipedia.org/wiki/M113_armored_personnel_carrier* the: The M113 is a fully tracked armored personnel carrier that was developed by Food Machinery Corp (FMC). The vehicle was first fielded by the United States Army's mechanized infantry units in Vietnam in April 1962. (2, Starry Page 21) The M113 was the most widely used armored vehicle of the U.S. Army in the Vietnam War, earning the nickname 'Green Dragon' by the Viet Cong as it was used to break through heavy thickets in the midst of the jungle to attack and overrun enemy positions, but largely known as an APC and ACAV (armored cavalry assault vehicle) by the allied forces. (3, Starry p. 73/Dunstan p. 107). The M113 introduced new aluminum armor that made the vehicle much lighter than earlier vehicles; it was thick enough to protect the crew and passengers against small arms fire but light enough that the vehicle was air transportable and moderately amphibious. In the U.S. Army, the M113 series have long been replaced as front-line combat vehicles by the M2 and M3 Bradley, but large numbers are still used in support roles such as armored ambulance, mortar carrier, engineer vehicle, command vehicle, etc. The Army's Heavy Brigade Combat Teams are equipped with around 6,000 M113s and 4,000 Bradleys. The M113's versatility spawned a wide variety of adaptations that live on worldwide, and in U.S. service. These variants together represent about half of U.S. Army armored vehicles today. To date, it is estimated that over 80,000 M113s of all types have been produced and used by over 50 countries worldwide; making it one of the most widely used armored fighting vehicles of all time (4, M113A3 Family of Vehicles BAE Systems). The Military Channel's "Top Ten" series named the M113 the most significant infantry vehicle in history (5, "The 10 Greatest Infantry Fighting Vehicles in Military History." The Military Channel. Web page: Top Ten Infantry Fighting Vehicles. Retrieved 26 November 2008). The U.S. Army planned to retire the M113 family of vehicles by 2018, seeking replacement with the GCV Infantry Fighting Vehicle program, (6, The ground combat vehicle strategy: Optimizing for the future." U.S. Army. Retrieved 14 December 2009), but now replacement of the M113 has fallen to the Armored Multi-Purpose Vehicle (AMPV) program (7, Army Mulls $1.7 Billion Effort To Replace 3,000 M113s - *Defense.AOL.com*, 29 May 2012.

Army of the Republic of Vietnam (ARVN). The Army of the Republic of Vietnam was also known as the South Vietnamese Army. The ARVN included the ground forces of the Republic of South Vietnam Military Forces. The ARVN was formed in 1955 and it fell to the NVA in 1975 when Saigon was captured. It is estimated to have suffered 1,394,000 casualties (killed and wounded) during the Vietnam War.

As Soon As Possible (ASAP). In Vietnam this normally meant to get the mission done now. ASAP is ambiguous and should not be used in military plans.

Ash and Trash. Sometimes referred to as "Hash and Trash" was a single ship utility helicopter mission to resupply base camps, troops in the field, and transport people, animals, equipment, spare parts, food, water, beer, and more.

Blood Chit. An emergency notice printed on a cloth about 24 inches by 24 inches and in local languages (Vietnamese, Cambodian,

Laotian, etc.), that is carried by the military, usually air crewmen, that displays messages aimed at the civilians that ask them to help the service member in case they are shot down and offers monetary $$$ rewards for aiding them to safety. The term "chit" is of Anglo-Indian origin and means "a note of a sum owed." An important piece of survival gear, a blood chit promises to reward civilians who assist downed aviators. The purpose of the blood chit is to provide a downed air crew member hope of survival in unknown territory.

Browning Automatic Rifle (BAR). The M1918 BAR was a 7.62mm (.3in), gas operated, limited 20 round magazine capacity, and effective squad level automatic weapon used by US Forces in WWII and Korea. It was obsolete to the US Army by 1968. It was really too heavy (16 to 24 pounds) and too long (47 inches long) for the small frame of the Vietnamese, but it was issued to and used in Vietnam by some South Vietnamese troops, especially Regional Forces and Popular Forces (RF/PF). The BAR did not become standard issue in the U.S. Army until 1938 when it was issued to squads as a portable light machine gun. The U.S. Army began phasing out the BAR in the late 1950s and was without a portable light machine gun until the introduction of the M249 Squad Automatic Weapon (SAW) in the mid-1980s. The US gangster Clyde Barrow loved his customized (sawed off barrel and shortened stock) version of the BAR.

Bullet Stoppers. The slang term used by Army Aviators to describe the Cobra front seat pilots (who were also the turret minigun and 40mm gunner) in the COBRA attack helicopters. Another sadistic name used to describe the front seat snake drivers was: "meat in the seat." Tragically, WO1 Larry Bodell, one of Danny Hickman's and Larry Dandridge's flight school classmates, was killed by a bullet in the front seat of a 235th Aerial Weapons Company Cobra's in the spring of 1969. This book is dedicated to Jerry Markland, Barry Alexander, Larry Bodell and other classmates killed in Vietnam.

Bungee Cords. Attached to the roof of the cabin of the UH-1B and C Model gunships, these cords or safety lines were also attached to the free M60 guns the door gunners used. These bungee cords helped door gunners and crew chiefs (who were also door gunners) from losing their M60 machine gun if they dropped the gun or were wounded. These cords were also used by utility helicopter door gunners in some earlier model slicks (UH-Ds), before they had hard mounted door guns. The Viking Crew Chiefs and Door Gunners did not use bungee cords.

Captain (CPT). Army and US Marine Corps Captain. 2nd (O-1) and 1st Lieutenants (O-2) commanded platoons. Captains (O-3) normally commanded companies——and not to be confused with a Navy and US Coast Guard Captain (CAPT) who is equivalent in rank to an Army or Marine Colonel (O-6). Majors commanded the aviation companies and air cavalry troops. Lt. Colonels commanded battalions and cavalry squadrons; Colonels commanded Brigades; Major Generals commanded Divisions, Lt. Generals commanded Corps; and Generals commanded Armies.

Cavalry (CAV). There are two types of cavalry units in the US Army in Vietnam, Armored Cavalry and Air Cavalry. Air Cavalry was an air mobile helicopter organization and its horses were the UH-1, AH-1, and OH-6 in 1968 and 1969. Air Cavalry was a new concept and played by far the predominant role in the Vietnam War. Blades of Thunder Book II of II will address more about the lessons of air cavalry.

Charlie or Charles. Slang for Viet Cong (VC). The VC was the military arm of the National Liberation Front . Charles was a highly motivated, illusive, and determined enemy of the South Vietnamese and US government.

Chicken Plate (or Chicken Board). Slang for an approximate 15 pound, ceramic, bullet resistant armor chest plate and back plate worn by US helicopter crew members. It was sometimes referred to as a "Chicken board." It saved many lives and prevented many wounds and injuries when worn properly in its tailor-made vest. The chicken plate was a ceramic armor chest and back plate in a carrier that slipped over your head and fastened in front with Velcro straps. One side had a snap fastener so you could get out of it in a hurry. Pilots did not need the back plate because the seat they sat in was made of the similar ceramic plate armor. The door gunner and crew chief (who was also a door gunner) sat on the back plates and wore chest plates or both back and chest plates in the UH-1 because the pilots' seats were the only armored seats in the aircraft. Pilots did not wear the back plates and really did not need the back plate when seated in their armored seats, but they cherished the chest plates. Unfortunately the chicken plates were not available to all pilots early in the Vietnam War (pre-1967) and many aviation crew members were killed and wounded due to the lack of this simple, yet highly effective armor. And the vests for the chicken plates were scarce in the 121st AHC in 1968 and 1969. Without the chicken plate vest (holder), the chicken plate was worn under the shoulder straps of the pilots, but this allowed the plate to become an "unguided and dangerous missile" in a helicopter crash. This unsheathed and improperly secured plate severely injured and probably killed many crew members in Vietnam helicopter crashes. This is what broke Larry Dandridge's jaw and nearly took his head off on 28 March 1969. To this day, the author is terribly disappointed that the Army did not provide the vest he needed for his chicken plate.

Chinook (CH-47). The name of the CH-47A, B, and C model, twin main rotor (with no tail rotor), twin turbine engine, medium lift, helicopter built by Boeing Vertol for the US Army. It was affectionately referred to by Army Aviators as the "Shit Hook" and "the only aircraft in the Army that could have a mid-air collision with itself," which happened if anything bad happened to the combining transmission or rotor systems that caused the rotors to get out of synchronization. The Chinook hauled all sorts of supplies, ammunition, troops, small vehicles, and other cargo and was frequently used to sling load downed UH-1s and OH-6s back for repair or cannibalization and destruction. It could sling load a 105mm howitzer or 33 troops. The CH-47 A model could carry about 7,000 pounds payload in the mountains of Vietnam and about 8,000 pounds of payload at sea level.

Cobra (AH-1G). The Bell Helicopter AH-1G Huey Cobra, nicknamed "snake," began replacing the Huey UH-1B and C Model gunships in 1967. It was a streamlined, tandem seated, state-of-the art attack helicopter that was narrow, fast, and had a stability augmentation system that allowed for very accurate rocket, minigun, and 40mm cannon fire and later optically sighted and wire guided (TOW) missile fire. The Aircraft Commander (AC) sat in back and pilot gunner in front seat. The AC flew the aircraft most of the time and operated the rocket system and the pilot/gunner sat in the front seat below the AC and operated the minigun and 40mm that was mounted in a turret below the nose of the helicopter. Snakes carried more fuel, more armament, and were fast enough to keep up with and fly ahead of the troop transports that they covered and they turned out to be one of the "largest cans of whip ass" on the battlefield. The Cobra was the Army's first helicopter designed to be an attack helicopter.

Command and Control (C&C) Helicopter. Commanders used C&C Huey UH-1D and H Model helicopters (sometimes called Charlie-Charlie aircraft) that had a special console and with several radios mounted in the crew compartment to observe and control ground and air operations. The Commander could, for example, use a UHF radio to talk to the slicks, a VHF radio to talk to the gunships, UHF and VHF to talk to USAF tactical air support, and an FM radio to talk to the ground troops and artillery.

Commander (CO). The Commissioned Officer in command of a Platoon; Company, Troop, or Battery; Battalion, Squadron, or Regiment; Brigade or Task Force; Division; Corps; or Army or Theater. Platoons were commanded by Lieutenants. Companies, troops, and batteries were commanded by Captains and Majors. Battalions and Squadrons were commanded by Lt. Colonels. Regiments were ceremonial units only. Brigades were commanded by Colonels. Divisions were commanded by Major Generals (two star generals), Corps were commanded by Lt. Generals (three star generals), and Armies and theaters were commanded by Generals (four star generals).

Chief Warrant Officer (CWO). There were four ranks of Warrant Officer during Vietnam (WO1, CW2, CW3, and CW4) and today there are five (WO1, CW2, CW3, CW4, and CW5). Almost all the Army pilots in Vietnam in 1968 and 1969 were WO1s, 1st Lieutenants, and Captains. Most were on their first combat tour of duty and had graduated from flight school within the past 12 months.

Frog. Term of endearment used by troops when referring to the UH-1B and UH-1C Huey Gunship armed with the M75 40 Millimeter (mm) grenade-launcher or "Thumper" turret systems installed on its nose and a 2.75 inch (70MM) Folding Fin Aerial Rocket (FFAR) pod installed on each side of the aircraft.

Geneva Conventions. According to *http://encyclopedia2.thefree-dictionary.com/Geneva+Convention+relative+to+the+Treat-ment+of+Prisoners+of+War,* "the Geneva Conventions are a series of four international agreements (1864, 1906, 1929, 1949) signed in Geneva, Switzerland, that established the humanitarian principles by which the signatory countries are to treat an enemy's military and civilian nationals in wartime. The first convention was initiated by Jean-Henri Dunant; it established that medical facilities were not to be war targets, that hospitals should treat all wounded impartially, that civilians aiding the wounded should be protected, and that the Red Cross symbol should serve to identify those covered by the agreement. The second convention amended and extended the first. The third stated that prisoners of war should be treated humanely and that prison camps should be open to inspection by neutral countries. The 1949 conventions made further provisions for civilians falling into a belligerent's hands. Guerrilla combatants were extended protection in two 1977 amendments, which the U.S. did not sign. Violations of the Geneva Conventions were among the crimes included in the jurisdictions of the international criminal tribunals for the former Yugoslavia (1993) and Rwanda (1994) and the International Criminal Court (2002). The NVA and VC did not recognize the Geneva Conventions and treated the US POWs terribly as war criminals and terrorists.

Gook (also called Dinks, Slant Eyes, and Slopes). A disparaging term for a North Vietnamese Army (NVA) soldier or Vietnamese Communist (VC) guerrilla in the Vietnam War. Some Americans also used the negative and disrespectful term to refer to all Vietnamese and even all Asians. A sign and symptom of the very poor training of most US troops on the culture, language, history, and importance of the Vietnamese.

Hog (and heavy hog). Hogs and "heavy hogs" referred to UH-1B and UH-1C Gunships and Cobras (attack helicopters) that were loaded with the maximum load of ordnance (rockets, minigun, 40mm, etc.) and as much fuel as possible. They were called hogs and heavy hogs because they were so loaded or most often over loaded that they handled sluggishly, could not climb very fast, had limited airspeed capability, and did not have enough power to hover—meaning they handled like a "hog."

Hootch. The term for the barracks, huts, tents, and other living quarters that aviation crews lived in back at their base camp or airfield. The local national women who were hired to come in during daylight hours to do our laundry and polish our boots were called "Hootch maids." Yes, the Vikings and Tigers started off with polished boots each morning.

Huey. Bell Helicopters rotary wing aircraft (helicopter) was the most widely used helicopter in the Vietnam War. The Army named this helicopter the UH-1 Iroquois. Its combat load was from six to 11 troops, but the UH-D and H Models hauled up to 25 troops in emergencies, if there was room for the helicopter to make a running take off. The UH-1A, B, C, D, and H model, two bladed, single rotor, and single-turbine engine powered helicopter was originally designed for medical evacuation, but quickly became the utility helicopter of choice of the US Army. In 1968 and 1969 the UH-1B and C models were used as gunships (attack helicopters) and UH-1D and H model were used for troops transport, cargo transport, medical evacuation, flare dispensing, smoke dispensing, defoliation, psychological operations, search and rescue, command and control, and many other missions. The UH-1H helicopters are 13 place helicopters, with a 9500 pound maximum gross weight, and powered by the Lycoming T53-L-13 engine. The maximum length of the UH-1D and H models with rotors turning was 57 feet 0.67 inches and the height of the aircraft was 13 feet and 7.40 inches which varied according to weight and how much the cross tubes were spread. The Huey was the work horse of Army Aviation and the most significant Army equipment innovation of the era. The H model had 200 more horse power, which was sorely needed in combat. In Vietnam it took about ten hours of maintenance for every single hour of flight time. By 1991, the US Army Aviation Center Maintenance Contractor was performing about 4 hours of maintenance for every one hour the Huey flew in peace time, versus about 27 hours per flight hour for the CH-47D Model Chinook and the AH-64A Apache helicopters.

Instrument Flight Rules (IFR). Pilots frequently said they were IFR when they were flying in bad weather (formally called instrument meteorological conditions) and on instruments and could not see the ground, the horizon, or anything other than the white clouds, rain, snow, smoke, dust, other obscuration, or black darkness surrounding the aircraft in flight.

Iroquois. The Bell UH-1 Iroquois A, B, C, D, and H Model helicopters were known as the Huey. The A and B model were designed for medical evacuation and later troop transport and could carry six passengers. The C Model was provided a more powerful engine and improved (enlarged) main rotor system and was designed to be a gunship armed with a large variety of armament and some time smoke dispensing equipment. The UH-1D and H model Hueys were longer versions of C models with larger engines and could carry 11 troops.

Klick. In Vietnam, troops referred to a "klick" as a distance of 1,000 meters, which is equal to one kilometer, or .62 miles. If a ground commander or helicopter pilot radioed that his position was two clicks south of hill 121, he was 2,000 meters (2 kilometers or 1.24 miles) south of hill 121. Most historians concur that the term first came into wide use in the U.S. Military during the Vietnam War. However, the exact origin of the term has been lost.

Lieutenant (Lt.). The two lowest (junior) ranking company grades of officers in the Army and Marine Corps are second lieutenants (gold bar) and first lieutenants (silver bar). Lieutenants and Captains (double silver bar) were and still are called "company grade officers" and Majors (gold leaf), Lt. Colonels (silver leaf), and Colonels (Eagles) are called "field grade officers" and Brigadier Generals (one star), Major Generals (two stars), Lt. Generals (three stars), and full Generals (four stars) were and still are called "general officers."

Light Observation Helicopter (LOH). The Hughes model OH-6 Cayuse (nicknamed and pronounced "Loach," after the requirement acronym LOH—Light Observation Helicopter) is a single-turbine engine, light helicopter with a four-bladed main rotor system used for reconnaissance, personnel transport, escort, and attack missions, and observation——and at times emergency medical evacuation. The OH-6 Cayuse was the high performance and most crashworthy sports car of combat helicopters. These little birds hovered like mad hornets just a few feet over elephant grass, over jungle and vegetation, over enemy bunkers and hootches, under trees and bridges, over NVA and VC spider holes, with skids in the water of rivers-canals-rice paddies looking for, finding, and killing the enemy. The use of "hunter-killer" helicopter teams of one to two OH-6s as the hunter (and frequently the killer), with a much more heavily armed Cobra killer or pair of Cobra killers covering above was perhaps the most productive killing machine in Vietnam. Nothing found and destroyed the enemy more often, nothing found and created more opportunities for US Cavalry and other Air Mobile forces to successfully block, trap, engage, and destroy enemy forces than the OH-6 and Cobra hunter killer teams. The downside of the LOACH mission was these courageous pilots and their brave gunners were wounded, injured, and killed more frequently than any other group of helicopter pilots.

Manioc. Manioc is a shrub. It belongs to the Spurge family of plants and it grows in tropical climates. Cassava, manioc, and yucca are all names for the same starchy tuber grown through-out South America, Africa, and Asia. It is cultivated for its edible root. The manioc must be cooked properly to detoxify it before it is eaten and can be used in dumplings, soups, stews and gravies. You might be more familiar with it in its dried and powdered form: tapioca. This root is a dietary mainstay in many parts of the world and forms the carbohydrate base for many excellent meals.

Maximum Allowable Gross Weight. The maximum allowable (safe) total weight of the helicopter prior to take-off which was the basic weight of the aircraft plus the crew, personnel equipment, special devices, passengers, cargo, and usable fuel and oil. This weight is limited by the structure, power available, and landing load and it was routinely exceeded due to mission necessity by both slicks and gunships in Vietnam.

Military Assistance Command Vietnam (MACV). Created on 8 February 1962, MACV was the command reorganization that responded to the increase in United States military assistance to South Vietnam. MACV was first implemented to assist the Military Assistance Advisory Group (MAAG) Vietnam. MACV commanded and controlled every advisory and assistance effort in Vietnam, but was reorganized on 15 May 1964. MACV absorbed MAAG Vietnam to its command when combat unit deployment became too large for an advisory group type control structure. General Creighton W. Abrams was the MACV US Commanding General when the authors, Larry Dandridge and Danny Hickman, were in Vietnam. The air crews in this book responded to many MACV advisor team requests for resupply, transport, MEDIVAC, reconnaissance, night flare illumination, defoliation, and attack helicopter (gunship) and other missions. The MACV advisors assigned to many small RF/PF units were very brave men operating in high risk situations, under very austere and hardship situations. The authors of this book salute them for their courage and outstanding service to our great nation and the Vietnamese people.

Mine Warfare. The NVA and VC used anti personnel mines, anti-tank, and other mines extensively—to the point our troops biggest fear was being killed or maimed by mines and booby traps. The Vietnam War is sometimes best described as a war against tens of thousands of mines, hundreds of thousands of punji stake traps, man traps, spike traps, bamboo whip traps, barbed spike plate traps, spiked rock traps, command detonated overhead mines, trip wire devices, and other types of booby traps. More US troops were killed and wounded by these devices than all other enemy weapons combined. The authors watched from the air as many leg units, airborne units, and other ground units would walk and trip these hideous man killers. The use of helicopter borne airmobile and air cavalry troops helped prevent these injuries by preventing the need for these sky troopers to have to do so much walking through these mined and booby trapped areas.

Mister or Mr. This is how other officers, warrant officers, non commissioned officers, and enlisted troops addressed a warrant officer. If the Warrant was a CW2, CW3, or CW4—they were also frequently called Chief instead of Mister.

Night Test Flying. The unsung heroes of Army Aviation in Vietnam and today are the maintenance soldiers who included test pilots, technical inspectors, crew chiefs, mechanics, armament and avionics specialists, and others who kept the helicopters flying in the most adverse heat, humidity, heavy rain, fog, dust, sand, mud, insect, rodent, and other conditions imaginable. Although night test flying was prohibited everywhere else, it was an absolute requirement in Vietnam because the aircraft usually flew all day and were worked on all night. The Crew Chiefs owned, slept, ate, protected, managed, and worked on these helicopters day and night and are the envy of all of the pilots who flew with them. Crew Chiefs served as one of the door gunners as an additional and major duty.

North Vietnamese Army (NVA). The NVA was North Vietnam's Regular Army (called the Vietnamese People's Army or VPA) in the Vietnam War with South Vietnam and the United States of America. According to WIKIPEDIA, URL: *http://en.wikipedia. org/wiki/Vietnam_People%27s_Army,* The Free Encyclopedia, Page 2, paragraph 1.3 titled "Vietnam War," "Regular formations were sent to Southern Vietnam from 1965 onwards; the 325th Division's 101B Regiment and the 66th Regiment of the 304th Division met U.S. forces on a large scale, a first for the VPA, at the Battle of Ia Drang Valley in November 1965. The 308th Division's 88A Regiment, the 312th Division's 141A, 141B, 165A, 209A, the 316th Division's 174A, the 325th Division's 95A, 95B, the 320A Division also faced the US forces which included the 1st Cavalry Division, the 101st Airborne Division, the 173d Airborne Brigade, the 4th Infantry Division, the 1st Infantry Division and the 25th Infantry Division. Those VPA formations were seen as extremely brave forces by the US forces. Many of those formations later became main forces of the 3rd Division (Yellow Star Division) in Binh Dinh (1965), the 5th Division (1966) of 7th Military Zone (Capital Tactical Area of ARVN), the 7th (created by 141st and 209th Regiments originated in the 312th Division in 1966) and 9th Divisions (first Division of National Liberation Front of Vietnam in 1965 in Mekong Delta), the 10th Dakto Division in Dakto – Highland in 1972 south of Vietnam. General Tran Van Tra, one time commander of the B2 Front (Saigon) HQ, confirms that even though the VPA and the NLFV were confident in their ability to defeat the regular ARVN forces, US intervention in Vietnam forced them to reconsider their operations. We understood that the U.S. Army was superior to our own logistically, in weapons and in all things. So strategically we did not hope to defeat the U.S. Army completely. Our intentions were to fight a long time and cause heavy casualties to the United States, so the United States would see that the war was unwinnable and would leave."[124]

Packs. The slang term for passengers (or troops) on board. For example, the UH-1D and H Model would frequently carry four crew members (two pilots, a door gunner and crew chief/door gunner) and six US "packs" (US troops) on combat assaults, unless it was a very hot and humid day and the aircraft was operating in mountains—where the air was less dense and the density altitude was too high. Mountain operations and operations where aircraft had to hover out of ground effect (as when a Dust-Off was operating a hoist/jungle penetrator) frequently required the Aircraft Commander to limit his load to much less than six packs. The record for troops carried by an H model slick is around 25 troops (probably small Vietnamese troops) with very low fuel on board and not much equipment, there is no known official record of combat troop lifts.

Perforated Steel Planking (PSP). Quick connecting steel planking used to quickly build runways and hard stands. Larry Dandridge and others built bunker roofs with PSP in Vietnam. PSP was not very safe for helicopter running landings as the skid shoes could catch and hang-up on the PSP connections and flip the helicopter. WO1 Air Craft Commander McKeche (spelling could be wrong) and Pilot Larry Dandridge successfully shot an emergency hydraulics out running landing a to the Vinh Long Army Airfield runway in late 1968 after experiencing a hydraulics failure.

Sapper (VC and NVA). Reference *http://vveoda.org/wp-content/uploads/2011/09/Impact-of-SAPPER-in-RVN-War.pdf,* "The Impact of the Sapper on the Viet-Nam War" by the US Mission in Vietnam, published in October 1969, "The sapper as used by the VC and NVA retains the combat engineer connotation; however, the VC and NVA sapper mission encompasses those tasks normally assigned to units of the "commando-raider-ranger type. Thus the VC and NVA sapper is in fact a combat arm of the VC and NVA military. With minimum military expenditures, the VC and NVA sappers had the potential to inflict costly military and political damage to US and ARVN forces. They used guerrilla tactics and appeared at anytime and at any place. The VC and NVA sapper unit main weapons were the AK-47, B-40 and B-41 rocket launcher, mines, and explosives.

South Vietnam Regional Forces and Provincial Forces (RF & PF). According to Wikipedia The Free Encyclopedia, URL: *http://en.wikipedia.org/wiki/South_Vietnamese_Regional_*

Force Page 1 and History Paragraph. "During the Vietnam War, the South Vietnamese Regional Forces were roughly akin to militias. Recruited locally, they fell into two broad groups - Regional Forces and Popular Forces. During the early 1960s the Regional Forces manned the country-wide outpost system and defended critical points, such as bridges and ferries. There were some 9,000 such positions, *half of them in the Mekong Delta region*. In 1964, the Regional Forces were integrated into the Army of the Republic of Vietnam (ARVN) and placed under the command of the Joint General Staff. When U.S. forces began to withdraw from South Vietnam during 1969 and the ARVN began the task of fighting the communist main force units, Regional forces took on a new importance. For the first time, they were deployed outside their home areas and were sometimes attached to ARVN units. By 1973 the Regional Forces had grown to 1,810 companies. Charged primarily with local defense, they were too lightly armed and equipped to withstand attack by regular People's Army of Vietnam units supported by tanks and artillery. The South Vietnamese Popular Force sometimes abbreviated PFPF or PF consisted of local militias that protected their home villages from attacks by first Viet Cong forces and later by People's Army of Vietnam units. Originally called the Civil Guard and the Self-Defense Corps, they were integrated into the Army of the Republic of Vietnam in 1964 and placed under the command of the Joint General Staff. The Popular Force was one of two broad groups of militia, the other being the Regional Forces. The American forces referred to both groups as 'Ruff-Puffs' referring to the abbreviation RFPF."

Rear Echelon Mother F#^*er (REMF). The slang, derogatory, and insulting term that combat soldiers (infantry, armor, artillery, combat engineers, aviators, door gunners, crew chiefs, and others) used to refer to troops who had much safer and much more comfortable jobs in the rear (administrative, food service, music, supply, ordnance, combat support, and almost all Air Force folks, etc.).

Revetments. Protective barricades made of dirt or cement filled 55 gallon drums that aircraft were parked in to prevent enemy small arms and fragmentation damage to aircraft from grenades, mortar fire, rockets, recoilless rifle, and artillery fire.

Rome Plow. The Rome plow is defined in Wikipedia at *http:// en.wikipedia.org/wiki/Rome_plow* as, The very large, armored, specially modified bulldozers used in South Vietnam by the United States military during the Vietnam War. First used in III Corps (Military Region III), major land clearing operations commenced in May 1967 upon the arrival of the 169th Engineer Battalion. Prior to plowing operations, preparatory machine-gun, mortar, and 90mm tank guns were fired into the forests and jungles, thus clearing a path for the Rome plows to commence their runs, clearing jungle vegetation and cover that could be used by the Viet Cong and North Vietnamese forces. The plows took their name from the city of Rome, Georgia, where they were made by the Rome Plow Company (now located in Cedartown, Georgia). The plows were equipped with a very sharp "stinger blade" which weighed more than two tons and was able to cut down trees, which were then burned. When fully equipped, a Rome plow weighed 48,000 pounds without the Rome plow kit. It was a major innovation used by the US Army in Vietnam.[125]

Rocket Propelled Grenade (RPG). The basic design of a rocket propelled shaped charge of the RPG was developed by the Soviets shortly after World War II in the form of the RPG-2. The VC and NVA RPG were similar in function to the US WWII bazooka and the Nazi German Panzerfaust. The VC and NVA made maximum use of this excellent, shoulder fired anti tank weapon in Vietnam.

Rung U-Minh. The legendary "Forest of Darkness," the U-Minh Forest. For centuries a safe haven for pirates, smugglers, bandits, and recently the Viet Cong. An area the French could not control or conquer, a place where the US and ARVN artillery and gunships had almost standing "free fire permission for almost every square mile." Hundreds of square miles of swamps, canals, rivers, heavy forests, high reeds, palms, ferns, POW Camps, and excellent cover for the VC to hide and operate. VC weapons manufacturing, VC ammunition and weapons stores, VC hospitals, and thousands of VC operated out of the U-Minh—where they also controlled the civilian population. The area was the target of many successful US and ARVN operations and it was also the target of B52 massive bombing. The VC reacted like angry hornets when American and ARVN troops came near the U-Minh.

Schlep. From German and Yiddish meaning to drag or haul (an object); to walk, esp. to make a tedious journey.

Short. Slang for about to complete a combat tour and less than one month left in Vietnam. To prevent the accompanying grief, shock, anxiety, and depression caused to all crew members, when a pilot, gunner, or crew chief was killed or seriously wounded or injured during their last weeks or days in Vietnam, most units grounded air crew members the last two weeks of their combat tour. Unfortunately and tragically, many units were short crew members and required crews to fly up until the last day or so in Vietnam—at least one of the authors beloved friends and classmates, WO1 Barry Alexander was killed in action flying in his last week in Vietnam.

Sortie. A sortie is a combat mission of an individual aircraft, starting when the aircraft takes off and ending on its return. If ten Army UH-1s take off in a flight and conduct one combat assault mission and return to their starting point, that equals ten sorties.

Warrant Officer (WO). There were four grades of aviation WOs in Vietnam. Warrant Officers were referred to as "Mister" by all other grades and enlisted men and women and junior WOs called warrants either sir or mister. "Wobbly One" was the nickname often used to refer to new Warrant Officers of the grade Warrant Officer One. There are five grades of Warrant Officers in today's Army.

Viet Cong (VC). According to Wikipedia, The Free Encyclopedia, URL: *http://en.wikipedia.org/wiki/Viet_Cong,* the term Viet Cong appeared in newspapers beginning in 1956. It is a contraction of *Việt Nam Cộng-sản,* (Vietnamese Communist). The Viet Cong was a political organization and army in South Vietnam and Cambodia that fought the United States and South Vietnamese governments during the Vietnam War from 1959 to 1975, and emerged on the winning side. It had both guerrilla and regular army units, as well as a network of cadres who organized peasants in the territory it controlled.

APPENDIX G:
ABOUT THE AUTHOR W. LARRY DANDRIDGE

Larry Dandridge is the founder, chief operating manager, editor, and a writer with Tigers, Vikings, and Vipers Publishing, LLC. His leadership, aerospace, business, and logistics articles have been published in over 24 magazines, journals, and newspapers and two books in the US, Germany, and England. He was also the founder and chief operating manager, principal owner, and board chairman of Community Loving Care (CLC) Hospice, LLC in Wentzville, MO. CLC Hospice LLC was one of the most successful hospices in MO from 2002 to 2012 based on quality of care, customer satisfaction, profitability, safety, and employee retention!

Larry is also a certified business process re-engineering specialist and lean six sigma black belt. Until he retired in June of 2014 he was the East Region Sample Data Collection and Analysis (SDCA) Manager, Proposals Manager, and a Program Manager, Senior Engineer, Logistician, and Analyst with QinetiQ North America, Inc. He is also a past program manager, scientist, industrial operations expert, and logistics innovator with Battelle Pacific NW Laboratory, Cobro Corporation, and Westar Aerospace and Defense Group, Inc.

He has successfully led the re-engineering and reinvention of over 15 businesses and government organizations including a textile manufacturing business, a vehicle remanufacturing facility, an aircraft maintenance facility, a police department, a federal law enforcement training center's logistics department, three Army logistics (DOL) operations, a food service operation, a mortuary, a university book store, a harbor craft operation, a vehicle maintenance operation, a medical services business, an ammunition supply operation, and other organizations. Larry also holds the record at QinetiQ North America, Incorporated's logistics sector and two of its legacy companies for most contracts sold or won (over 125) in a five year period. Larry's programs also set the company record for most industry awards (4) and most nominations (55) in a ten year period.

Larry Dandridge is also an Army ex-enlisted infantryman; ex-aviation Warrant Officer; ex-combat attack, utility, and scout helicopter pilot; ex-Army fixed wing single and multi-engine pilot, flight examiner, maintenance test pilot, and instructor pilot. He is a retired Army Master Aviator. He has a commercial pilot's license in helicopters, airplanes, and instruments, and is an FAA Certified Flight Instructor (CFI) in airplanes, helicopters, instruments, and basic ground academics. He has worked as a multi and single engine commercial (air taxi) pilot. He served in combat in Vietnam in 1968 and 1969 with the 121st Assault Helicopter Company (Air Mobile Light) and the 235th Armed Helicopter Company (Cobra aerial weapons company).

He served as the US Army Aviation Center's Chief of Aircraft Maintenance and at various locations worldwide as an Army flight instructor and instrument flight examiner, safety officer, flight training company commander, an aviation intermediate maintenance company (375 troops) commander, airport manager and commander, a battalion operations and intelligence officer, a battalion executive officer, a US-German negotiator, logistics advisor in Iran, cobra attack helicopter assistant fielding team chief, aviation POMCUS (long term humidity controlled storage of attack helicopters) science project officer, depot transportation officer, 101st Airborne Division material officer, and locomotive operator. His military decorations include the Purple Heart, German Silver Cross of Honor, two Vietnamese Crosses of Gallantry, the Legion of Merit, the Defense Joint Meritorious Service Medal, five Army Meritorious Service Medals, 15 Combat Air Medals, the Army Commendation Medal, and others.

He is also an honors graduate of three police academies and has served as a motorcycle officer and patrol officer for police departments in Missouri and Alabama. He was the only recruit in his St. Louis County and Municipal Police Academy Class to fire expert in both the pistol and shotgun combat courses. In his year with the Bridgeton Police Department in Missouri he set records in arrests, especially DUI arrests, and in ten years as a police officer had no complaints made against him. He was commended numerous times for his outstanding performance as a police officer.

He is a graduate of the electronics and carpentry shops of Charleston, SC's Murray Vocational High School. He has a BS degree in Aeronautical Science with a minor in business from Embry Riddle Aeronautical University and a MS degree in Transportation Management from Florida Institute of Technology. He is a graduate of the Army Transportation Officer Advanced Course, Armed Forces Staff College, Haus Rissen Institute (international political/ strategic think tank), and over 20 other military specialty schools, including logistics, instructor pilot, academic instructor, contracting and procurement, special operations, command and staff, and others.

He has a California Community College Teaching Credential in Aeronautics, Business, Industrial Operations, and Military Science. He also has worked as a federal law enforcement training center (FLETC) consultant, and college business, economics, industrial operations, technical report writing, military science, and aeronautics instructor for the Embry Riddle Aeronautical University, University of Maryland, Chapman University, and Lassen Community College. Larry also served with great success as an extension division director for Lassen Community College and Chapman University in Herlong, CA.

As the past Association of the US Army (AUSA) Charleston, SC President, he guided the chapter to best small chapter in 2009 and runner-up small chapter for four years. He is a current Vice President at Large of the AUSA 3rd Region and the Vice President for Veteran Affairs of the Charleston, SC AUSA Chapter. He is an active volunteer, patient advisor, and patient and family centered care (PFCC) instructor and member of the Strategic Planning Team, the Customer Service Council, and the PFCC Committee with the Ralph H. Johnson VA Medical Center in Charleston, SC. He is a VA, State of SC, and American Legion Trained Veterans Service Officer and an Army Combat Related Service Compensation Ambassador in training.

A member of the "West Point Logistics Hall of Fame (inducted in 2002)," his awards include the "2006, 2007, 2008 AUSA Exceptional

Service Awards," "2009 AUSA 3rd Region Brenda M. Dougherty Award," the "2009 AUSA Chapter President's Award," "2009 Ralph H. Johnson VA Medical Center Volunteer and Sponsor of the Year Award," "2010 MOAA Charleston SC Chapter Robert J. Lahm Award," "2011 AUSA 3rd Region Significant Achievement Award," the "2013 AUSA 3rd Region's President's Award," "the VA Special 2012 Volunteer Award," and the "Runner-up for the 2012 VA Spirit Award." He has also received three "Silver Quill Awards" for writing.

He is a member of the Vietnam Helicopter Pilots Association (VHPA), Army Aviation Association of America (AAAA), Association of the US Army (AUSA), Military Officers Association of America (MOAA), Vietnam Helicopter Crew Members Association (VHCMA), Military Order of Purple Heart (MOPH), American Legion, Disabled America Veterans (DAV), 121st Aviation Association, and a past member of the Military Order of World Wars (MOWW), Women in Defense (WID), the Charleston, SC Exchange Club, and Wentzville, MO Rotary.

He is married to Judith Ann (Siegel) Dandridge and the proud father of five children, including: two nurse practitioners, one dietitian, one lawyer, and one computer programmer. He is also very proud of his nine grandchildren. He is the owner of two Italian Greyhounds. He likes to play tennis and basketball and he enjoys grandchildren, traveling, fishing, writing, history, public speaking, swimming, and reading. He is currently writing book II on Army Helicopter Pilots, Crew Chiefs, and Door Gunners in Vietnam titled *Blades of Thunder Book II* which should be published in 2016.

APPENDIX H: THE JOINT LIBRARY OF CONGRESS AND VETERANS ADMINISTRATION'S VETERANS HISTORY PROJECT

Many Americans and some of the news media did not support our troops or their families during the Vietnam War, and after. And less than one percent of Americans today serve in the military. Most Americans have very little education on US military history (especially WWI, WWII, the Korean War, and Vietnam War) and world geography and events. The United States of America needed a program that educates the public on what our military stands for and what our military has done for this great nation and the world in general. To help correct this ignorance and to show the tremendous contributions of Veterans, the VA and the Library of Congress started the "Veterans History Project" to help educate the public on the tremendous contributions our troops and their families make to our wonderful country.

This Veterans History Project is similar to what Steven Spielberg is trying to do with Holocaust victims. Only instead of Holocaust victims, the VA and Library of Congress are documenting our veterans' history and contributions before the veteran expires. That is, the VA and the Library of Congress want to interview and record all the veterans that they can, before they expire or become too ill to interview. The VA wants to interview Veterans from all generations including WWII, Greece, Congo (Zaire), Korea, Vietnam, Dominican Republic, Guatemala, Philippines, Nicaragua, El Salvador, Iran, Panama, Desert Storm, Granada, Bosnia and Kosovo, Somalia, Desert Storm, Iraq, Afghanistan, and other wars, insurgencies, and campaigns. The VA and Library of Congress then want to file these interviews in the Library of Congress for all Americans to see on-line our nation's veterans' contributions to this great nation and the world during times of peace and war.

The VA will come to the Veteran's home, assisted living home, or skilled nursing facility, if the Veteran cannot get to the local VA Medical Center. The VA will also conduct joint interviews of Veterans if the Veterans prefer a group interview instead of a one-on-one interview. These low stress and enjoyable interviews take from 30 minutes to an hour and will be cherished by the Veteran and his or her family members and friends. The VA will give copies of the interview on a Compact Disc to the Veteran to share with his or her immediate family members.

The author of this book encourages all living US military Veterans from all branches of the military and from all wars and eras of military service to go to *http://www.loc.gov/vets/* and read about how to enroll in the joint Library of Congress and Veterans Administration's "Veterans History Project," and then, schedule a taped (filmed, recorded, and digitized) interview with the local Veterans Medical Center (hospital), Public Affairs Office (PAO), and Volunteer Activity. *We especially need to get our beloved WWII and Korean War Vets in to make these recordings before they are all gone!* If you live in lower state SC and the area covered by the Ralph H. Johnson VA Medical Center (from the SC-NC border to Hinesville, GA and Savannah, GA and from Orangeburg, SC to Charleston, SC), you should contact the Ralph H. Johnson VA Medical Center's Chief of Volunteer Services, Mr. Fred Lesinski, at 109 Bee Street, Charleston SC 29401, Office Phone: 843-789-7488, Cell Phone: 843-200-3350, Fax: 843-789-6132, and Email: *Edmund. Lesinski@va.gov* to schedule a Veteran History Project interview and recording. Copies of the interview will be given to the veteran and his or her family will cherish this interview!

APPENDIX I:
PLEASE SUPPORT FISHER HOUSE CHARLESTON, THE RALPH H. JOHNSON VA MEDICAL CENTER, AND THE RHJ VA MED CENTER'S PATIENTS AND FAMILIES

Besides wanting to write an interesting, informative, accurate, and thought provoking book, the reason I wrote this book is to help raise money to purchase approved property for the construction of the **Fisher House Charleston** near to the Ralph H. Johnson (RHJ) VA Medical Center in Charleston, SC. All 2015 profits from the sale of this book will go to Fisher House Charleston.

The Fisher House Charleston project is a joint effort, led by Durbin and Trux Emerson and between Fisher House and local patriots. The Fisher House Charleston will provide comfortable refuge for families of patients who are being treated at the Ralph H. Johnson (RHJ) VA Medical Center. The RHJ VA Medical Center supports over 64,000 veteran families (and a few military families) in 22 coastal counties from Hinesville, GA and Savannah, GA to the NC-SC border and westward to Orangeburg, SC.

Many veterans and their families cannot afford the cost of lodging at America's favorite vacation destination, historic Charleston, SC. Located in historic downtown Charleston, the 117-bed RHJ VA Medical Center provides first class and acute medical, surgical, and psychiatric inpatient care, as well as outpatient primary and mental healthcare at its main facility and six community-based and annex outpatient clinics in Savannah, Hinesville, Myrtle Beach, Goose Creek, Beaufort, and the Trident Annex.

There are more than 4,500 inpatient stays annually at the RHJ VA Medical Center. Having family nearby is greatly beneficial to those battling illness, wounds, or injuries. The length of time a patient spends in the hospital is greatly reduced when family is near. The frequency of readmission also decreases when family members closely participate in the recovery process. Shorter stays in the hospital and less frequent readmissions benefit the hospital as well as the patient and taxpayers, allowing more veterans to be treated annually. Family involvement results in fewer patient falls, reduced stress and depression, improved patient privacy, confidentiality, improved communication and social support, and increased patient satisfaction. The patient load at Charleston is increasing by approximately 7 per cent per year.

Trux and Durbin Emerson are leading this wonderful charitable project and they are determined to raise the over $4.25 million dollars that it will take to purchase land to donate to the VA so that Fisher Foundation[126] (which has pledged the over $10 million to build the facility) can build this lodging facility near the RHJ VA Medical Center. As of February of 2015 over $2 million dollars has been raised and paid towards the purchase of the land for Fisher House Charleston.

This unique public/private partnership will assure Fisher House Charleston is forever funded to continue to operate. To make donations to Fisher House Charleston, go to *http://fisherhousecharleston. org/* and donate on line or make checks payable to: **Fisher House Charleston, Inc., PO Box 829, Johns Island, SC 29457.**

APPENDIX J:
TIGER, VIKING, STOGIE, RAT PACK, AND DUST OFF (MEDICAL EVACUATION) MINI-BIOGRAPHIES (ENDNOTES)

i - George Taylor, Captain.

First Lieutenant George Taylor grew up in an Army family. George was born in Michigan in 1944 while his Dad was serving in Europe. George never considered any one place home due to moving around as a dependent so much, until he moved to Montana. George's dad was a full bird colonel in Vietnam at the same time George was serving in the Tigers and Vikings. George was promoted to captain and became an accomplished slick and gunship AC, fire team leader, and Viking platoon leader (call sign Viking 26). George is remembered by all his friends as having a slow Texas drawl and his use of "ole Partner" when he addressed his fellow aviators. He was cool and calm under fire, no matter how bad things got. He and Captain Bubba Segrest became good friends while they were in the 121st. George stuck with aviation and helicopters after his separation from the Army in 1970. Initially, he spent a good bit of time working overseas. He was single and living out of a suitcase, so working where ever sounded interesting, uncomplicated, and attractive to him. After becoming a civilian in 1970, he joined Air America and went back to Southeast Asia, Vietnam initially and then Laos for three years and finally back to Vietnam through the evacuation of Vietnam—"departing" on the USS Midway. He then worked in the "oil patch" in Indonesia and Abu Dhabi as a pilot. He spent a couple of years in Saudi Arabia flying geological survey teams around "the Kingdom" before deciding it was time to come back to America.

George discovered western Montana in the early '70s and he really liked it and always felt that would be a place he would live someday as he never viewed the ex-patriot lifestyle as something long term. Although there wasn't much in the way of helicopter work, he moved to the Flathead Valley (Whitefish) in the early 1980s and worked summer seasons in Alaska. He met his future bride, an OR nurse, in Whitefish over a winter break and George said, "She must have been real bored as we started hanging out together." George and his wife went to Florida for a couple of years where he worked a contract in Central America until the hospital in Kalispell finally had an opening for an Emergency Medical Services (EMS) pilot. He and his wife moved back to Montana and the Flathead valley and he worked with them for 20 years leaving in 2008. During that time George and his wife had a daughter making them a family of four including a step daughter. George is still involved in the business employed part time at a Fixed Bas Operator (FBO) in Kalispell in their aircraft charter operation. George has flown more than 14,000 hours in the UH-1, and Bell 204, 205, 212, 206, 407,429 helicopters and Hughes 500 and 530 helicopters. Most of his flying has been "bush" work in remote areas with some off-shore and Emergency Medical Service also. George is not flying much anymore and mostly doing paperwork, but thankful to be employed as his youngest has a year of school left to finish her Masters in England. George says, "It's all been good; I've got no complaints or regrets and am blessed with three great ladies in my life!"

ii - Sid Seitz, Captain

Sid Seitz, Captain was drafted into the Army in February 1965. He was bused from his home town in Omaha, Nebraska, to Ft. Leonard Wood, MO, for induction and all the shots.

After graduating from basic combat training, Private Sietz was shipped to Ft Jackson, SC, for Infantry Officers' Candidate School (OCS). He was then shipped to Ft Benning, Georgia. Sid says OCS and Fort Benning was his "Comeuppance." Sid made it through OCS and applied for Army Flight School. He was one of Bubba Segrest's TAC Officers when Bubba went through OCS. Bubba was one of the best officer candidates in Sid's company. After graduating from Flight School at Fort Rucker, Alabama, Sid was sent to Vietnam. He landed in Vietnam on January 1, 1969. After a couple of Air Force C130 rides he ended up in Soc Trang, South Vietnam assigned to the 121st Assault Helicopter Company. He was put up in a two story barracks building and was scared of being mortared or rocketed in a wooden barracks. Sure enough, Sir Charles (the VC) decided to lob a few mortar rounds in that night. The mortars were a rude welcome from the VC. Sid was appointed as the Blue Tiger Platoon Commander. Tiger Surprise was assigned to his platoon. He hated flying in combat assaults, because his flight position was "Trail." Sid said, "The VC usually couldn't hit his ass with both hands but it was the To Whom It May Concern rounds that got him excited." (The VC had a habit of shooting at the leading aircraft in a flight and hitting one of the aircraft in the rear of the flight.)

On March 28, 1969, it was Sid who would fly his aircraft back to the LZ to rescue and medical evacuate Brian King, Larry Dandridge, and the enlisted crew members of crashed Viking 21. Sid said, "Our mission was always twofold: Kill the bad guys and save the good guys." Sid said, "I didn't put a clock on it, but I believe it took a good five minutes to get back to the LZ. The longest time was getting the wounded and injured guys from that terribly broken Huey B Model gunship to my slick. Once on board, I pushed the pedal to the metal. My crew chief yelled at me to slow down or the transmission would blow. I can't think the flight was much more than 15, maybe 20 minutes from the LZ to Binh Thuy." Sid was later transferred to the Vikings. He became Viking 26, the Viking Gunship Platoon Leader. Later in his tour and much to Sid's displeasure, he was assigned to the 164th Aviation Group Staff in Can Tho. As a Tactical Operations Center (TOC) Officer, his shifts were two days, two nights, and then two days off. Captain Sietz would jump a flight back home to Soc Trang and go out on missions the next day, most always with George Taylor or Bill Ferguson. After Fergie (Captain Bill Ferguson) got shot and George left Vietnam, Sid stopped going back. Sid left Vietnam on December 29, 1969. He flew approximately 1,500 hours in Vietnam and after. His military awards include the Bronze Star, Army Commendation Medal, over 25 Combat Air Medals, and others. Sid completed the Infantry Officer's Advanced Course at Fort Benning, GA and got out of the Army in August of 1973.

After the Army Sid graduated from St Martin's College in Lacy, WA. Sid then worked 36 years for Michelin Tire Corporation as a manager and store owner. Sid and his wife had two beloved children; a son (now deceased) who attended West Point and Harvard Business School and a daughter. He and his wife live in Kirkland, WA. Sid has been married to his beloved wife for almost 51 years. Sid says, "1969 was a chapter in my life that I would like to forget at times. Then there are the times that I am so proud to have served with such great men as the Tigers and Vikings I bust buttons off my shirt. I still wear a black t-shirt (a part of the Viking uniform) from time-to-time and I am very proud to do so!"

iii - Brian King, Chief Warrant Officer 2

Brian King, Chief Warrant Officer 2 is from Ocala, FL and he flew Tiger slicks and Viking gunships in Vietnam. In June 1965, Brian attended community college in GA and FL, and then joined the Army. He completed flight school with Warrant Officer Rotary Wing Aviation Class (WORWAC) 68-7A3 on July 1, 1968. He served in the 121st Assault Helicopter Company as a slick and gunship pilot, wing ship aircraft commander, and fire team leader. He also flew two weeks in the 235th Aerial Weapons Company as a Cobra pilot. After Vietnam Brian King retired as a Chief Warrant Officer (CW2) in September of 1970. He spent most of his military time as a patient after the gunship crash of March 28, 1969. His military awards include the Combat Air Medal with 28th Oak Leaf Clusters, Army Commendation Medal, and Vietnam Cross of Gallantry with Bronze Star (two awards).

He was married on June 16, 1970. Brian went back to college and received a baccalaureate degree in business in 1973. In 1974 he went to a Bob Jones University (and says he became a Christian) and received his Master's Degree in 1976. He taught and led the Insurance Department at a Community College for a few years and in 1978 he went into business, bought several insurance agencies, and achieved much success. Brian and his wife have lived in the Orlando area since 1988. Brian retired from business completely in 2006. There are three children in the family; two daughters and one son. The oldest daughter is a teacher in central Florida. The younger daughter is an actress and casting director in the region. His son is an Army Chief Warrant Officer and helicopter Apache flight instructor. Brian is a volunteer staff member of his church in Longwood, Florida. Larry Dandridge and Brian have remained lifelong friends.

iv - Bill Ferguson, Captain

Bill Ferguson is from Greenville, SC. He was a Tiger and Viking in the 121st. He flew over 1,100 hours during his Vietnam combat tour in 1968 and 1969. He served in a Cavalry unit between his assignments at Soc Trang. He got out of the Army in September 1973. Bill and Larry Dandridge were assigned together at Hunter Army Airfield, GA, between 1969 and 1972 and they have been lifelong friends. Bill completed college at the University of Tampa, FL, in 1974. His military decorations include the Silver Star, the Purple Heart, the Air Medal with V device for Valor, the Vietnamese Cross of Gallantry, the Army Commendation medal, and others. He retired in 2013 in the Charlotte, NC area after a highly successful career with a large company that sold electrical cable and wire. He is happily married and has a beloved daughter who is an attorney. Bill is an avid and loyal fan of the Clemson University Tiger athletic teams and he was honored at the Clemson Football Home Coming Game in 2014 as a "Vietnam Veteran, Hero, and Patriot Extraordinaire." This was quite special to Bill and his family since there was not any welcome home in 1969 when he returned seriously wounded from Vietnam. Bill and his wife own a camper and they travel frequently and are enjoying our beautiful country.

v - Crew Chief George Quackenbush, Specialist 5 (E-5)

George Quackenbush was raisd in the foothills of central California, studied Aeronautics at Reedley College, was drafted into the US Armywhen he left college to work to finance continuing his education. Immediately after basic training and Advanced Individual Training (Honor Graduate), he was sent to Vietnam as a component repairman in the 121 AHC at Soc Trang in November 1967. While in maintenance, he quickly moved up to shop lead, then hangar supervisor for second shift. He was quickly bored with maintenance, so requested a transfer into the Viking gun platoon as gunner during his second tour of duty in Vietnam. This experience was the start of a lifelong love of helicopter aviation and a constantly advancing career in aviation. On returning to the USA, he continued his aeronautical studies to get his FAA airframe and power plant mechanic license, FAA Inspection Authorization, and FAA advanced ground instructor licenses.

As soon as studies were completed, his first job offer was to ferry a Bell 205 helicopter to Peru for flight support for an offshore oil exploration project. The ferry was to Panama where the helicopter met the drilling ship as it was exiting the Pan Canal and floated to Peru. Peru was just the start as Columbia, Panama, Nicaragua, Iran, Mexico, Brazil, back to Peru and Chile followed as mechanic, inspector, instructor, director of maintenance, aviation adviser for the US State Department. He later became a Bell Helicopter technical representative and Vice President of Latin Operations for a large helicopter repair facility. George's work has taken him off shore, on shore, in the jungle, in the desert, in mountains, at garden spots and dung holes. He has worked in beautiful hangars and under large trees. George says it has all been interesting and challenging. His travels have taken him to every country in North, Central and South America and numerous countries in Europe and he will travel to Antarctica in the next few months.

He married a very special lady from Peru that has followed him and stayed by his side through thick and thin all over the world. He and his wife have two wonderful daughters. George says, "Looking back, I had no idea how much Vietnam changed my life and had no idea that life could be so much fun because of those changes. I thought that because we all flaunted rules and had no use for rank on the flight line that we were not destined for much, but to be a Viking you had to have other positive qualities including: being hard working 24/7, reliable, a team player, adventurous, able to accept risk, able to conquer fear, willing mentors as well as students, able to think outside of the box, and have high ethical and moral standards. With these qualities, it should be no surprise that so many of the Viking crews have excelled in their chosen professions. Their successes make me proud to have been a part of that gun platoon. A true band of brothers!" George also says, "He is the luckiest SOB on this planet as he didn't get so much as a hang nail during two years in Vietnam while so many others were killed or seriously injured and that luck continues today in love and health. What a ride!"

vi - Jim Saunders, Specialist 5 (E-5)

Jim Saunders, Specialist 5 (E-5) served in the 121st Assault Helicopter Company as a Viking gunship crew chief and door gunner and in the 7/1st Air Cavalry Squadron as a crew chief and door gunner. Jim flew over 1600 combat hours and was awarded the Purple Heart with one Oak Leaf Cluster (two awards), the Army Commendation Medal with three Oak Leaf Clusters (four medals total) and "V" device for valor, over 20 Combat Air Medals and other awards. Jim Saunders is from Colorado, returned to Colorado, and spent 42 years in law enforcement. He retired as a lieutenant for a large sheriff's office and was the chief of police for two smaller agencies. His final job was as the undersheriff for a mid-sized county. He and his wife retired and live in California today.

vii - Daniel T. Eisman, Specialist 5

Daniel T. Eisman, Specialist 5 was wounded twice in Vietnam and extended his tour of duty there. He flew over 2,000 flight hours as a door gunner and crew chief on UH-1D Tiger slicks and UH-1B Model Viking gunships. He also served as a crew chief on Cobras. After leaving the Army he went to law school and accepted Jesus Christ as his personal Lord and Savior. One of the most successful Vikings today, he became the Chief Justice of the Idaho State Supreme Court. He has written an excellent book, titled "Freedom Is Your Destiny!" that uses his combat experiences to relate to his strong religious education and beliefs. His book information follows: ISBN: 978-0-9897133-9-9, Library of Congress Control Number: 2013945042, published and can be ordered from Desert Sage Press, P.O. Box 357, Eagle, Idaho 83616 or *www.desertsagepress.com*. His E-book is also available from *www.amazon.com*.

viii - Jim Zeitler, Chief Warrant Officer 4

Jim Zeitler, Chief Warrant Officer 4 (Ordnance Corps) flew door gunner in Tiger slicks and Viking gunships in Vietnam. He separated as a Specialist 5 (E-5) from the Army in July, 1970, and went back to New York, married, and worked as a truck mechanic. He went back into the Army in February, 1976. Unfortunately, he couldn't return to the aviation field, so he became a highly successful tank and automotive, wheeled and tracked vehicle, engineer equipment, power generation (generators), and material handling equipment (MHE) technician. He was appointed a warrant officer in July, 1978. He retired from the Army in October, 1994 as a Chief Warrant Officer 4. After his highly successful Army career he worked as a Fleet Manager for Ryder, First Group America, L3, and other fleet maintenance management companies. Jim retired again in January, 2014, and now does things he didn't have enough time to do when he was working. Jim and his wife live in the Fayetteville, NC area.

ix - Specialist 5 Keith Brinnon

Specialist 5 Keith Brinnon served in the 121st AHC from April 1, 1968 to November 17, 1969 as a Tiger and Viking crew chief and door gunner. Keith flew over 2,800 combat hours in Vietnam. His military decorations included the Purple Heart, Air Medal with the V device for valor and the 28 oak leaf clusters, several Army Commendation Medals, and other awards. Keith got out of the Army in September of 1970. He returned to his home town of Springfield, OH, where he started his career in the tool and die maker field. In August of 1984, he went to work for the United States Air Force as a civil servant and retired in December of 2013 after 29 years. His last position in the Air Force was the Chief of the Commander's Action Group (CAG) at Wright Patterson Air Force Base. After retirement Keith started an investment company that purchased and flipped foreclosed homes. Keith married in January, 1976 and divorced several years later. Shortly after his divorce, he was reintroduced to his Lord Jesus Christ. He met his second wife shortly after and has been married ever since. Keith has three sons and three grandsons and a granddaughter. Keith also did mission work which involved taking Vietnam veterans back to Vietnam to help them with their healing process of the war. Keith made a total of five trips back to where so many of his war memories are.

x - Specialist 5 Michael Dewey

Specialist 5 Michael Dewey was a Tiger slick and Viking gunship crew chief and door gunner in Vietnam. He was born in Cleveland, OH, and grew up in Cincinnati, OH. He was attending Palm Beach Junior College (now Palm Beach Community College) when he decided to join the US Army in August of 1967. He was inducted into the Army at Fort Jackson, SC and completed basic training at Fort Gordon, GA. In November of 1967 he was transferred to Fort Eustis, VA, where he completed helicopter mechanic training and graduated with the Military Occupational Specialty (MOS) of 67N20. After helicopter mechanic training he deployed to Vietnam in March 1968 where he was assigned to the famous 121st Assault Helicopter Company (Air Mobile Light) at Soc Trang, Vietnam. He worked as a phase inspection team mechanic and applied for a crew chief job, as he wanted to fly and serve as a crew chief and door gunner on a Tiger Huey.

After serving five months in the hangar on a maintenance team, he was assigned his own UH-1D Huey aircraft and became a key flight crew member under the command of Warrant Officer Joe Casanova. It was July of 1968 when Mike Dewey teamed up with Specialist 4 John Romero, a very brave door gunner, to become the two enlisted crew members on Casanova's Huey. After flying an estimated 1,000 hours in slicks and distinguishing himself on many missions, Mike volunteered to fly in the 121st Viking gun platoon. He then flew another approximate 1,000 hours as a Viking Crew Chief and Door Gunner, until he was seriously wounded by a gunshot through the back and out of his left shoulder on December 19, 1969. He voluntarily extended his combat tour twice in Vietnam.

Michael Dewey's contributions to the Tigers and Vikings were exemplary. He helped saved a number of downed helicopter crews and his positive attitude and kindness are legendary among Tigers and Vikings. He was wounded twice in the Vikings. The first wound was a Plexiglas shard that was blown out of the front wind shield by enemy ground fire. The large Plexiglas shard seriously cut his head and required five stitches. He flew all day with that first wound and was flying again the next day with stitches in his head. Mike was a beloved member of the elite Vikings and he helped train dozens of new pilots and door gunners during his time at Soc Trang. His military decorations include the Bronze Star, the Purple Heart (two awards), over 40 Combat Air Medals, three Army Commendation Medals, and one Army Commendation Medal with V for valor. On the day he was shot, he was medically evacuated to Can Tho and stabilized and then sent on to the 249th

General Hospital, at Camp Zama, Japan for surgery and recovery. After about a month in Japan, Mike was medical evacuated to Walter Reed Army Medical Center in Washington, DC where he was allowed to go home for two months to recover at his parent's home in DC. After he was released from the hospital at Walter Reed, he was assigned to Fort Wolters, Texas to serve his final five months in the Army.

Specialist 5 Mike Dewey was discharged from the Army in August of 1970. He went back to college and finished his undergraduate degree in Florida. He moved to Savannah, GA, and worked there in the maritime industry. After about four years in the maritime industry he went into the hardware business for a couple of years and then entered the food service industry where he worked until he retired in 2009. In 1980 he married. His marriage resulted in three sons, Brian, Jason, and Robert. Mike and his wife put their sons through college and each son has been very successful. The oldest son is working as a Bank Vice President, the second son is working as a Physical Therapist, and the youngest son is finishing his second master's degree and working as an audiologist. He has never forgotten his exciting days and nights with the Tigers and Vikings in Vietnam. Today Mike is retired and lives in Savannah, GA and does volunteer work helping disabled friends and neighbors.

xi - Larry Gray, Specialist 5 (E-5)

Larry Gray, Specialist 5 (E-5) got out of the Army in 1969, went to work with IBM as a typewriter mechanic, and spent three years there. He then attended the University of Illinois and graduated in 1976 with a degree in accounting and minor in automated data processing. To earn extra money during his college years, Larry worked as a college veteran's advisor and was active in the local Veterans Association. He has since had a highly successful career in logistics and information technology working for IBM, NCR, Bristol Myers, GE, Oracle, and now Boar's head. He got his masters degree in business administration and marketing in 1993 from St. Francis University. Today he is an expert in material requirements planning (MRP), MRP II, and enterprise resource planning (ERP), and Lean Six Sigma. In 1970 he met Cindy, the love of his life, and they married quickly. Larry and Cindy have two children (Karl and Kate) and six grandchildren. Both children are Army veterans. Karl served in Iraq in 2003, as an infantryman and received the Combat Infantrymen's Badge. Katie served three years that included 18 months in Korea, as a supply specialist. Katie is currently married to a US Army Chaplain. Larry and Cindy live in Sarasota county Florida. Larry and Cindy are active members of Good Shepard Episcopal Church where Larry is a vestry member. Larry is still working and continues to live a successful and rewarding life with his family.

xii - Wayne Zander, Chief Warrant Officer (Ret)

Wayne Zander, Specialist 5 (E-5) flew as a crew chief and door gunner in the Vikings for 20 months. He has over 1,700 hours of combat flight time. His Army decorations include the Army Meritorious Service Medal, Army Commendation Medal with V device for valor, the Combat Air Medal with 34 Oak Leaf Clusters, Vietnam Service Medal (4 campaigns), and others. He was raised on a farm in North Dakota, retired from the National Guard as a Chief Warrant Officer and now lives in Chandler, AZ with his wife Linda. His decorations include the Combat Air Medal and many others. Wayne made a most profound statement to the author of this book in 2012, "We guys in the back seat always knew that the decisions you guys, in the front seat, made were probably going to get us killed. Now we know that the decisions you guys made also kept us alive!"

xiv - Jim Preston, Aviation Master Warrant Officer (CW4)

Jim Preston, Aviation Master Warrant Officer (CW4) was born January 22, 1943 in Bessemer, Alabama to Chief Warrant Officer 4 James Preston and Edna Preston. He entered the Army June 15, 1960, and went to Germany as an infantry Private. He was selected for warrant officer training and flight school in October, 1966 (WORWAC Class 67-9) and graduated June 30, 1967, as a warrant officer. He was next assigned to Ft Knox, KY with C Troop 7/1 Air Cavalry and deployed to Vietnam with them in January, 1968. He was assigned to the 121st Assault Helicopter Company in June, 1968. He flew slicks with the White Tigers until the end of January, 1969. Jim Preston was the air craft commander of Viking Surprise when they changed the name to Tiger Surprise. He flew 1,000 combat hours in Vietnam—750 with the Tigers and Vikings and 250 with the cavalry. He flew 750 combat hours in six months with the 121st and he said, "We flew our tails off in the 121st!" After Vietnam, Jim went back to Fort Rucker as a contact instructor pilot (IP) until returning to Vietnam on his second tour with the Cobra New Equipment Training Team (NETT). His military awards and decorations include the Legion of Merit, Army Meritorious Service Medal with two oak leaf clusters (3 awards total), Combat Air Medal, Army Commendation Medal, Good Conduct Medal, and others.

During his meritorious and highly successful Army career, he was stationed at Ft Hood, TX twice, Ft Knox, KY, Ft Campbell, KY, Ft Belvoir, VA and Ft Benning, GA and Germany twice and Iran. He went to the fixed wing (airplane) school (Q course) in March 1980 and completed his Army career as a C-12 (twin-engine turboprop aircraft based on the Beech Craft Super King Air and Beech Craft 1900) driver for the Commanding General at Fort Benning, GA. Jim was selected to the first Master Warrant Officer list and was promoted in 1989 to Chief Warrant Officer 4. He was the Lawson Army Air Field (AAF) Operations Officer when he retired in November 1990 with a little over 7,000 rotary wing and fixed wing flight hours. Jim says, "The love of his life put up with him through all of this. She was his high school sweetheart and they celebrated their 50th Anniversary this past January." Jim and his wife have two sons and four grandchildren. Mr. Jim Preston distinguished himself for 30 years in the US Army. He retired in 1990 as a Chief Warrant Officer 4 (a Master Warrant Officer and Master Army Aviator). Larry Dandridge and Jim Preston helped to deploy one of the first Apache Attack Helicopter Battalions from Fort Rucker, through Fort Benning, and to Southwest Asia during Desert Shield in 1991. Jim and his wife have been enjoying their Recreational Vehicle ever since he retired, traveling around this great nation and visiting family and old friends.

xv - Rick Thomas, Army Warrant Officer/Commissioned Officer and later US Coast Guard Captain (0-6)

Rick Thomas, Army Warrant Officer/Commissioned Officer and

later US Coast Guard Captain (0-6) arrived in Soc Trang and the 121st AHC on December 17, 1967 as a warrant officer fresh from flight school. His Tiger slick was the famous Tiger 777 – "The Good Widow Mrs. Jones" with an Alberto Vargas, 1964 centerfold painting, on the nose cone, from Playboy magazine. He went through the tremendous challenge of the VC 1968 TET offensive, served as a Tiger AC and Viking AC and was a great source of information and advice to all the new and older 121st AHC pilots. He later married a lovely Vietnamese lady that we (Tigers and Vikings) called "Sam" who worked in our Soc Trang Officers Club and Post Exchange. He served two and one half combat tours in Vietnam and was a UH-1D and H Model Utility (slick) and UH-1B Model Gunship, OH-6 Light Observation Helicopter, and OH-58 Kiowa Scout Standardization Instructor Pilot (IP) for the 13th Combat Aviation Battalion (CAB), and later a CH-47 Chinook pilot. He received a direct commission to 1st Lieutenant in 1970 and got out of the active Army as a Captain in February, 1972. He joined the Army Reserve shortly after and then went on leave of absence to fly for Air America from January through November, 1973, in Vientiane, Laos and Saigon, Vietnam.

He then came home in January, 1974, settled in the city of Hoquiam, in Washington State and worked for the police department and the Army National Guard as a tank company commander. He transferred into a CH-47 company at Pain Field (Everett, WA.) and flew with them until 1983 when a bad hearing loss kicked him off flight status. He went into the Army's Individual Ready Reserve (IRR) and worked as a police officer until retiring in April, 2006, with the last 10 years as the Chief of Police. Later, in 1983 he joined the US Coast Guard (USCG) as a Lieutenant Junior Grade (O2) doing law enforcement and intelligence work. Captain Thomas retired in April, 2006, with ten years of active duty and 30 years of military reserve time. In the USCG, he took his Port Security Unit 313 to Kuwait and Iraq in 2003. He worked his way up to Captain (O-6 – equal to an Army Colonel). He stayed as the commander until April 2006 and retired from the military with 40 years of service (20 Army/20 Coast Guard). He is now very active in the Reserve Officers Association (ROA) and he has been the Department of Washington (state) Commander twice, local Reserve Officers Association Chapter President multiple times, and is currently sitting on two of their national committees. Rick is a graduate of Saint Martin's University (Lacey, WA.), the FBI Academy, and multiple military schools. Rick and Sam have been married for 44 years, have two children and five grandchildren, and are enjoying retired life in Aberdeen, Washington State.

xvi - Mike Shakocius (Shaky), Chief Warrant Officer 2

Mike Shakocius (Shaky), Chief Warrant Officer 2 was a Blue Tiger from October, 1967, to October, 1968. Mike's Father was a B-17 Flight Engineer during World War 2. Mike always had an interest in aviation as a child. Mike got his private pilot's license in southern California during his early college years. He graduated from US Army Flight School with Class 67-3 and was assigned to Fort Benning. At Fort Benning he was assigned to 235th Aerial Weapons Company and trained on UH-1H's and later on UH-1C's which he helped pickup at the Bell Factory. Once the time had arrived for deployment to Vietnam he and his fellow 235th pilots ferried for five days all 25 of is unit's aircraft to Stockton, CA, for further transport to the Republic of Vietnam. Mike and his unit boarded the Troop Transport Ship MSTS General Walker in Alameda NAS, San Francisco, in October, 1967 and they arrived in Vung Tau, South Vietnam four weeks later. He went ashore in a landing craft.

He eventually arrived in Can Tho in IV Corps. He was fortunate to be assigned to the Soc Trang Tigers. During his combat tour he flew 1,241 Combat Hours. During TET he flew 188 hours in a 30 day period. During TET, together with the crew of Tiger 777, he spent an interesting several days in the Outpost of Tieu Can (C5) after receiving numerous hits to his aircraft from enemy small arms fire during a resupply mission. His Commanding Officer, Maj Carl McNair providing Command and Control (C&C), along with a Vietnamese Air Force (VNAF) airstrike and the 235th Cobras gave covering fire and a Trusty Tiger Huey with a brave crew got Mike and his crew safely out.

After Vietnam he flew CH-34 helicopters in Germany and served his four years of total regular Army time. Germany is where Mike met his future wife, learned the German language, and received his European discharge. Germany and Europe impressed him and this helped him decide his future. He joined the Army reserves and maintained military proficiency with Reserve duty in Germany as a CW4 Master Army Aviator. He acquired his German Air Line Transport License (TPLH), and together with his US Federal Aviation Agency (FAA) License was able to work, fly, and travel to all seven continents, including an expedition in the Antarctic. He retired at age 65 in Germany, accident free, with just over 20,000 hours! He is grateful to all the great aviation people he met and worked with, especially those from the Tigers and Vikings who have provided special memories of "Good Friends". Mike says, "Being in the 121st in Vietnam is something he will never forget!"

xvii - Jim Noblin, Warrant Officer

Jim Noblin, Warrant Officer was a Blue Tiger slick pilot. He arrived at Soc Trang March 13, 1968, and went home in October, 1969, with 2,000 plus combat flight hours in-country. His decorations include the Combat Air Medal with V device for valor, over 45 Combat Air Medals, the Vietnamese Cross of Gallantry (Bronze), the Vietnamese Cross of Gallantry (Silver), the US Army Broken wing Award, a MACV Advisor Honorary Paddy Rat Award, and others. He rotated ships nearly daily, but he was mainly assigned Silver Eagle, "Tiger 29er", flying for the ARVN senior advisor. Don Peterson was his rating officer. As an additional duty, he was an Assistant Motor Pool officer working with Captain Bill Schmidt. When Jim returned from Vietnam, he married his wife (Lyola) and they raised three sons together. He returned to work on the ramp for Western Airlines in Anchorage, AK, just in time to take part in the air cargo support for the Trans Alaska Pipeline as a cargo supervisor with a crew of 20 employees. Jim joined the Alaska Army National Guard and tried to fly in the newly organized 1898th Aviation Company but could not arrange enough training time to meet minimum flight requirements. Jim went into the inactive ready reserve and worked for Western Airlines (later Delta) and retired from Delta air cargo in September, 2011. He joined Alaska Communications as a wireless representative after his airline career, and retired from Alaska Communications in 2014.

xviii - Eugene A. "Gene" Booth, Captain

Eugene A. "Gene" Booth, was a Tiger and Viking combat pilot in Vietnam. He was born in Baton Rouge, Louisiana in 1944. The family moved to Texas in 1948. His father worked in the petrochemical industry and they moved several times, eventually ending up in LaPorte, Texas. In the fall of 1962 he enrolled in Louisiana State University (LSU) majoring in engineering, then business, and then general studies. He applied for and was granted his commission as a Second Lieutenant in the US Army Infantry in March 1967. The Army waived the degree requirement (Vietnam was heating up). He reported to Ft. Benning, Georgia, for the Combat Infantry Officer's Basic Course in July, 1967. After Ft. Benning he went to Ft. Wolters, Texas for Primary Rotary Wing Training and then Ft. Rucker, Alabama for Advanced Rotary Wing training. Upon completion of flight school, he reported to Vietnam the first week of September, 1968, where he was assigned to the 121st Assault Helicopter Company at Soc Trang. He became a co-pilot flying transport (slicks) Hueys. He had gone through the gunnery school at Ft. Rucker and lobbied hard to be transferred to the Viking Gun Platoon. In December, 1968, he was assigned to the Viking Gun Platoon as the new platoon leader, Viking 26. He flew with the Vikings for the remainder of his tour. He flew over 1,100 hours with the Tigers and Vikings. He was awarded the Distinguished Flying Cross, the Combat Air Medal with 30 Oak Leaf Clusters, the Army Commendation Medal, and other awards during his combat tour. When his tour was completed, he was assigned to Hunter Army Airfield in Savannah, Georgia, where he served from September, 1969, until released from active duty in August, 1971. While stationed at Hunter AAF he completed his degree in Business Administration.

He returned to LSU to attend Law School, graduated in June, 1974 and has practiced law in Baton Rouge, Louisiana, since. He had a successful private practice until 1992 when he accepted a position as an attorney for the East Baton Rouge Parish Attorney's Office. He has been the Director of Risk Management for the Parish Attorney's Office for the last seven years. He also owned a private business, "Red Stick Sports" since 1981, which grew from a small retail athletic store to a major supplier for team equipment and uniforms for most of Louisiana and southern Mississippi. Gene

Booth is married and has four sons and two step-sons.

Today Gene volunteers as a middle school coach and he is a member of the Baton Rouge Bar Association, the Louisiana State Bar Association, the American Trial Lawyers Association, the Louisiana Trial Lawyers Association, National Football Foundation and Hall of Fame, the Distinguish Flying Cross Society, the Vietnam Helicopter Pilots Association, and the Catholic High School Men's Club. All of his children have served successfully and honorably in the military, except one who could not serve due to medical reasons. One son retired as a USAF Lt. Colonel and F-16 pilot. Another son graduated from West Point and served in the Army as a Field Artillery Captain. One of his step sons is an architect and was an Engineer in the Army and another son was a Sergeant in the US Marine Corps. The other step son, now a minister, was an Army Chaplain. Gene and his wife are active in their church and it is a very important part of their lives. Gene is very proud to have served with so many fine young men in Vietnam. Although the Vikings and Tigers suffered many serious combat wounds and injuries in 1968 and 1969, none of Gene's soldiers were killed.

xix - Bill Schmidt, Captain and Later Major

Bill Schmidt, Captain served as a Tiger platoon leader, assistant operations officer, slick pilot, unit instructor pilot, motor officer, and much more in the 121st Assault Helicopter Company. He flew over 1,300 hours of combat time in Vietnam and his decorations include the Bronze Star, Meritorious Service Medal, Air Medal with "V" for Valor, Army Commendation Medal, the Republic of Vietnam Training Medal, and many others. Originally from Indiana, he left Soc Trang and the Tigers to serve in Germany. There he commanded a Field Artillery Battery. His command time was cut short with orders to the Aviation Safety Course and Chinook transition prior to returning to combat. He completed his graduate degree while on active duty, remained on active duty for 10 years, and spent another ten years in the Army Reserves retiring as a Major. After leaving active duty, Bill was a pharmaceutical representative for 28 years for Abbott Laboratories in Texas. He has two daughters and two grandsons. He is retired, resides in Pearland, TX (suburb of Houston), and does volunteer work with the Pearland Police Department.

xx - Tom Jameson, Lieutenant Colonel (Ret)

Tom Jameson, 1st Lt. and Captain served as a Tiger slick aircraft commander and leader in the 121st in Vietnam. He served two combat tours in Vietnam. His military decorations include the Legion of Merit (2 awards), Bronze Star, Meritorious Service Medal, Combat Air Medal with V for valor, Air Medal with 50 Oak Leaf Clusters, Army Commendation Medal, Purple Heart, Vietnamese Cross of Gallantry with Star, and others. Tom flew 1288 Huey combat hours with the 121st during his first tour in Vietnam and 250 hours of Chinook time with the 164th Aviation Group during his combat second tour for a total of 1,528 flight hours. He had a highly successful Army engineer career and retired as a US Army LTC in 1990. He is married and the father of two children, a grandfather of five, and a great grandfather of one. He served another tour in combat in Vietnam as a Chinook pilot, commanded an award winning Engineer Company, served as a battalion logistics officer and facilities engineer, mastered test pilot school and completed his graduate education while on active duty. After retiring from the Army he had another successful career as the Director of Facilities at California University of PA, and is a Project Manager today at Management Engineering Corporation.

xxi - Bob Ennis, Chief Warrant Officer (CW2)

Bob Ennis, Chief Warrant Officer (CW2) flew as a Tiger and Viking combat pilot in Vietnam. His gunship call sign was Viking 21. He was seriously wounded and helped save the lives of some of his wounded comrades. He spent a couple of weeks in the hospital at Can Tho, then a couple of days in a Saigon hospital, then two weeks in a hospital in Japan, a day in San Francisco, and 11 months in the hospital at Fort Lewis, WA. He saved his pay while he was hospitalized. When he got out of the Army bought an XKE and headed to Palm Springs. Bob went back to college and finished his degree, worked for Evergreen Helicopters up in Alaska, and then was the backup Pilot for Boeing's Corporate Helicopter. He got rated in 727s and 737s but once reality set in, as none of the airlines were hiring, he joined the business world. He plans to work two more years and retire. Bob and his wife are empty nesters. He has had the same great wife for the past 38 years. He and his wife have three wonderful high achieving children, three terrific grandkids and another on the way.

xxii - Roger Howell, Chief Warrant Officer 2

Roger Howell, Chief Warrant Officer 2 was a combat slick and gunship pilot in Vietnam in the 187th Assault Helicopter Company. His combat awards include the Purple Heart, numerous Combat Air Medals, and other awards. He flew 600 hours of combat time in Vietnam. Roger Howell was born in Wilkes Barre, PA in 1946. His father was a Special Agent in the FBI and his family moved to several different areas before settling to Washington, D. C. in 1955. He attended grade school, high school, and a local Community College in Montgomery County, Maryland before enlisting in the Army in the Aviation Warrant Officers Candidate program on January 22, 1967. Upon graduation he was assigned to the 187th Assault Helicopter Company in Tay Ninh, RVN. He flew as a slick pilot and later as a gun and smoke ship pilot and aircraft commander. He was severely wounded December 28, 1968. After medical rehabilitation he was assigned to U.S Army Transportation School at Ft. Eustis, Virginia and was honorably discharged on October 9, 1970. Roger returned to Maryland and married in 1975. He and his wife are happily married with two children and two grandchildren. He retired in June 2010 as owner of a Mechanical Contracting Company and moved to Kissimmee, FL in September 2013 and enjoying retirement.

xxiii - Paul McClymonds, Chief Warrant Officer 2

Paul McClymonds, Chief Warrant Officer 2 was born in north east Ohio and went to Ohio State for a year. He had a chance to take a short ride in a small plane once as a teenager and fell in love with flying. He went into the Army helicopter training program at 19 and, after basic flight school, was assigned to Cobra school. He served in the 121st AHC from February, 1969 to February, 1970. He was sent to Soctrang because they were going to get Cobras any day. He flew with the Tigers for about two months and then went to the Viking' gunships. Fortunately, he was never wounded, but once had a bullet come through the chin bubble and hit him on the leg. The round did not break the skin on his leg. When he left

Soctrang they were still going to get Cobras any day. He completed his enlistment as an instructor pilot (IP) training Vietnamese pilots to fly gunships at Hunter Army Air Field, GA. He is one of the few Army pilots who has never been to Fort Rucker, AL. He met his wife at Hunter Army Air Field. They have been married for 44 years. The McClymonds have one son. After the Army, he worked for Marriott as a restaurant manager for seven years. Then he moved his family to Phoenix in 1978. He recently retired after a successful 32 year career with UPS. His military awards include the Bronze Star, the Vietnamese Cross of Gallantry with Bronze star, and more than 20 Combat Air Medals. He flew 1,044 hours in Vietnam and a total of 2,000 hours in the Army.

xxiv - Ken Roies, Specialist 5

Ken Roies, Specialist 5 (nicknamed Rhody) was a White Tiger and Viking door gunner and crew chief. He grew up in Tiverton, Rhode Island and graduated from high school in nearby Paul River, Massachusetts. He joined the Army right after high school graduation and went to basic training at Fort Jackson, SC. He went to aviation maintenance school at Fort Rucker, AL and was awarded the military occupational specialties of 67A1F (door gunner) and 67N2F (crew chief). He arrived at Soc Trang in December, 1968, and served in the White Tigers and Vikings until June of 1970. He flew more than 1,400 combat hours in Vietnam and was awarded the Distinguished Flying Cross, four Air Medals with V device for Valor, 28 Air medals, two Purple Hearts, two Army Commendation Medals, and others. He is one of the enlisted heroes of the 121st Assault Helicopter Company. He was with CPT Bill Ferguson when Bill was shot in the chest. He was with CPT Bubba Segrest when Bubba was shot through the knee and hand. Roies was injured by a bullet and debris when an AK47 round came through the chin bubble. It shot off the heel of CPT George Taylor's boot and blew bullet fragments and metal aircraft fragments into his eyes, face, and shoulder.

His second wound was much more serious when he was flying as crew chief and gunner with Warrant Officer McKeatch (spelling maybe wrong). A VC, in a spider hole, shot him through the upper leg near his hip with an AK-47 at close range. He also helped rescue Major James Rowe by serving as crew chief on the Tiger aircraft that flew Major Rowe from the U-Minh Forest to safety. After Vietnam, Ken Roies served in the 14th Armored Cavalry in the Fulda Gap, Germany. After leaving the Army, he worked as a Stone Mason and Iron Worker in the Marble Setters Union and Iron Workers Union all over the USA. He married in 1975. He and his wife (recently deceased) had three beloved children— two boys and a girl. Ken retired from the Iron Workers Union in 2005. Today Ken works part-time at Home Depot and is raising one of his grandsons.

xxv - US Army Brigadier General (Ret) Danny Hickman

US Army Brigadier General (Ret) Danny Hickman. Danny Hickman served in Vietnam as a Warrant Officer flying slicks, Cobras, and occasionally scouts while in B Troop, 3/17th Air Cavalry Squadron. He later served in various Instructor Pilot (IP) and Standardization Instructor Pilot (SIP) positions after returning from Vietnam. General Hickman took a "Direct Demotion" (as he calls it) from Chief Warrant Officer 2 to 2nd Lieutenant, Infantry in 1975. He served with great distinction in ground assignments in the Army National Guard for the next 30 years. General Hickman completed his 35 year career as commander of the 30th Separate Armor Brigade serving in combat, in Operation Iraqi Freedom (OIF), in Iraq, from 2003 to 2005. During the Iraq war, he led his Brigade Combat Team (BCT) into Iraq's Sunni Triangle with responsibility for combat operations over an area of operation the size of Connecticut. He not only commanded over 5,000 US troops in his famous brigade, but he also had control over two to three Iraqi Army brigades simultaneously. General Hickman's awards include the Legion of Merit, the Distinguished Flying Cross, two Bronze Stars, two Meritorious Service Medals, and twenty-six Air Medals plus one Air Medal with a V for Valor. He is married with a daughter and two sons. After his Army career, he retired as the Executive Vice President of Cape Fear Community College and is now living in Wilmington, NC. General Hickman and the author have been close friends since 1967.

xxvi - US Army Colonel (Ret) Sam DeLoach

Sam DeLoach who acted as the author's technical editor for

lessons learned, served as his (Larry Dandridge's) mentor and best friend throughout his Army career, and served in Vietnam as a combat Dust Off and Cobra pilot, maintenance test pilot, and maintenance detachment commander. He also flew Black Hawk and Apache Helicopters after Vietnam and served in many high impact and important command and staff positions in his Army career. His decorations include the Bronze Star Medal with one Oak Leaf Cluster (OLC), Meritorious Service Medal with 5 OLC, Air Medal with V for Valor, and many others. Col (Ret) DeLoach is an Army War College graduate. His last job in the Army was as the Apache Helicopter Program Manager. He had a highly successful second career as the Senior Vice President of a major flight parts manufacturing company. He is now retired. Sam served two combat tours in Vietnam, one tour with the 498th Medical Evacuation Company and one with famed 1st of the 9th Air Cavalry. One of his Cavalry stories "What is a Pink Team" will be in Book II of Blades of Thunder. He is married with two sons. He lives at Smith Mountain Lake, VA and Edisto Beach, SC. Larry Dandridge and Sam are from Charleston, SC and have been close friends since 1969.

xxvii - US Army Ex-Captain Laurie "Bubba" Segrest

US Army Ex-Captain Laurie "Bubba" Segrest flew Tiger slicks and Viking gunships in Vietnam. His decorations include the Bronze Star, Purple Heart and the Air Medal. He is medically retired from two Vietnam gunshot wounds, one through the leg and one through the hand, and finger amputations received in Vietnam in 1969. Bubba is married with two daughters and the owner and operator of a successful tour business "Charms of Charleston" in Charleston, SC. If you ever visit beautiful Charleston, Bubba gives the best tour available! Bubba and Larry have been great friends since their days together at the Baptist College at Charleston (now Charleston Southern University) in 1966 and 1967.

APPENDIX K: FOOTNOTES

1

William Shakespeare, Henry V, Act IV, speech of Henry V on eve of the battle of Agincourt, in the year 1415 wrote "We few, we happy few, we Band of Brothers. For he to-day that sheds his blood with me, shall be my brother."

2

Wikipedia The Free Encyclopedia, URL: *http://en.wikipedia.org/wiki/Fog_of_war* The **fog of war** (German: Nebel des Krieges) is the uncertainty in situational awareness experienced by participants in military operations(from the Joint Service Command and Staff College, advanced command and staff course notes dated 2001). The term seeks to capture the uncertainty regarding one's own capability, adversary capability, and adversary intent during an engagement, operation, or campaign. The concept was introduced by the Prussian military analyst Carl von Clausewitz in his posthumously published book, *Vom Kriege* (1837), which appeared in English translation in 1873 under the title *On War*. The nature of the ambiguity described as the fog of war varies according to the level at which participants are engaged.

3

The Viking "23" call sign was made up by the author. Regretfully, neither the author nor CW2 Brian King could remember the Viking wing ship's call sign on 28 March 1969.

4

The US Military has come a long way since Vietnam towards developing much improved 2.75-inch FFAR systems and munitions.

Today's Army attack pilots have impact detonating and airburst war heads with much faster Hydra 70 rockets with a huge variety of warheads to chose from including, 10- pound High Explosive (HE), 17- pound HE and HE anti-armor, Flechette, Infrared (IR) Flare/Illumination, Red Phosphorous (marking and incendiary), Smoke Screening, Multipurpose Submunition, Smoke Practice, Practice, High Explosive Remote Set (HERS) for canopy-bunker-and open targets, and soon there will be guided 2.75- inch folding fin aerial rockets.

5

http://www.vietnamgear.com/Article.aspx?Art=91 and 1. Military Specification MIL-C-43544. (20 September 1967), 2. Personnel Armor Handbook by LT R. A. Green, J. A. Parish (US Naval Weapon Laboratory June 1971), and 3. Body Armor for Aircrewmen by Edward R. Barron, Anthony L. Alesi and Alice F. Park. (US Army Natick Laboratories January 1969). The 1968 designed version of the aircrew small arms protective body armor carrier featured large envelopes to accommodate a front torso protector for pilots or front and rear plates for gunners, who did not have the benefit of armored seats. It had a front pocket for maps (or the Secret Operating Instruction – [SOI]), stretchable webbing sides and, unlike the 1967 standardized carrier, quick-release snap fasteners with non-slip buckles on both shoulders.1 Attached to the outside overlapping waistband was an elastic loop with a snap fastener that prevented opening in the wind stream. Army aircrews were issued the carrier with aluminum oxide ceramic plates. Ceramic plates were backed by reinforced plastic, had a front spall shield with rubber edging around the periphery and were available in three materials; aluminum oxide (class I), silicon carbide (class II) and boron carbide (class III). Some crew members wore an M1952A flak vest over or under their torso armor because the spall and fragment protection provided by the T65-2 carrier was inadequate.

6

Reference the M60 Operator's Manual, TM 9-1005-224-10, dated October 1970. The M60 is air-cooled and has fixed head space allowing quick change barrel changes for cooling and maintenance when required. In order to extend the life of the barrels, retain accuracy, and allow continuous firing for prolonged periods, two barrel assemblies are issued with each gun. The maximum range of the M60 is 3,725 meters (12,106 feet). The maximum grazing range is 600 meters and the tracer burn out is approximately 900 meters. The M60 fires the NATO 7.62mm armor piercing (M61), ball (M80), and red/orange tracer (M62) ammunition. Gun comes with asbestos mitten, wrench, screw driver, reamer, cleaning rods, cleaning brushes, spare barrel, carrying case, and ruptured cartridge extractor. Field Manual 23-67 covers the use of the machine gun and TM 9-1005-224-24 covers Support Maintenance and Parts.

7

The Crew Chief probably had numerous other injuries, but Larry Dandridge and Brian King never saw him again and could not verify all of his injuries. Both pilots would like to thank Malcolm Rose for his selfless and courageous service. If anyone has his address, phone number, or email address, please send it to the author at *Ldandridge@earthlink.net.*

8

See Technical Manual™ 9-1005-224-10, Operators Manual, for details on use and operator maintenance on the M60 7.62mm Machine Gun, NSN 1005-00605-7710. Also see Field Manual (FM) 23-67 M60 Machine Gun.

9

Picture courtesy of Brian King and Bill Ferguson.

10

Sam DeLoach actually graduated from Flight School in 1967 with WORWAC Class 66-23.

11

Picture 13 courtesy of Larry Dandridge.

12

The primary antiaircraft weapon fielded by the NVA and VC in 1968 and 1969 was the Soviet made, 12.7mm DshKM38/46 heavy machine gun and its Chinese made Type 54 copy was effective at up to 1,200 meters and fired at a rate of 540 to 600 rounds per minute. The tracers from these guns were described by many helicopter pilots as looking like "basketballs" or "soft balls" coming up at them and, in mountains, sometimes coming down at them.

13

In Aviation units, especially attack units, taking the point position is almost always where the flight leader or fire team leader needs to be. However the operation commander over ground and total air assets is usually in a command and control (C&C) aircraft above the battle. Frequently a slick flight leader will fly trail to be able to see what is happening to his or her total flight. It would not be wise for a ground company commander to frequently try to take the point position of a rifle company in jungle or anywhere else, as he could not see the total battle well and would subject the radio operator and himself to potential quick elimination in an ambush or battle. Ground unit commanders need to survive the battle to be able call in artillery, naval gun fire, gunships, reserves, and air strikes and medical evacuation, and direct the maneuvering of his or her troops on the ground, thus they are frequently located at the center of their formation with their radio man. With that said, a commander who has never walked in the shoes of his troopers, especially the high-risk point position, is one who is less skilled and admired by his troops.

14

Val Berger, Hank Fagerskog, Judith Ann (Siegel) Dandridge, Meredith Miller, Jim Frownfelter, Les Phillips, Timmy Brown, David Cohn, Luther Bergen, Marci and Brent Wood, Lisa and Jaco LaCroix, Lori Stoney, Harold Ramey, Brian King, Bill Schmidt, Keith West, Ray Johnson, George Lincoln, Stacy Martin, Eleanor Wood, Dylan LaCroix, Tom Connell, Reid Daughtry, Jonah Wood, Rocky Cassano, First Sergeant Ed Cassel, Cecil Bradshaw, Payton Daughtry, Eugene Williams, Janet Huddleston, John DeGrazia Jr., Ben Callis, Juanita Vann, Raymond Ackerman, Grace Picicci, Fred Lesinsky, Joy Fealy-Kalar, Kim Boone, Ron McCollum, Charlie Mingus, Mike Sakole, Steve Wooten, Faye Crowe, Bob Wacker, Denny Fluharty, Angela Gallagher, Herbert Curry, Irma Snider, Hans J. Kaufhold, Phyllis Kaplan, Maria and Penny Kyramarios, Barbara Stevenson, Charlie Mingus, Robert Murray, Peggy Orrell, Pat O'Malley, Denny Roodman, Debbie Rast, Ben and Ryan LaCroix, Letitia Addison Dandridge, Jeff Silkwood, Fuzz Sanders, Bill Wallace, Bubba Segrest, and all the officers, warrent officers, and enlisted men mentioned in this book.

15

From John Stewart Mill, British philosopher, political economist and civil servant, born May 20, 1806, and died May 8, 1873. He was an influential contributor to social theory, political theory and political economy. He said, "Life has a certain flavor for those who have fought and risked all that the sheltered and protected can never experience." See *http://www.brainyquote.com/quotes/quotes/j/ johnstuart143730.html#g362GJ6Qj51PfIoj.99 and http://en.wikipedia.org/wiki/John_Stuart_Mill.*

16

This leadership article and speech is based on an award winning speech given by LTC (Ret) Dandridge at the Armed Forces Staff College in 1983. Various versions of this speech have been published in over 20 magazines, professional journals, and news papers and two books in the US, Germany, and England. The article has been used by dozens of military, civil service, and industry schools to stimulate thought on leadership.

17

Wikipedia The Free Encyclopedia, URL: *http://en.wikipedia.org/ wiki/Leaving_on_a_Jet_Plane. "Leaving on a Jet Plane"* is a song written by John Denver in 1966 and most famously recorded by Peter, Paul, and Mary. The original title of the song was "Babe, I Hate to Go" but Denver's then producer Milt Okun convinced him to change the title. That same year, Denver chose this song along with fifteen others and, with his own money, had 250 copies pressed onto vinyl. He distributed the copies to friends and family. Peter, Paul and Mary were so impressed with the song that they chose to record it themselves and released it on their 1967 album, 1700. Notably, it didn't become a hit for them until they released it as a single in 1969. The song was also recorded in 1967 by the Chad Mitchell Trio and then later that same year by Spanky and Our Gang. It was performed for the very first time live at The Cellar Door in Washington, D.C. in 1966 by the Chad Mitchell Trio, with John Denver substituting for Chad Mitchell. John Denver recorded his own version of the song for his debut solo album, Rhymes & Reasons, and re-recorded it in 1973 for John Denver's Greatest Hits. It turned out to be Peter, Paul, & Mary's biggest (and final) hit, becoming their only #1 on the Billboard Hot 100 chart in the United States.

18

http://en.wikipedia.org/wiki/Revetment_(aircraft. A **revetment**, in military aviation, is a parking area for one or more aircraft that is surrounded by blast walls on two or three sides. These walls are as much about protecting neighboring aircraft as they are to protect the aircraft within the revetment. If a combat aircraft fully loaded with fuel and munitions was to somehow be set on fire, by accident or design, then it could start a chain reaction, as the destruction of individual aircraft could set ablaze its neighbors. The blast walls around a revetment are designed to channel blast and damage upwards and outwards away from neighboring aircraft. Most of the IV Corps revetments were made of 55 gallon drums filled with dirt or sand and anchored together.

19

Originally formed as Delta Aviation Battalion in July 1963, at Can Tho it was activated as the 13th Battalion in September 1964. In December 1967 it was assigned to the 164th Group to support the three ARVN divisions in the Delta and other units. It moved to Soc Trang in October 1968, and remained there until March 1972.

20

This short and incomplete history is based on the 121st Aviation Organization web site at *http://www.121avn.org/history/history.aspx* home page, "History Tab" and official historical accounts of the 121st Aviation Company recorded in Box 614, RG 472, Stack Area 270, row 33, Compartment 7, Shelf 11 of the National Archives and Records Administration (NARA) in College Park, MD.

21

The 164th Aviation Group was activated in Vietnam in December 1967 and located in Can Tho. The 164th CAG had about 3,700 personnel. Main infantry groups supported were the US 9th Infantry, the ARVN units and the 5th Special Forces. IV Corps was the delta area consisting of rice patties and swampy ground which was covered with water six months a year during rainy season. The corps was heavily populated, consisting of many small towns and villages. During the 1968 Tet offensive, aviation companies of the 164th CAG played vital and deciding roles in the liberation of Soc Trang, Can Tho, Bac Lieu, Vinh Long, and in preventing the VC from occupying many other major cities in the Delta. During the Cambodian Incursion in April and May 1970, the 164th CAG participated in numerous combat operations in Cambodia, accounting for over 900 killed by air.

22

"Blood Chit" is a notice printed on a cloth about 24 inches by 24 inches and in local languages (Vietnamese, Cambodian, Laotian, etc.), that is carried by the military, usually air crewmen, that displays messages aimed at the civilians that ask them to help the service member in case they are shot down and offers monetary $$$ rewards for aiding them to safety. The term "chit" is of Anglo-Indian origin and means "a note of a sum owed." An important piece of survival gear, a blood chit promises to reward civilians who assist downed aviators. The purpose of the blood chit is to provide a downed air crew member hope of survival in unknown territory. Army Aviators in Vietnam were each issued a "Blood Chit" to carry in the event they were shot down, crashed, or became separated from their aircraft and crew members and needed help from locals returning to friendly (US or Army of the Republic of South Vietnam) safe havens. Blood chits were squares of cloth made of silk or rayon. The term "chit" is of Anglo-Indian origin and means "a note of a sum owed." The concept of blood chits may have been prompted by French balloonists experimenting with flight during the late eighteenth century and were first developed for wide spread military use by the British Royal Air Force toward the end of World War I.

They have messages in various languages that identify the person's military affiliation and promise to reward anyone who assists the aviator in returning to friendly control. Militaries across the world have issued blood chits to their air crew members. The blood chit has one main purpose: to provide a downed air crew member hope of survival in unknown territory. For more information on blood chits, check out "Last Hope: The Blood Chit Story," by R.E. Baldwin and Thomas Wm. McGarry. The Army Vietnam Era Aviator's "blood chit" was in 14 languages with the following message printed under an American Flag picture: I am a citizen of the United States of America. I do not speak your language. Misfortune forces me to seek assistance in obtaining food, shelter, and protection. Please take me to someone who will provide for my safety and see that I am returned to my people. My Government will reward you. The 14 languages on the blood chit were English, Burmese, Thai, Laotian, Cambodian, Vietnamese, Malayan, Indonesian, Chinese, Chinese (Modern), Tagalog, Visayan, French, and Dutch.

23

Wikipedia The Free Encyclopedia, URL: *http://en.wikipedia.org/wiki/Tar-Baby*. Variations on the tar baby legend are spread in folklore of more than one culture. The mythical West African hero Anansi is recorded as once being similarly trapped.[4] In a Spanish language version told in the mountainous parts of Colombia, an unnamed rabbit is trapped by the "Muñeco de Brea" (tar doll). A Buddhist myth tells of Prince Five-weapons (the Future Buddha) who encounters the ogre Sticky Hair in a forest.

24

Wikipedia The Free Encyclopedia, URL: *http://en.wikipedia.org/wiki/Four_Hole_Swamp*. Four Holes Swamp is a small black water river that is a tributary to the Edisto River in South Carolina. The swamp rises in Calhoun County and flows 62 miles to the confluence, in an unusual braided pattern. The river/swamp has no well-defined channel, but multiple channels that start and disappear, yet maintain a flow. The swamp is the home of the Francis Beidler Forest, a 16,000-acre nature preserve of virgin cypress and tupelo forest owned and operated by the Audubon Society. Some of the trees are over 1,000 years in age, and the forest is the home of a number of rare or endangered species.

25

Aircraft Commander's name has been changed for privacy reasons.

26

Department of the Army, Vietnam Studies, Tactical and Materiel Innovations, Chapter 1, page 5, by Lieutenant General John H. Hay, Jr. Washington, D.C. 1974.

27

DoD GEN-25, Handbook for US Forces in Vietnam, 10 June 1966, General William C Westmoreland, pages 1 and 2.

28

DoD GEN-25, Handbook for US Forces in Vietnam, 10 June 1966, General William C Westmoreland, pages 1 and 2.

29

DoD GEN-25, Handbook for US Forces in Vietnam, 10 June 1966, General William C Westmoreland, pages 1 and 2.

30

DoD GEN-25, Handbook for US Forces in Vietnam, 10 June 1966, General William C Westmoreland, pages 1 and 2.

31

The exact Tiger call sign could not be recalled by the author, so "Tiger 99" is a fictional call sign. The two slick platoons did use Tiger as the beginning of their call sign and the head of a Tiger was painted on the pilots' doors of each 121st "slick" aircraft.

32

Soldier, Sailor, Airman, and Marine Argument Joke, Unknown source. This funny story (joke) about which military service is the best is not the joke that Bob told 47 years ago, as the author cannot remember the actual joke that was told. However, the story is typical of the frequent jokes crew members told each other to break the ice and relieve stress on missions. This particular joke about God signing a letter as "US Army Aviation Retired" is typical of how very proud Army aviators are of their branch of the Army, their flying skills, and their contributions to this great nation.

33

The U Minh Forest is a vast, very dense, VC held, and foreboding place. A place where US and ARVN troops and before them the French played hell trying to defeat the VC. Its area is approximately 2,000 square kilometers. It locates at the position where its back leans southwest and face is directed toward Thai Lan Bay. The U Minh Forest stretches from the Ong Doc River, Ca Mau province to the Cai Lon River, Kien Giang province. The Trem Trem River and Cai tau River divide U Minh into two approximate parts that are U Minh Thuong in the North and U Minh Ha in the South. Major Rowe was hidden and tortured here much of his five years in captivity. Navy Seals spent a lot of time here—doing very scary work!

34

DoD GEN-25, Handbook for US Forces in Vietnam, 10 June 1966, General William C Westmoreland, pages 4 and 5.

35

Example: When another aircraft or a ground unit wanted to tell your FM radio frequency over the radio and in the clear, they would say go up 2.5 from Jack Benny's age (39.0) to get you to go to 40.5 on the FM radio.

36

VIETNAM STUDIES, Tactical and Materiel Innovations, Published by LTG John H. Hay, Jr., Department of Defense, Washington, DC, 1974.

37

GI is a term (noun) used especially in the Second World War and after to refer to all soldiers and airman and sometimes other branches of servicemen and women. Originally meant "General Issue" and before that "Galvanized Iron" which many military items were made of. Also used frequently as a verb to describe deep cleaning of something. For example: The Sergeant ordered us to G.I. the barracks and latrines until they shined.

38

From Wikipedia The Free Encyclopedia, List of English words of Yiddish origin, <u>schmuck:</u> (vulgar) a contemptible or foolish person; a jerk; literally means 'penis.'

39

Unknown original source. COL Frank Giazdowski told this story to the author in 1980, at Fort Campbell, KY. Jokes and frequently morbid jokes were told by soldiers both in base camps, bases, and in the bush to relieve stress and turn troops attention away from the harsh conditions and situations troops were in.

40

Vietnam: The 10,000 Day War, TV Documentary "Vietnam: The Ten Thousand Day War," a 26-part Canadian television documentary on the Vietnam War, was produced in 1980 by Michael Maclear. The series aired in Canada on CBC Television, in the United States and in the United Kingdom on Channel 4.

41

Vietnam Helicopter Pilots Association (VHPA), Killed In Action (KIA) Statistics Tab, URL: *http://www.vhpa.org/KIA/D05_KIA_stix.htm* and Helicopter Losses Tab, URL: *http://www.vhpa.org/heliloss.pdf* 28 January 2013.

42

Vietnam Helicopter Pilots Association (VHPA), Killed In Action (KIA) Information by Name Tab, URL: *http://www.vhpa.org/KIA/KIAINDEX.HTM* 28 January 2013.

43

Vietnam Helicopter Pilots Association (VHPA) Helicopter Losses Tab, URL: *http://www.vhpa.org/heliloss.pdf*, 28 January 2013.

44

Military.Com Website, *http://usmilitary.about.com/od/theorder-lyroom/f/faqklickdef.htm*. In, military terms, defines a klick as a distance of 1,000 meters (one kilometer, or .62 miles). Most historians concur that the term first came into wide use in the US Military during the Vietnam War. However, the exact origin of the term is lost.

45

Wikipedia The Free Encyclopedia, URL: *http://en.wikipedia.org/wiki/B%E1%BA%A3y_N%C3%BAi*, "Bay Nui," Introduction, Page 1.

46

Wikipedia The Free Encyclopedia, URL: *http://en.wikipedia.org/wiki/B%E1%BA%A3y_N%C3%BAi*, "Bay Nui," History, Page 1.

47

Wikipedia The Free Encyclopedia, URL: *http://en.wikipedia.org/wiki/Peter_Lorre*. **Peter Lorre** was born 26 June 1904 and died 23 March 1964. He was an Austrian-born American actor of Jewish descent.[1] In enforced exile in Hollywood, he later became a featured player in many Hollywood crime and mystery films. *The Maltese Falcon* (1941), his first film with Humphrey Bogart and Sydney Greenstreet, was followed by *Casablanca* (1942).

48

DoD GEN-25, Handbook for US Forces in Vietnam, 10 June 1966, General William C. Westmoreland, page 7.

49

Aircrews call out enemy fire by the hour location on the clock. Taking fire six o'clock means taking fire from the direct rear of the aircraft, and taking fire three o'clock means taking fire from the right side (perpendicular) of the aircraft, and so on.

50

Squads of infantry work as a team. If one does not get off the aircraft he is placing his entire squad in harm's way and is an act of cowardice.

51

The caliber of a bullet is the measurement of the diameter of the slug (or projectile) part of the bullet cartridge. In some situations, the bullet casing will be wider than the slug itself. But the caliber is specifically describing the width of the slug portion. Caliber does not refer to the length or power of the bullet (in most cases), but simply the diameter of the bullet. Calibers can be metric or American measurement. A nine millimeter (9mm) is 9mm in diameter. The American measurement is a little different. A twenty-two (or 0.22) is twenty-two one hundredths (22/100's) of an inch in diameter–or a little less than a quarter of an inch. Similarly, a 0.44 is 44/100's of an inch, a .50 caliber is a half inch, etc.

52

Obviously, there was more than one poisonous Vietnam snake species referred to as the "two-step" in Vietnam. See the "Living Hazards Data Base" Vietnam page at *http://www.afpmb.org/content/venomous-animals-country-v#Vietnam* published by the Armed Forces Pest Management Board, US Army Garrison, 2460 Linden Lane, Building 172, Silver Spring, MD 20910. Also see Snakes of the Orient: A Checklist, Welch, K.R.G. 1988. Robert E. Krieger Publishing Company, Malabar, Florida. vii + 183 pp. and *http://en.wikipedia.org/wiki/List_of_snakes_of_South_Asia*. The Web carries all kinds of two-step stories, among them: *https://answers.yahoo.com/question/index?qid=20060729054443AAaefUa* and: *https://answers.yahoo.com/question/index?qid=20101114103933AAOpzVN*

53

Meal, Combat, Individual (MCI) replaced the C-ration beginning in 1958 and was used extensively in Vietnam. Troops in Vietnam called the MCI "C Rations or C Rats." MCIs used the same metal contain-ers as C-rations. Each MCI weighed approximately 2.7 pounds and contained about 1,200 calories. Components of the MCI were almost identical to the C-ration components, but with more variety. MCIs came in 12 different meals per case with increased variety of canned meats. MCI's were less monotonous and helped (but did not prevent) menu fatigue. The B1 Units meat choices (in small cans) were: beef steak, ham and eggs, chopped ham slices, and turkey loaf. The fruit included in the B1 Unit was either: applesauce, fruit cocktail, peach-es, pears. The rest of the B1 included 7 crackers, peanut butter, candy disc, chocolate, solid chocolate, cream, and coconut. All C rats came with an accessory pack that included a: plastic spoon, salt, pepper, instant coffee, sugar, non-dairy creamer, two Chicklets of gum, pack of four cigarettes, moisture resistant matches, and a small packet of toilet paper. The B2 Units meat choices were in larger cans and in-cluded either: beans and wieners, spaghetti and meatballs, beefsteak with potatoes and gravy, ham and lima beans, meatballs and beans, and four crackers, cheese spread, processed caraway, pimento, fruit cake, pecan roll, pound cake, and an accessory pack. The B3 Units Meat choices in small cans included: boned chicken, chicken and noodles, meat loaf, spiced beef, white bread, four cookies, cocoa beverage powder, jam (apple, berry, grape, mixed fruit, or strawber-ry), and an accessory pack.

54
The Religions of Vietnam, COMMAND INFORMATION PAM-PHLET 11-67, MACV Office of Information APO 96222, April 1968, see *http://www.history.navy.mil/library/online/religions.htm*, Unknown author.

55
CPT Segrest nor the author could recall the call sign, so "Tiger 88" is a fictional call sign. The two slick platoons did use Tiger as the beginning of their call sign and the head of a Tiger was painted on the pilots' doors of each slick aircraft in the 121st. We Tigers used Tiger followed by the last three tail numbers on our aircraft for call signs.

56

According to Federal Aviation Pamphlet titled Density Altitude, FAA–P–8740–2 • AFS–8 (2008), "Density altitude has a significant (and inescapable) influence on aircraft and engine (and wing and rotor blade) performance, so every pilot needs to thoroughly understand its effects. Hot, high, and humid weather conditions (high density altitude conditions) increases stall speeds, degrades engine performance, and can cause a routine takeoff or landing to become an accident in less time than it takes to tell about it."

57

Wikipedia The Free Encyclopedia, URL: *http://en.wikipedia.org/ wiki/Tr%E1%BA%A7n_H%C6%B0ng_%C4%90%E1%BA%A1o*, Trần Hưng Đạo (1228–1300) was the supreme commander of Vietnam during the Trần Dynasty. He commanded the Dai Viet armies that repelled three major Mongol invasions in the 13th century. His triple victories over the mighty Mongols under Kublai Khan are considered among the greatest military feats in world history. General Tran Hung Dao's military brilliance and prowess are reflected in many warfare treatises that he authored. He is regarded as one of the most accomplished military tacticians in history.

58

Last Printed Issue of Infantry Journal was in 2013. Exact issue of Infantry Journal is unknown. Quote can be found at: *http://www.joe-ks.com/archives_dec2006/Military_Humour. htm; http://www.murphys-laws.com/murphy/murphy-war.html; http://www.twinbeech.com/humor.htm; http://www.post768.org/ MilitaryWit&Wisdom.htm*; and many others.

59

9th Infantry Division Society web site. URL: *http://9thinfdivsociety. org/9thvn.html, 30 January 2013* and Wikipedia Free Encyclopedia. URL: *http://en.wikipedia.org/wiki/9th_Infantry_Division_ (United_States)*, 30 January 2013. The 9th Infantry Division began withdrawing in the summer of 1969, leaving its 3rd Brigade behind as a separate unit (under command of 25th Infantry Division) until October 1970.

60

Wikipedia, The Free Encyclopedia, URL: *http://en.wikipedia.org/wiki/Radio_propaganda*, paragraph titled "Vietnam." The first Vietnamese-language radio transmission was made on September 2, 1945, when Ho Chi Minh read out the Declaration of Independence. Prior to 1945, Vietnamese people were banned from owning radio receivers. Broadcasting was under control of the French colonial government, which established the first radio station in Vietnam, Radio Saigon, in the late 1920s. Vietnam's national radio station, now called the Voice of Vietnam, started broadcasting from Hanoi the week after declaration of the Democratic Republic of Vietnam, stating, "This is the Voice of Vietnam, broadcasting from Hanoi, the capital of the Democratic Republic of Vietnam." During the Vietnam War, Radio Hanoi operated as a propaganda tool of North Vietnam. Following reunification, all radio stations were combined into the Voice of Vietnam, which became the national radio station in 1978. "Hanoi Hannah" or Trịnh Thị Ngọ, was a Vietnamese radio personality best known for her work during the Vietnam War, when she made English-language broadcasts for North Vietnam directed at US troops. (*"The Search for Hanoi Hannah."* Don North. Retrieved 28 October 2012.) During the Vietnam War in the 1960s and 1970s, Ngo became famous among US. soldiers for her propaganda broadcasts on Radio Hanoi. She made three broadcasts a day, reading the list of the newly killed or imprisoned Americans, attempting to persuade US troops that the US involvement in the Vietnam War was unjust and immoral and playing popular US anti-war songs in an attempt to incite feelings of nostalgia and homesickness amongst US troops. Although she used the alias Thu Huong, the GIs usually called her *"Hanoi Hannah"* or *"The Dragon Lady."* (*"The Search for Hanoi Hannah."* Don North. Retrieved 28 October 2012.) Few were believed to have been influenced by her propaganda work and the soldiers often mocked her tactics, but they were also impressed by her military intelligence, especially when she mentioned the location of their own unit or listed specific US casualties. After the war, she returned to live in Ho Chi Minh City with her husband where her voice was better known in the US than in her own country. According to war correspondent Don North's assessment: By zapping the truth through an ostrich-like policy censorship, deletions, and exaggerations US Armed Forces Radio lost the trust of many GIs when they were most isolated and vulnerable to enemy propaganda. It wasn't that Hanoi Hannah always told the truth—she didn't. But she was most effective when she did tell the truth and US Armed Forces Radio was fudging it.

61

Wikipedia and The Free Encyclopedia. URL: *http://en.wikipedia. org/wiki/Ben_Tre_Province*, Geography, 30 January 2013.

62

Wikipedia, The Free Encyclopedia. URL: *http://en.wikipedia.org/ wiki/We_Gotta_Get_out_of_This_Place*, "We Gotta Get out of This Place," occasionally written "We've Gotta Get out of This Place," is a rock song written by Barry Mann and Cynthia Weil, and recorded as a 1965 hit single by The Animals. It has become an iconic song of its type and was immensely popular among United States Armed Forces during the Vietnam War. It was frequently requested of, and played by, American Forces Vietnam Network disc jockeys. During 2006 two University of Wisconsin–Madison employees, one a Vietnam veteran, began an in-depth survey of hundreds of Vietnam veterans, and found that "We Gotta Get out of This Place" had resonated the strongest among all the music popular then: "We had absolute unanimity in this song being the touchstone. This was the Vietnam anthem. Every bad band that ever played in an armed forces club had to play this song." Just such a band played the song in an episode ("USO Down," by Vietnam veteran Jim Beaver) of the American television series about the war, Tour of Duty, and the song is reprised in the episode's final scene."

63

Wikipedia, The Free Encyclopedia. URL: *http://en.wikipedia.org/ wiki/Time_Is_on_My_Side*, *"Time Is on My Side"* is a song written by Jerry Ragovoy (under the pseudonym of Norman Meade). First recorded by jazz trombonist Kai Winding and his Orchestra in 1963, it was covered (with additional lyrics by Jimmy Norman) by both soul singer Irma Thomas and The Rolling Stones in 1964. When the Rolling Stones performed "Time Is on My Side" during their first guest spot on The Ed Sullivan Show, Sullivan was shocked by their appearance, because long hair on men was considered outrageous to older people in the United States at that time, and declared that they would never be invited onto the show again. He subsequently invited them back several times.

64

Wikipedia, The Free Encyclopedia. URL: *http://en.wikipedia.org/wiki/Peter_Arnett,* Peter Gregg Arnett, ONZM (born 13 November 1934, Riverton, New Zealand) is a New Zealand journalist. Arnett's most famous act of reporting from the Vietnam War was a story published on 7 February 1968, about the provincial capital Bến Tre: "'It became necessary to destroy the town to save it,' a United States Army major said today. He was talking about the decision by allied commanders to bomb and shell the town regardless of civilian casualties, to rout the Vietcong." The quotation was distorted in subsequent publications, eventually becoming the more familiar, "We had to destroy the village in order to save it." March 5, 2014.

65

Wikipedia The Free Encyclopedia, List of English words of Yiddish origin, **schlimazel** also **schlemazl**: a chronically unlucky person.

66

http://www.writing.upenn.edu/~afilreis/50s/rebel-quotes.html and *http://www.cosmopolis.ch/english/cosmo6/rebel.htm.* The film "Rebel Without a Cause" is directed by Nicholas Ray and based on his story and the screenplay by Stewart Stern, adapted by Irving Schulman. It is one of the classic movies of the 1950s. The scene at the planetarium with the professor (scientist) explaining the universe to his students is the key to understanding their feelings as they reach adulthood: "The Earth will one day disappear in a burst of gas and fire. [...] In the immensity of our universe and the galaxies beyond, the Earth will not be missed. Through the infinite reaches of space the problems of man seem trivial and naive indeed. And man, existing alone, seems himself an episode of little consequence." These feelings could be compared to some of our troops feelings in Vietnam in 1968 and 1969.

67

This letter was written by Larry Dandridge, not Sam DeLoach. None of the original letters these aviators wrote to each other survived. Although the letter is fiction, it does contain the kind of things Army aviators wrote in letters to each other. Locations and events and other information (code of conduct, the guys kidding each other, both Sam and Larry liking fishing, etc.) are factual.

68

This mission actually took place in November 1967. The date was changed to support the book's story line and time line and to include a "Dust Off" mission in the book and to give credit to the author's very dear and lifelong friend COL (Ret) Sam DeLoach. Sam DeLoach is a great American, soldier, aviator, family man, businessman, son, brother, and friend. He is an excellent example of what we troops call "a mustang," an officer who came up through the ranks from private to chief warrant officer, and on to highest field grade officer rank (O-6 or full bird Colonel). One of the goals of this book was to include at least one story about each type (slick, dust off, scout, gunship, Cobra attack, and cargo) of Army helicopter in Vietnam in 1968 and 1969. Book II of Blades of Thunder will have a Flying Crane, heavy lift cargo helicopter and a Chinook, Medium Lift Cargo Helicopter story in it.

69

That altitude and airspeed where it is impossible to make a successful emergency landing (auto-rotation) without an operating engine. Engine failures in the dead man's curve area of flight meant you were going to crash and hard.

70

This Dust Off 22 mission actually took place in 1967. Sam DeLoach graduated from flight school with WORWAC Class 66-23 in February 1967. The date was changed in this book solely to accommodate the story time line of 1968 and 1969, and to allow the author to include a Dust Off Story that was commanded by his dear friend COL (Ret) Sam DeLoach—then Warrant Officer1 Sam DeLoach. Sam DeLoach and Larry Dandridge remain best friends today. Sam DeLoach and Bubba Segrest went to high school together and both drove school buses for St. Andrews High School as young teenagers in Charleston, SC. Larry Dandridge played football for the high schools of Charleston, SC (the Bantams) against Bubba Segrest and his St. Andrew's Rocks. Larry Dandridge played basketball for Murray Vocational High School's Tigers against Sam DeLoach and the Saint Andrew's Rocks. Bubba Segrest and Larry Dandridge became good friends as freshmen at the Baptist College at Charleston before joining the Army. Sam would go on to accept a direct commission in the Transportation Corps and return to Vietnam to serve in the famous 1st of the 9th Cavalry as a maintenance detachment commander, test pilot and later as a Cobra Attack helicopter pilot where he distinguished himself. Sam would rise to the rank of colonel where he culminated his outstanding career as the Army's Apache Helicopter Program Manager. With Sam's one year seniority on Larry Dandridge, he served as a great military and personal mentor for Larry throughout Larry's career in everything but fishing. Larry tried to teach him the many skills required of that highly skilled recreational activity.

71

From my (Larry Dandridge's) memories of my King James and \ Methodist (my Dad's family) child hood Bible teachings and my Catholic Church participation (My Stepdad's family).

72

Note: The above story was told and reviewed by Roger Howell and written and edited by Larry Dandridge. Roger Howell gave his permission by phone and email to publish this story in Blades of Thunder.

73

(c) 1979, Jan Michael Joncas. Published by Oregon Catholic Press (OCP). 5536 NE Hassalo, Portland, OR 9721. All rights reserved. Used with permission. Wikipedia and The Free Encyclopedia. URL: *http://en.wikipedia.org/wiki/On_Eagle's_Wings*, January 14, 2014, First chorus of "On Eagles' Wings" is a devotional song composed by Michael Joncas, a priest, in 1979. Its words are loosely based on Psalm 91 and Isaiah 40:31. The song was published by North American Liturgy Resources and was later purchased by New Dawn Music, a subsidiary of Oregon Catholic Press. It quickly proved to be quite popular as a contemplative song at Catholic masses as well as at Protestant services; it is now sung in churches of many denominations including Pentecostal churches and was performed at many of the funerals of victims of September 11. It is often performed either at the beginning or the ending of a Roman Catholic Funeral Mass. Father Joncas has stated that his preference for the title would be "On Eagle's Wings," indicating that the wings belong to a single eagle which is metaphorically related to God, but he said he could make an argument for "On Eagles' Wings," indicating wings that belong to many eagles, since there would be many wings needed to lift up the multiple people in covenant with God.

74

(c) 1979, Jan Michael Joncas. Published by Oregon Catholic Press (OCP). 5536 NE Hassalo, Portland, OR 9721. All rights reserved. Used with permission. Wikipedia The Free Encyclopedia. URL: *http://en.wikipedia.org/wiki/On_Eagle's_Wings,* January 14, 2014, First chorus of **"On Eagles' Wings"** is a devotional song composed by Michael Joncas, a priest, in 1979. Its words are loosely based on Psalm 91 and Isaiah 40:31. The song was published by North American Liturgy Resources and was later purchased by New Dawn Music, a subsidiary of Oregon Catholic Press. It quickly proved to be quite popular as a contemplative song at Catholic Masses as well as at Protestant services; it is now sung in churches of many denominations including Pentecostal churches and was performed at many of the funerals of victims of September 11. It is often performed either at the beginning or the ending of a Roman Catholic Funeral Mass.

75

http://en.wikipedia.org/wiki/Air_America_(airline. **Air America** was an American passenger and cargo airline established in 1950 and covertly owned by the United States Government and was initially a CIA project for intelligence operations in China. The CIA did not have enough work to keep the asset afloat and the National Security Council farmed the airline out to various government entities that included the USAF, U.S. Army, USAID and for a brief time the French Republic. Essentially, Air America was used by the U.S. Government covertly and clandestinely to conduct military operations, posing as a civilian air carrier, in areas the U.S. Armed forces could not go due to treaty restraints contained in the 1954 and 1962 Geneva Accords. The pilots and crews of Air America were a patriotic and professional group.

76

The New York Times Obituary Section, April 22, 1989, by Glenn Fowler, stated: "Col. James N. Rowe, a United States Army officer who spent five years as a prisoner in Vietnam before escaping in 1968, was shot to death yesterday by gunmen near Manila, where he was a military adviser to the Philippine armed forces. He was 51 years old. Colonel Rowe was being driven to work at the Joint United States Military Advisory Group headquarters in Quezon City, a suburb of Manila, shortly after 7 a.m. when at least two hooded gunmen in a stolen car fired more than 20 bullets into his vehicle... In the ensuing years, as domestic opposition to the war in Vietnam increased, he became an outspoken defender of the American effort, at one point demonstrating a copy of the cage in which he was held. He wrote a book dealing with his imprisonment *Five Years To Freedom*... In 1985, Colonel Rowe was placed in command of the First Special Warfare Training Battalion at Fort Bragg, a post he held until last May, when he went to the Philippines. Unfortunately, the communist never forgot the American hero they could not break and could not hold on to and the communists in the Philippines had close ties with the Vietnamese Communists. *Five Years To Freedom,* copyright James N. Rowe, published by First Ballentine Books June 1984, 13th printing June 1991, ISBN 0-345-31460-3, has been in print since its first publication and continues today as a must-read for all soldiers and, in the authors' opinions, a must-read for all US citizens.

77

Wikipedia The Free Encyclopedia, URL: *http://en.wikipedia.org/ wiki/Military_Affiliate_Radio_System,* Military Auxiliary Radio

System (MARS), Page 1. The Military Auxiliary Radio System (MARS) is a United States Department of Defense sponsored program, established as a separately managed and operated program by the United States Army, Navy, and Air Force. The program is a civilian auxiliary consisting primarily of licensed amateur radio operators who are interested in assisting the military with communications on a local, national, and international basis as an adjunct to normal communications. MARS members work by the slogan "Proudly serving those who serve."

78

It is possible that the other aircraft commander was the flight lead, but I remember Joe being the flight leader. Forty-seven years ago is a long time back!

79

Signal operating instructions (SOI) or **Communications-Electronics Operation Instructions** (CEOI) are US military terms for a type of combat order issued for the technical control and coordination of communications within a command. They include current and up-to-date information covering radio call signs and frequencies, a telephone directory, code-words (for rudimentary encryption), and visual and sound signals. A designated battalion signal officer prepares the battalion SOI in conformance with the SOI of higher headquarters. (US Army FM 55-30). Units maintained two copies of the SOI: a training version and a "go-to-war" version. During operations, SOI are changed daily. Since the fielding of the SINCGARS system, however, the paper SOI has generally faded from Army use. Electronic SOI are now generated, distributed and loaded along with cryptographic keys.

80

The call signs in this story are fictitious as the author could not remember the actual call signs from over 47 years ago. Joe Casanova was on the mission. Joe was an outstanding soldier, officer, pilot, and person. The author never knew the names of the advisors and never saw them again.

81

The US Army used not only the 105mm howitzer in Vietnam, but also the 155mm towed and self propelled gun systems with a range of 14,600 meters and firing a shell weighing 95 pounds (three times the weight of the 105 round), the eight inch howitzer, and the 175mm gun which fired a 174 pound projectile almost 33 kilometers (19.8 miles). The eight inch gun and 175 mm gun fired the same ammunition (projectile) but had different gun tubes.

82

Vietnam Helicopter Pilots Association (VHPA) Helicopter Losses Tab, URL: *http://www.vhpa.org/heliloss.pdf*, 28 January 2013.

83

Viking door gunners and crew chiefs left their cleaned and ready M14 rifles in the gunships, but Tigers took them back to their hooch each day after the last mission. From the Viking ready shack on the flight line, the Vikings had 24-hour surveillance of the gunship flight line. There were Viking crew chiefs and door gunners' working day and night on the gunship flight line. Many nights the Viking enlisted crews slept on or near the aircraft.

84

Flying slicks was also a very dangerous mission. However, it was the gunships that went looking for trouble and operated below 1,500 feet most of the time. Guns and slicks were almost always going to the "sounds of the guns."

85

FREEDOM IS YOUR DESTINY!, ISBN: 978-0-9897133-9-9, Library of Congress Control Number: 2013945042, by Daniel T. Eismann (an ex-121st AHC Tiger Slick and Viking Gunship Crew Chief/Door Gunner), published by Desert Sage Press, P. O. Box 357, Eagle, Idaho 83616, Copyright 2013-14.

86

The cyclic control is the control stick between the pilot's legs used to bank (and turn) the aircraft left or right and used to push the nose of the helicopter up or down. The forced trim was a "poor man's" auto pilot which crudely held the cyclic in the same place once it was set. The Huey (UH-1), Cobra (AH-1G), Cayuse (OH-6), Kiowa (OH-58), and other Army single main rotor helicopters used in the 1960s and 70s had to be flown all the time, with both hands (left hand on the collective pitch and throttle and right hand on cyclic control), and with both feet on the anti-torque pedals (left foot on left pedal and right foot on right pedal) or the aircraft would fly off course, bank, and descend until it was out of control. Helicopters are very different from airplanes and more difficult to fly.

87

There were two primary ways to climb in a single main rotor helicopter. The normal way was to add pitch to the main rotor blades by pulling up on the collective pitch control with the left hand and arm, holding the cyclic steady, and adding a little left pedal to counter torque. The other way to climb and climb very rapidly was to pull quickly and smoothly back on the cyclic control (the control stick between the pilot's legs) with the right hand and creating a cyclic climb. The cyclic was used (in conjunction with other controls—pedals, collective, and throttle) to bank, accelerate, decelerate, climb, and dive the aircraft.

88

From Wikipedia The Free Encyclopedia List of English words of Yiddish origin, list of English words of Yiddish origin: **chutzpah**: nerve, guts, daring, audacity, effrontery.

89

WO1 Larry A. Bodell [CP] Cobra shot by small arms fire and killed in action, in An Xugen Province, near Rach Gia, in IV Corps, flying with the 235 Aerial Weapons Company, in Cobra attack helicopter tail number 66-15331.

90

Vietnam Helicopter Pilots Association (VHPA) Helicopter Losses Tab, URL: *http://www.vhpa.org/heliloss.pdf*, 28 January 2013.

91

Compared to airplanes, helicopters are quite complicated (wings that rotate, transmissions, gear boxes, and much more) with thousands more parts—and everything vibrating like crazy. For every hour a Huey flew, maintenance had to expend about five or more man-hours inspecting and repairing things that go wrong, reach their finite life, or wear out. Gunships required twice as much work as slicks as the armament systems created more vibrations and work.

93.

I would suffer from PTSD for the next 40 years from this incident. It was a stuck point that I could not reconcile, justify, or forgive myself for until I asked a fine Physiologist, Doctor Rachel Darrow, at the Ralph H. Johnson VA Medical Center to help me solve this problem and treat this horrific injury. Dr. Barrow's treatment was successful and my nightmares are much less frequent today and I understand what happened and how I must deal with this tragic incident. *Blades of Thunder Book II* will provide veterans information on how to get help for their PTSD.

94

"The letter and story titled "Milk Run" is copy righted © 2014 to BG (Ret) Dan Hickman and is printed in this book with his permission.

95

"The letter and story titled "Milk Run" is copy righted © 2014 to BG (Ret) Dan Hickman and is printed in this book with his permission.

96

Although ground unit morale was suffering from the effects of sensationalized and inaccurate media reporting, civil rights injustices in the US, and the anti-war movement—most US Army Aviation units morale and esprit de corps remained high throughout the war.

97

Vietnam Helicopter Pilots Association (VHPA), Killed In Action

(KIA) Statistics Tab, URL: *http://www.vhpa.org/KIA/D05_KIA_stix.htm* and Helicopter Losses Tab, URL: *http://www.vhpa.org/heliloss.pdf 28 January 2013.*.movement—most US Army Aviation units morale and esprit de corps remained high throughout the war.

98

Armed Forces Pest Management Board Website *http://www.afpmb.org/content/venomous-animals-country-v#Vietnam:Lists* 43 specifies of venomous snakes (34 land snakes and 9 water/sea snakes) in Vietnam including: Stokes' sea snake, Spiny-headed sea snake, Fea's Viper, Mangrove Snake, Himalayan Krait, Malayan Krait, Banded Krait, Red-Headed Krait, Many-Banded Krait, McClelland's Coral Snake, Speckled Coral Snake, Malayan Pit Viper, Russell's Pit Viper (accounts for 50 percent of all venomous snake bites today), Beaded Sea Snake, Annulated Sea Snake, Gray's sea Snake, Yellow Sea Snake, Shaw's Sea Snake, Short Sea Snake, Yellow Lipped Sea Krait, Chinese Sea Snake, Chinese Cobra, Monacled Cobra, Spectacled Cobra, Thai Spitting Cobra, King Cobra, Mountain Pit Viper, Tonkin Pit Viper, Yellow-Bellied sea Snake, Banded Keelback Snake, Hubei Keelback Snake, Red-Necked Keelback Snake, Tiger-Wassemotter Snake, Schmidt's Sea Snake, Three-Horned Viper, White-Lipped Tree Viper, Kramer's Pit Viper, Gumprecht's Green Pit Viper, Chinese Green Tree Viper, and Bamboo Pit-Viper. Also see SURVIVAL CARDS FOR SOUTHEAST ASIA, GTA 21-7-1, dated 1 April 1968, Card 49: Asiatic Cobra; Card 50: Malayan Krait and Russell's Viper; Card 51: Malayan Pit Viper and Wagler's Pit Viper; Hook-Nosed Sea Snake and Hardwick's Sea Snake (note these cards only listed 7 of 43 poisonous snakes) and see *https://sites.google.com/site/venomousdangerous/snakes/asia-s-most-venomous-snakes*

99

Survival Card 46, STINGING TREE (Man ong voi; Nan tia to), of SURVIVAL CARDS for SE ASIA, GTA 21-7-1, 1 April 1968: Small tree 10 to 16 feet high; wild in forest. Leaves are oblong-lanceolate, six- to-12 inches long; two to four inches wide; dark; glossy on top, lighter beneath. Bearing poisonous hairs on upper surface and many more as well stinging spines on the veins below. Contact causes itching, prickling, and then red spots, followed by stabbing, radiating pain which may last for three hours; then duller pain, swelling, and enlarged lymph nodes which may persist for three days. Extreme and prolonged contact can prove fatal. May itch from being near tree when it is in bloom. Water and rubbing do not relieve pain but intensify it.

100

Not all troops carried all of these things, but each was heavily burdened with equipment in the best of situations. For examples: Cavalry troops frequently carried little or no C-rations as they expected helicopter resupply. Also they were helicopter-transported the longer distances rather than made to walk the way leg infantry was. Few troops carried both a pistol and rifle. Mortars and recoilless rifles were also frequently left in the rear. Only one soldier per platoon carried a primary radio. Sleeping bags were used only in coldest areas –such as in the central highland mountains. Troops carried only one primary weapon (M16, shotgun, M60, M79, etc.).

101

Reference the "NATIONAL ARCHIVES, **DCAS Vietnam Conflict Extract File record counts by CASUALTY CATEGORY (as of April 29, 2008)**—938 (one and one half percent) of the 58,220 who died in Vietnam expired from illnesses.

102

Tropical impetigo (Tropical bacterial pyodermas) was a leading cause of disability among American soldiers in Vietnam. The lesions yielded group A β-hemolytic streptococci on cultures. Pyodermas were more than 21/2 times as prevalent in whites as in those with darker skins. Systemic addition of penicillin to standard topical treatment significantly reduced healing time.

103

Dengue is a major threat to military troops operating in areas to which it is endemic. Dengue often occurred in US troops in Vietnam, the Philippines, Somalia, and Haiti. Attack rates run as high as 80% and periods of convalescence up to 3-1/2 weeks beyond the acute illness. Dengue will remain a problem for military personnel until an effective vaccine is provided.

104

According to the National Archives, DCAS Vietnam Conflict Extract File record counts by MEMBER SERVICE CODE (Branch of Service) (as of April 29, 2008) at *http://www.archives. gov/research/military/vietnam-war/casualty-statistics.html*, of the 58,220 US KIAs in Vietnam: 38,224 (66%) were Army, 14,844 (25%) were USMC, 2,586 (4%) were USAF, 2,559 (4%) were USN, and 7 (less than 1%) were USCG.

105

Wikipedia The Free Encyclopedia, URL: *http://wiki.answers.com/Q/ How_many_veterans_were_still_alive_after_the_vietnam_war.*

106

The American War Library, The American War Library (amervets. com), 16907 Brighton Avenue, Gardena CA 90247-5420, Phone/ Fax: 1-310-532-0634, URL: *www.americanwarlibrary.com/ personnel/vietvet.htm.*

107

Veterans History Project URL: *http://www.loc.gov/vets/*. The Veterans History Project of the American Folklife Center collects, preserves, and makes accessible the personal accounts of American war veterans so that future generations may hear directly from veterans and better understand the realities of war. Just contact your local VA Medical Center's Volunteer Office.

108

Vietnam Helicopter Pilots Association (VHPA), Killed In Action (KIA) Information by Name Tab, URL: *http://www.vhpa.org/ KIA/KIAINDEX.HTM,* 28 January 2013.

109

Vietnam Helicopter Pilots Association (VHPA) Helicopter Losses Tab, URL: *http://www.vhpa.org/heliloss.pdf,* 28 January 2013.

110

Vietnam Helicopter Pilots Association (VHPA) Helicopter Losses Tab, URL: *http://www.vhpa.org/heliloss.pdf*, 28 January 2013.

111

Vietnam Helicopter Pilots Association (VHPA) Helicopter Losses Tab, URL: *http://www.vhpa.org/heliloss.pdf*, 28 January 2013.

112

Wikipedia The Free Encyclopedia, URL: *http://en.wikipedia.org/ wiki/Vietnam_War*, Page 1.

113

Wikipedia The Free Encyclopedia, URL: *http://en.wikipedia.org/ wiki/Vietnam_War*, Page 1.

114

http://data.bls.gov/cgi-bin/cpicalcpl?cost1=120&year1=1973&year2=2014 the "CPI Inflation Calculator" $120 billion in 1973 is worth $641.7 billion in 2014. According to Dave Manual.com $1 worth of 1973 dollars is now worth $5.32. $5.32 x 120 billion = $638.4 billion. See *http://www.davemanuel.com/inflation-calculator.php.*

115

Wikipedia The Free Encyclopedia, URL: *http://en.wikipedia.org/ wiki/Vietnam_War*, Page 1.

116

The first female Army helicopter pilot was Colonel (Retired) Sally D. Murphy, who graduated from flight school as a 2nd Lieutenant in 1974. There were no female Army Aviators in Vietnam as the war ended in 1973. However, female aviators have contributed greatly to the Army and this great nation since 1974 and there will be many books written to honor those brave US Army women warriors.

117

Wikipedia The Free Encyclopedia, URL: *http://wiki.answers.com/Q/ How_many_veterans_were_still_alive_after_the_vietnam_war.*

118

Fire ants are a major problem in the southern regions of the United States and account for billions of dollars in damage to crops, farm equipment and residential property. They were accidentally introduced in the 1930s through cargo that came to the USA via the port in Mobile, Alabama and rapidly expanded.

119

Cockroaches thrive in warm conditions, especially in the southern USA. 78 to 98 percent of urban homes have cockroaches with as many as 900 to 330,000 per home. They are nocturnal and run away when exposed to light. Some have been known to live up to 3 months without food or water. They have many negative effects on human health because of allergens found in their feces, saliva, and body parts that cause asthma and they transport all sorts of pathogens (bacteria and viruses).

120

Water hyacinth is found globally in the tropics and subtropics, but its spread is limited by severe cold. Its leaves re-grow after moderate freezes and the plant can grow very fast. Populations can double in as little as six days. Within 70 years of reaching Florida, where the plant is predominantly located, water hyacinth has come to cover 126,000 acres of waterways.

121

The negative effects of Kudzu (Pueraria Montana) on the Southeastern economy have been extensively documented. Kudzu is a very large problem for the forestry industry. Invasions are difficult to eradicate and can rapidly spread over large areas. Ten years ago the total productivity lost by agricultural and the forestry business was over $500 million. This does not include the crop damage caused by diseases carried by kudzu. Once it arrives—it never goes away.

122

VHPA 2009 Membership Directory, Volume 26 October 2009, Copyright 2009 Vietnam Helicopter Pilots Association.

123

Note: Barry K. Alexander and the author, Larry Dandridge, joined the Army together and were sworn in at Fort Jackson, SC in late August 1967. They shoveled coal together into the furnace of a WWII era wooden barracks, went through basic infantry training together and went through snow bird, preflight, and flight training together at Fort Wolters, TX. Barry Alexander went to Fort Rucker to finish flight school. Larry Dandridge went to Hunter Army Airfield, Savannah, GA to complete flight school. They never saw each other again after they left Fort Wolters, TX. Barry was a fine young man and officer and Larry has been searching for his parents ever since 1969 to tell them how great a soldier, officer, pilot, American, and person their son was. If anyone can help Larry Dandridge find a member of Barry K. Alexander's family, please contact Larry at ldandridge@earthlink.net or cell phone (843) 276-7164.

124

Wikipedia The Free Encyclopedia, Vietnam War, page 2. Paragraph 1.3.

125

Wikipedia The Free Encyclopedia, URL: *http://en.wikipedia.org/wiki/Rome_plow,* Rome plow, page 1.

126

Private donations and a Congressionally-approved Trust Fund for each branch of the US military service support operations of each Fisher House in this unique public-private partnership. 64 Fisher Houses worldwide serve over 22,000 veterans and their families annually. Since its inception in 1990, Fisher House Foundation has saved veterans and their families an estimated $235 million in lodging and transportation expenses. Over four million days of free lodging has been provided by Fisher Houses.

Blades of Thunder Book II of II is scheduled for publication in late 2016. It will contain the story of Viking 26, Captain Gene Booth's attack on a North Vietnamese Army Base Camp in Cambodia and his aircraft and crew surviving over 200 hits from enemy small arms fire. Book II will also include CW4 (Ret) Wes Komulainen's CH-54A Flying Crane mission in Laos where his aircraft and crew were attacked by two MIGs fighters. Many other exciting Viking, Tiger, and other Army helicopter unit missions, including the story of Captain Bubba Segrest and how he was wounded while covering a helicopter defoliation mission in IV Corps, are included as well.

All 2015 profits from the sale of this book will go to Fisher House Charleston, SC! Fisher House will serve the families of veterans undergoing treatment at the VA Medical Center in Charleston, SC. To make donations to Fisher House Charleston, go to http:// fisherhousecharleston.org/ and donate on line or make checks payable to:
Fisher House Charleston, Inc.,
PO Box 829, Johns Island, SC 29457